N EVANGELION
A C DAYS

BY FUMINO HAYASHI

BASED ON AN ORIGINAL STORY BY GAINAX

VOLUME 3

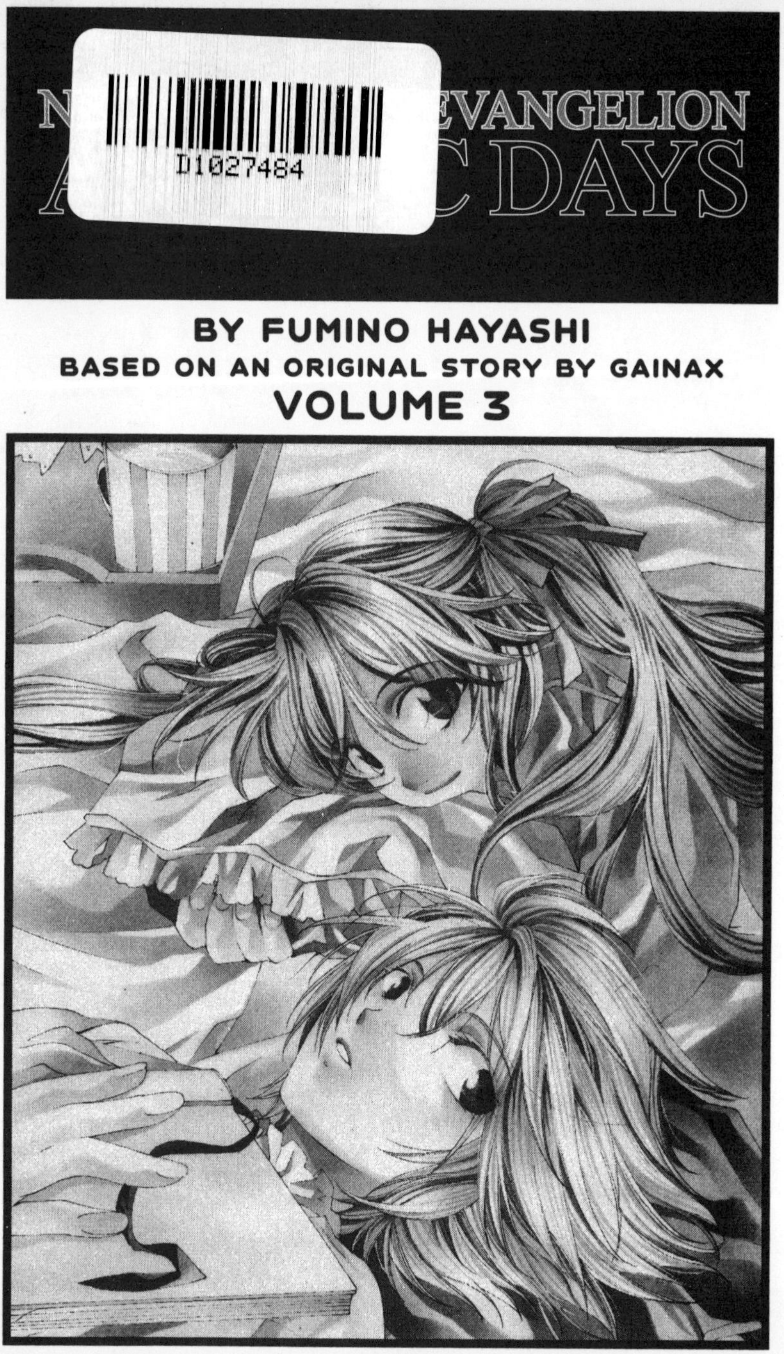

REI AYANAMI
A beautiful and mysterious transfer student. Rei has a practical outlook and a lively personality.

SYNOPSIS AND INTRODUCTION TO THE CHARACTERS

2015, New Tokyo-3. Shinji Ikari is a student of First Municipal Junior High. Accompanied by his childhood friend Asuka and the rest of his classmates, he has enjoyed a relatively normal school life... but ever since a girl named Rei transferred to his school, Shinji hasn't been able get her off of his mind. One day, a chance encounter at Lake Ashi brings Shinji and the others face to face with a series of artificial humans called the Evangelion. Shinji and Rei pilot Evangelion of their own to successfully fight off an unknown life form that appeared in New Tokyo-3, but the resulting psychological scars will not be so easily healed...

KAWORU NAGISA
A handsome boy who never loses his cool. He seems to have a special fondness for Shinji.

MISATO KATSURAGI
Homeroom teacher for Shinji and his classmates. Misato's cheerful and easygoing personality makes her a hit with the students.

RITSUKO AKAGI
The intelligent, calm and collected school nurse of First Municipal Junior High. She is Misato's long-time friend.

SHINJI IKARI
Timid, quiet and easily influenced. He is Asuka's childhood friend.

ASUKA LANGLEY SOHRYU
Shinji's self-appointed chaperone. Asuka has a strong will and a clear sense of right and wrong.

TOJI SUZUHARA
Shinji's classmate. Originally from Osaka. Toji is having a (secret) romance with Hikari.

HIKARI HORAKI
President of Shinji's class. The serious-minded Hikari is head over heels for Toji.

KENSUKE AIDA
Friendly and intelligent. Kensuke's hobby is playing with his camcorder.

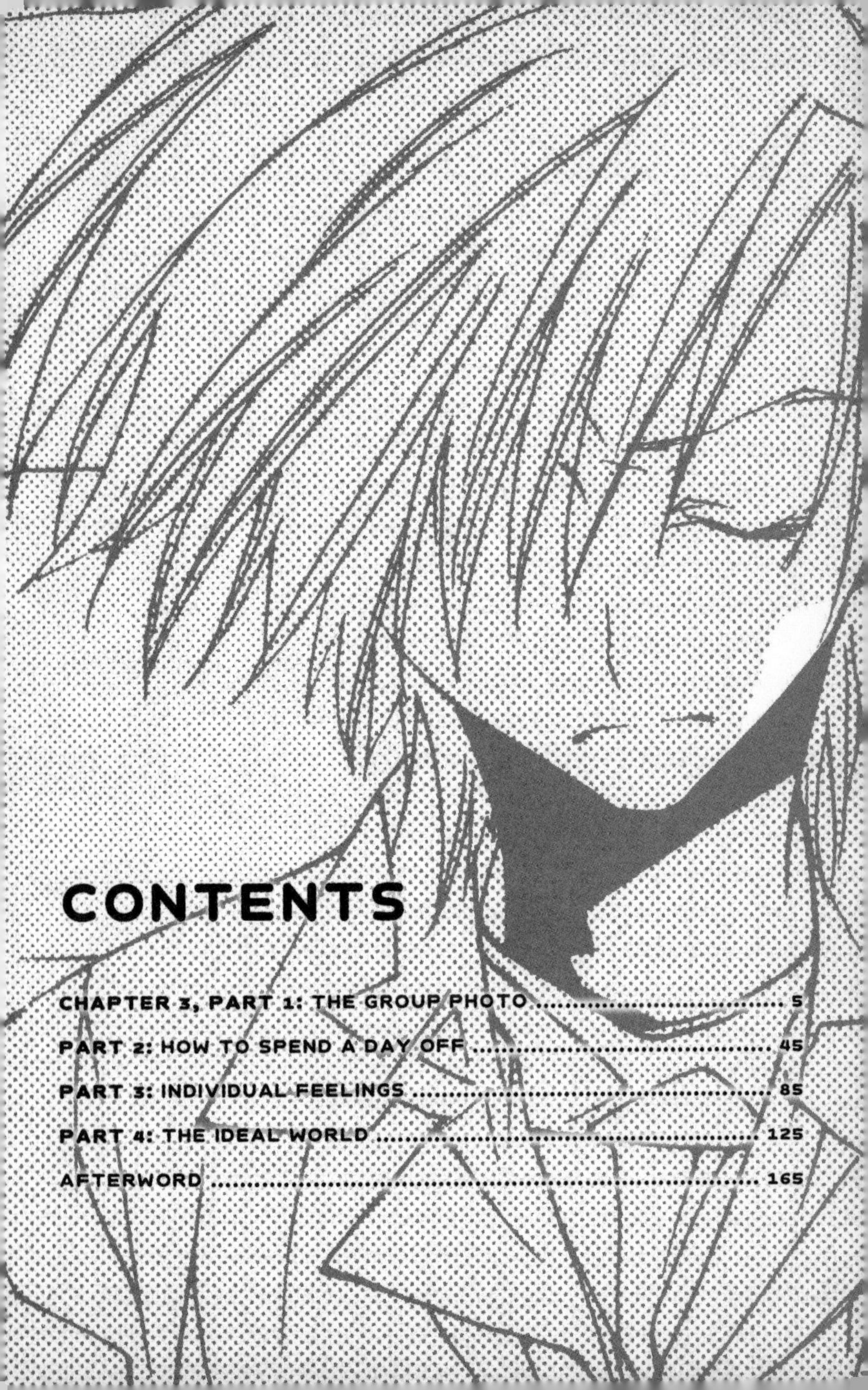

CONTENTS

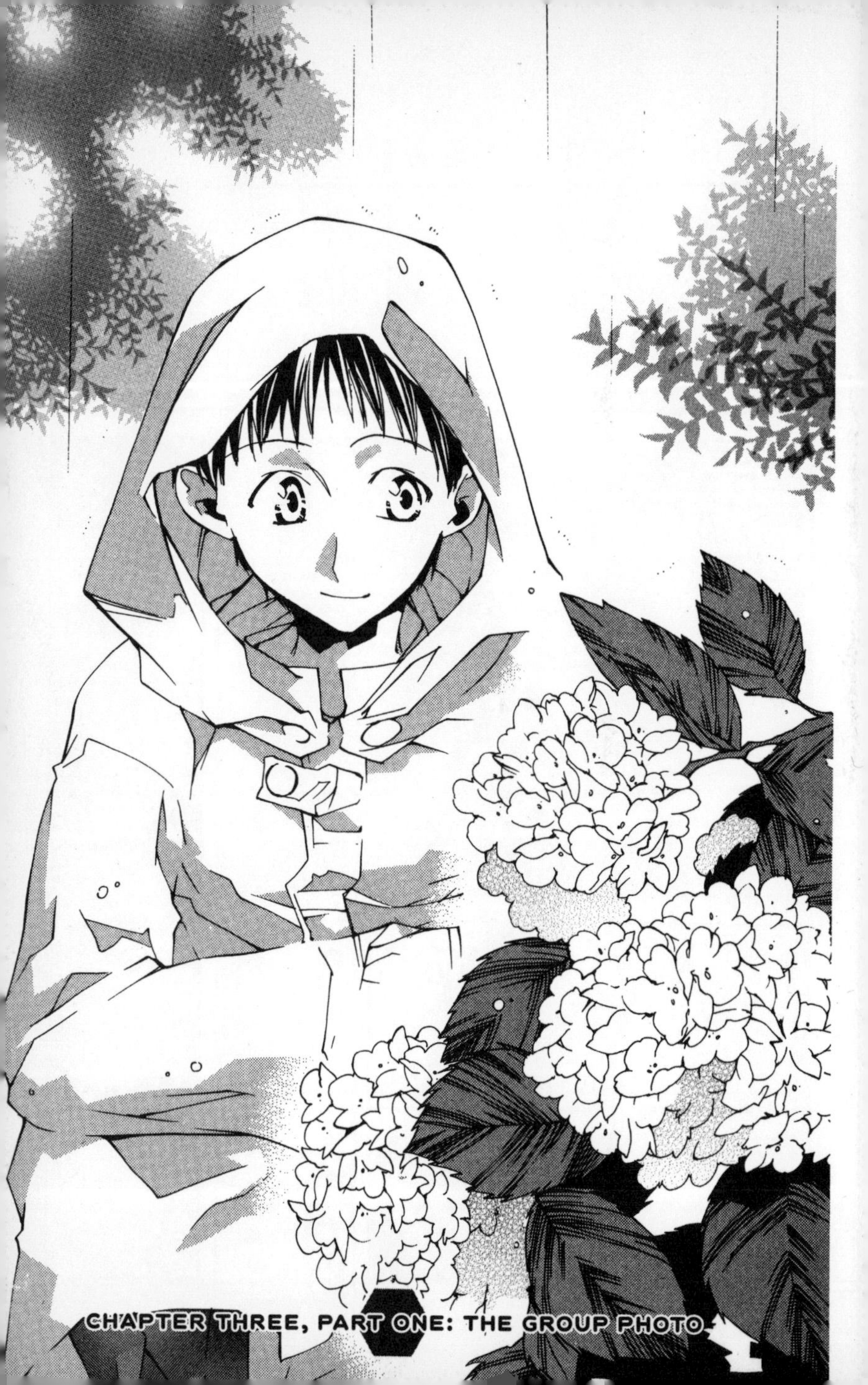
CHAPTER THREE, PART ONE: THE GROUP PHOTO

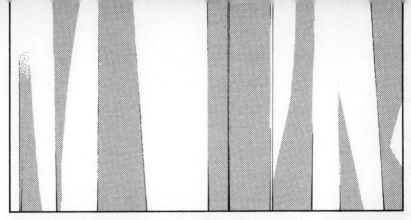

Pi

CLICK Pi

Pi

Pi

I HAVE

TO GET TO SCHOOL.

Pi

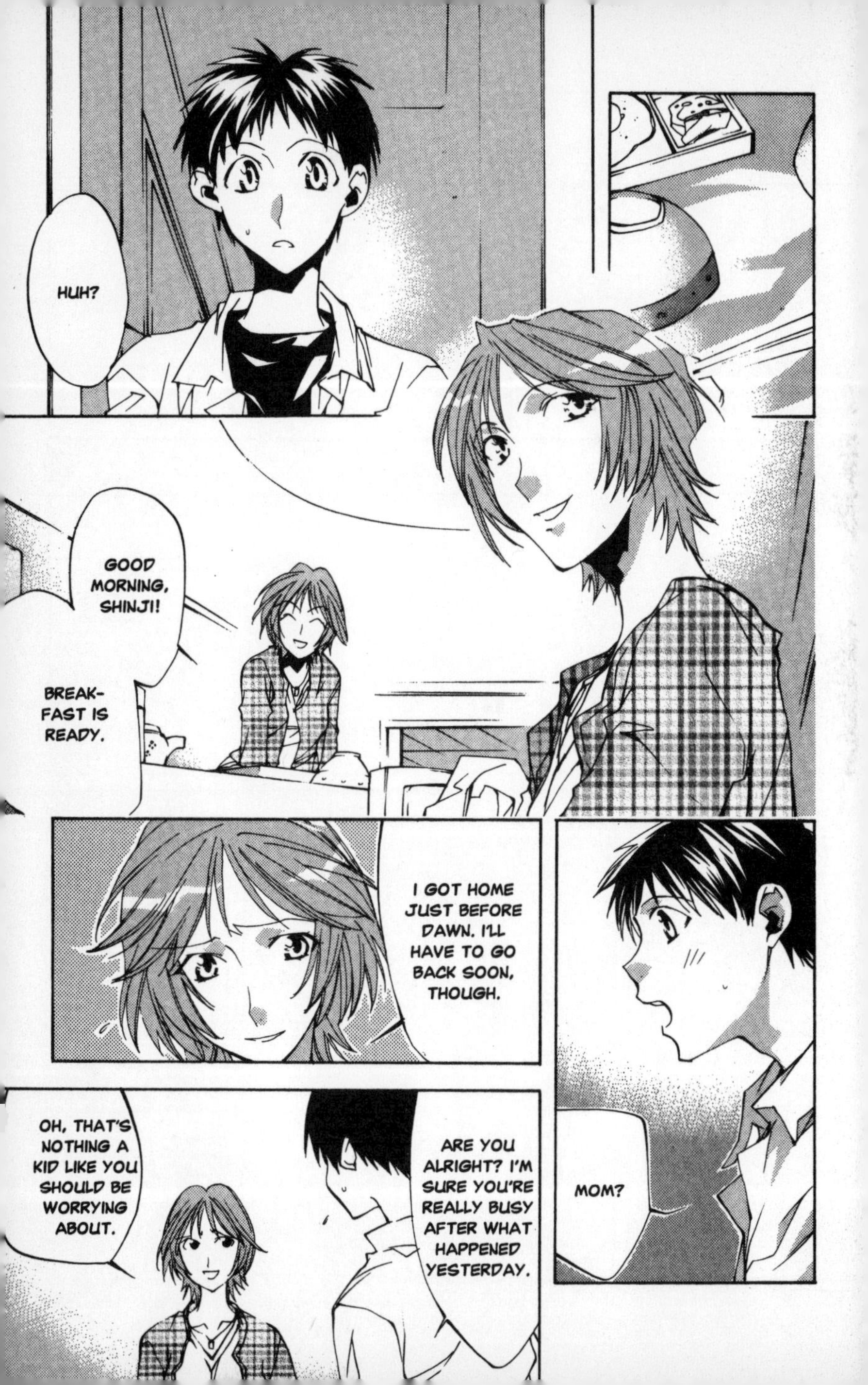
HUH?
GOOD MORNING, SHINJI!
BREAK-FAST IS READY.
MOM?
I GOT HOME JUST BEFORE DAWN. I'LL HAVE TO GO BACK SOON, THOUGH.
ARE YOU ALRIGHT? I'M SURE YOU'RE REALLY BUSY AFTER WHAT HAPPENED YESTERDAY.
OH, THAT'S NOTHING A KID LIKE YOU SHOULD BE WORRYING ABOUT.

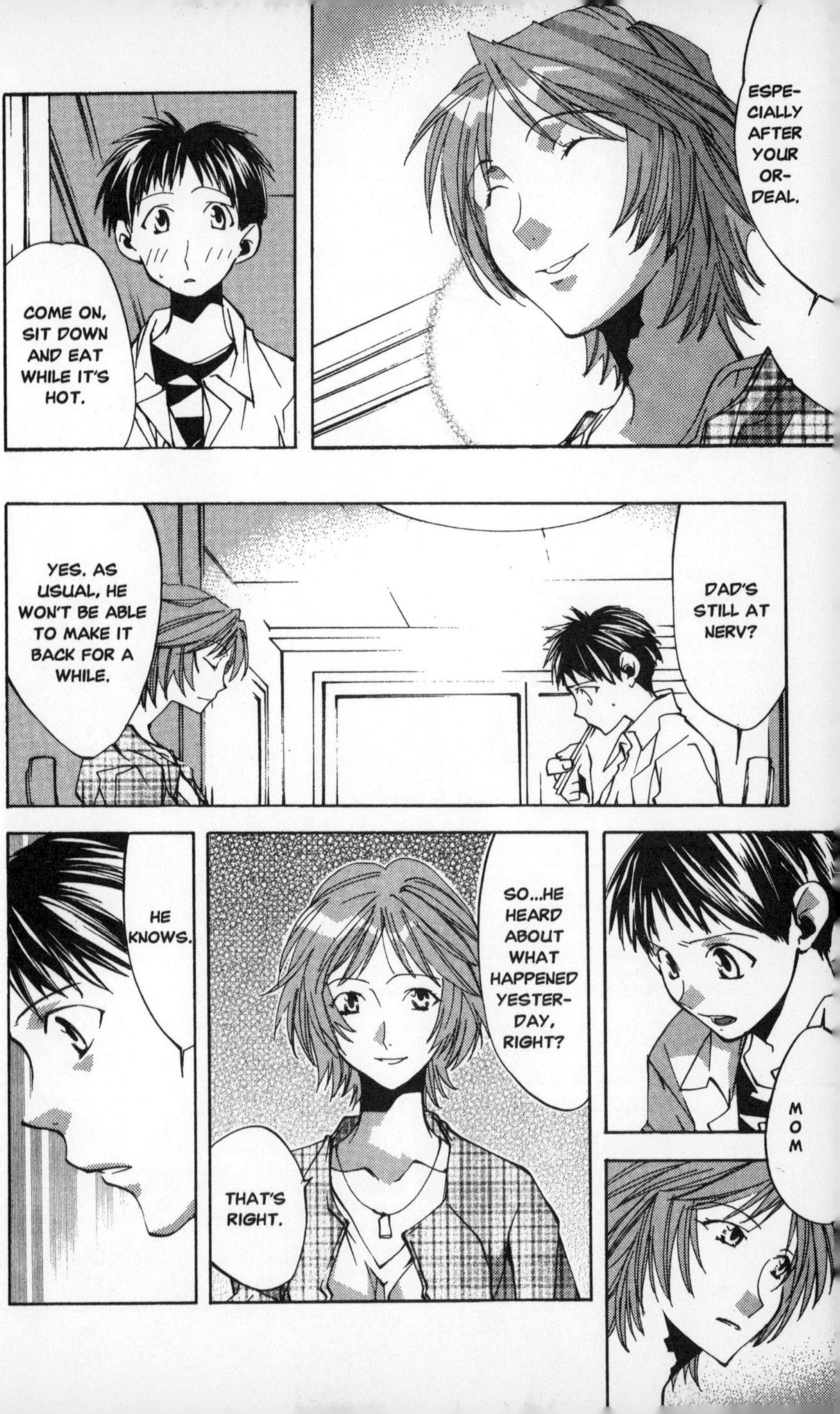
ESPE-CIALLY AFTER YOUR OR-DEAL.
COME ON, SIT DOWN AND EAT WHILE IT'S HOT.
DAD'S STILL AT NERV?
YES. AS USUAL, HE WON'T BE ABLE TO MAKE IT BACK FOR A WHILE.
MOM
SO...HE HEARD ABOUT WHAT HAPPENED YESTER-DAY, RIGHT?
THAT'S RIGHT.
HE KNOWS.

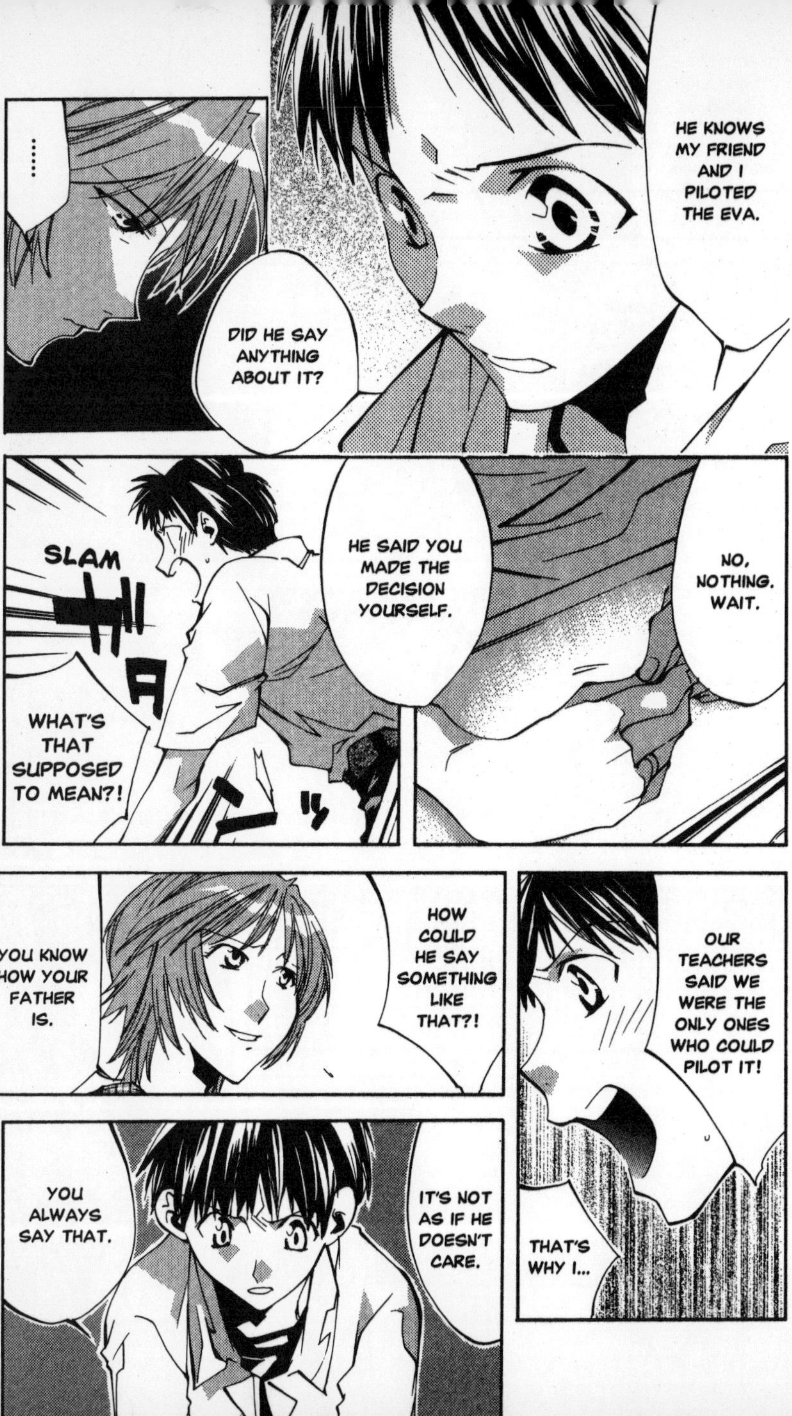
HE KNOWS MY FRIEND AND I PILOTED THE EVA.
DID HE SAY ANYTHING ABOUT IT?
......
NO, NOTHING. WAIT.
HE SAID YOU MADE THE DECISION YOURSELF.
SLAM
WHAT'S THAT SUPPOSED TO MEAN?!
OUR TEACHERS SAID WE WERE THE ONLY ONES WHO COULD PILOT IT!
THAT'S WHY I...
HOW COULD HE SAY SOMETHING LIKE THAT?!
YOU KNOW HOW YOUR FATHER IS.
IT'S NOT AS IF HE DOESN'T CARE.
YOU ALWAYS SAY THAT.

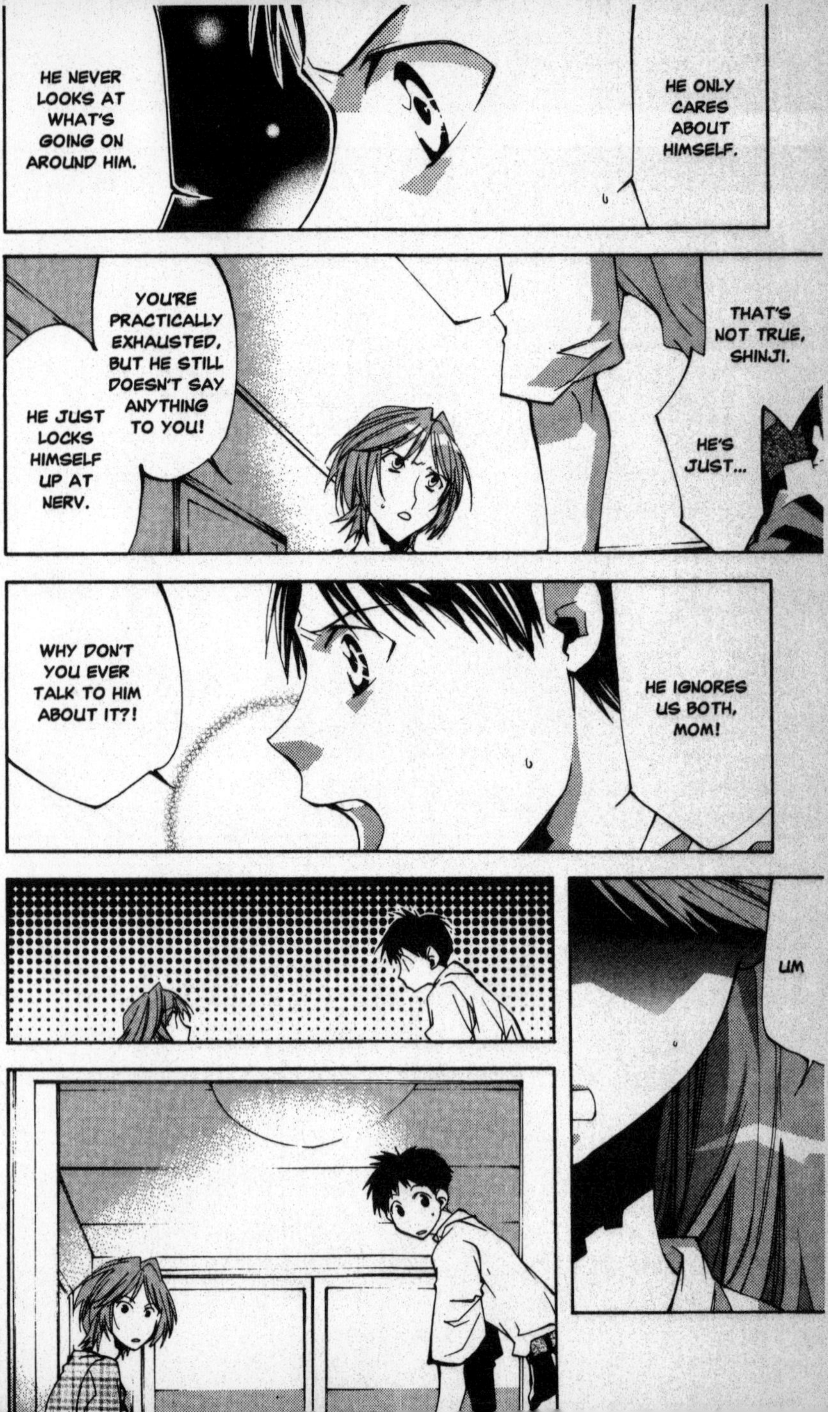

HE ONLY CARES ABOUT HIMSELF.
HE NEVER LOOKS AT WHAT'S GOING ON AROUND HIM.
THAT'S NOT TRUE, SHINJI.
HE'S JUST...
YOU'RE PRACTICALLY EXHAUSTED, BUT HE STILL DOESN'T SAY ANYTHING TO YOU!
HE JUST LOCKS HIMSELF UP AT NERV.
HE IGNORES US BOTH, MOM!
WHY DON'T YOU EVER TALK TO HIM ABOUT IT?!
UM

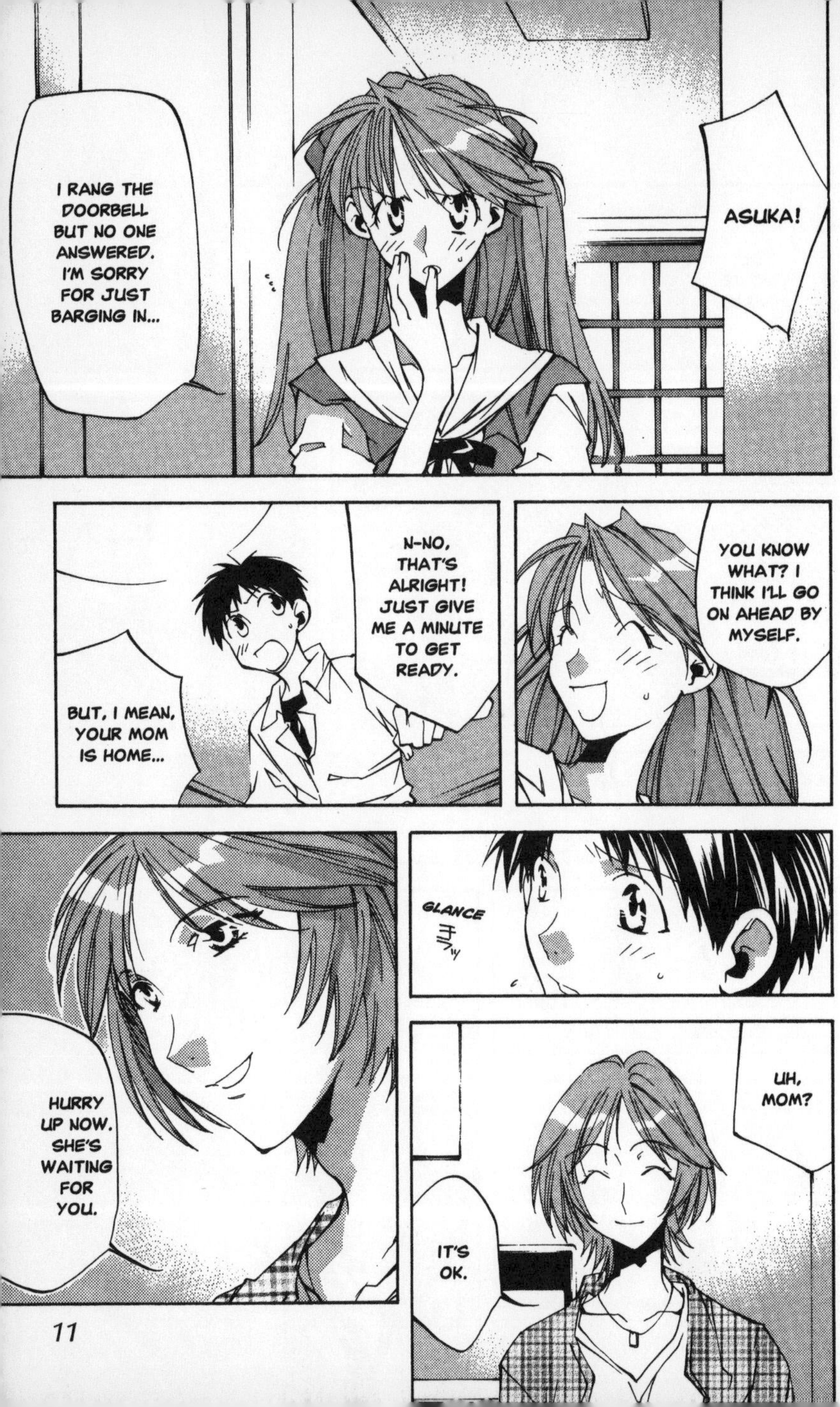
ASUKA!
I RANG THE DOORBELL BUT NO ONE ANSWERED. I'M SORRY FOR JUST BARGING IN...
YOU KNOW WHAT? I THINK I'LL GO ON AHEAD BY MYSELF.
N-NO, THAT'S ALRIGHT! JUST GIVE ME A MINUTE TO GET READY.
BUT, I MEAN, YOUR MOM IS HOME...
GLANCE
UH, MOM?
IT'S OK.
HURRY UP NOW. SHE'S WAITING FOR YOU.

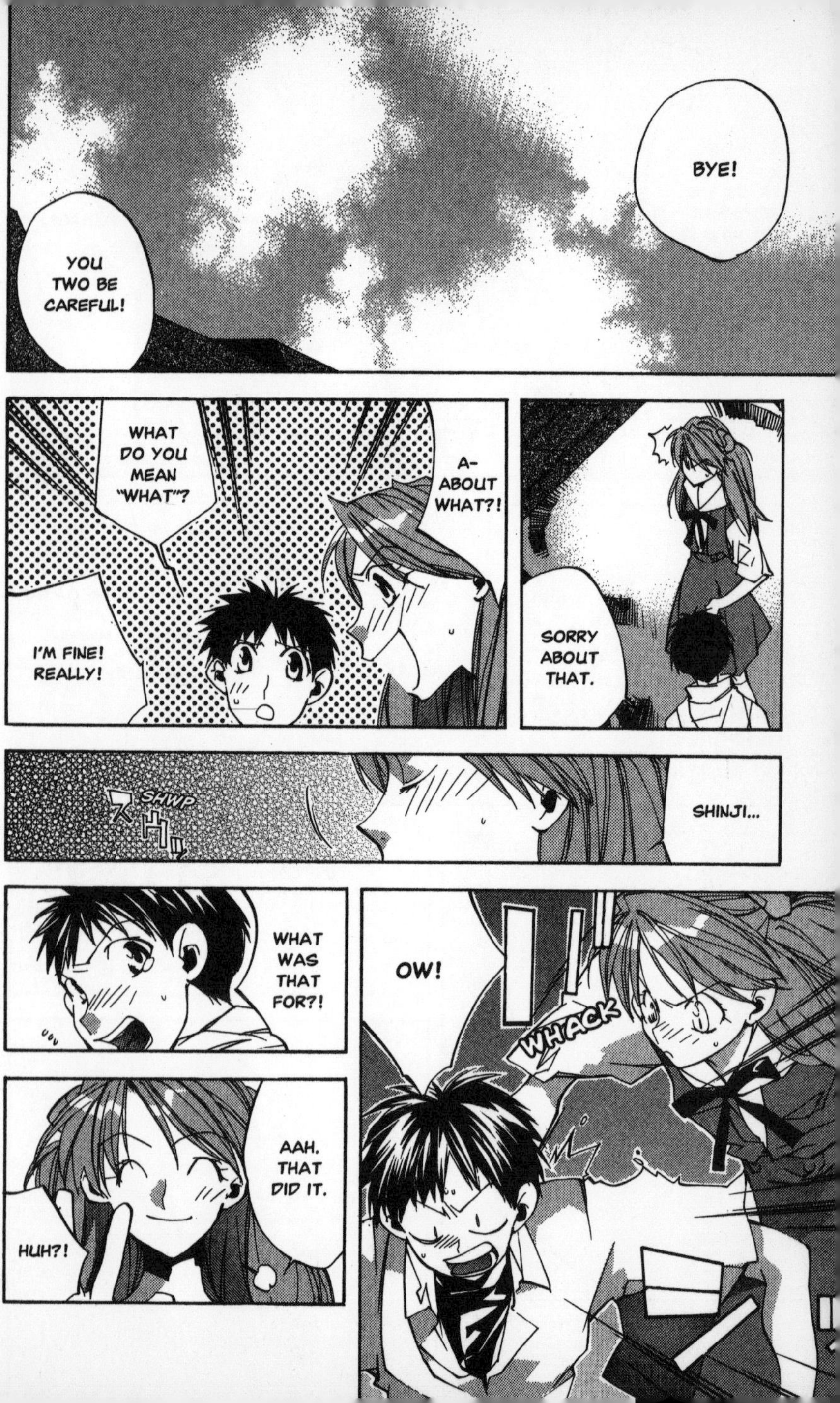
BYE!
YOU TWO BE CAREFUL!
SORRY ABOUT THAT.
A- ABOUT WHAT?!
WHAT DO YOU MEAN "WHAT"?
I'M FINE! REALLY!
SHINJI...
SHWP
OW!
WHACK
WHAT WAS THAT FOR?!
AAH. THAT DID IT.
HUH?!

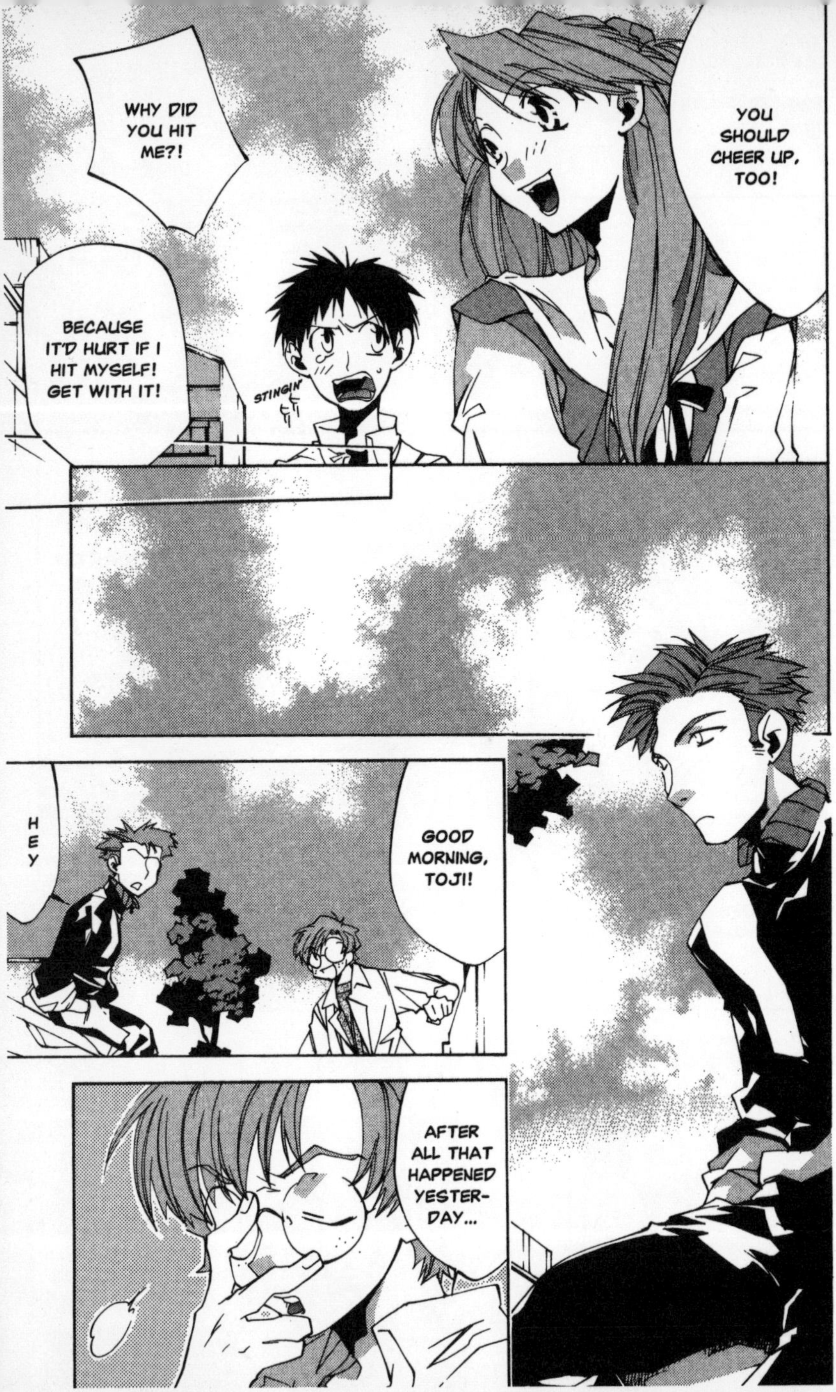
YOU SHOULD CHEER UP, TOO!
WHY DID YOU HIT ME?!
BECAUSE IT'D HURT IF I HIT MYSELF! GET WITH IT!
STINGIN'
GOOD MORNING, TOJI!
HEY
AFTER ALL THAT HAPPENED YESTER-DAY...

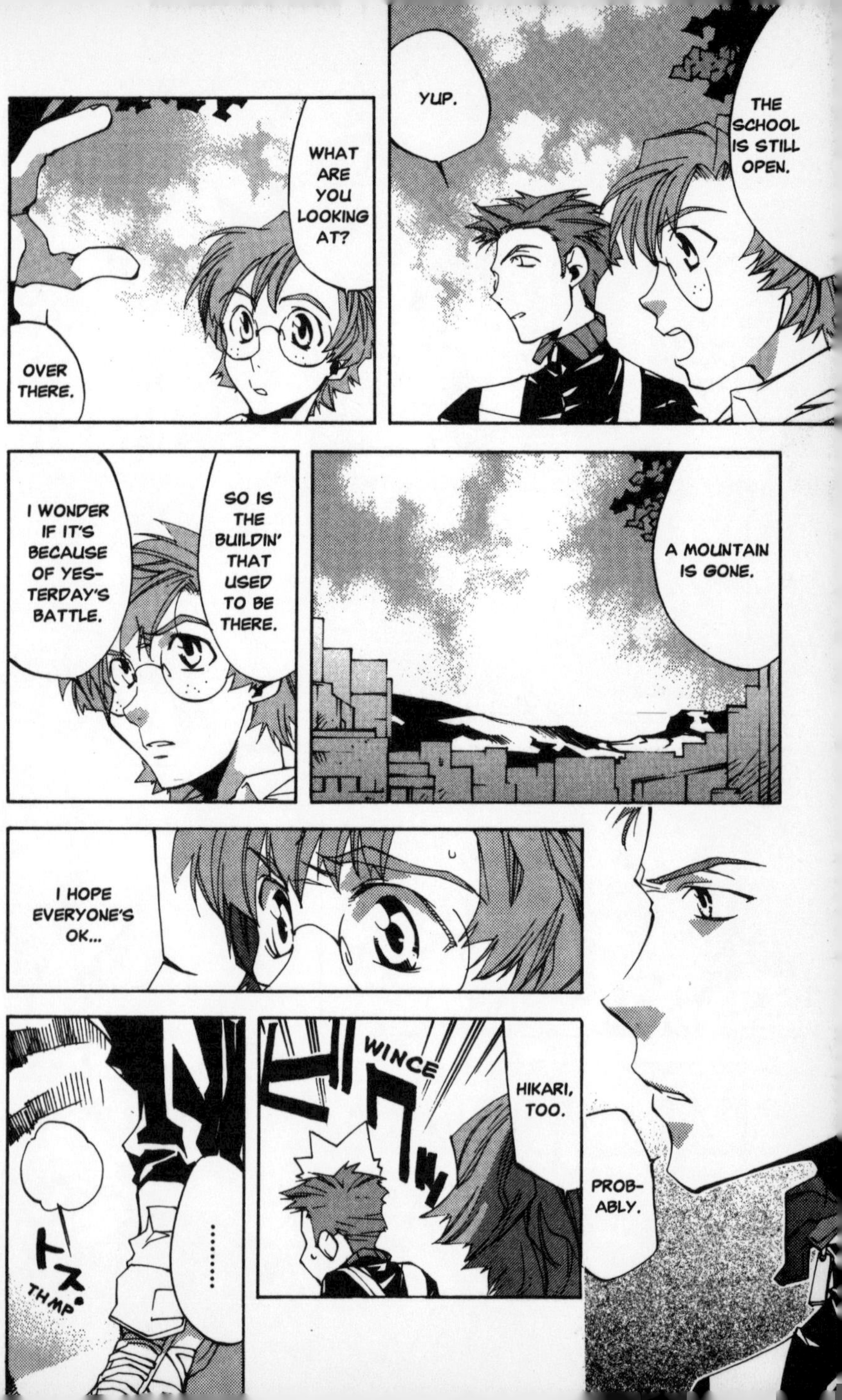
THE SCHOOL IS STILL OPEN.
YUP.
WHAT ARE YOU LOOKING AT?
OVER THERE.
A MOUNTAIN IS GONE.
SO IS THE BUILDIN' THAT USED TO BE THERE.
I WONDER IF IT'S BECAUSE OF YES-TERDAY'S BATTLE.
I HOPE EVERYONE'S OK...
HIKARI, TOO.
PROB-ABLY.
WINCE
......
THMP

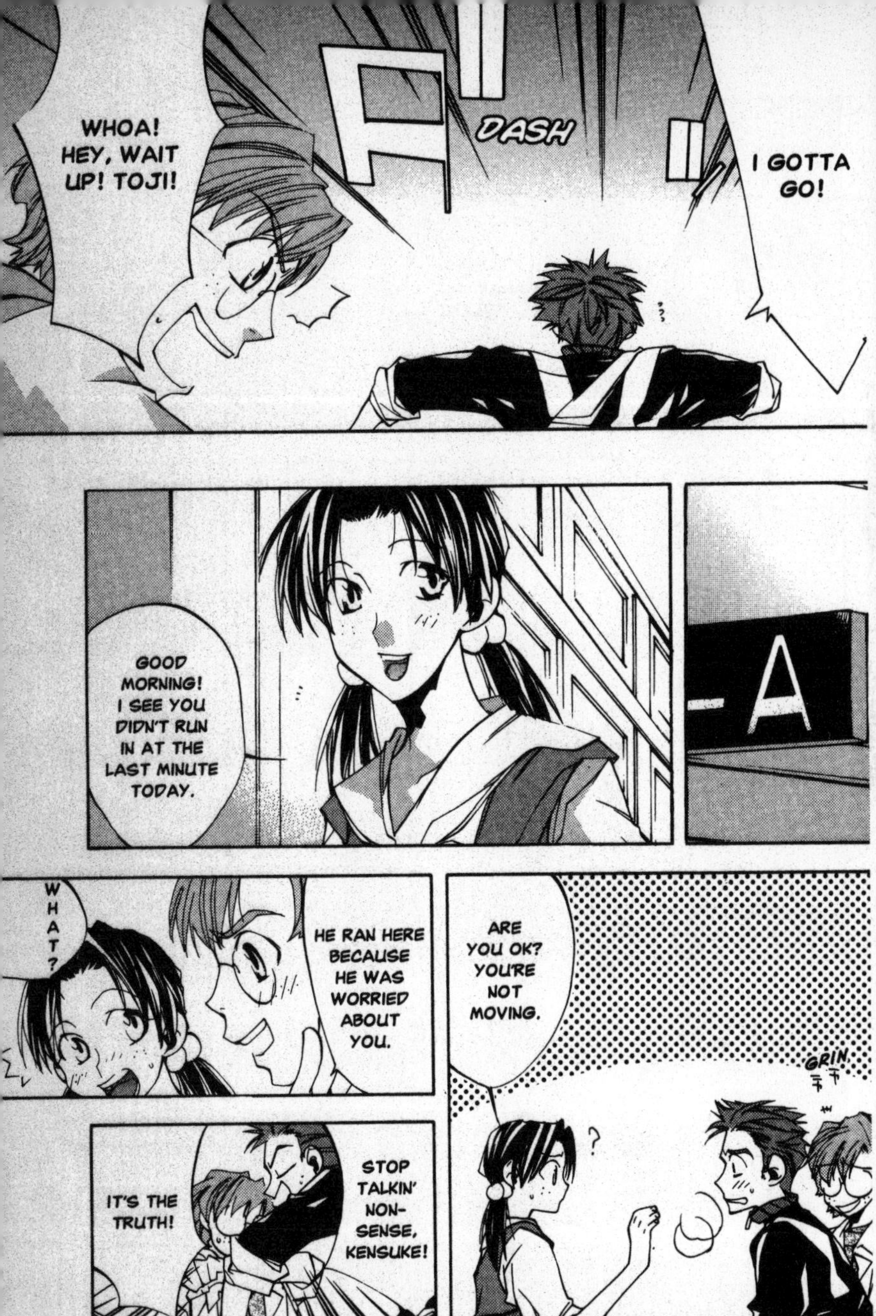
I GOTTA GO!
DASH
WHOA! HEY, WAIT UP! TOJI!
GOOD MORNING! I SEE YOU DIDN'T RUN IN AT THE LAST MINUTE TODAY.
ARE YOU OK? YOU'RE NOT MOVING.
GRIN
HE RAN HERE BECAUSE HE WAS WORRIED ABOUT YOU.
WHAT?
STOP TALKIN' NON-SENSE, KENSUKE!
IT'S THE TRUTH!

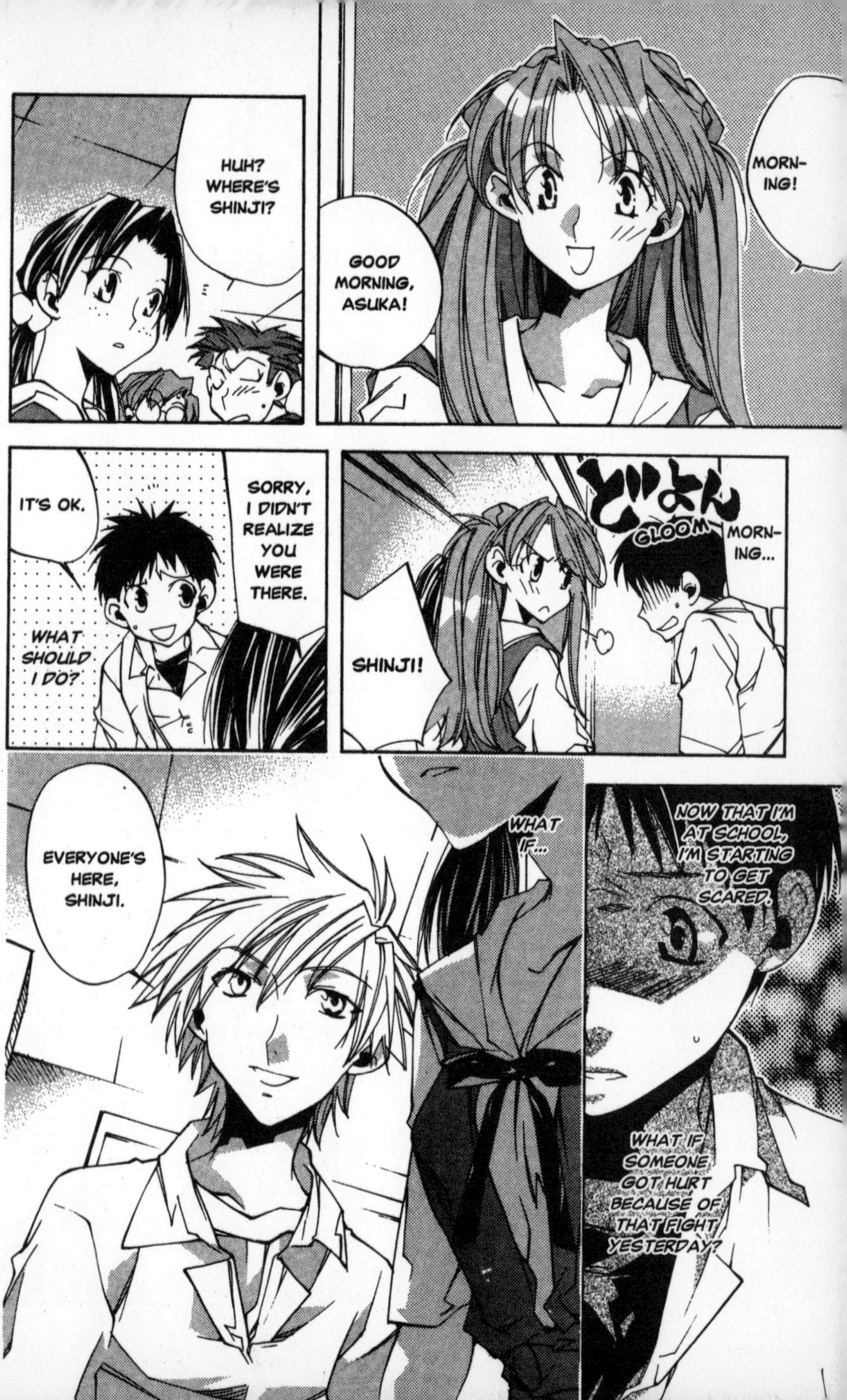
MORN-ING!
GOOD MORNING, ASUKA!
HUH? WHERE'S SHINJI?
SHINJI!
とほほん
GLOOM
MORN-ING...
SORRY, I DIDN'T REALIZE YOU WERE THERE.
IT'S OK.
WHAT SHOULD I DO?
NOW THAT I'M AT SCHOOL, I'M STARTING TO GET SCARED.
WHAT IF SOMEONE GOT HURT BECAUSE OF THAT FIGHT YESTERDAY?
WHAT IF...
EVERYONE'S HERE, SHINJI.

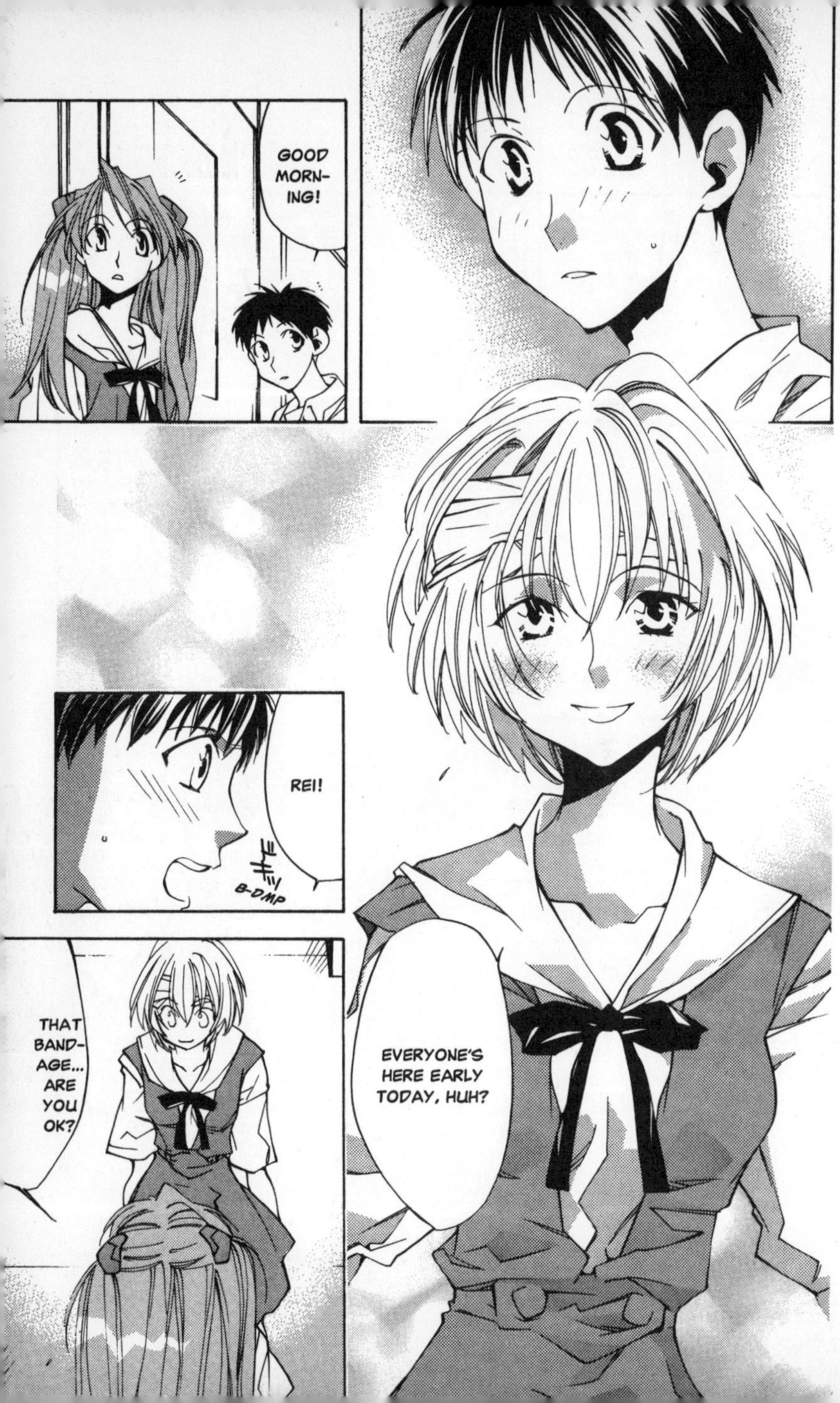
GOOD MORNING!
REI!
B-DMP
EVERYONE'S HERE EARLY TODAY, HUH?
THAT BANDAGE... ARE YOU OK?

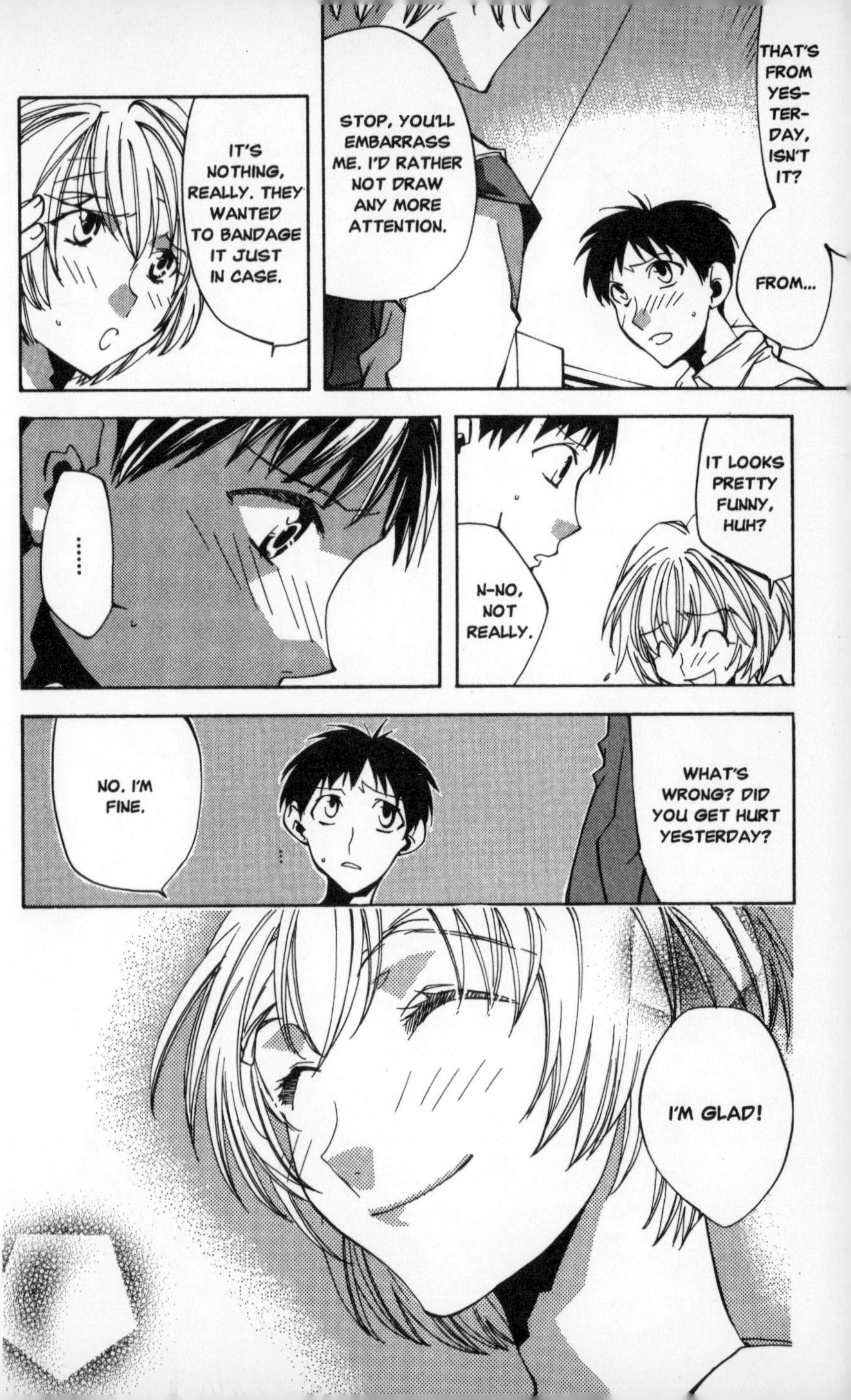

THAT'S FROM YES-TER-DAY, ISN'T IT?
FROM...
STOP, YOU'LL EMBARRASS ME. I'D RATHER NOT DRAW ANY MORE ATTENTION.
IT'S NOTHING, REALLY. THEY WANTED TO BANDAGE IT JUST IN CASE.
IT LOOKS PRETTY FUNNY, HUH?
N-NO, NOT REALLY.
......
WHAT'S WRONG? DID YOU GET HURT YESTERDAY?
NO. I'M FINE.
I'M GLAD!

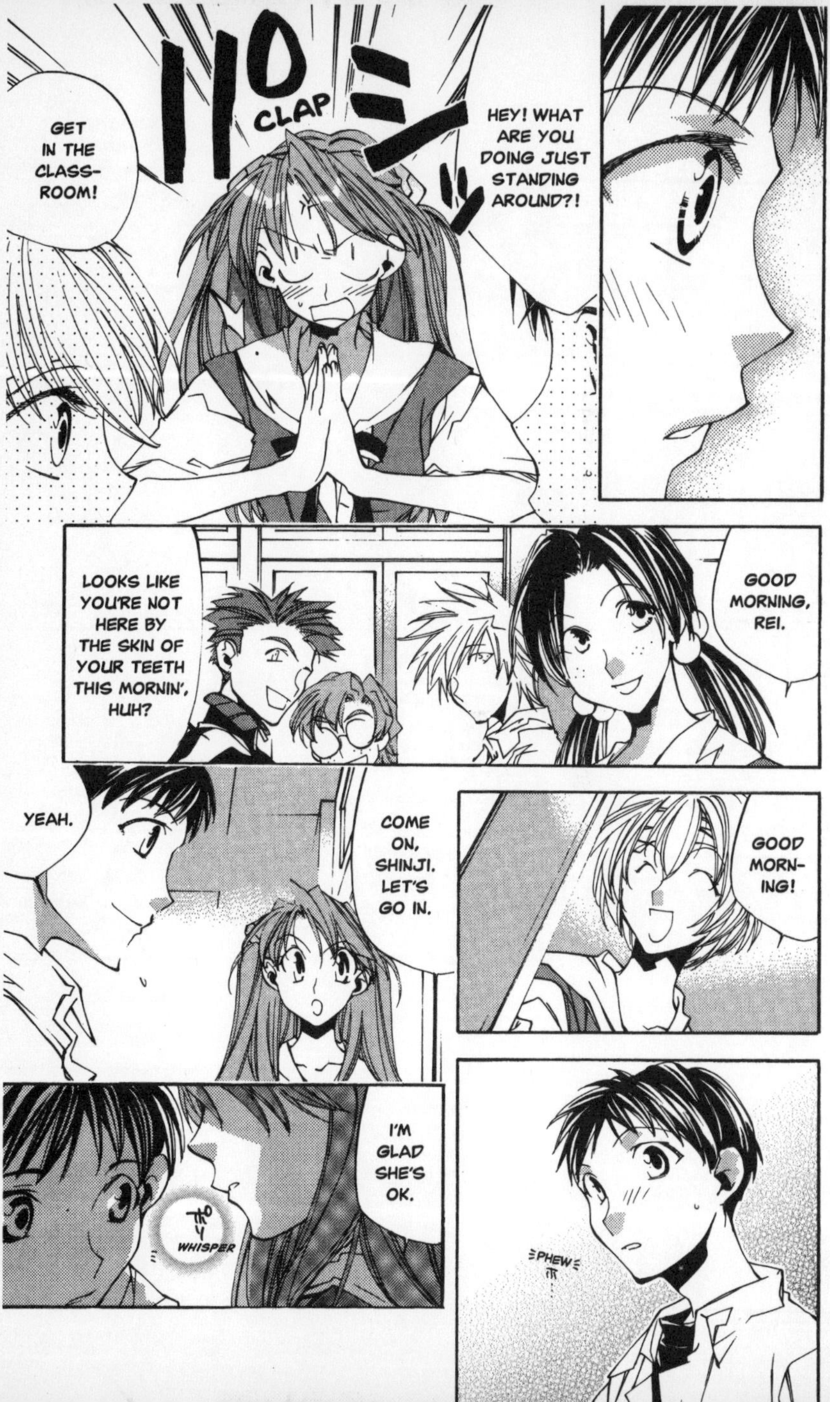
HEY! WHAT ARE YOU DOING JUST STANDING AROUND?!
CLAP
GET IN THE CLASS-ROOM!
GOOD MORNING, REI.
LOOKS LIKE YOU'RE NOT HERE BY THE SKIN OF YOUR TEETH THIS MORNIN', HUH?
GOOD MORN-ING!
COME ON, SHINJI. LET'S GO IN.
YEAH.
PHEW
I'M GLAD SHE'S OK.
WHISPER

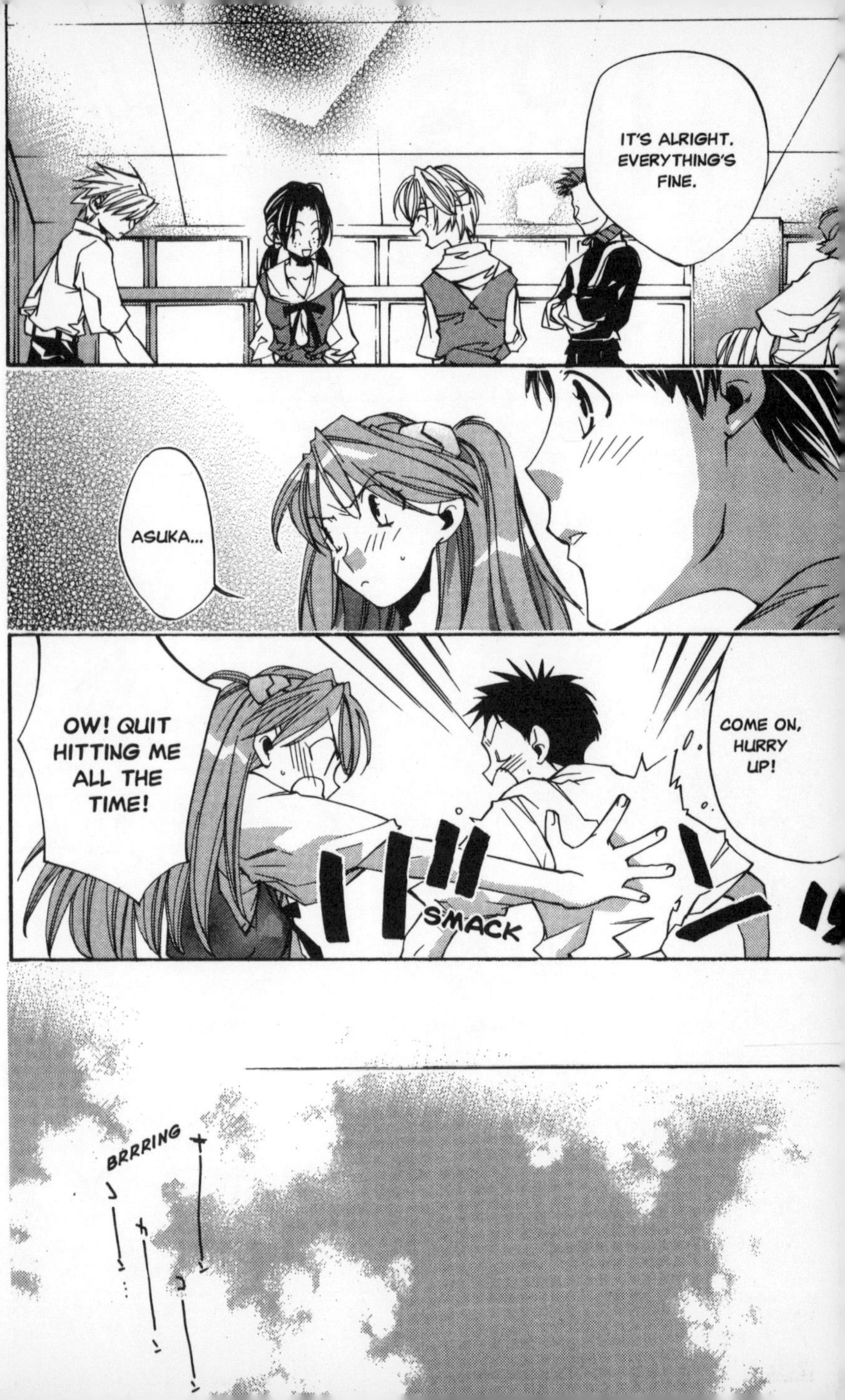
IT'S ALRIGHT. EVERYTHING'S FINE.
ASUKA...
COME ON, HURRY UP!
OW! QUIT HITTING ME ALL THE TIME!
SMACK
BRRRING

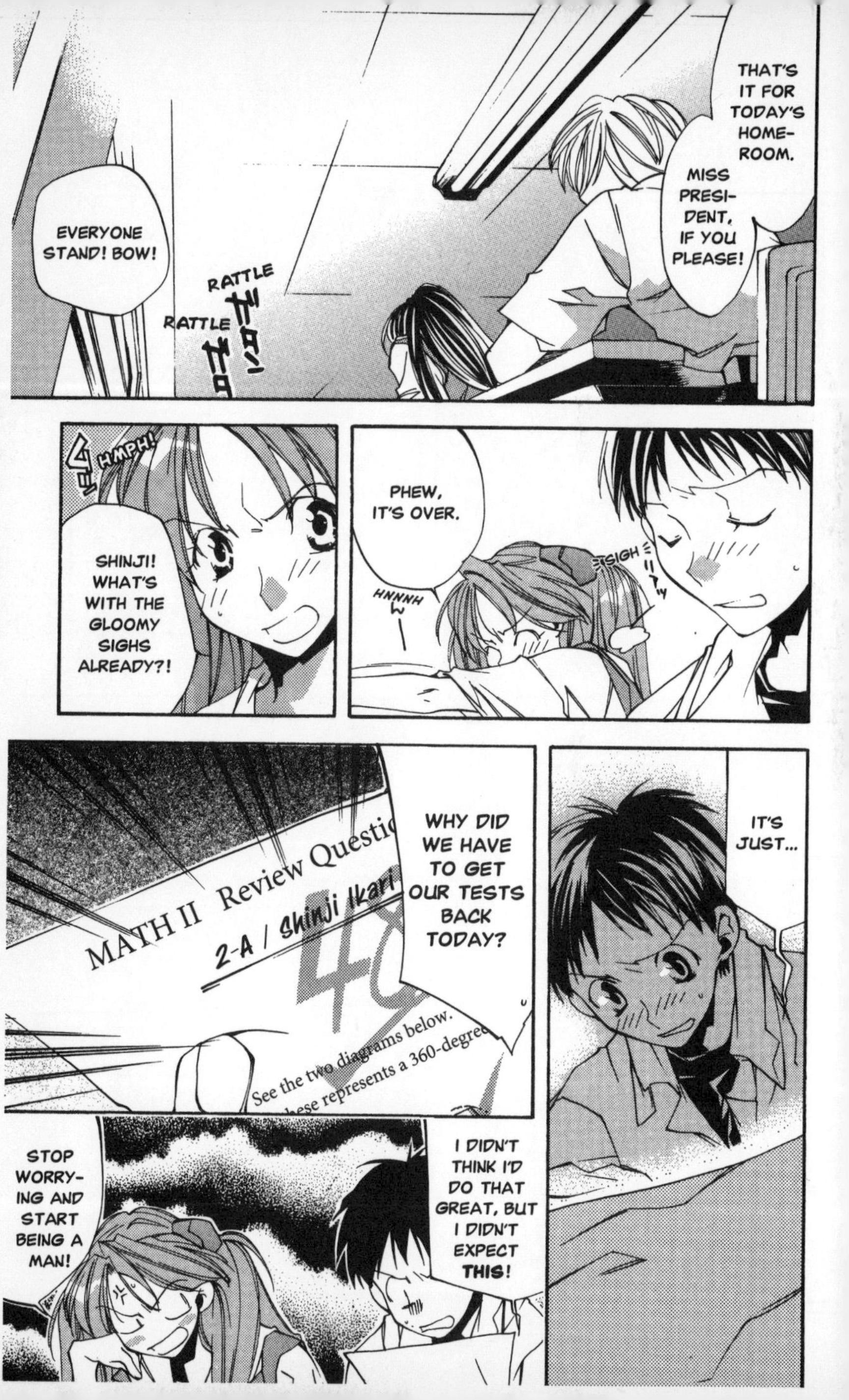
THAT'S IT FOR TODAY'S HOME-ROOM.
MISS PRESI-DENT, IF YOU PLEASE!
RATTLE
RATTLE
EVERYONE STAND! BOW!
PHEW, IT'S OVER.
SIGH
HNNNH
HMPH!
SHINJI! WHAT'S WITH THE GLOOMY SIGHS ALREADY?!
IT'S JUST...
WHY DID WE HAVE TO GET OUR TESTS BACK TODAY?
MATH II Review Questio
2-A / Shinji Ikari
See the two diagrams below.
these represents a 360-degre
I DIDN'T THINK I'D DO THAT GREAT, BUT I DIDN'T EXPECT **THIS**!
STOP WORRY-ING AND START BEING A MAN!

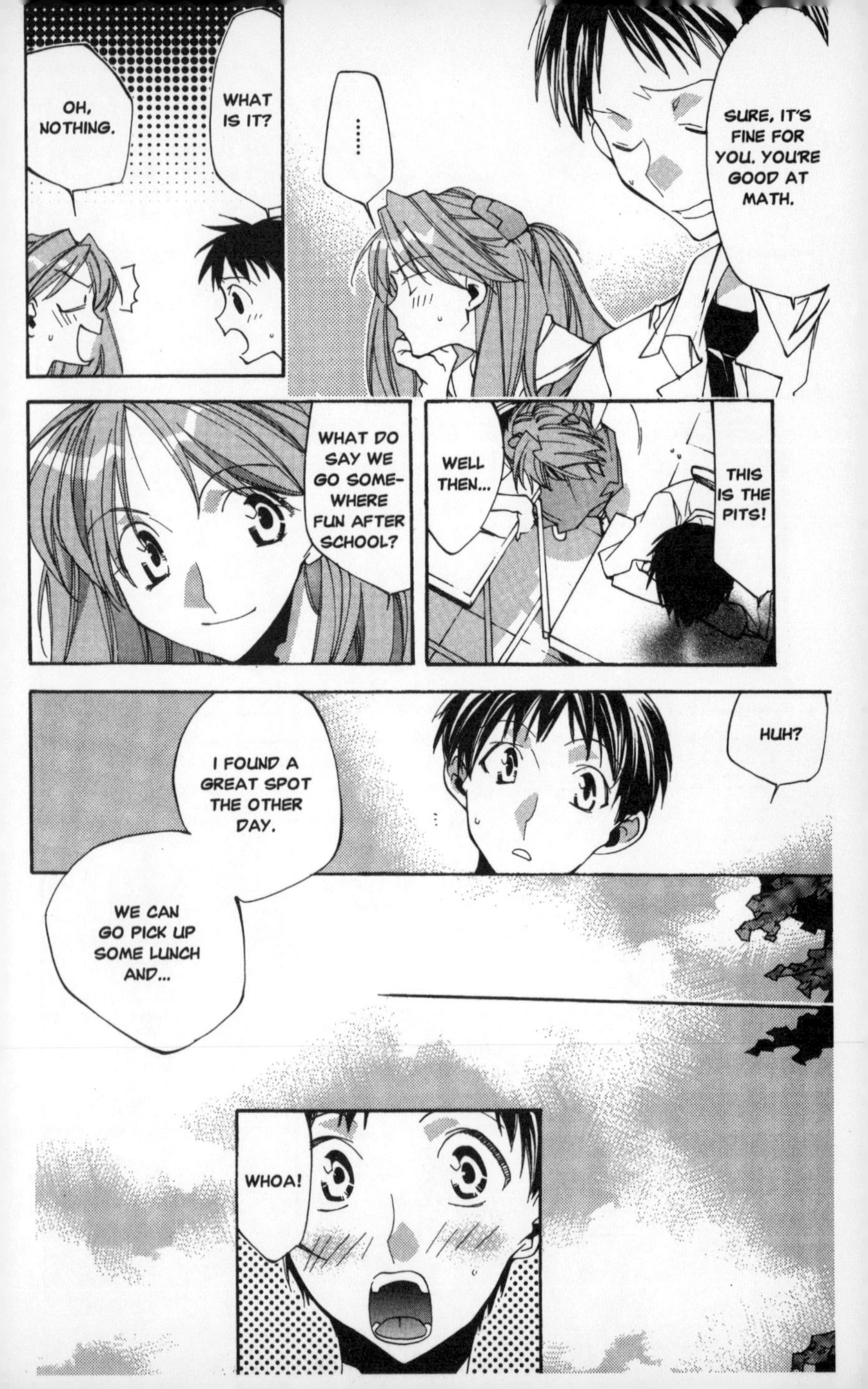
SURE, IT'S FINE FOR YOU. YOU'RE GOOD AT MATH.
......
WHAT IS IT?
OH, NOTHING.
THIS IS THE PITS!
WELL THEN...
WHAT DO SAY WE GO SOME-WHERE FUN AFTER SCHOOL?
HUH?
I FOUND A GREAT SPOT THE OTHER DAY.
WE CAN GO PICK UP SOME LUNCH AND...
WHOA!

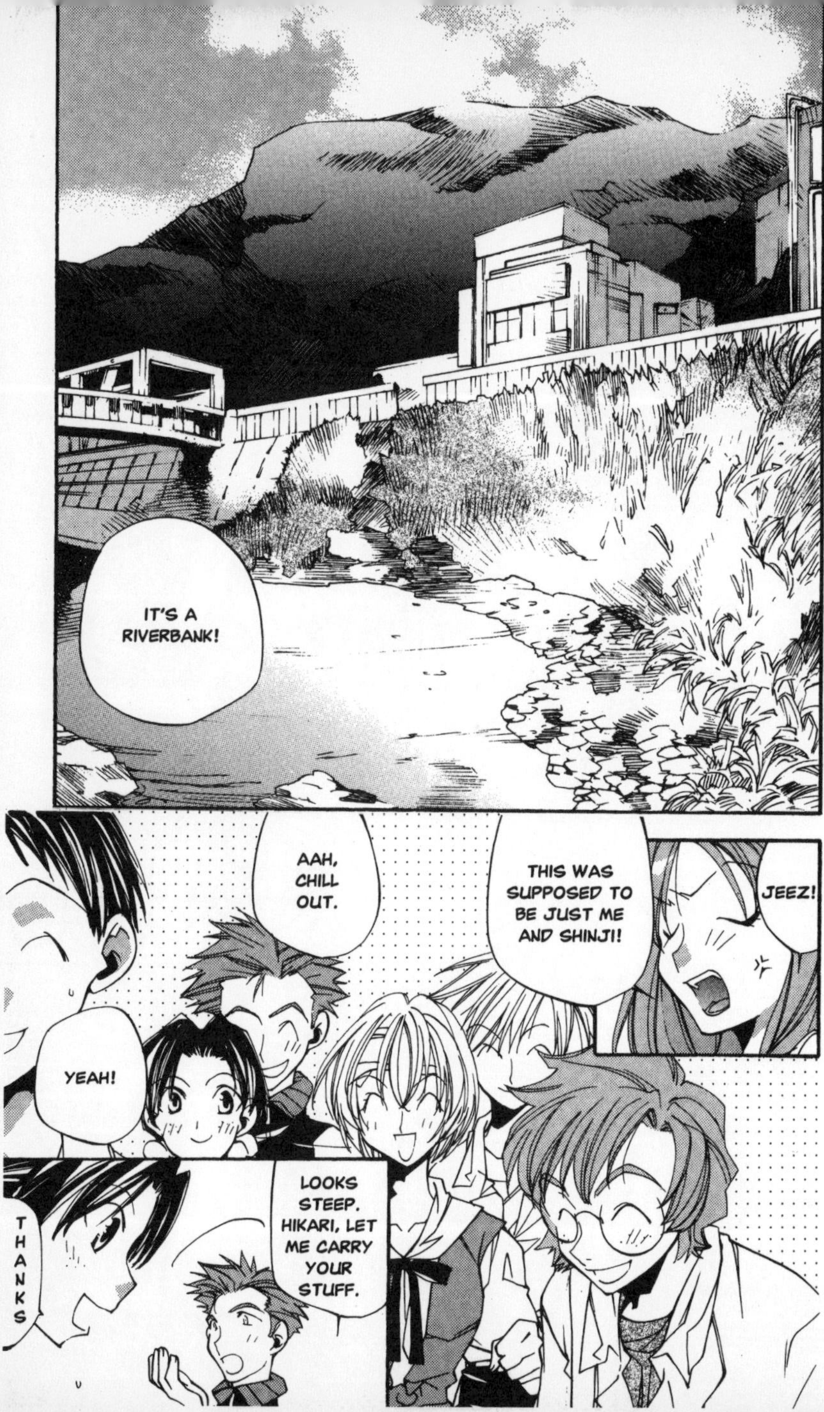
IT'S A RIVERBANK!
JEEZ!
THIS WAS SUPPOSED TO BE JUST ME AND SHINJI!
AAH, CHILL OUT.
YEAH!
LOOKS STEEP. HIKARI, LET ME CARRY YOUR STUFF.
THANKS

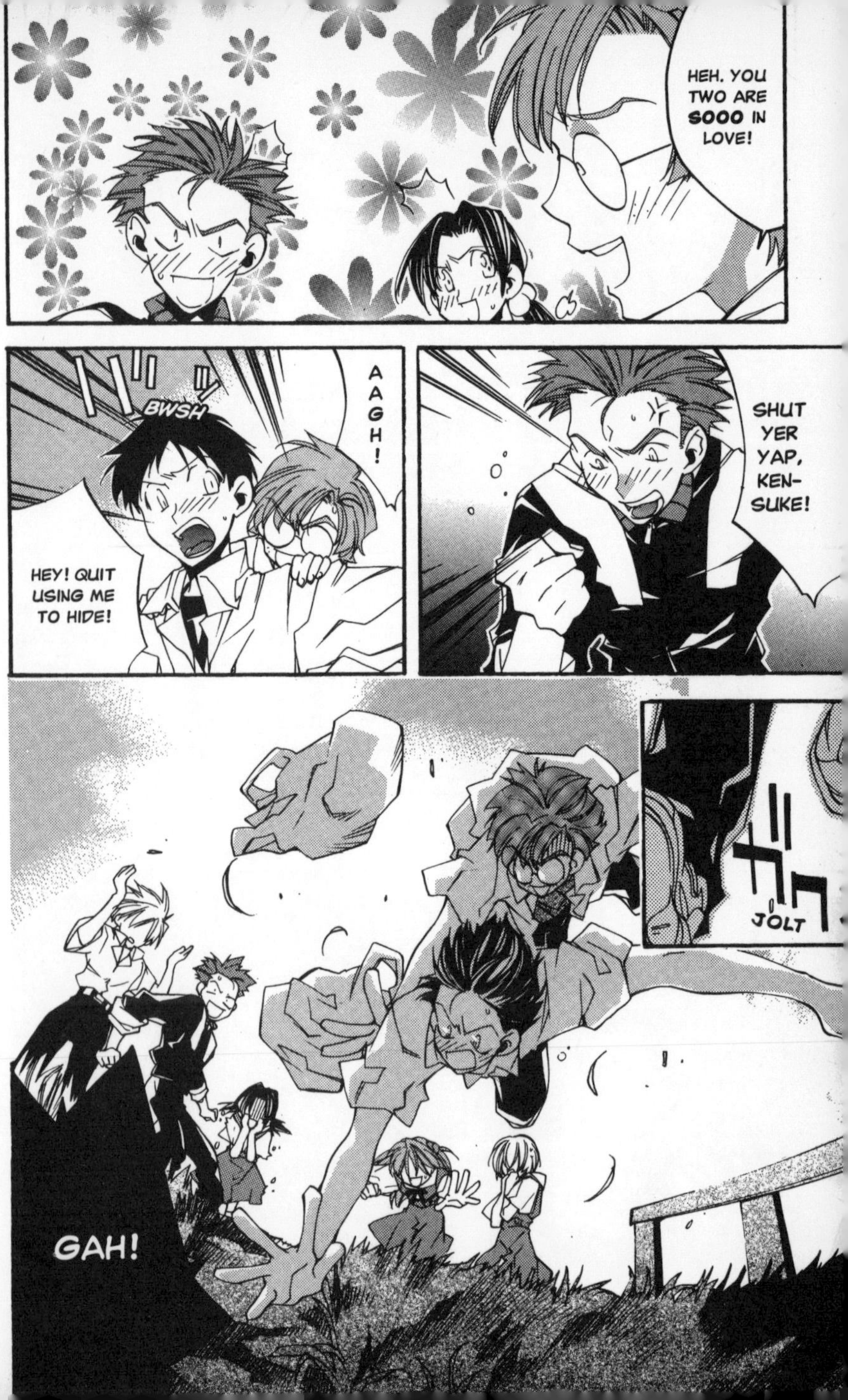
HEH. YOU TWO ARE SOOO IN LOVE!
SHUT YER YAP, KEN-SUKE!
AAGH!
BWSH
HEY! QUIT USING ME TO HIDE!
JOLT
GAH!

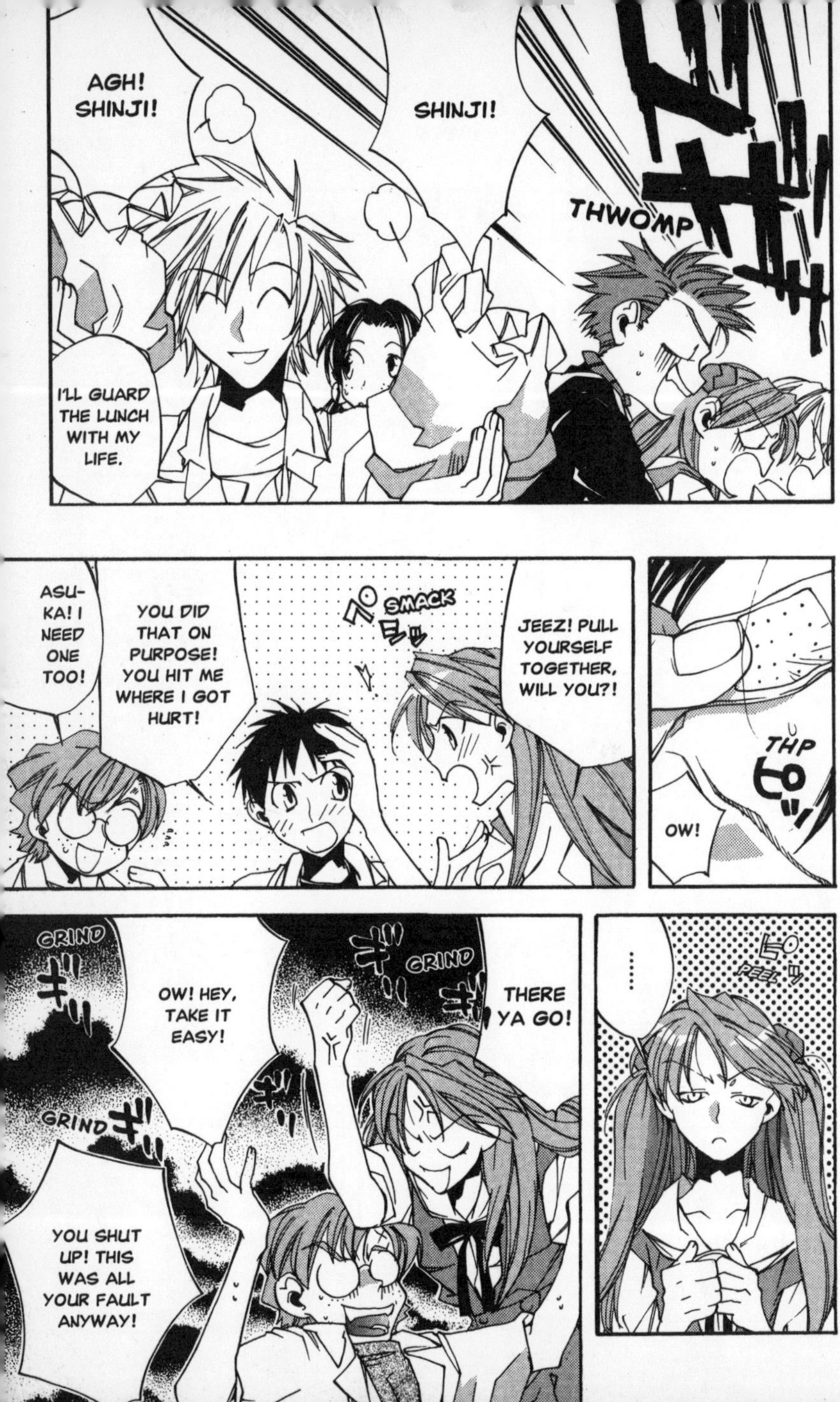
THWOMP
SHINJI!
AGH! SHINJI!
I'LL GUARD THE LUNCH WITH MY LIFE.
THP
OW!
JEEZ! PULL YOURSELF TOGETHER, WILL YOU?!
SMACK
YOU DID THAT ON PURPOSE! YOU HIT ME WHERE I GOT HURT!
ASU-KA! I NEED ONE TOO!
PEEL
......
THERE YA GO!
GRIND
OW! HEY, TAKE IT EASY!
GRIND
GRIND
YOU SHUT UP! THIS WAS ALL YOUR FAULT ANYWAY!

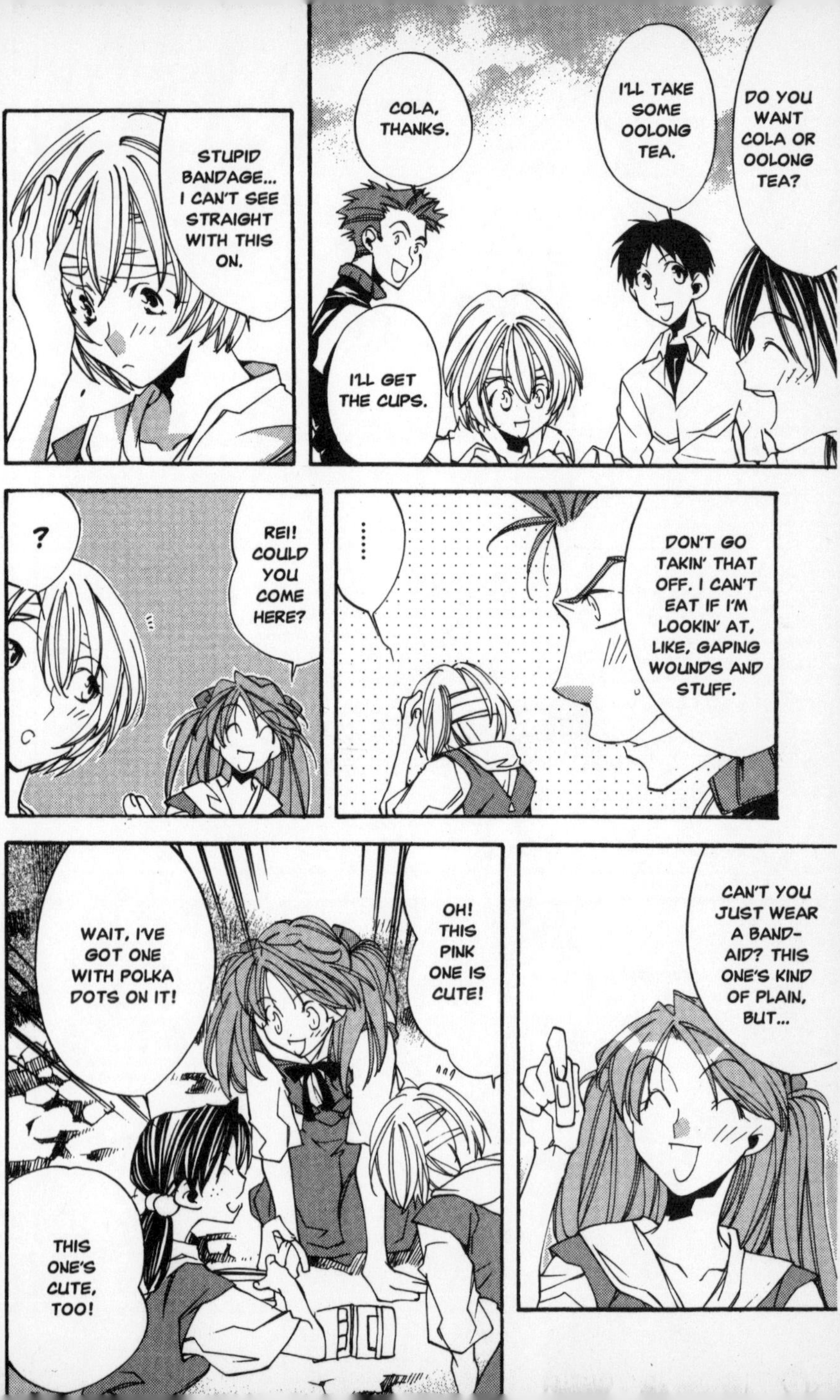
DO YOU WANT COLA OR OOLONG TEA?
I'LL TAKE SOME OOLONG TEA.
COLA, THANKS.
I'LL GET THE CUPS.
STUPID BANDAGE... I CAN'T SEE STRAIGHT WITH THIS ON.
DON'T GO TAKIN' THAT OFF. I CAN'T EAT IF I'M LOOKIN' AT, LIKE, GAPING WOUNDS AND STUFF.
......
REI! COULD YOU COME HERE?
?
CAN'T YOU JUST WEAR A BAND-AID? THIS ONE'S KIND OF PLAIN, BUT...
OH! THIS PINK ONE IS CUTE!
WAIT, I'VE GOT ONE WITH POLKA DOTS ON IT!
THIS ONE'S CUTE, TOO!

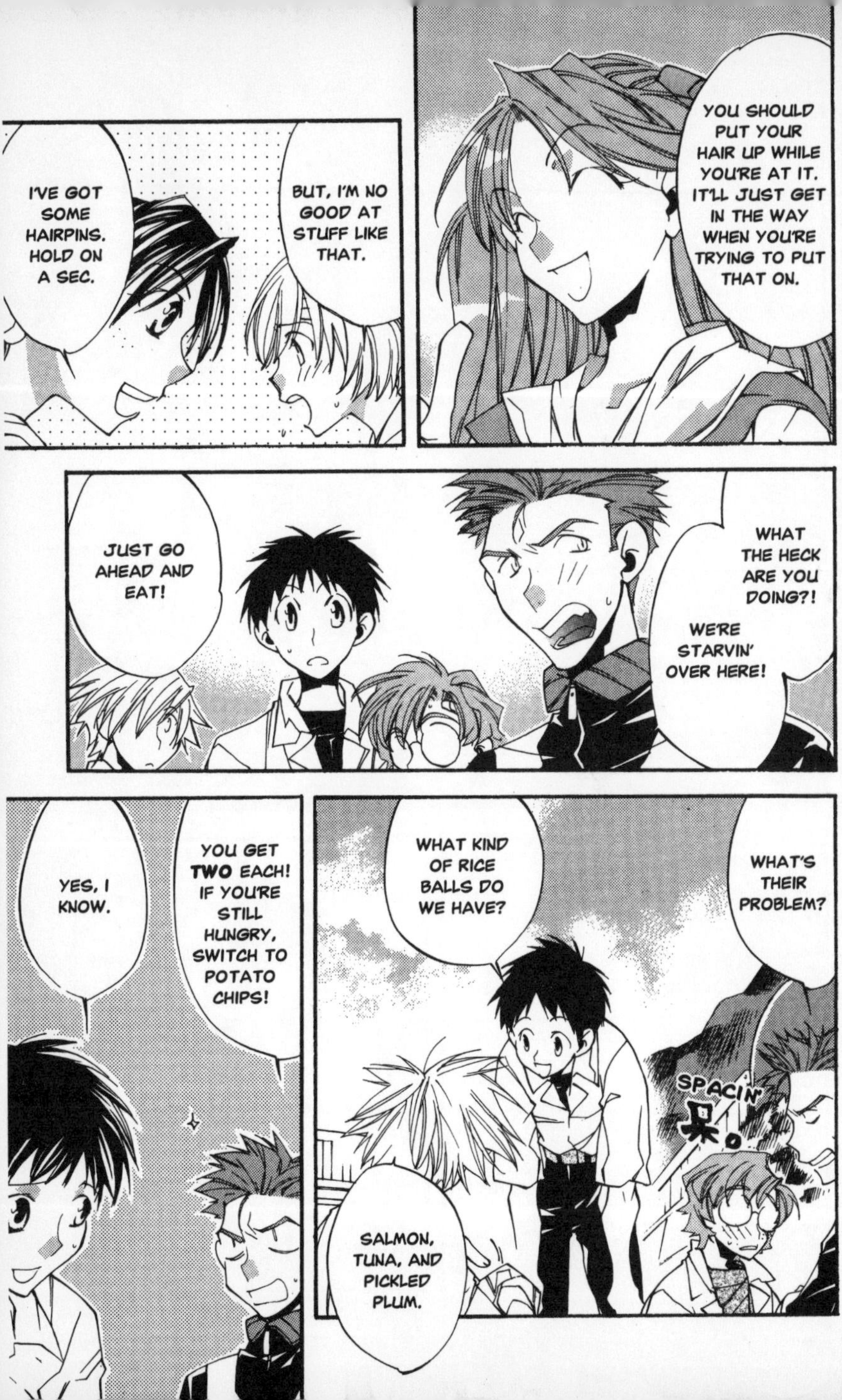
YOU SHOULD PUT YOUR HAIR UP WHILE YOU'RE AT IT. IT'LL JUST GET IN THE WAY WHEN YOU'RE TRYING TO PUT THAT ON.
BUT, I'M NO GOOD AT STUFF LIKE THAT.
I'VE GOT SOME HAIRPINS. HOLD ON A SEC.
WHAT THE HECK ARE YOU DOING?!
WE'RE STARVIN' OVER HERE!
JUST GO AHEAD AND EAT!
WHAT'S THEIR PROBLEM?
WHAT KIND OF RICE BALLS DO WE HAVE?
SPACIN'
SALMON, TUNA, AND PICKLED PLUM.
YOU GET **TWO** EACH! IF YOU'RE STILL HUNGRY, SWITCH TO POTATO CHIPS!
YES, I KNOW.

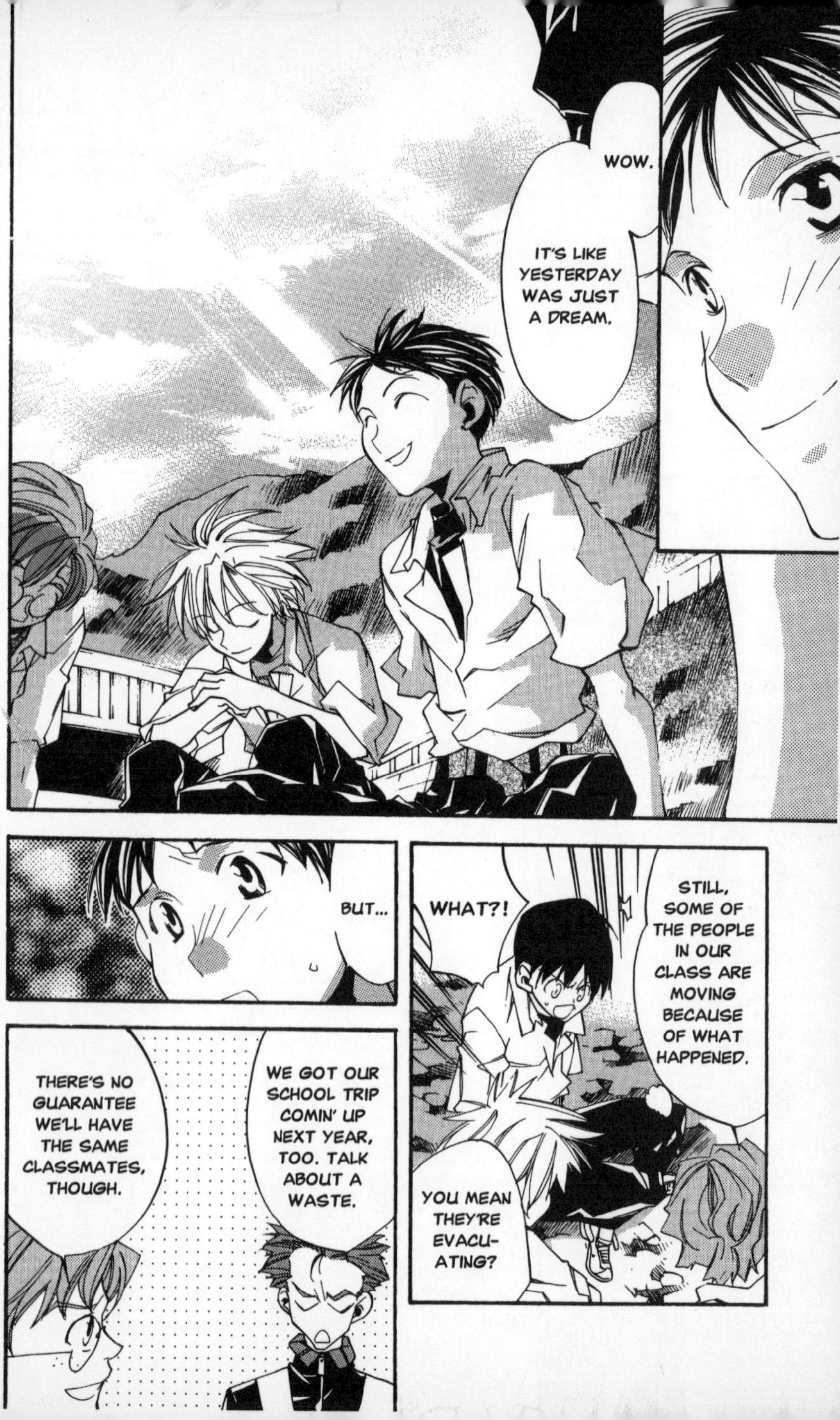
WOW.
IT'S LIKE YESTERDAY WAS JUST A DREAM.
BUT...
STILL, SOME OF THE PEOPLE IN OUR CLASS ARE MOVING BECAUSE OF WHAT HAPPENED.
WHAT?!
YOU MEAN THEY'RE EVACU-ATING?
WE GOT OUR SCHOOL TRIP COMIN' UP NEXT YEAR, TOO. TALK ABOUT A WASTE.
THERE'S NO GUARANTEE WE'LL HAVE THE SAME CLASSMATES, THOUGH.

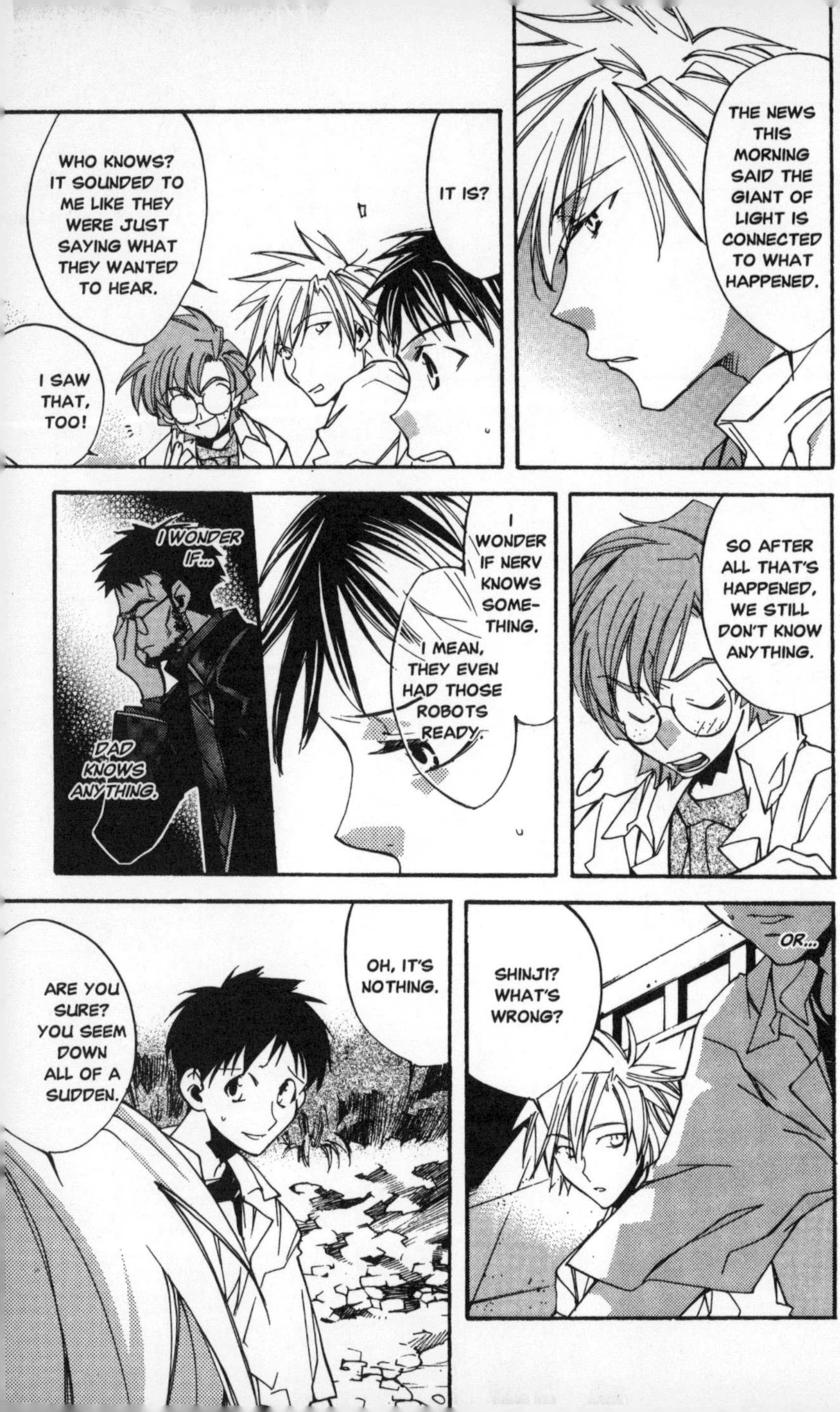
THE NEWS THIS MORNING SAID THE GIANT OF LIGHT IS CONNECTED TO WHAT HAPPENED.
IT IS?
WHO KNOWS? IT SOUNDED TO ME LIKE THEY WERE JUST SAYING WHAT THEY WANTED TO HEAR.
I SAW THAT, TOO!
SO AFTER ALL THAT'S HAPPENED, WE STILL DON'T KNOW ANYTHING.
I WONDER IF NERV KNOWS SOMETHING.
I MEAN, THEY EVEN HAD THOSE ROBOTS READY.
I WONDER IF...
DAD KNOWS ANYTHING.
...OR...
SHINJI? WHAT'S WRONG?
OH, IT'S NOTHING.
ARE YOU SURE? YOU SEEM DOWN ALL OF A SUDDEN.

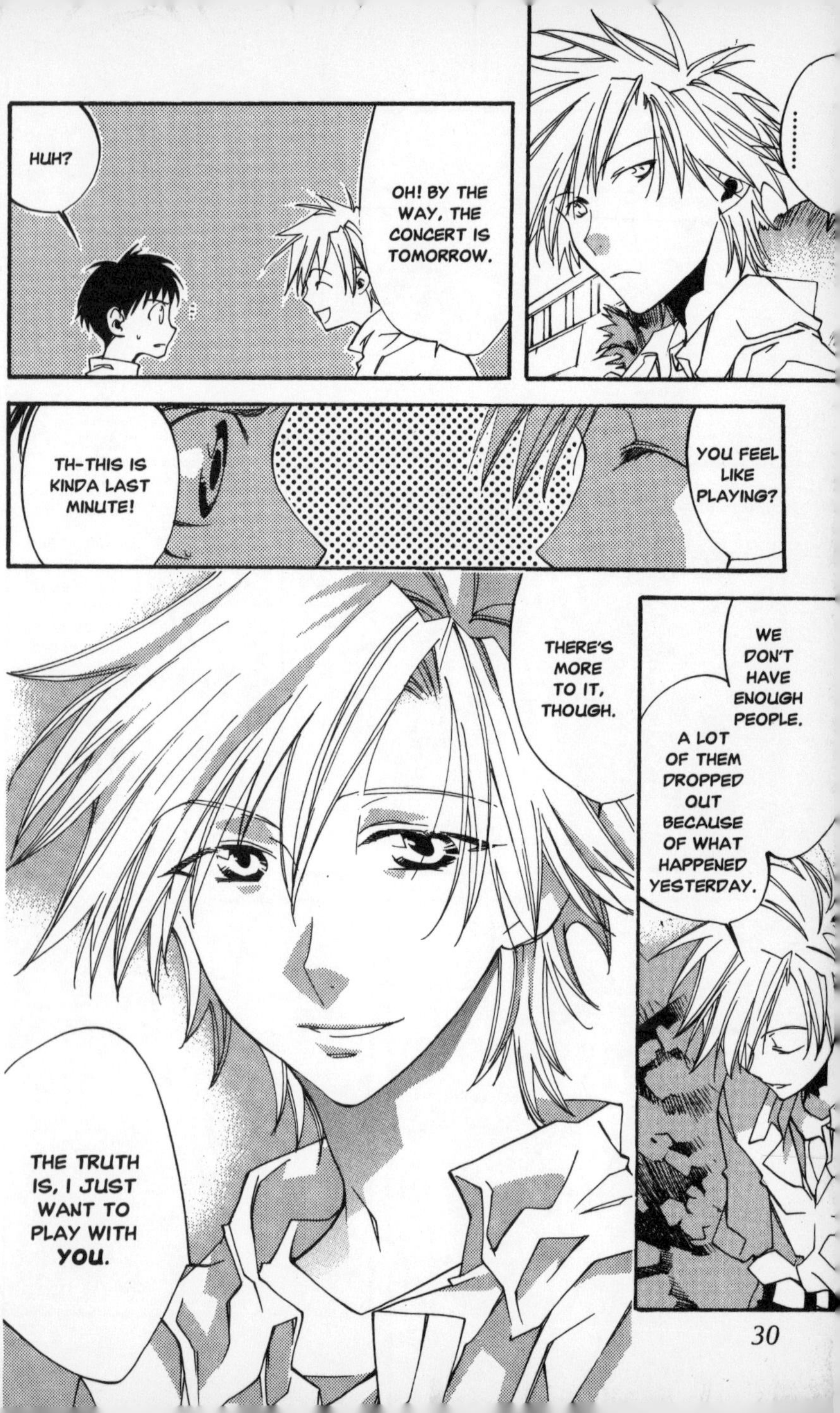
......
OH! BY THE WAY, THE CONCERT IS TOMORROW.
HUH?
YOU FEEL LIKE PLAYING?
TH-THIS IS KINDA LAST MINUTE!
WE DON'T HAVE ENOUGH PEOPLE.
A LOT OF THEM DROPPED OUT BECAUSE OF WHAT HAPPENED YESTERDAY.
THERE'S MORE TO IT, THOUGH.
THE TRUTH IS, I JUST WANT TO PLAY WITH **YOU**.

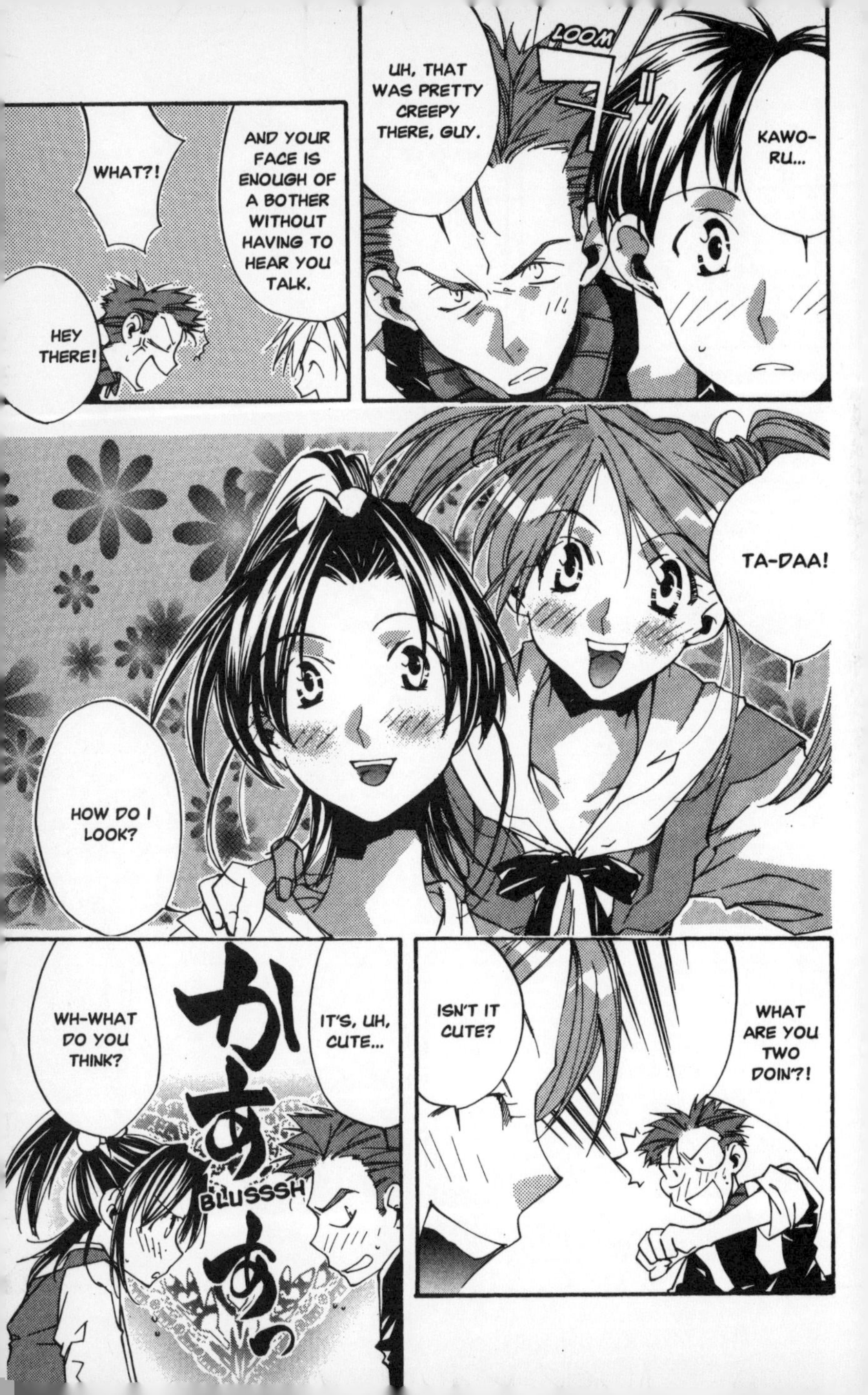
KAWO-RU...
LOOM
UH, THAT WAS PRETTY CREEPY THERE, GUY.
AND YOUR FACE IS ENOUGH OF A BOTHER WITHOUT HAVING TO HEAR YOU TALK.
WHAT?!
HEY THERE!
TA-DAA!
HOW DO I LOOK?
WHAT ARE YOU TWO DOIN'?!
ISN'T IT CUTE?
IT'S, UH, CUTE...
かあっ
BLUSSSH
WH-WHAT DO YOU THINK?

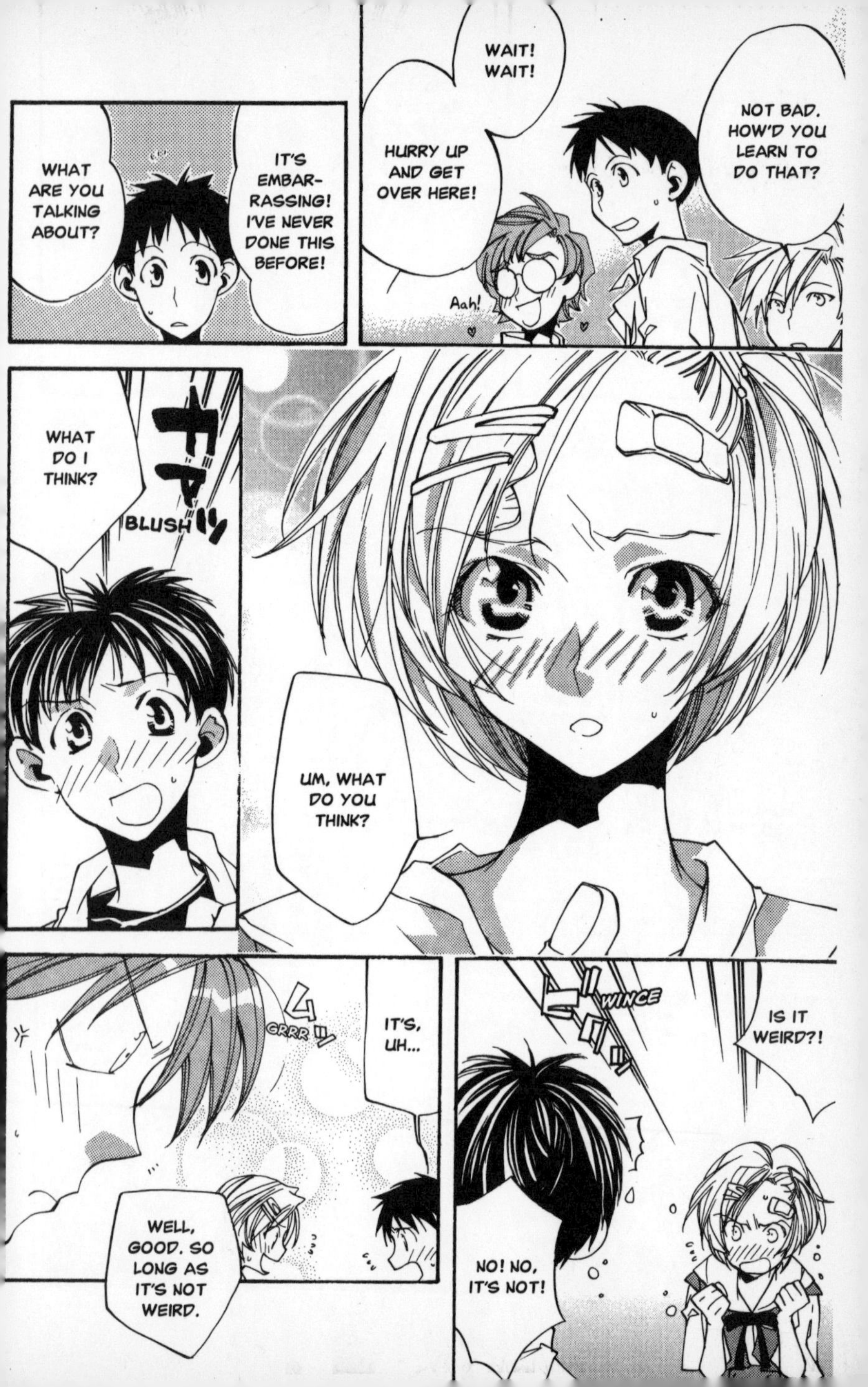
NOT BAD. HOW'D YOU LEARN TO DO THAT?
WAIT! WAIT!
HURRY UP AND GET OVER HERE!
Aah!
IT'S EMBARRASSING! I'VE NEVER DONE THIS BEFORE!
WHAT ARE YOU TALKING ABOUT?
UM, WHAT DO YOU THINK?
WHAT DO I THINK?
BLUSH
IS IT WEIRD?!
WINCE
NO! NO, IT'S NOT!
GRRR
IT'S, UH...
WELL, GOOD. SO LONG AS IT'S NOT WEIRD.

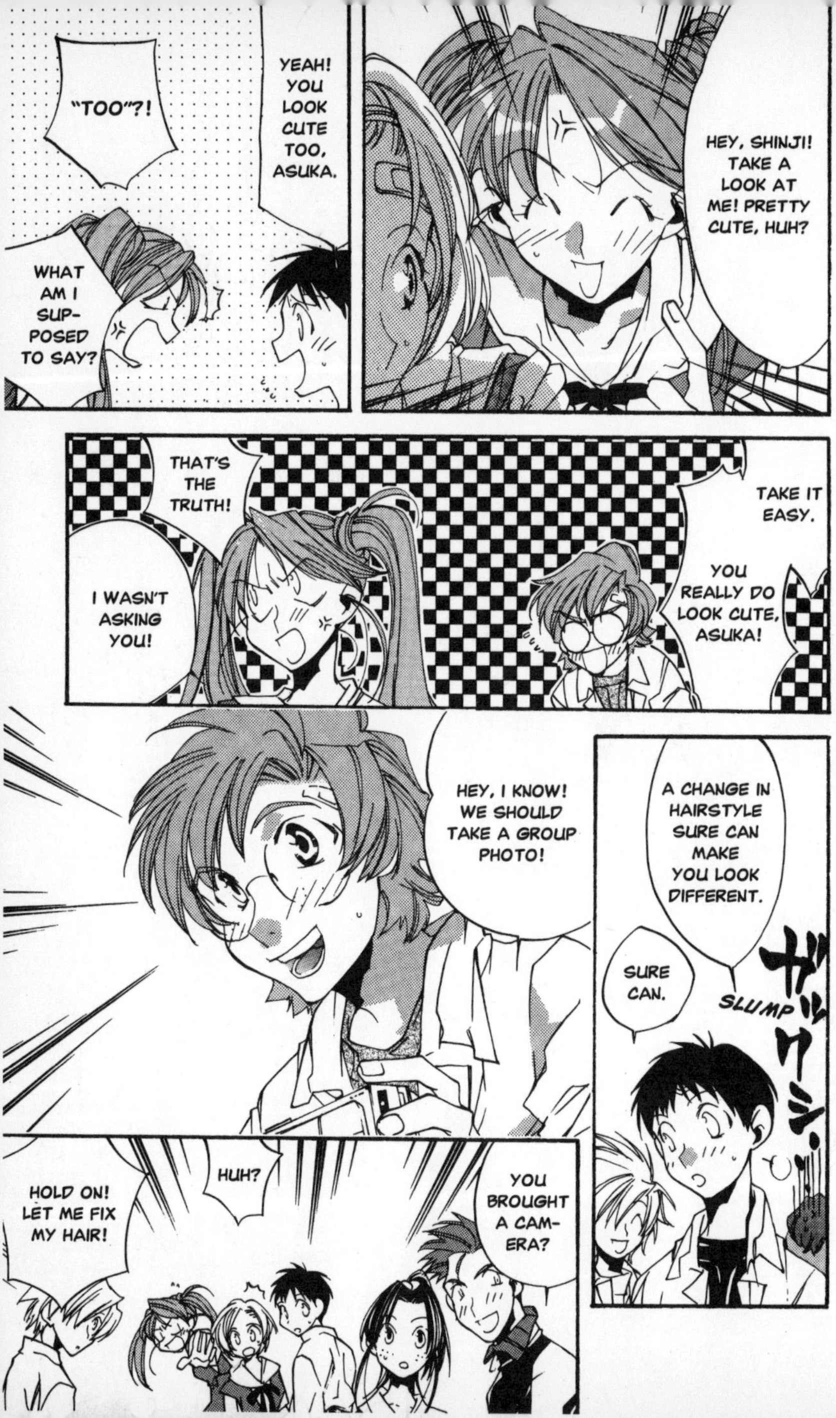
HEY, SHINJI! TAKE A LOOK AT ME! PRETTY CUTE, HUH?
YEAH! YOU LOOK CUTE TOO, ASUKA.
"TOO"?!
WHAT AM I SUP-POSED TO SAY?
TAKE IT EASY.
YOU REALLY DO LOOK CUTE, ASUKA!
THAT'S THE TRUTH!
I WASN'T ASKING YOU!
A CHANGE IN HAIRSTYLE SURE CAN MAKE YOU LOOK DIFFERENT.
SURE CAN.
SLUMP
HEY, I KNOW! WE SHOULD TAKE A GROUP PHOTO!
YOU BROUGHT A CAM-ERA?
HUH?
HOLD ON! LET ME FIX MY HAIR!

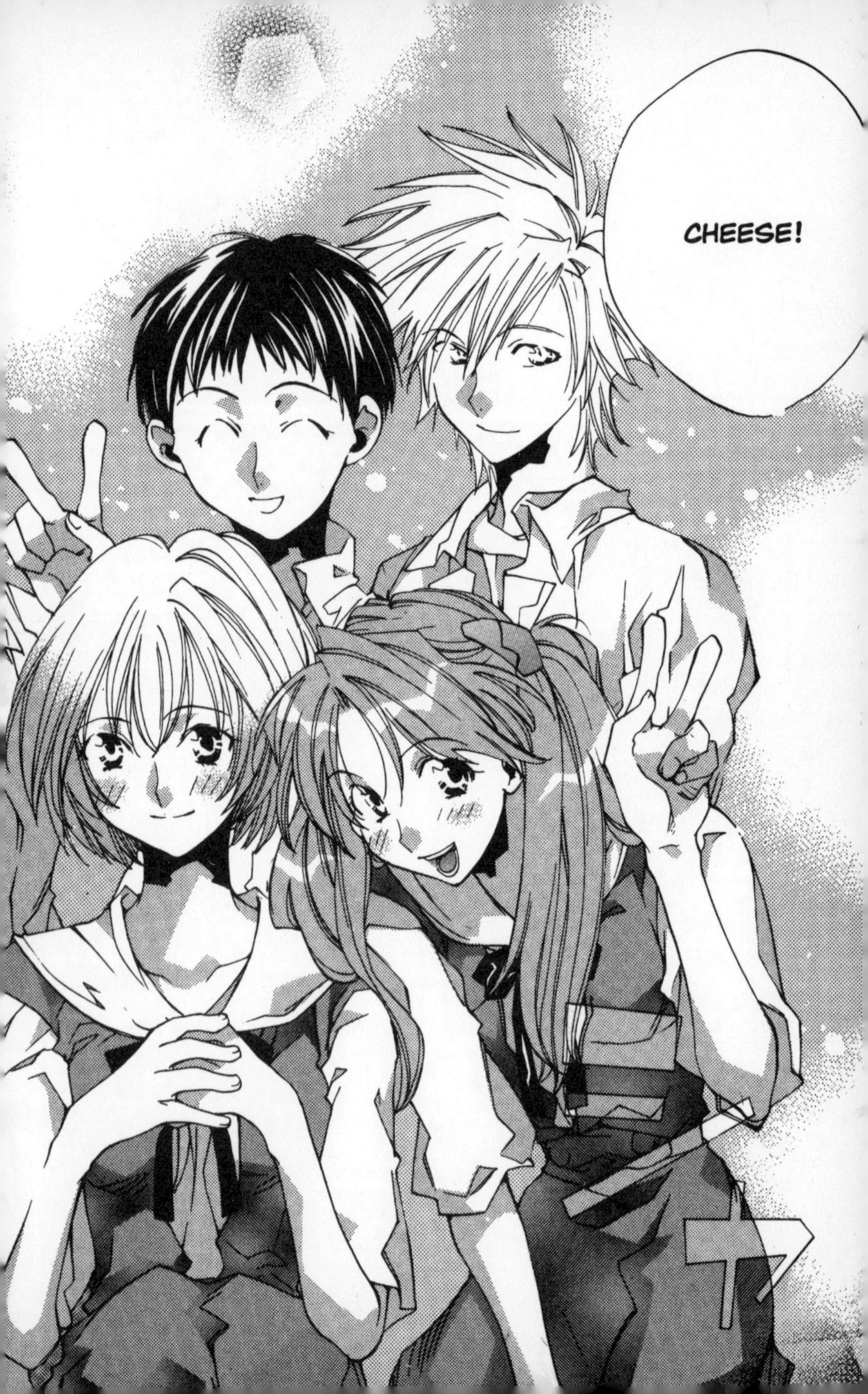
CHEESE!

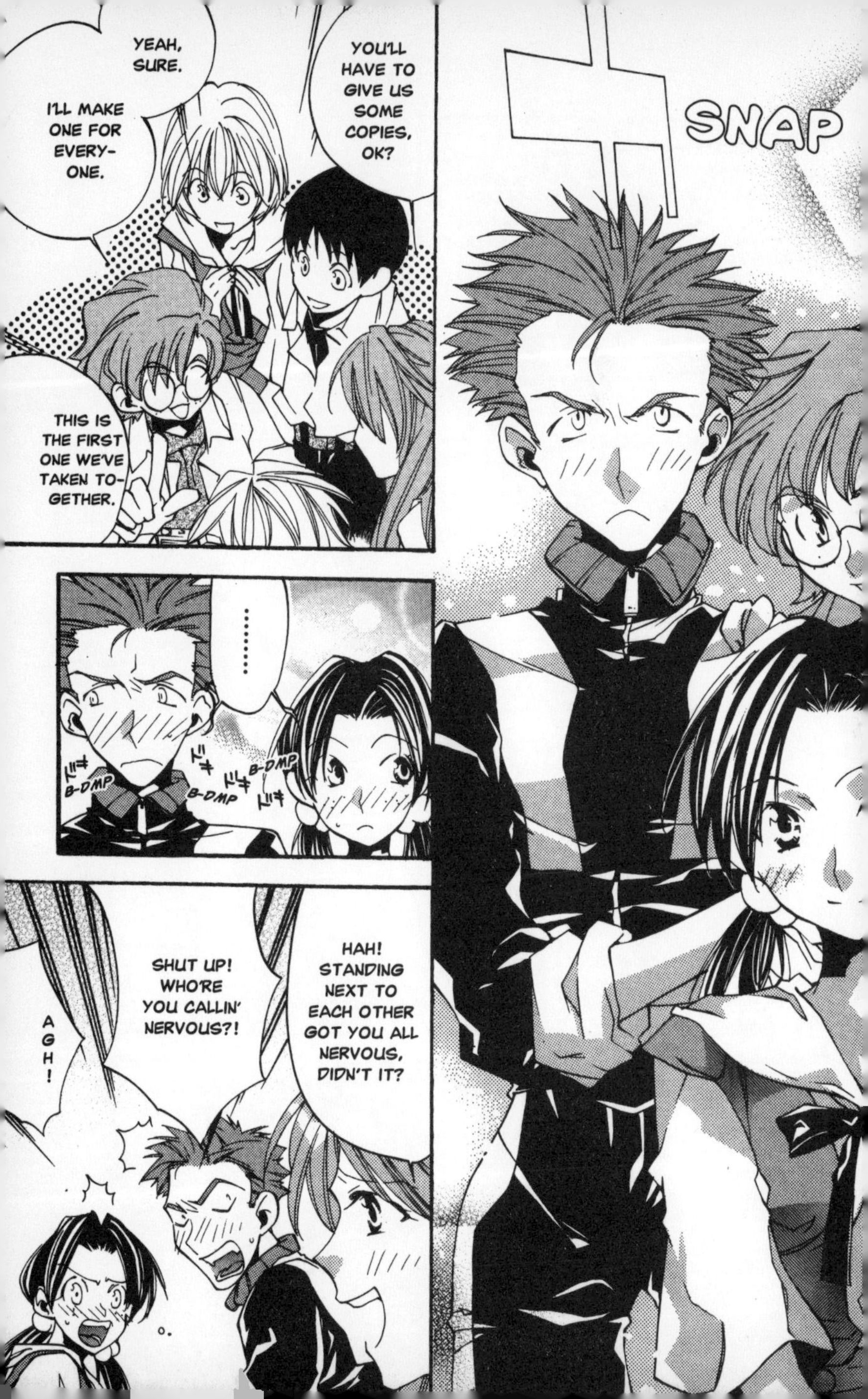
SNAP
YOU'LL HAVE TO GIVE US SOME COPIES, OK?
YEAH, SURE.
I'LL MAKE ONE FOR EVERY-ONE.
THIS IS THE FIRST ONE WE'VE TAKEN TO-GETHER.
....
ドキ B-DMP
ドキ B-DMP
ドキ B-DMP
ドキ B-DMP
HAH! STANDING NEXT TO EACH OTHER GOT YOU ALL NERVOUS, DIDN'T IT?
SHUT UP! WHO'RE YOU CALLIN' NERVOUS?!
AGH!

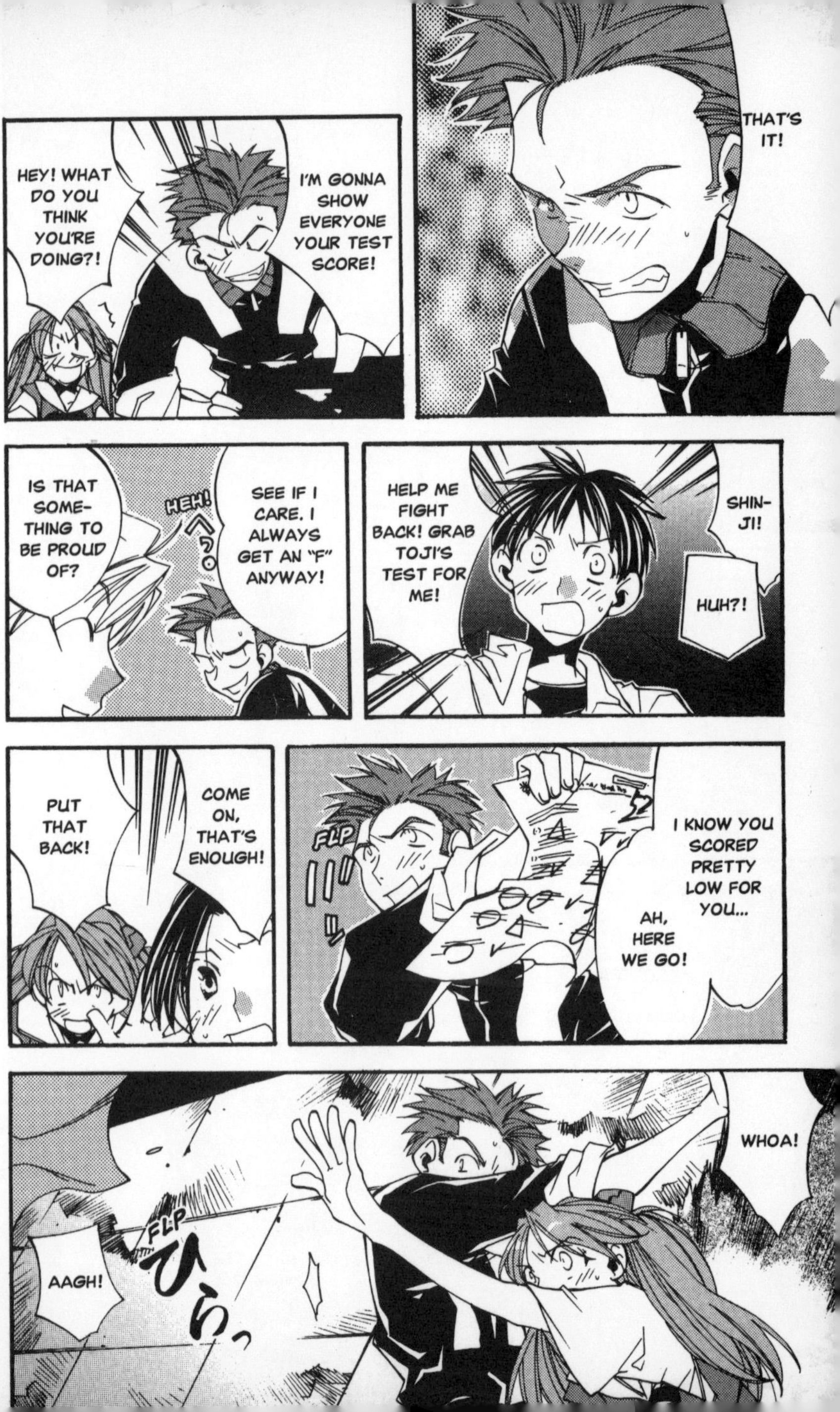

THAT'S IT!
I'M GONNA SHOW EVERYONE YOUR TEST SCORE!
HEY! WHAT DO YOU THINK YOU'RE DOING?!
SHIN-JI!
HUH?!
HELP ME FIGHT BACK! GRAB TOJI'S TEST FOR ME!
SEE IF I CARE. I ALWAYS GET AN "F" ANYWAY!
HEH!
IS THAT SOME-THING TO BE PROUD OF?
I KNOW YOU SCORED PRETTY LOW FOR YOU...
AH, HERE WE GO!
FLP
COME ON, THAT'S ENOUGH!
PUT THAT BACK!
WHOA!
FLP
AAGH!

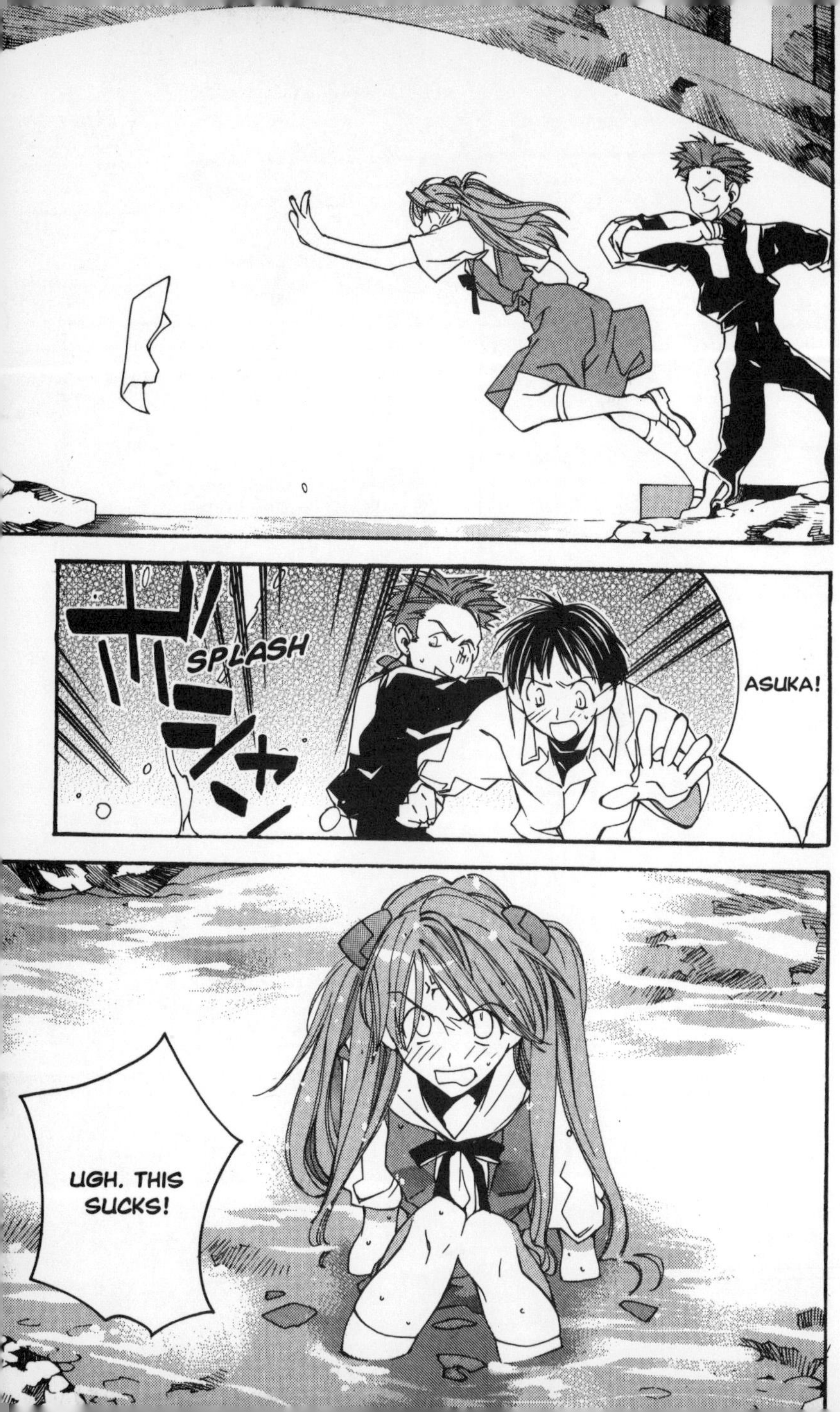
SPLASH
ASUKA!
UGH. THIS SUCKS!

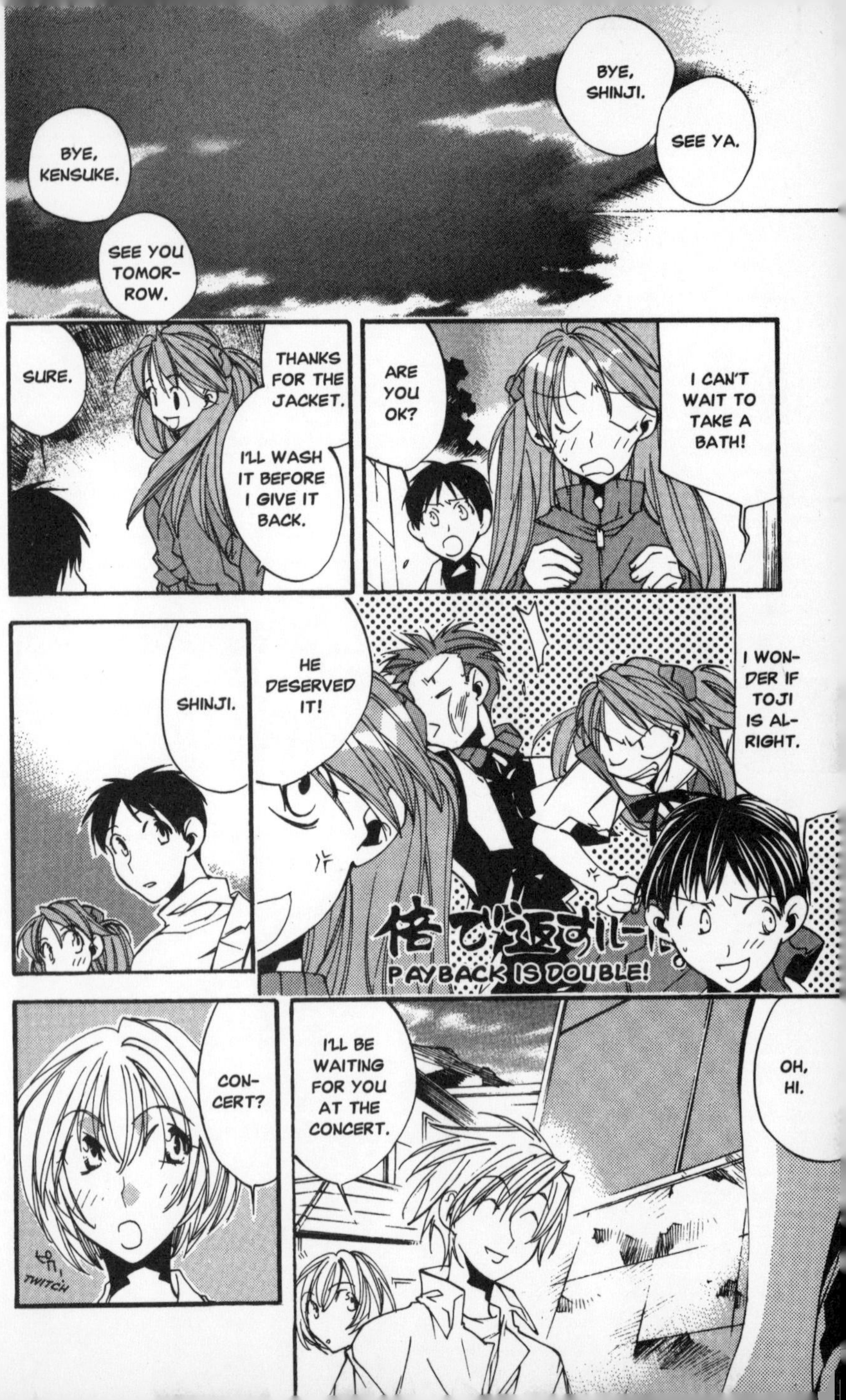
BYE, SHINJI.
SEE YA.
BYE, KENSUKE.
SEE YOU TOMOR-ROW.
I CAN'T WAIT TO TAKE A BATH!
ARE YOU OK?
THANKS FOR THE JACKET.
I'LL WASH IT BEFORE I GIVE IT BACK.
SURE.
I WON-DER IF TOJI IS AL-RIGHT.
HE DESERVED IT!
PAYBACK IS DOUBLE!
SHINJI.
OH, HI.
I'LL BE WAITING FOR YOU AT THE CONCERT.
CON-CERT?
TWITCH

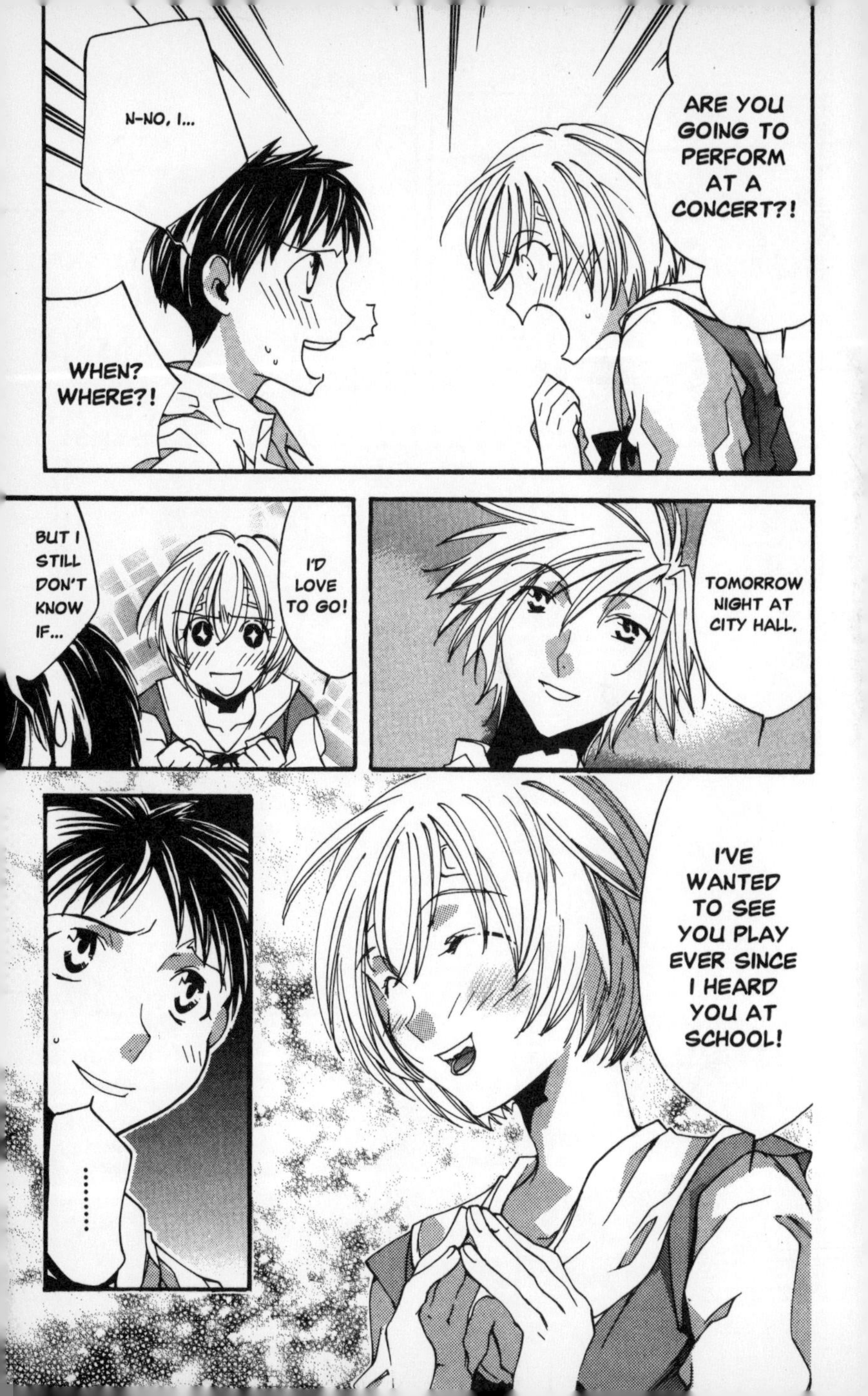
ARE YOU GOING TO PERFORM AT A CONCERT?!
N-NO, I...
WHEN? WHERE?!
TOMORROW NIGHT AT CITY HALL.
I'D LOVE TO GO!
BUT I STILL DON'T KNOW IF...
I'VE WANTED TO SEE YOU PLAY EVER SINCE I HEARD YOU AT SCHOOL!
....

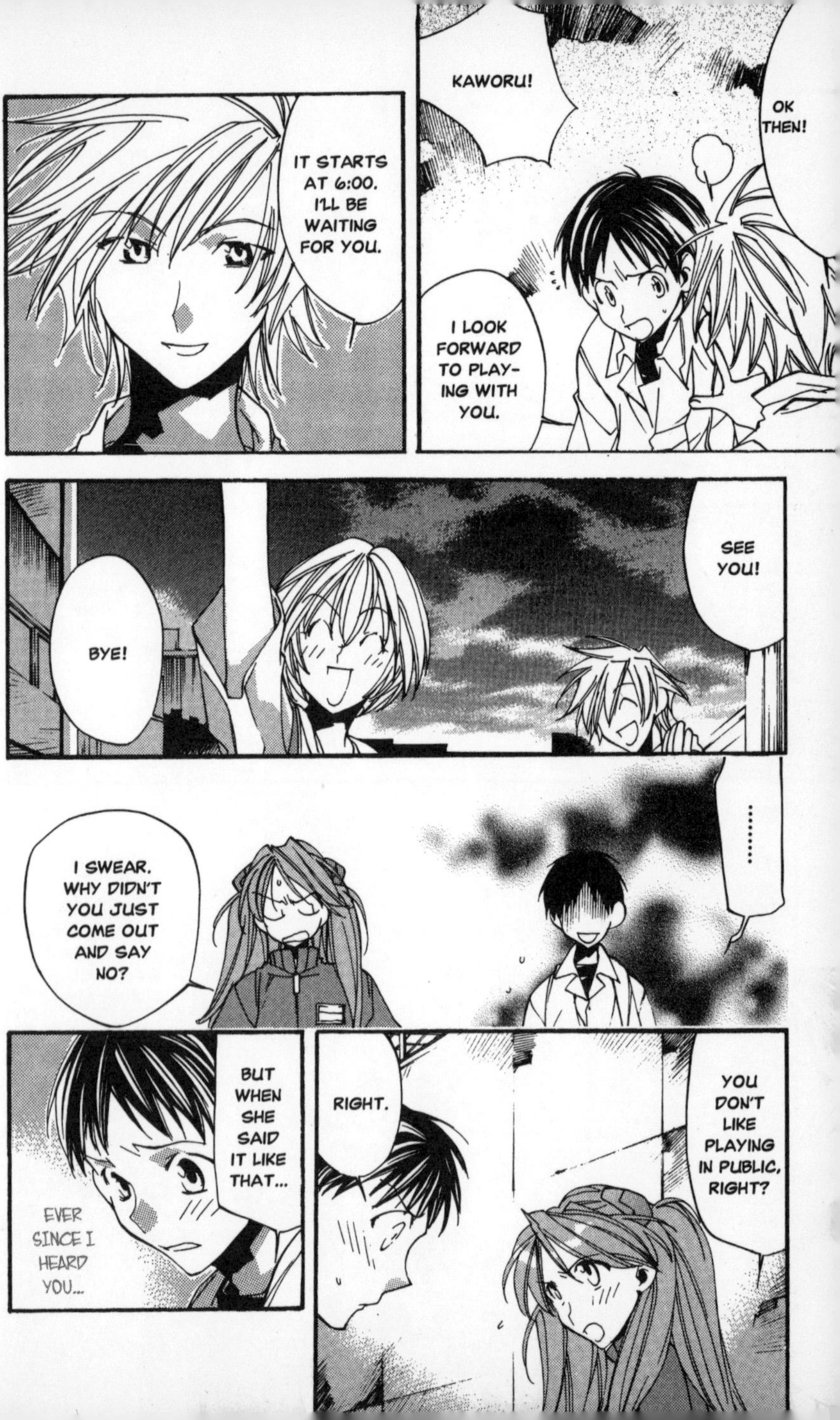
OK THEN!
KAWORU!
I LOOK FORWARD TO PLAYING WITH YOU.
IT STARTS AT 6:00. I'LL BE WAITING FOR YOU.
SEE YOU!
BYE!
......
I SWEAR. WHY DIDN'T YOU JUST COME OUT AND SAY NO?
YOU DON'T LIKE PLAYING IN PUBLIC, RIGHT?
RIGHT.
BUT WHEN SHE SAID IT LIKE THAT...
EVER SINCE I HEARD YOU...

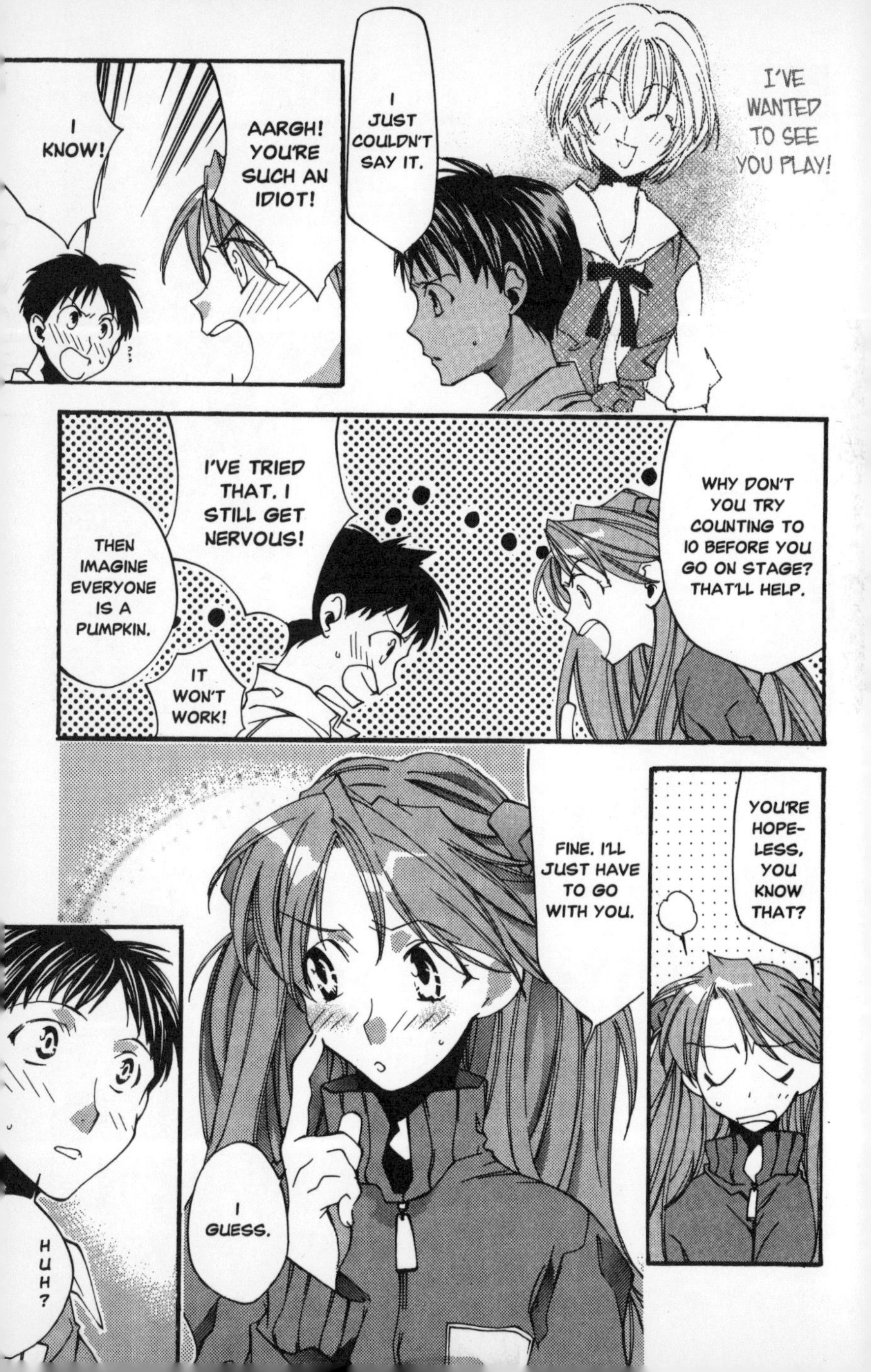
I'VE WANTED TO SEE YOU PLAY!
I JUST COULDN'T SAY IT.
AARGH! YOU'RE SUCH AN IDIOT!
I KNOW!
WHY DON'T YOU TRY COUNTING TO 10 BEFORE YOU GO ON STAGE? THAT'LL HELP.
I'VE TRIED THAT. I STILL GET NERVOUS!
THEN IMAGINE EVERYONE IS A PUMPKIN.
IT WON'T WORK!
YOU'RE HOPE-LESS, YOU KNOW THAT?
FINE. I'LL JUST HAVE TO GO WITH YOU.
I GUESS.
HUH?

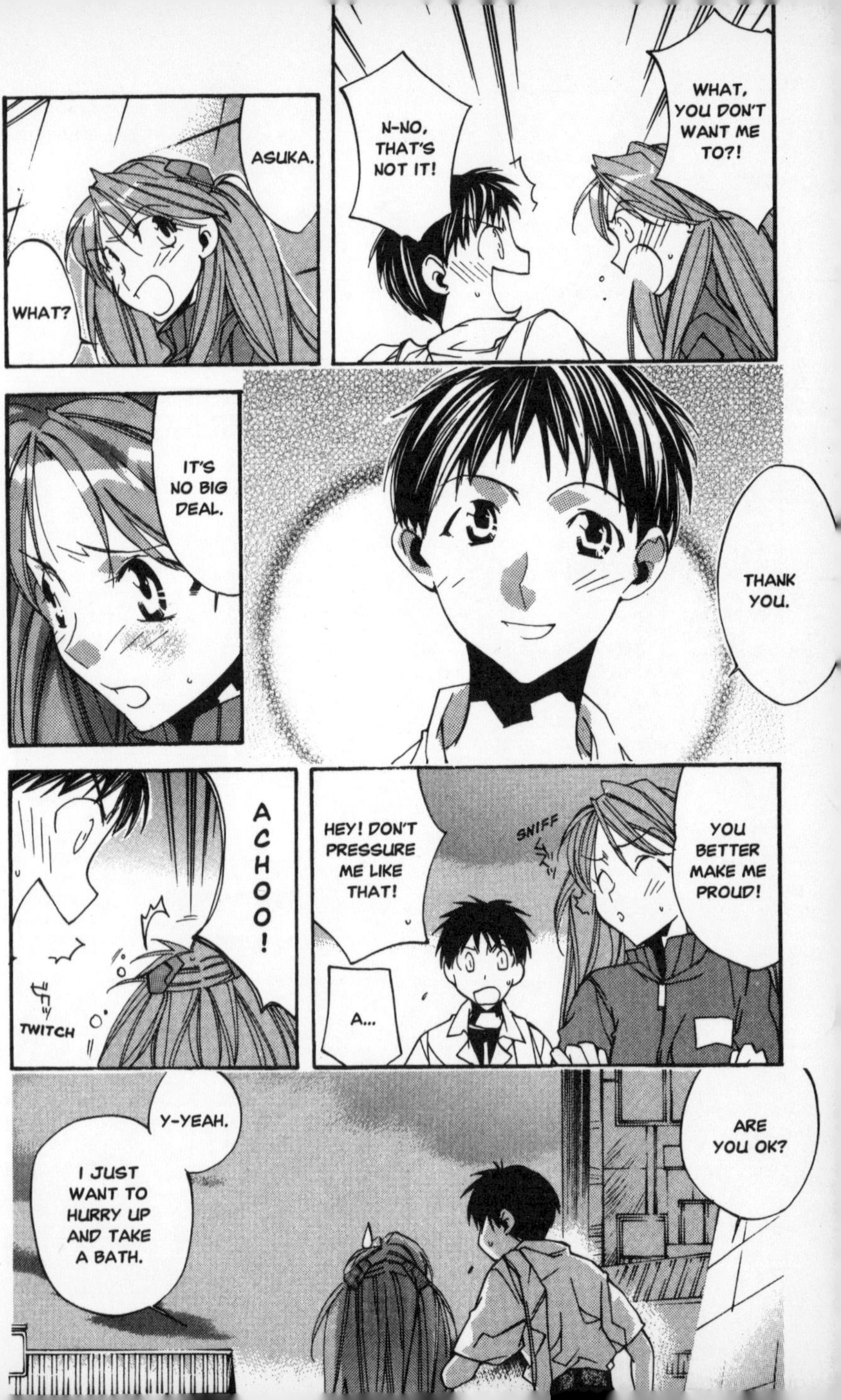
WHAT, YOU DON'T WANT ME TO?!
N-NO, THAT'S NOT IT!
ASUKA.
WHAT?
THANK YOU.
IT'S NO BIG DEAL.
YOU BETTER MAKE ME PROUD!
SNIFF
HEY! DON'T PRESSURE ME LIKE THAT!
A...
ACHOO!
TWITCH
ARE YOU OK?
Y-YEAH.
I JUST WANT TO HURRY UP AND TAKE A BATH.

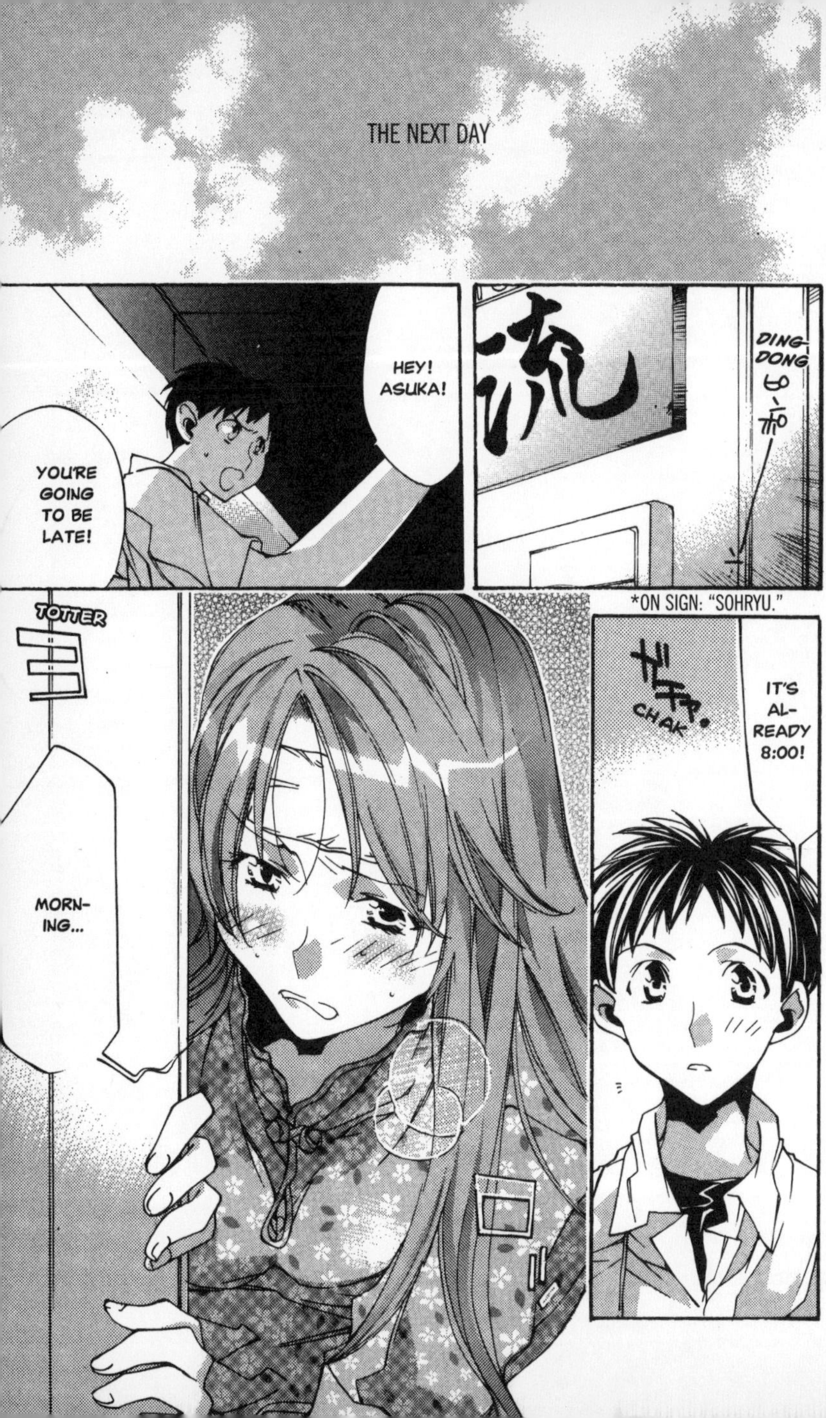
THE NEXT DAY
DING DONG
HEY! ASUKA!
YOU'RE GOING TO BE LATE!
*ON SIGN: "SOHRYU."
CHAK
IT'S AL- READY 8:00!
TOTTER
MORN- ING...

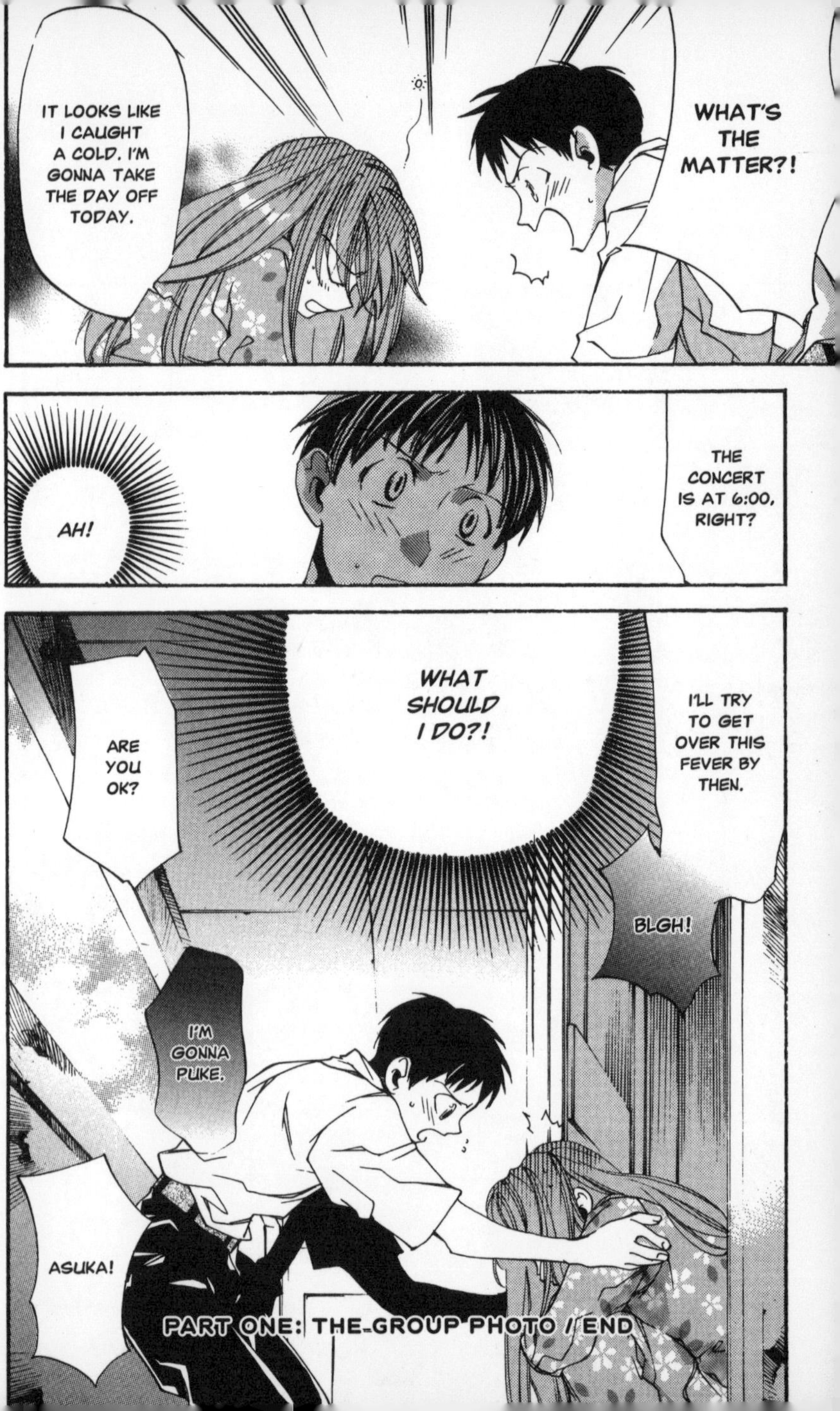
WHAT'S THE MATTER?!
IT LOOKS LIKE I CAUGHT A COLD. I'M GONNA TAKE THE DAY OFF TODAY.
THE CONCERT IS AT 6:00, RIGHT?
AH!
I'LL TRY TO GET OVER THIS FEVER BY THEN.
WHAT SHOULD I DO?!
ARE YOU OK?
BLGH!
I'M GONNA PUKE.
ASUKA!
PART ONE: THE GROUP PHOTO / END

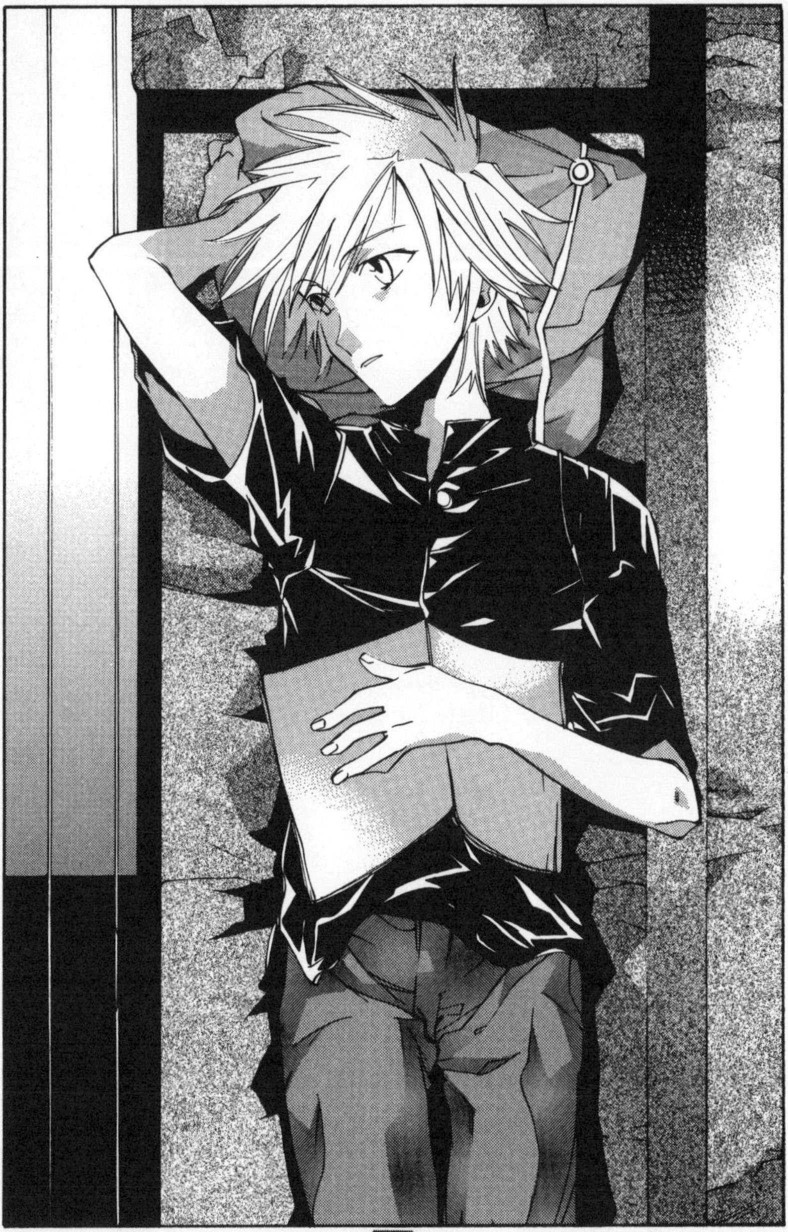

CHAPTER THREE, PART TWO: HOW TO SPEND A DAY OFF

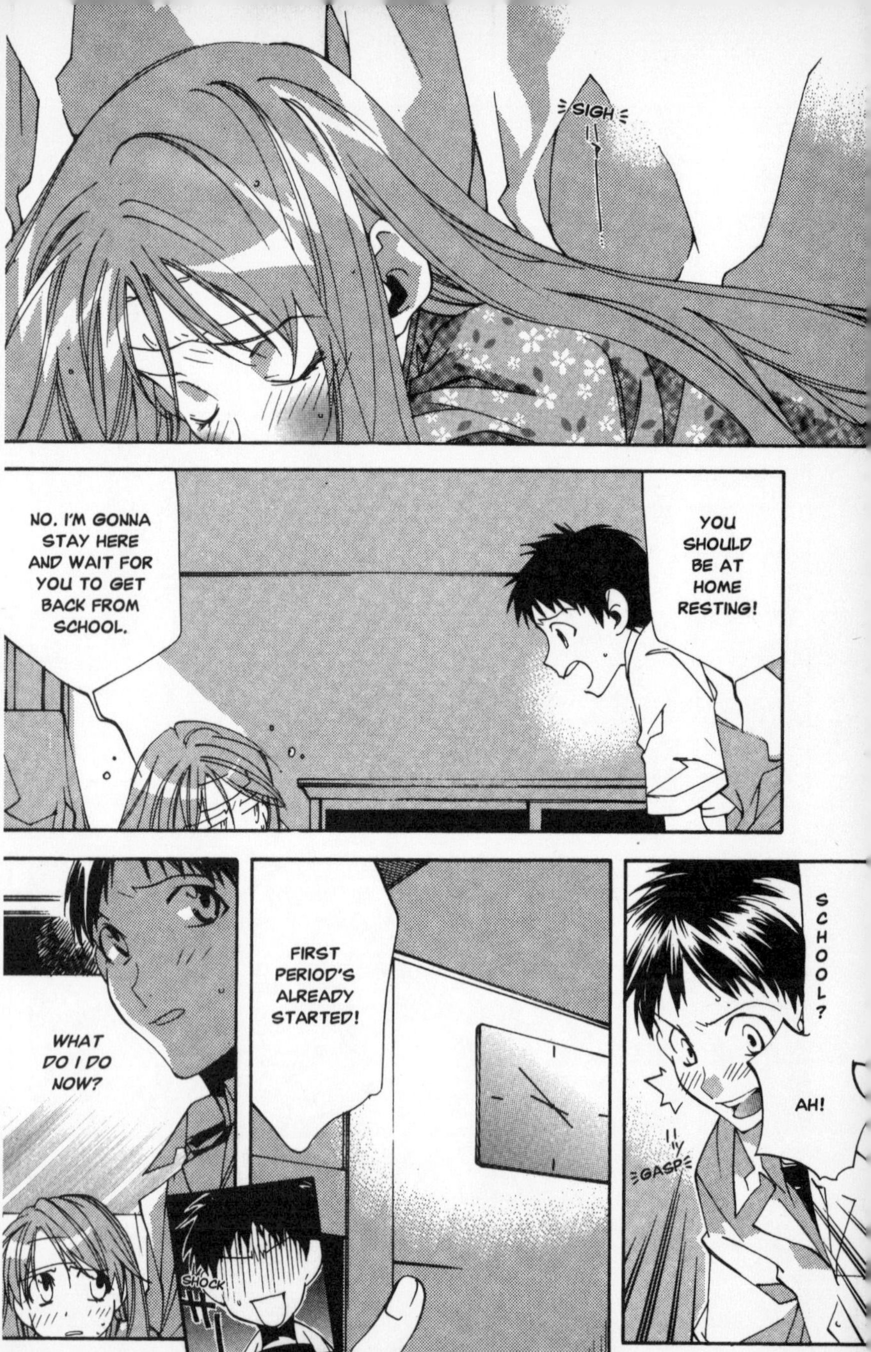
SIGH
YOU SHOULD BE AT HOME RESTING!
NO. I'M GONNA STAY HERE AND WAIT FOR YOU TO GET BACK FROM SCHOOL.
SCHOOL?
AH!
GASP
FIRST PERIOD'S ALREADY STARTED!
WHAT DO I DO NOW?
SHOCK

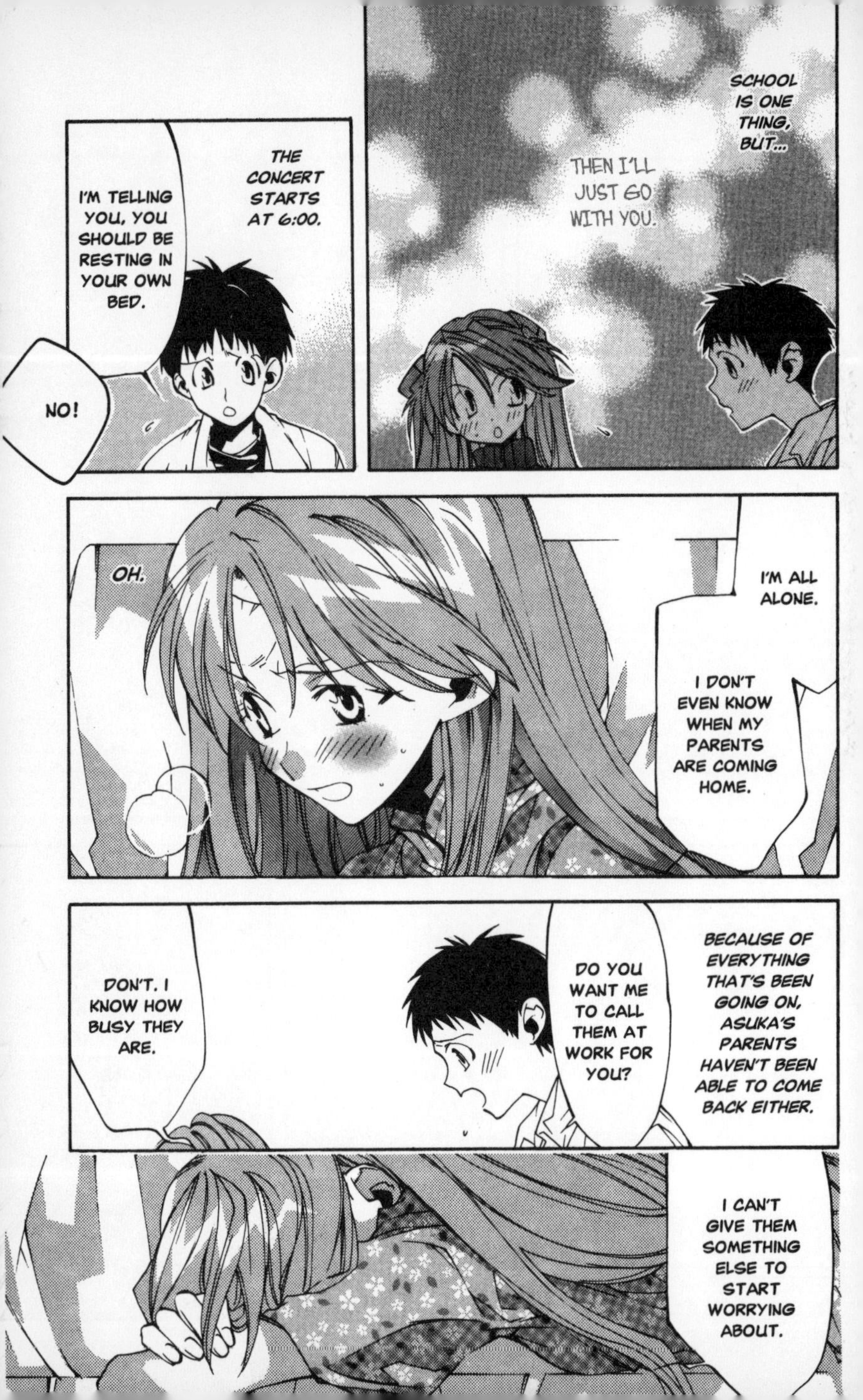
SCHOOL IS ONE THING, BUT...
THEN I'LL JUST GO WITH YOU.
THE CONCERT STARTS AT 6:00.
I'M TELLING YOU, YOU SHOULD BE RESTING IN YOUR OWN BED.
NO!
I'M ALL ALONE.
I DON'T EVEN KNOW WHEN MY PARENTS ARE COMING HOME.
OH.
BECAUSE OF EVERYTHING THAT'S BEEN GOING ON, ASUKA'S PARENTS HAVEN'T BEEN ABLE TO COME BACK EITHER.
DO YOU WANT ME TO CALL THEM AT WORK FOR YOU?
DON'T. I KNOW HOW BUSY THEY ARE.
I CAN'T GIVE THEM SOMETHING ELSE TO START WORRYING ABOUT.

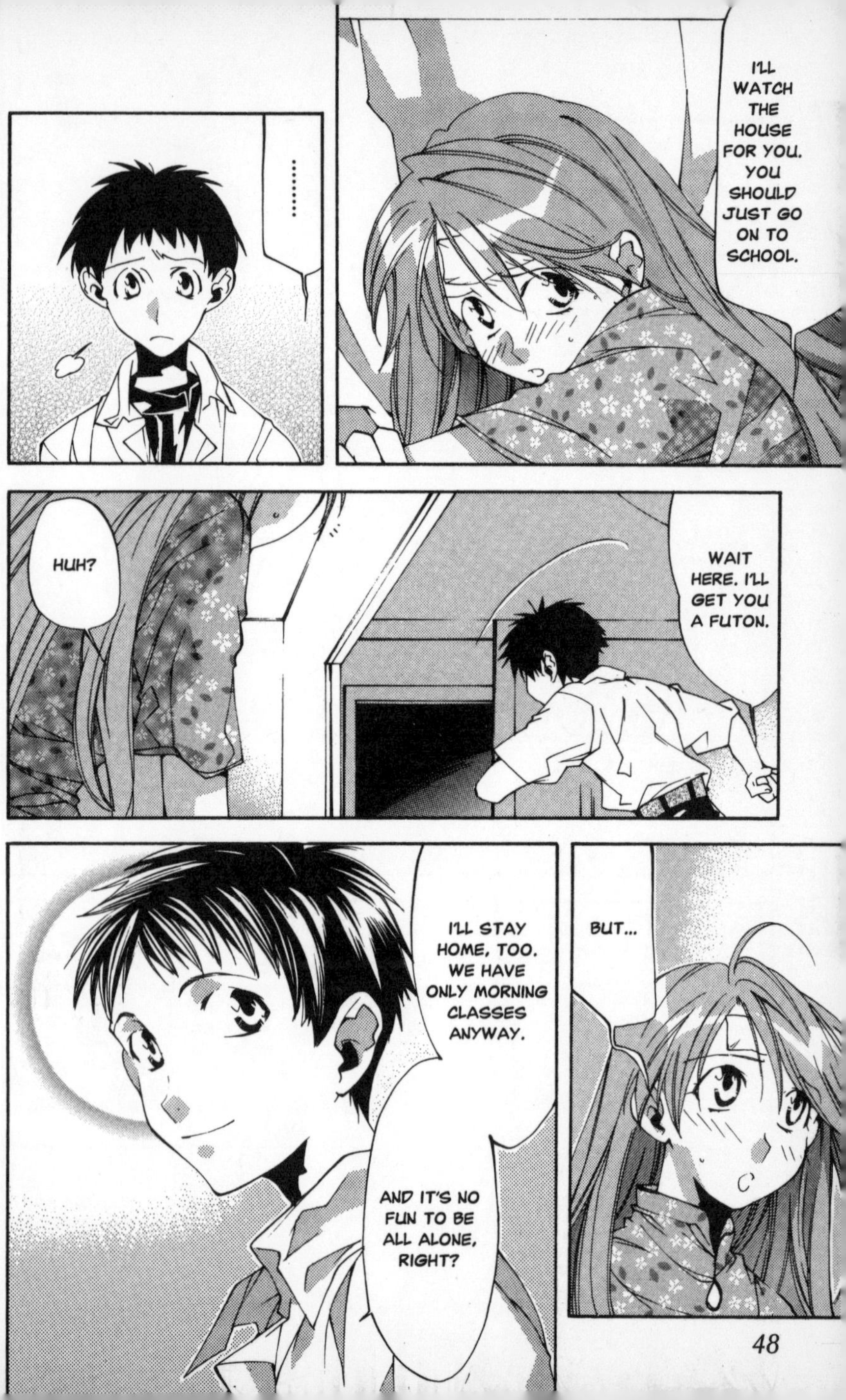
I'LL WATCH THE HOUSE FOR YOU. YOU SHOULD JUST GO ON TO SCHOOL.
....
WAIT HERE. I'LL GET YOU A FUTON.
HUH?
BUT...
I'LL STAY HOME, TOO. WE HAVE ONLY MORNING CLASSES ANYWAY.
AND IT'S NO FUN TO BE ALL ALONE, RIGHT?

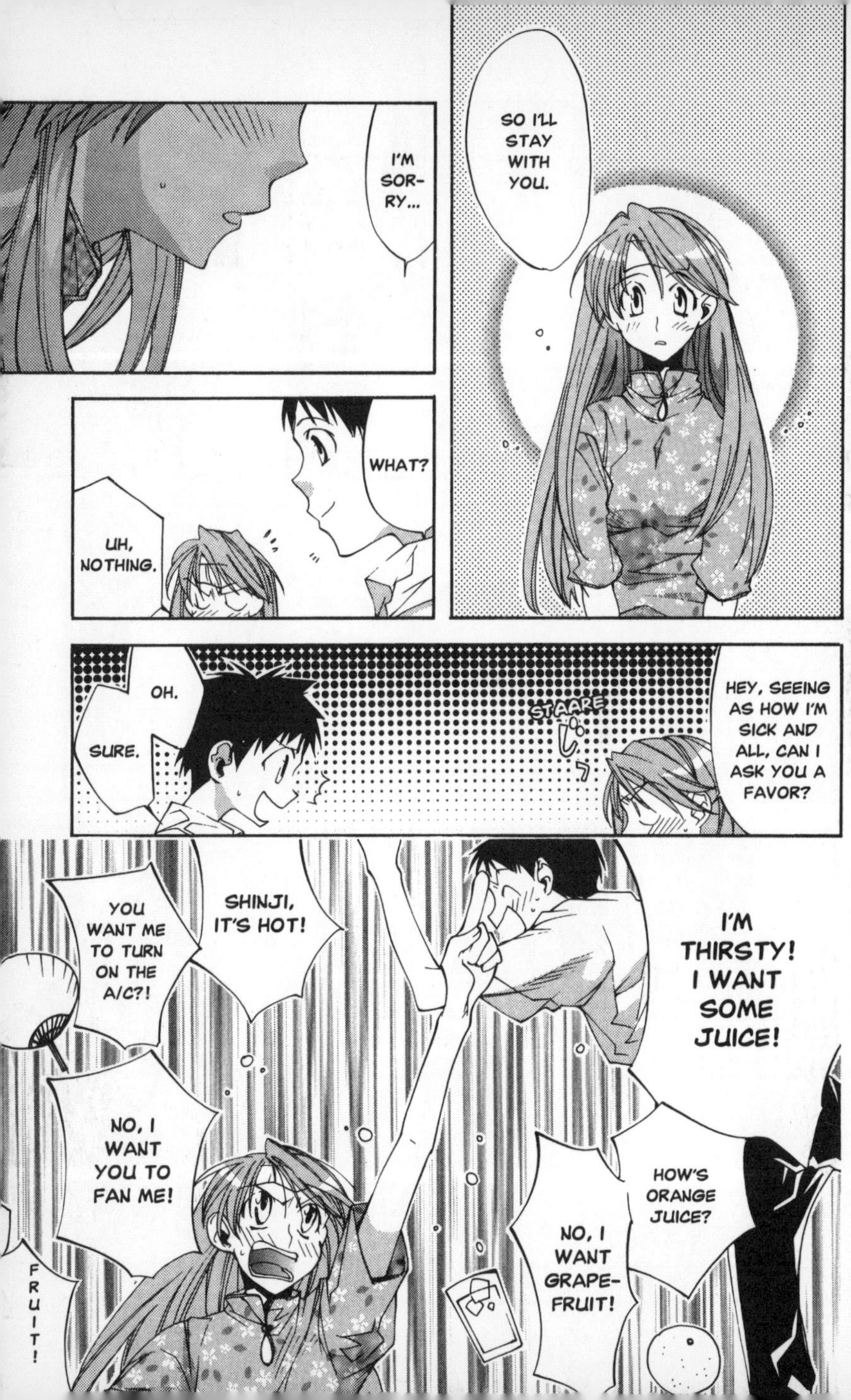
SO I'LL STAY WITH YOU.
I'M SOR-RY...
WHAT?
UH, NOTHING.
HEY, SEEING AS HOW I'M SICK AND ALL, CAN I ASK YOU A FAVOR?
STAARE
OH.
SURE.
I'M THIRSTY! I WANT SOME JUICE!
SHINJI, IT'S HOT!
YOU WANT ME TO TURN ON THE A/C?!
HOW'S ORANGE JUICE?
NO, I WANT GRAPE-FRUIT!
NO, I WANT YOU TO FAN ME!
FRUIT!

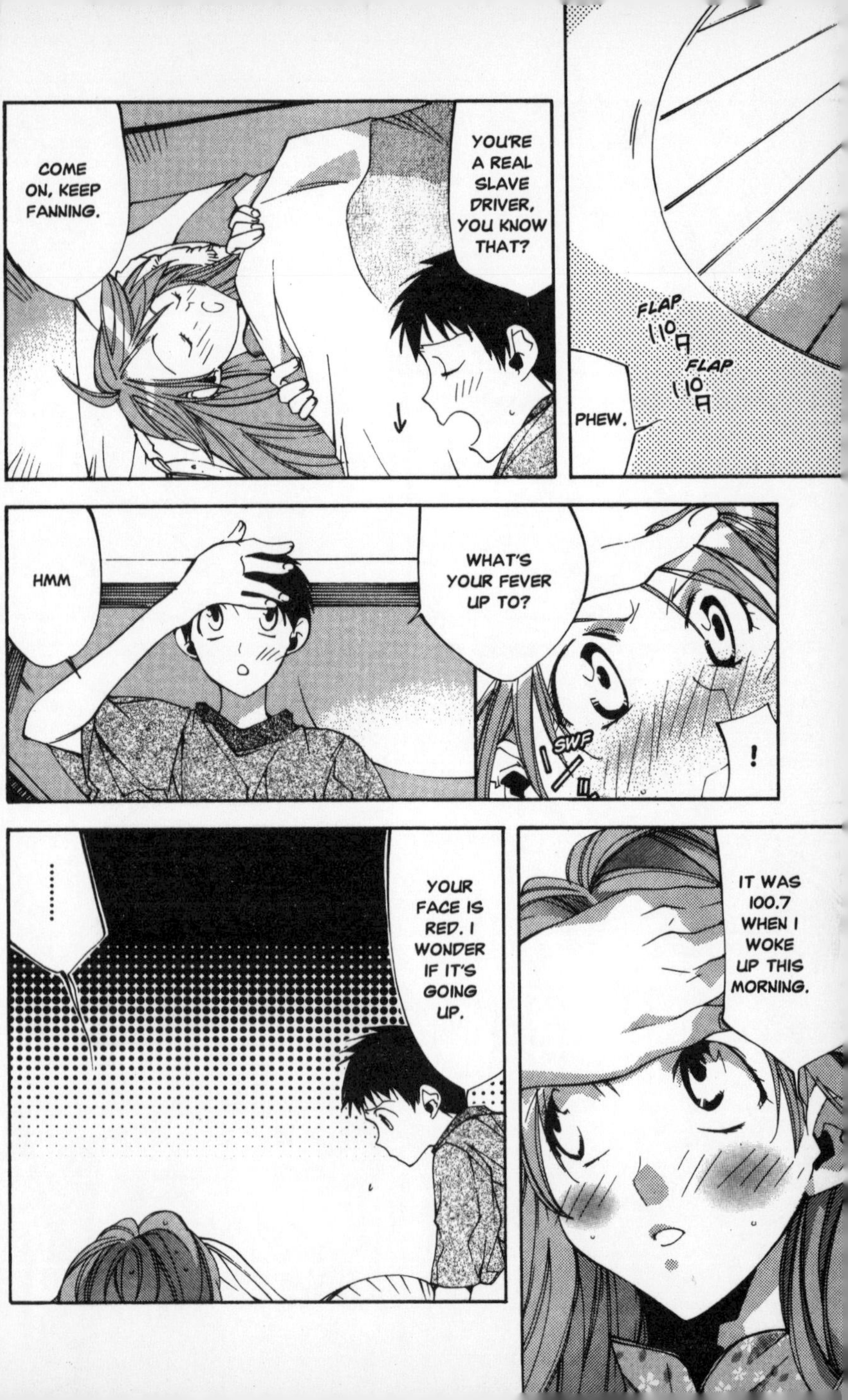
FLAP
FLAP
PHEW.
YOU'RE A REAL SLAVE DRIVER, YOU KNOW THAT?
COME ON, KEEP FANNING.
!
SWF
WHAT'S YOUR FEVER UP TO?
HMM
IT WAS 100.7 WHEN I WOKE UP THIS MORNING.
YOUR FACE IS RED. I WONDER IF IT'S GOING UP.
....

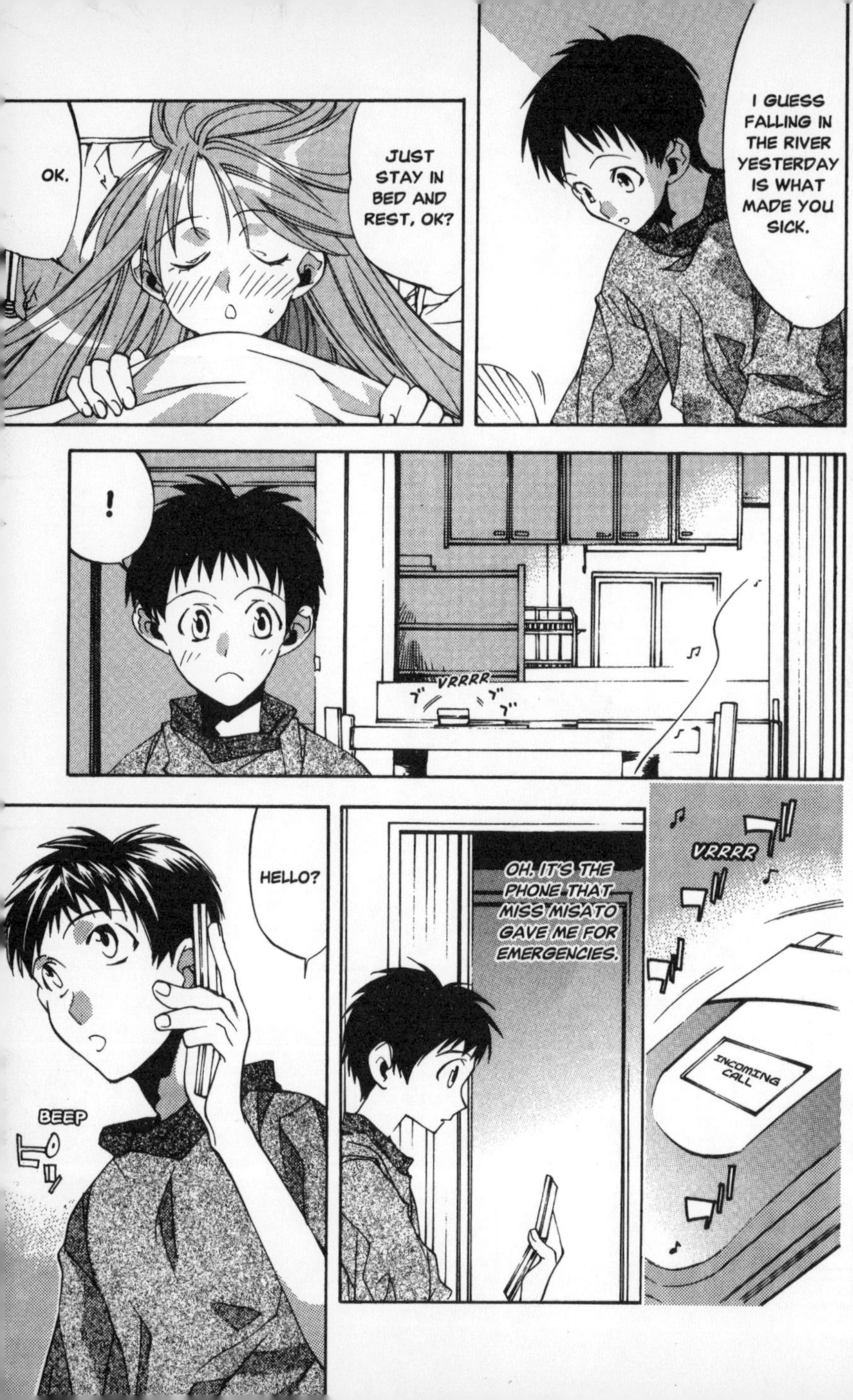
I GUESS FALLING IN THE RIVER YESTERDAY IS WHAT MADE YOU SICK.
JUST STAY IN BED AND REST, OK?
OK.
VRRRR
!
VRRRR
INCOMING CALL
OH. IT'S THE PHONE THAT MISS MISATO GAVE ME FOR EMERGENCIES.
HELLO?
BEEP

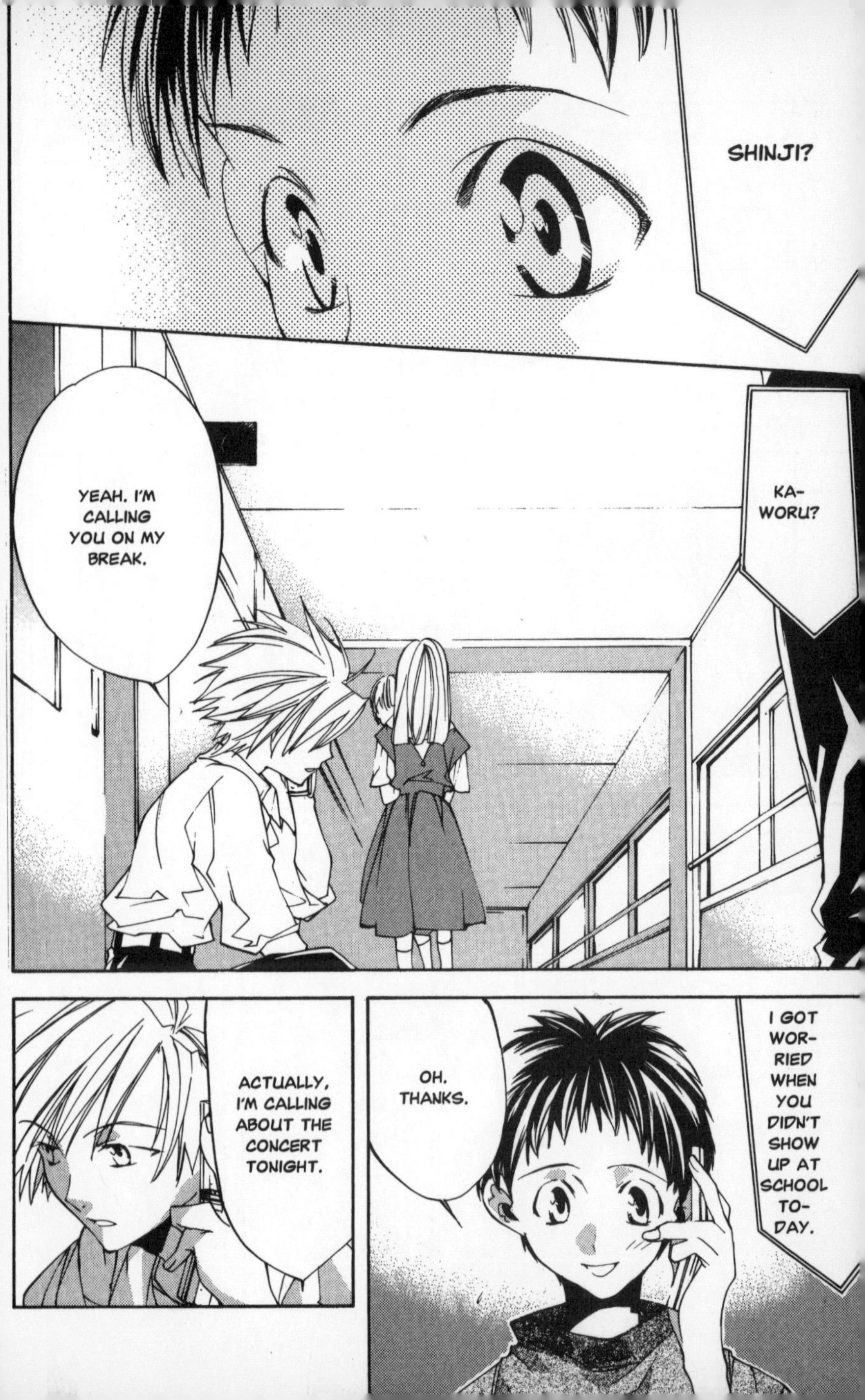
SHINJI?
KA-WORU?
YEAH. I'M CALLING YOU ON MY BREAK.
I GOT WOR-RIED WHEN YOU DIDN'T SHOW UP AT SCHOOL TO-DAY.
OH. THANKS.
ACTUALLY, I'M CALLING ABOUT THE CONCERT TONIGHT.

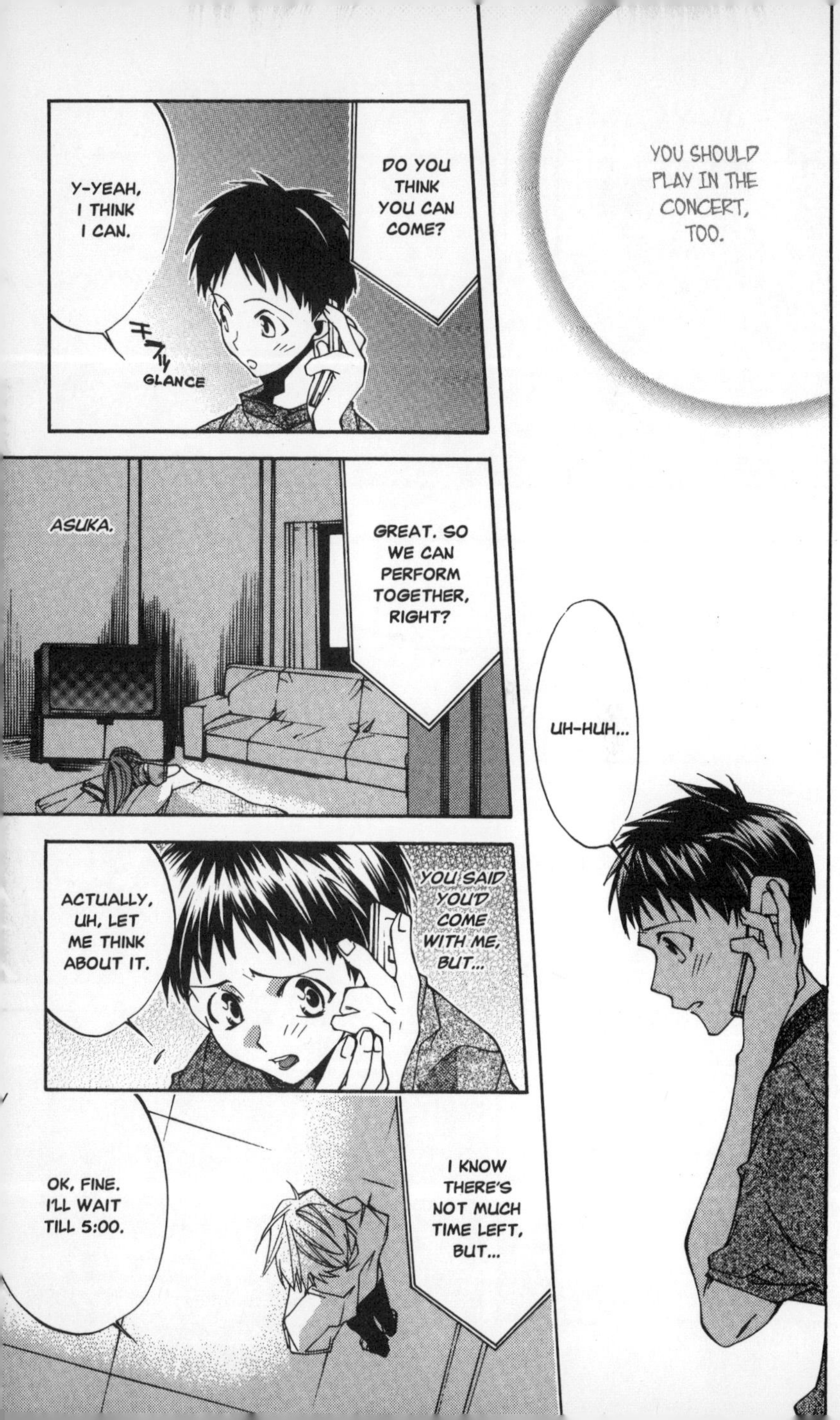

YOU SHOULD PLAY IN THE CONCERT, TOO.
DO YOU THINK YOU CAN COME?
Y-YEAH, I THINK I CAN.
GLANCE
GREAT. SO WE CAN PERFORM TOGETHER, RIGHT?
ASUKA.
UH-HUH...
YOU SAID YOU'D COME WITH ME, BUT...
ACTUALLY, UH, LET ME THINK ABOUT IT.
I KNOW THERE'S NOT MUCH TIME LEFT, BUT...
OK, FINE. I'LL WAIT TILL 5:00.

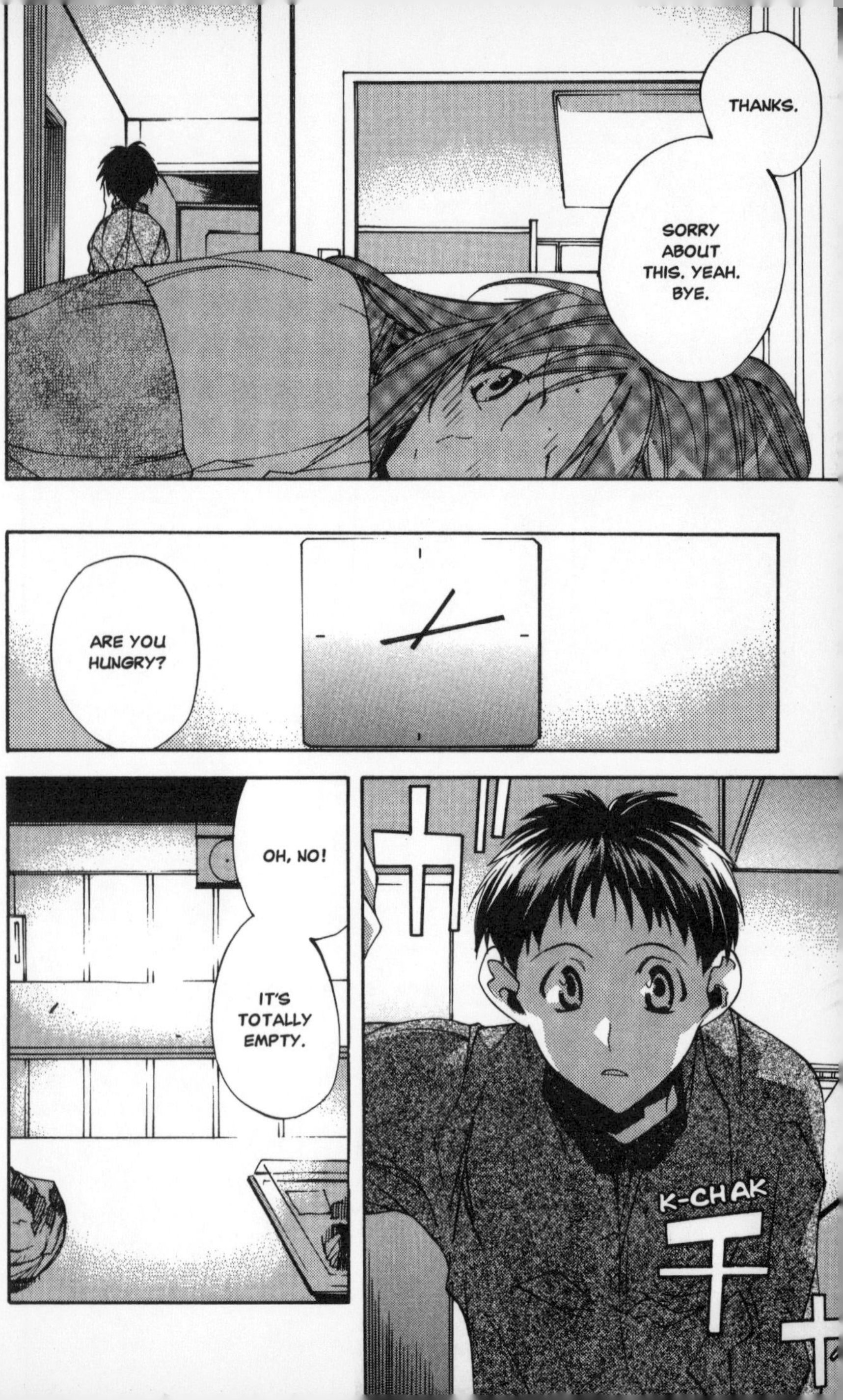
THANKS.
SORRY ABOUT THIS. YEAH. BYE.
ARE YOU HUNGRY?
OH, NO!
IT'S TOTALLY EMPTY.
K-CHAK

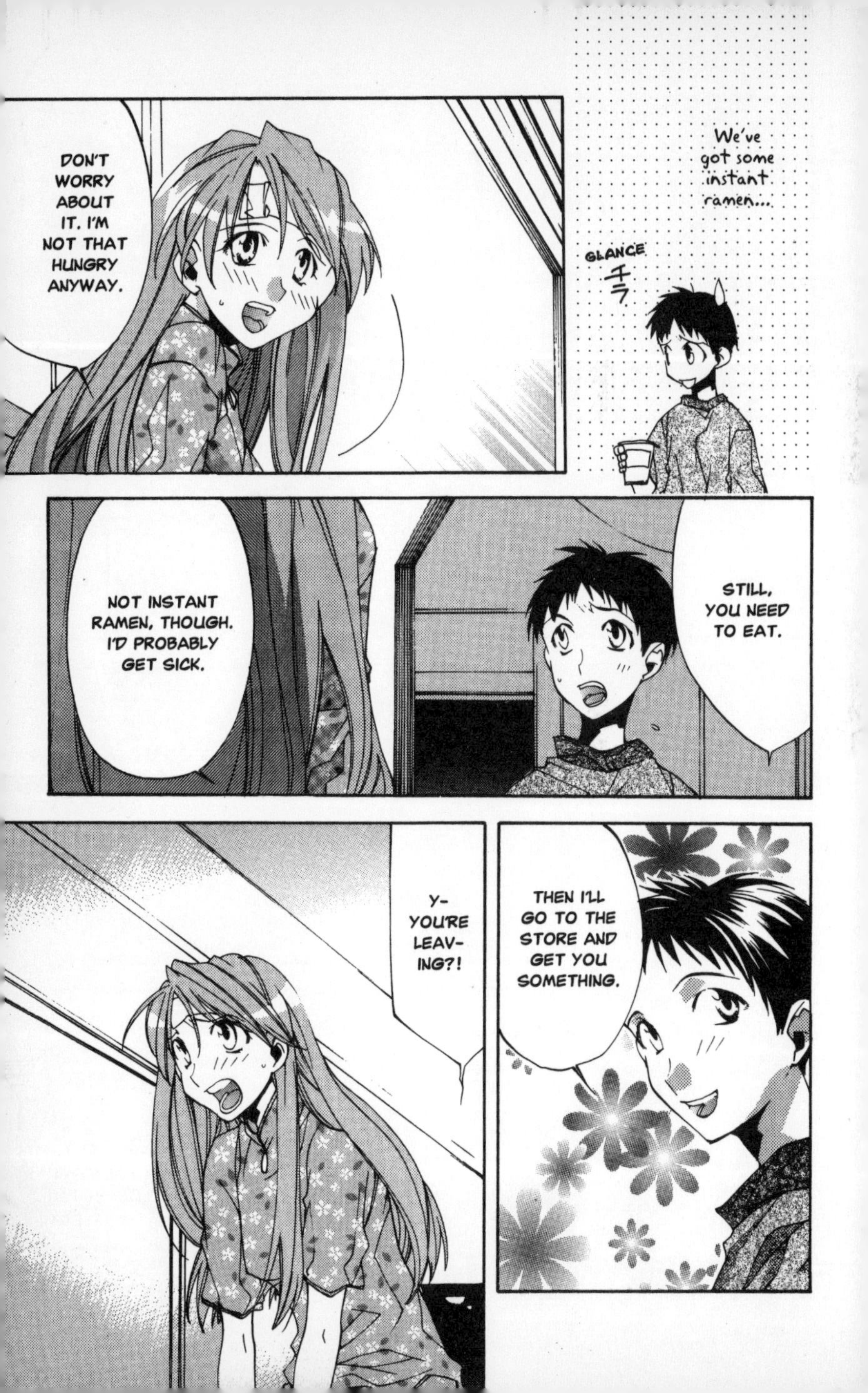
We've got some instant ramen...
GLANCE
チラ
DON'T WORRY ABOUT IT. I'M NOT THAT HUNGRY ANYWAY.
STILL, YOU NEED TO EAT.
NOT INSTANT RAMEN, THOUGH. I'D PROBABLY GET SICK.
THEN I'LL GO TO THE STORE AND GET YOU SOMETHING.
Y- YOU'RE LEAVING?!

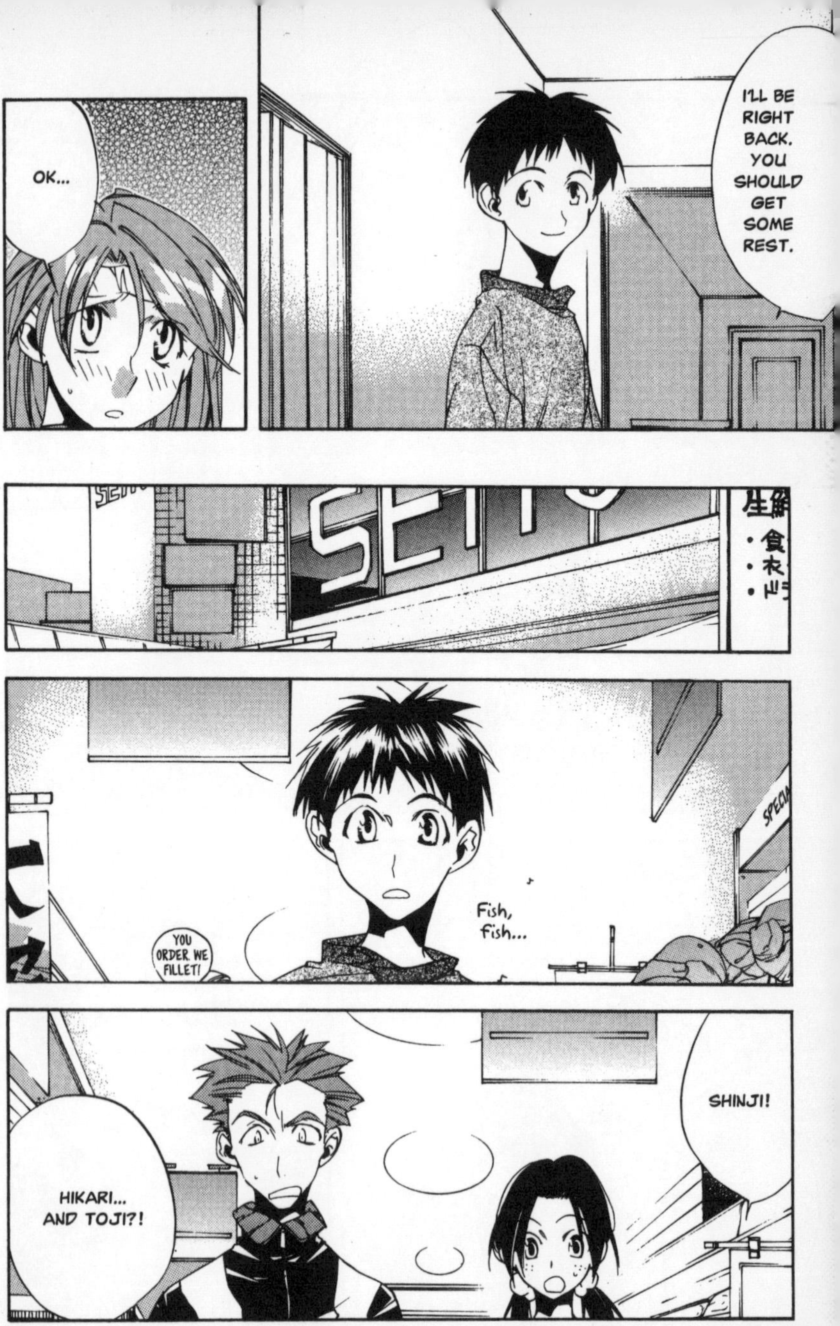
I'LL BE RIGHT BACK. YOU SHOULD GET SOME REST.
OK...
Fish, fish...
YOU ORDER WE FILLET!
SHINJI!
HIKARI... AND TOJI?!

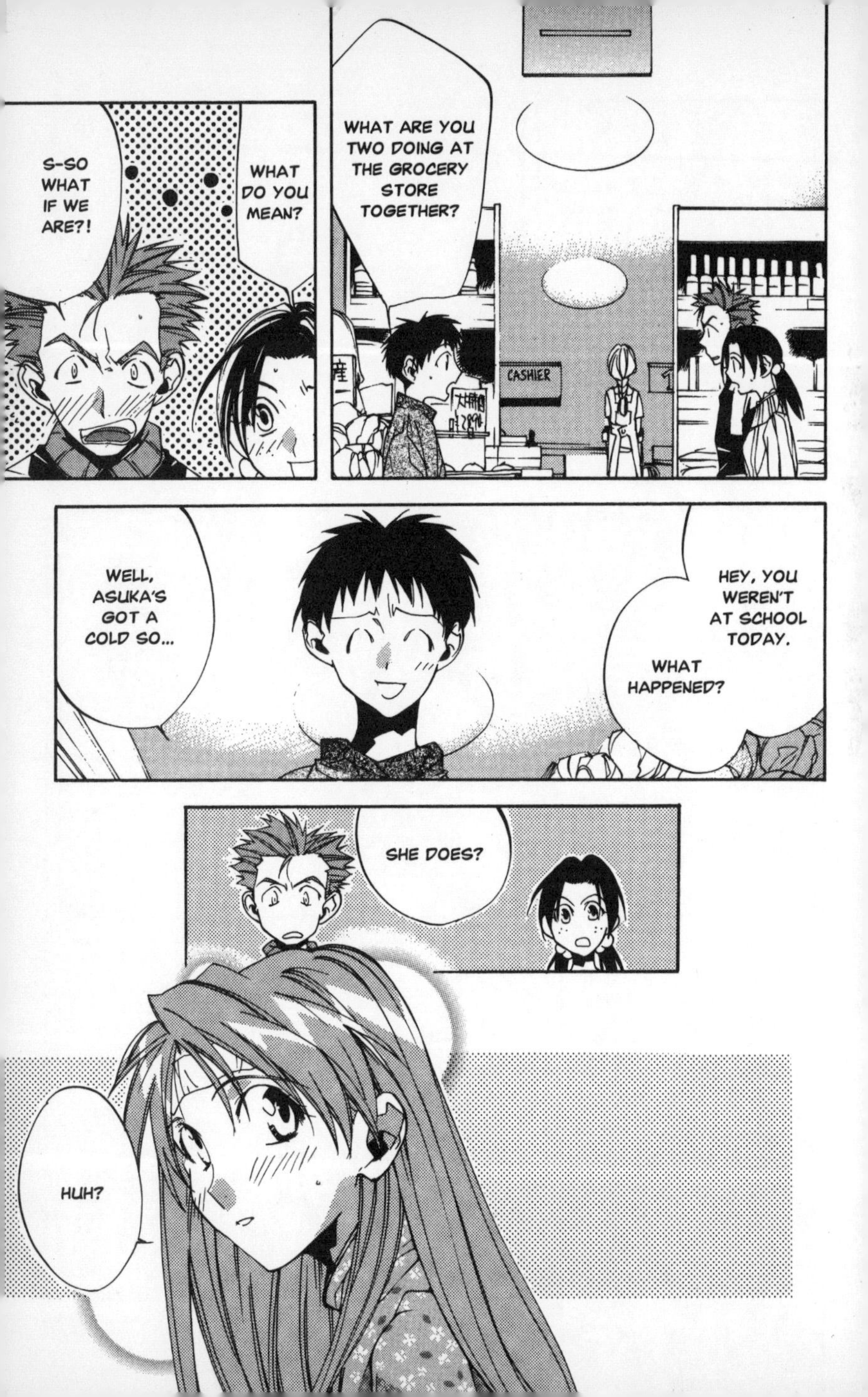
WHAT ARE YOU TWO DOING AT THE GROCERY STORE TOGETHER?
CASHIER
WHAT DO YOU MEAN?
S-SO WHAT IF WE ARE?!
HEY, YOU WEREN'T AT SCHOOL TODAY.
WHAT HAPPENED?
WELL, ASUKA'S GOT A COLD SO...
SHE DOES?
HUH?

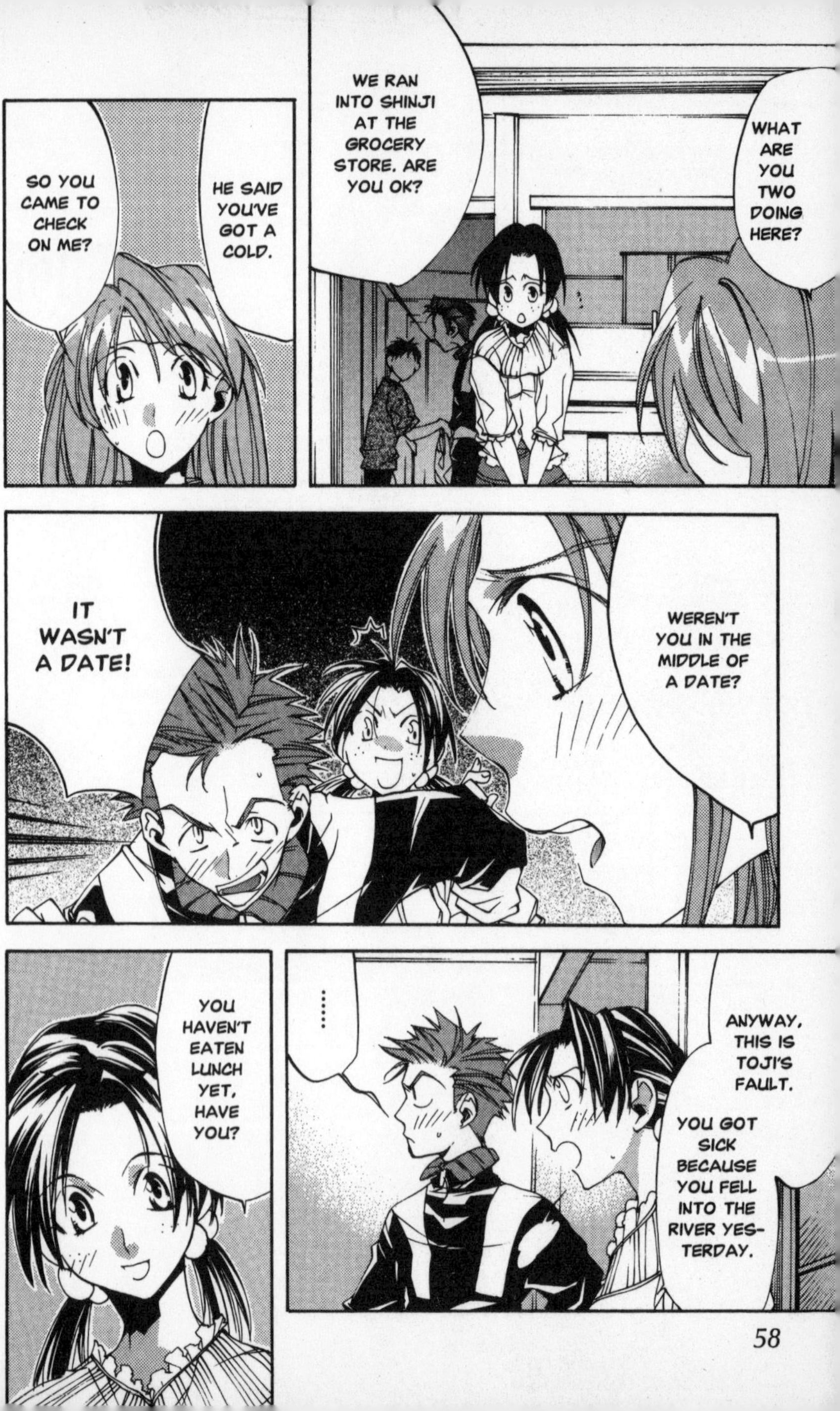
WHAT ARE YOU TWO DOING HERE?
WE RAN INTO SHINJI AT THE GROCERY STORE. ARE YOU OK?
HE SAID YOU'VE GOT A COLD.
SO YOU CAME TO CHECK ON ME?
WEREN'T YOU IN THE MIDDLE OF A DATE?
IT WASN'T A DATE!
ANYWAY, THIS IS TOJI'S FAULT.
YOU GOT SICK BECAUSE YOU FELL INTO THE RIVER YES-TERDAY.
......
YOU HAVEN'T EATEN LUNCH YET, HAVE YOU?

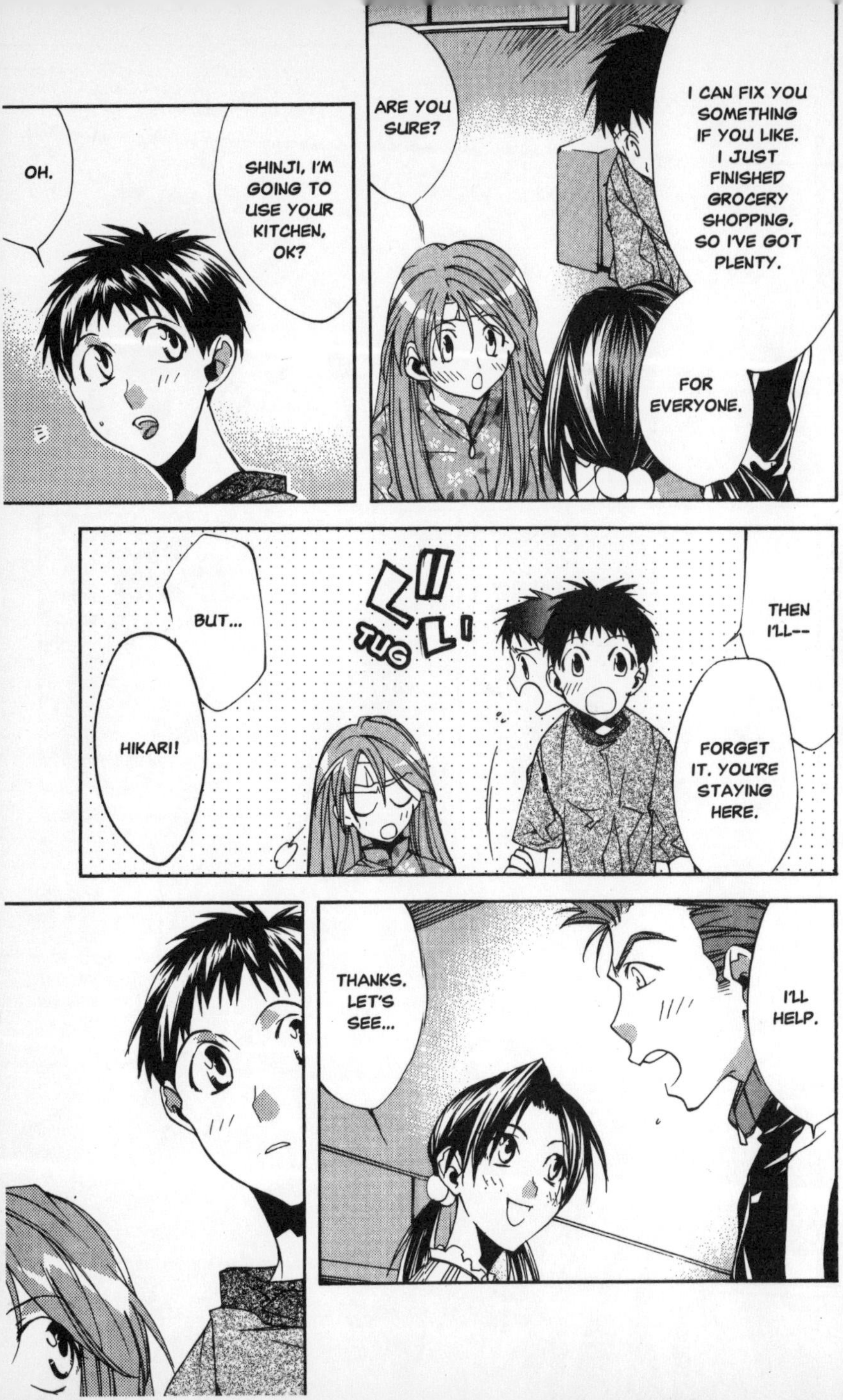
I CAN FIX YOU SOMETHING IF YOU LIKE. I JUST FINISHED GROCERY SHOPPING, SO I'VE GOT PLENTY.
FOR EVERYONE.
ARE YOU SURE?
SHINJI, I'M GOING TO USE YOUR KITCHEN, OK?
OH.
THEN I'LL--
FORGET IT. YOU'RE STAYING HERE.
TUG
BUT...
HIKARI!
I'LL HELP.
THANKS. LET'S SEE...

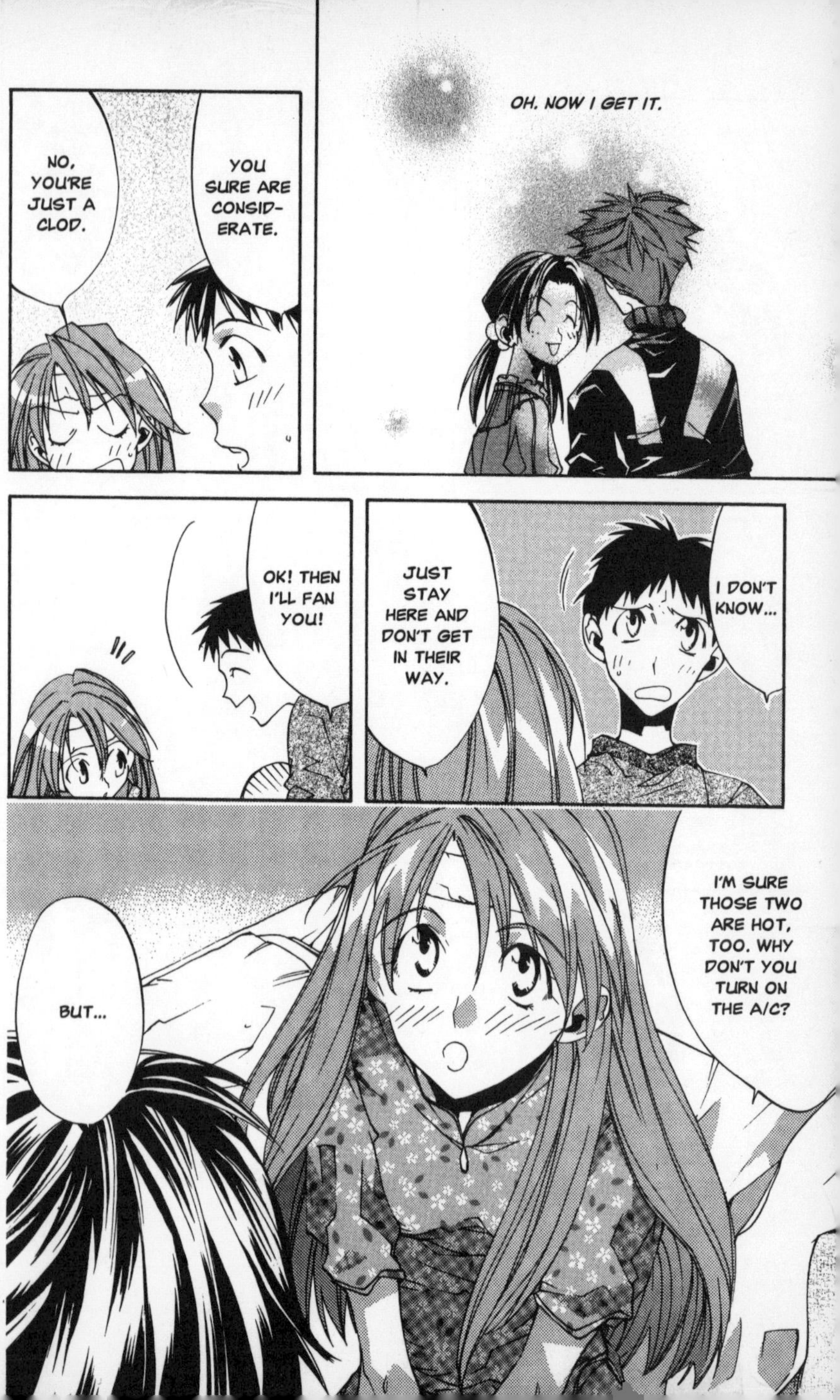
OH. NOW I GET IT.
YOU SURE ARE CONSID-ERATE.
NO, YOU'RE JUST A CLOD.
I DON'T KNOW...
JUST STAY HERE AND DON'T GET IN THEIR WAY.
OK! THEN I'LL FAN YOU!
I'M SURE THOSE TWO ARE HOT, TOO. WHY DON'T YOU TURN ON THE A/C?
BUT...

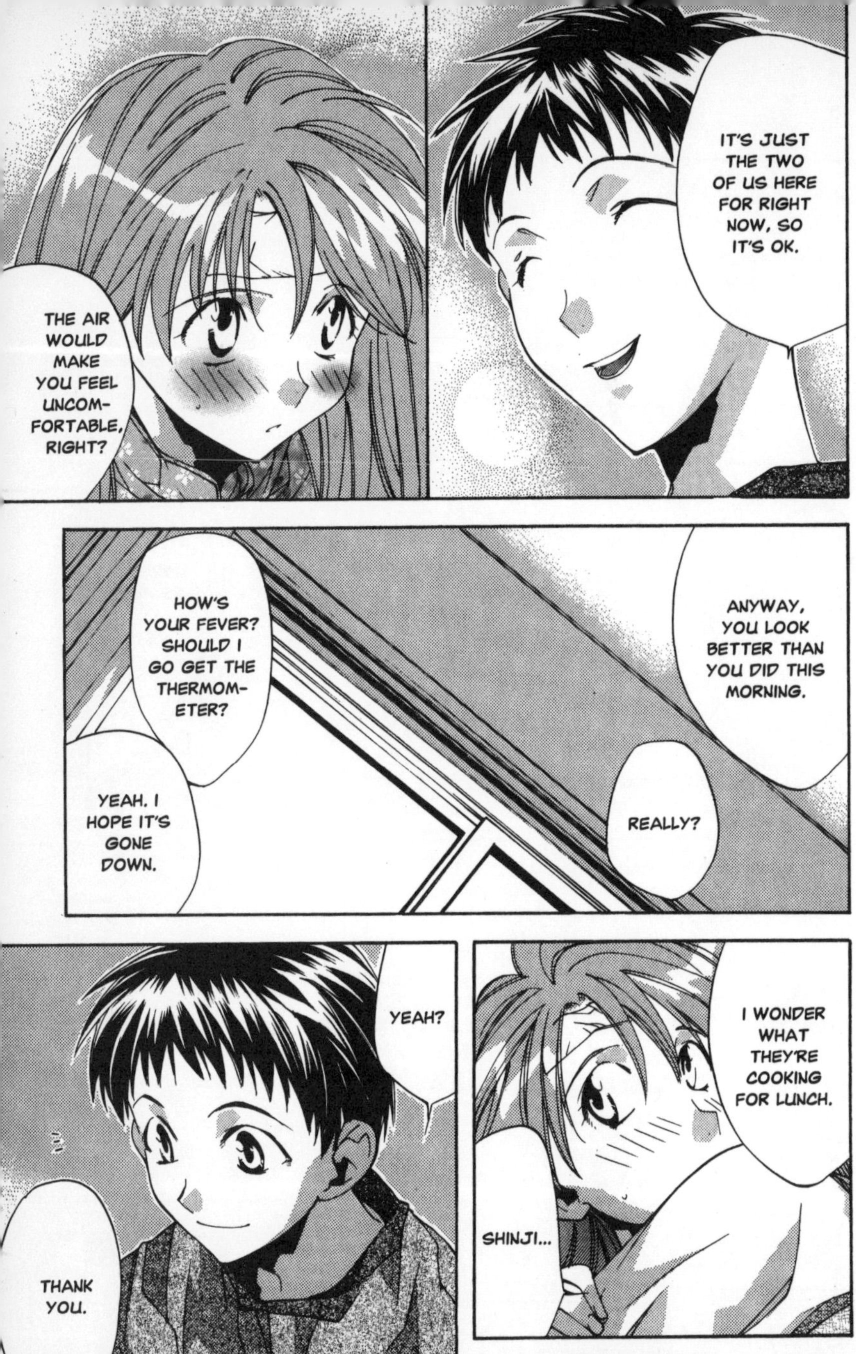
IT'S JUST THE TWO OF US HERE FOR RIGHT NOW, SO IT'S OK.
THE AIR WOULD MAKE YOU FEEL UNCOM-FORTABLE, RIGHT?
ANYWAY, YOU LOOK BETTER THAN YOU DID THIS MORNING.
REALLY?
HOW'S YOUR FEVER? SHOULD I GO GET THE THERMOM-ETER?
YEAH. I HOPE IT'S GONE DOWN.
I WONDER WHAT THEY'RE COOKING FOR LUNCH.
SHINJI...
YEAH?
THANK YOU.

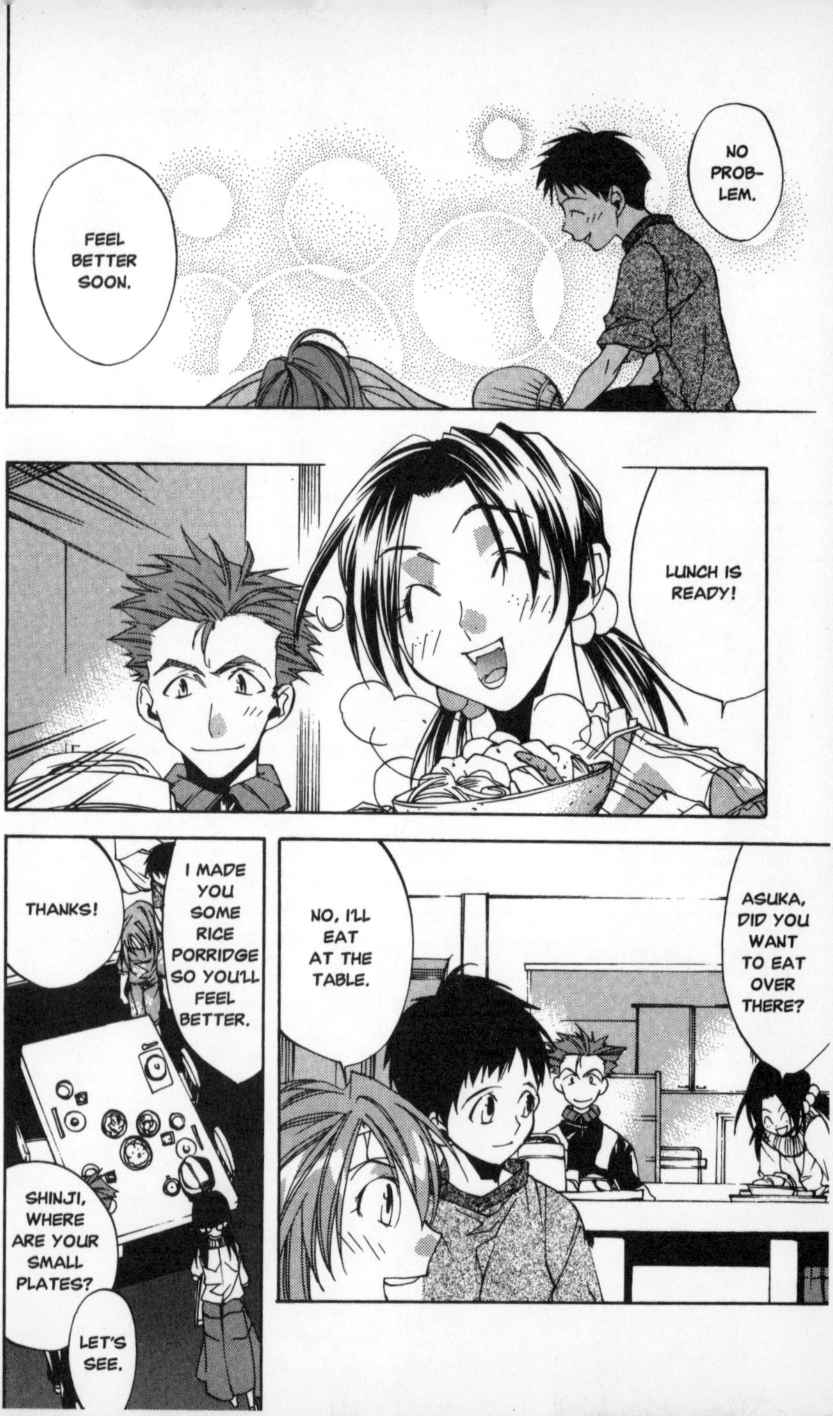
NO PROB-LEM.
FEEL BETTER SOON.
LUNCH IS READY!
ASUKA, DID YOU WANT TO EAT OVER THERE?
NO, I'LL EAT AT THE TABLE.
I MADE YOU SOME RICE PORRIDGE SO YOU'LL FEEL BETTER.
THANKS!
SHINJI, WHERE ARE YOUR SMALL PLATES?
LET'S SEE.

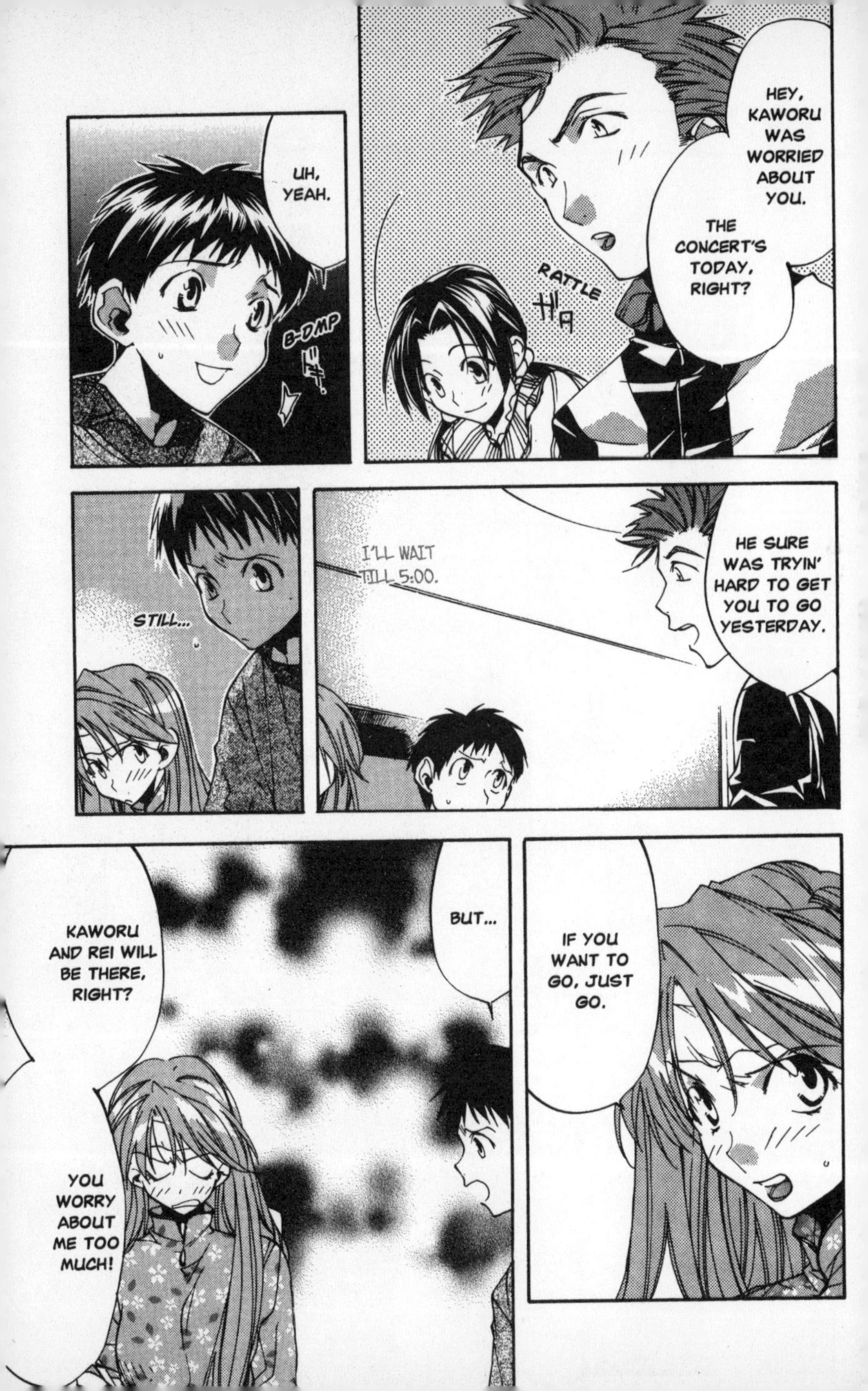
HEY, KAWORU WAS WORRIED ABOUT YOU.
THE CONCERT'S TODAY, RIGHT?
RATTLE
UH, YEAH.
B-DMP
HE SURE WAS TRYIN' HARD TO GET YOU TO GO YESTERDAY.
I'LL WAIT TILL 5:00.
STILL...
IF YOU WANT TO GO, JUST GO.
BUT...
KAWORU AND REI WILL BE THERE, RIGHT?
YOU WORRY ABOUT ME TOO MUCH!

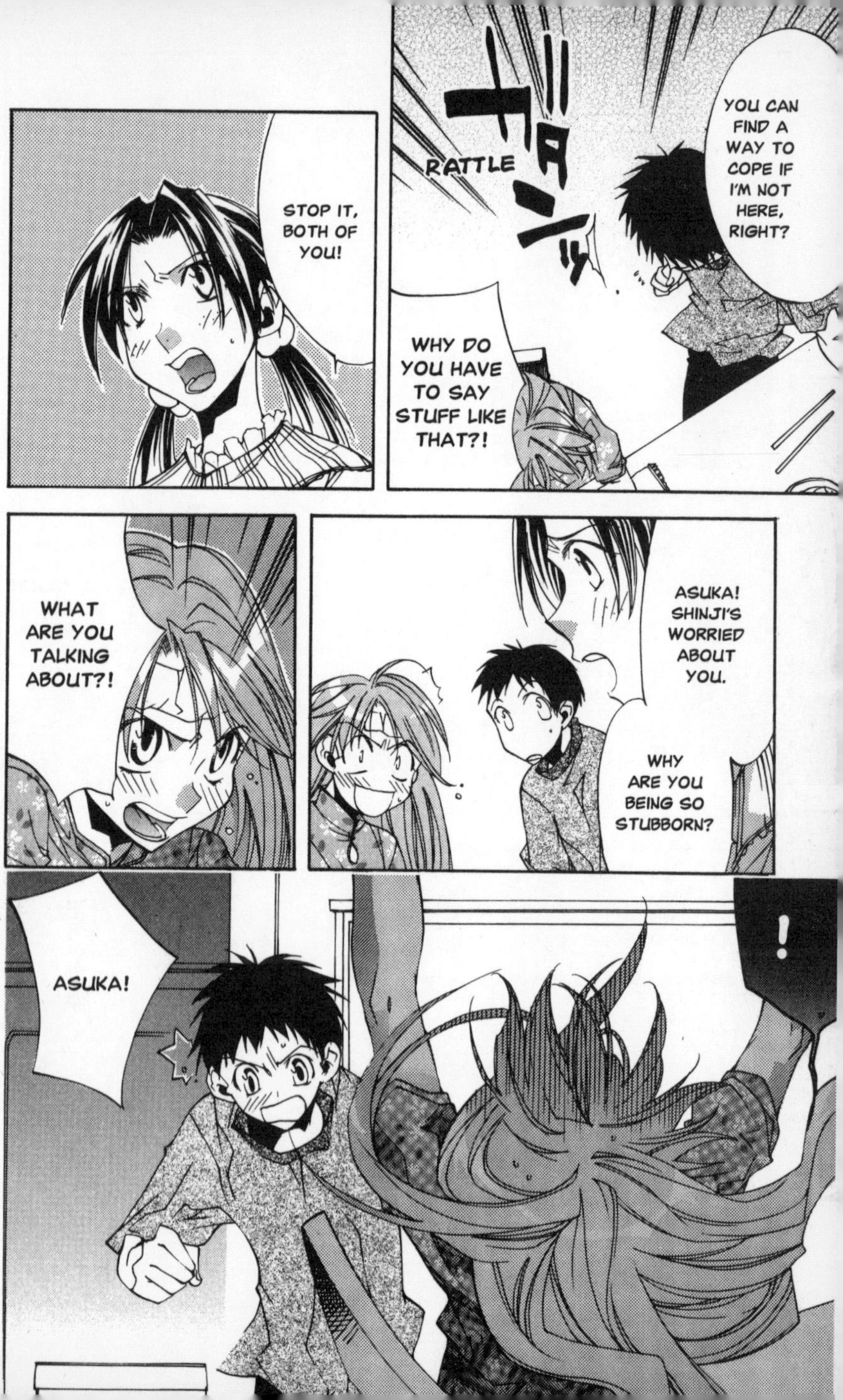
YOU CAN FIND A WAY TO COPE IF I'M NOT HERE, RIGHT?
RATTLE
WHY DO YOU HAVE TO SAY STUFF LIKE THAT?!
STOP IT, BOTH OF YOU!
ASUKA! SHINJI'S WORRIED ABOUT YOU.
WHY ARE YOU BEING SO STUBBORN?
WHAT ARE YOU TALKING ABOUT?!
!
ASUKA!

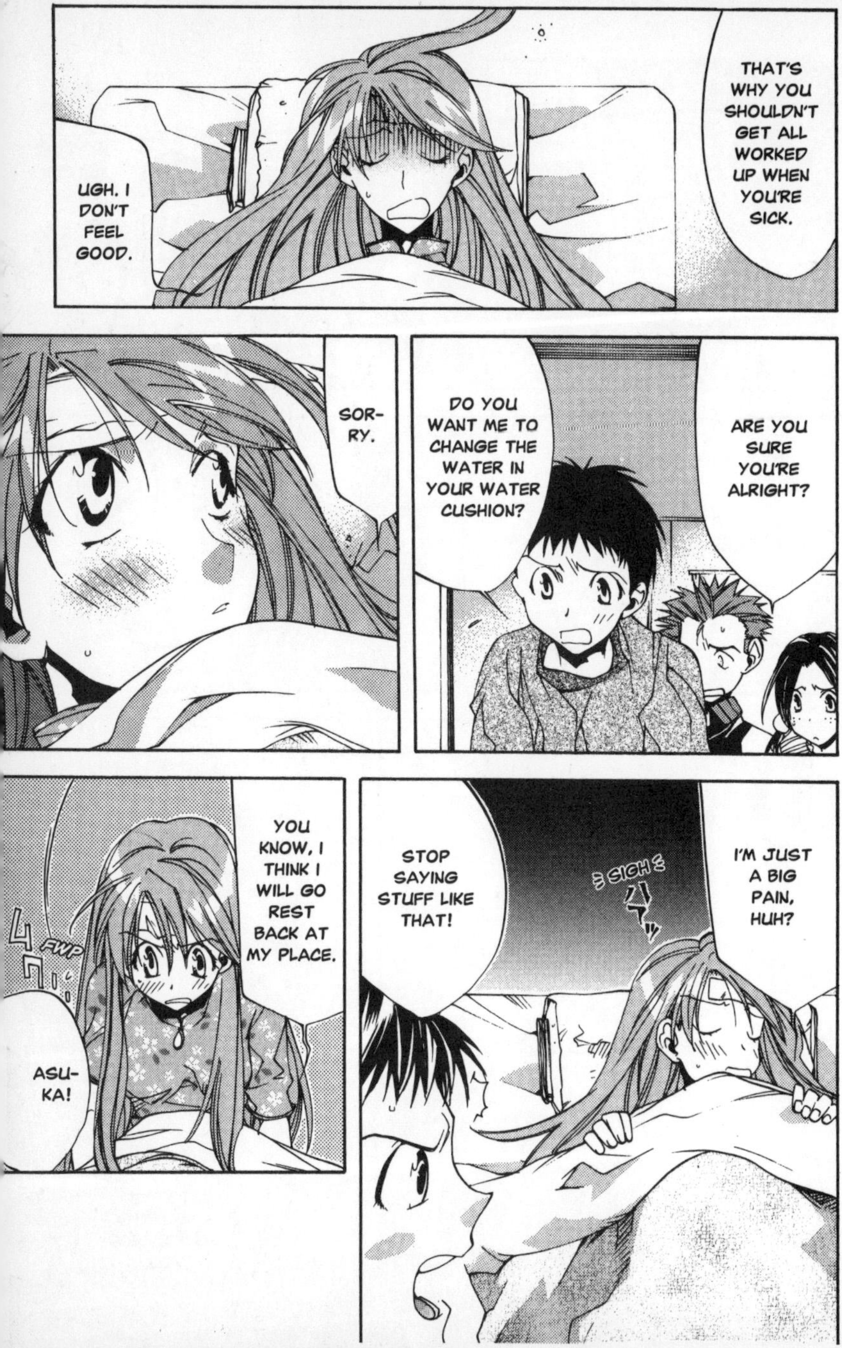
THAT'S WHY YOU SHOULDN'T GET ALL WORKED UP WHEN YOU'RE SICK.
UGH. I DON'T FEEL GOOD.
ARE YOU SURE YOU'RE ALRIGHT?
DO YOU WANT ME TO CHANGE THE WATER IN YOUR WATER CUSHION?
SOR-RY.
I'M JUST A BIG PAIN, HUH?
SIGH
STOP SAYING STUFF LIKE THAT!
YOU KNOW, I THINK I WILL GO REST BACK AT MY PLACE.
FWP
ASU-KA!

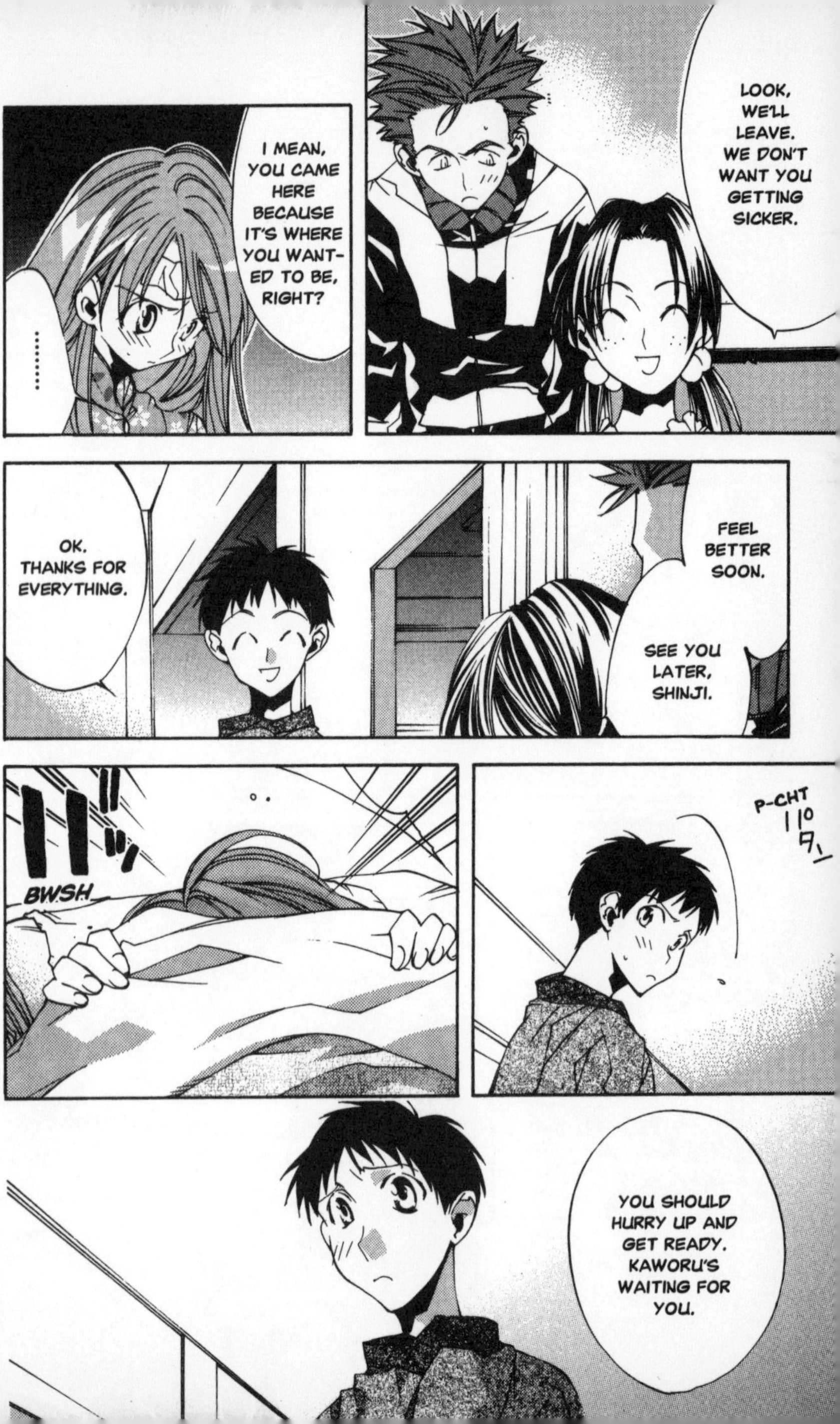
LOOK, WE'LL LEAVE. WE DON'T WANT YOU GETTING SICKER.
I MEAN, YOU CAME HERE BECAUSE IT'S WHERE YOU WANTED TO BE, RIGHT?
....
FEEL BETTER SOON.
SEE YOU LATER, SHINJI.
OK. THANKS FOR EVERYTHING.
P-CHT
BWSH
YOU SHOULD HURRY UP AND GET READY. KAWORU'S WAITING FOR YOU.

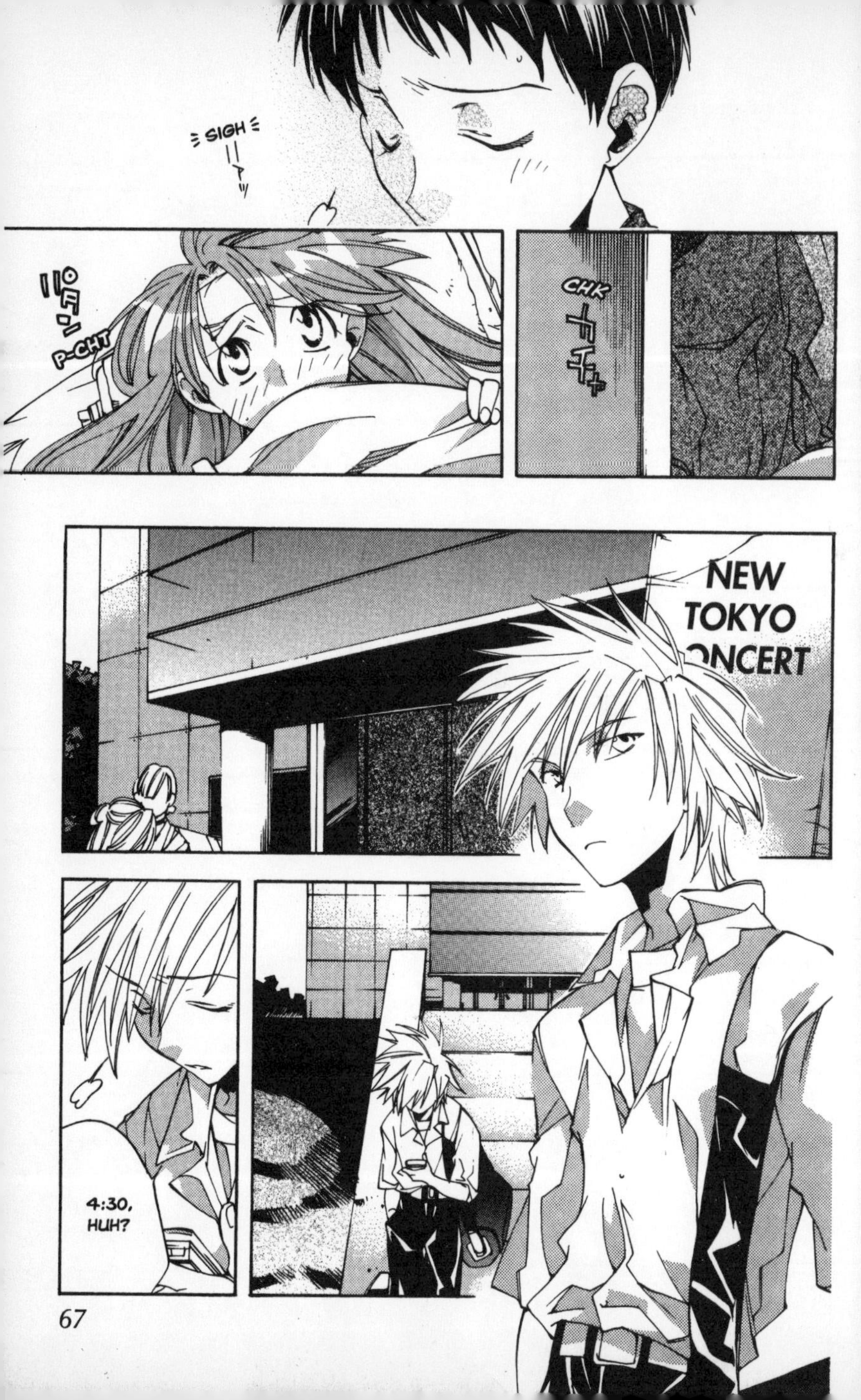
SIGH
P-CHT
CHK
NEW
TOKYO
ONCERT
4:30, HUH?

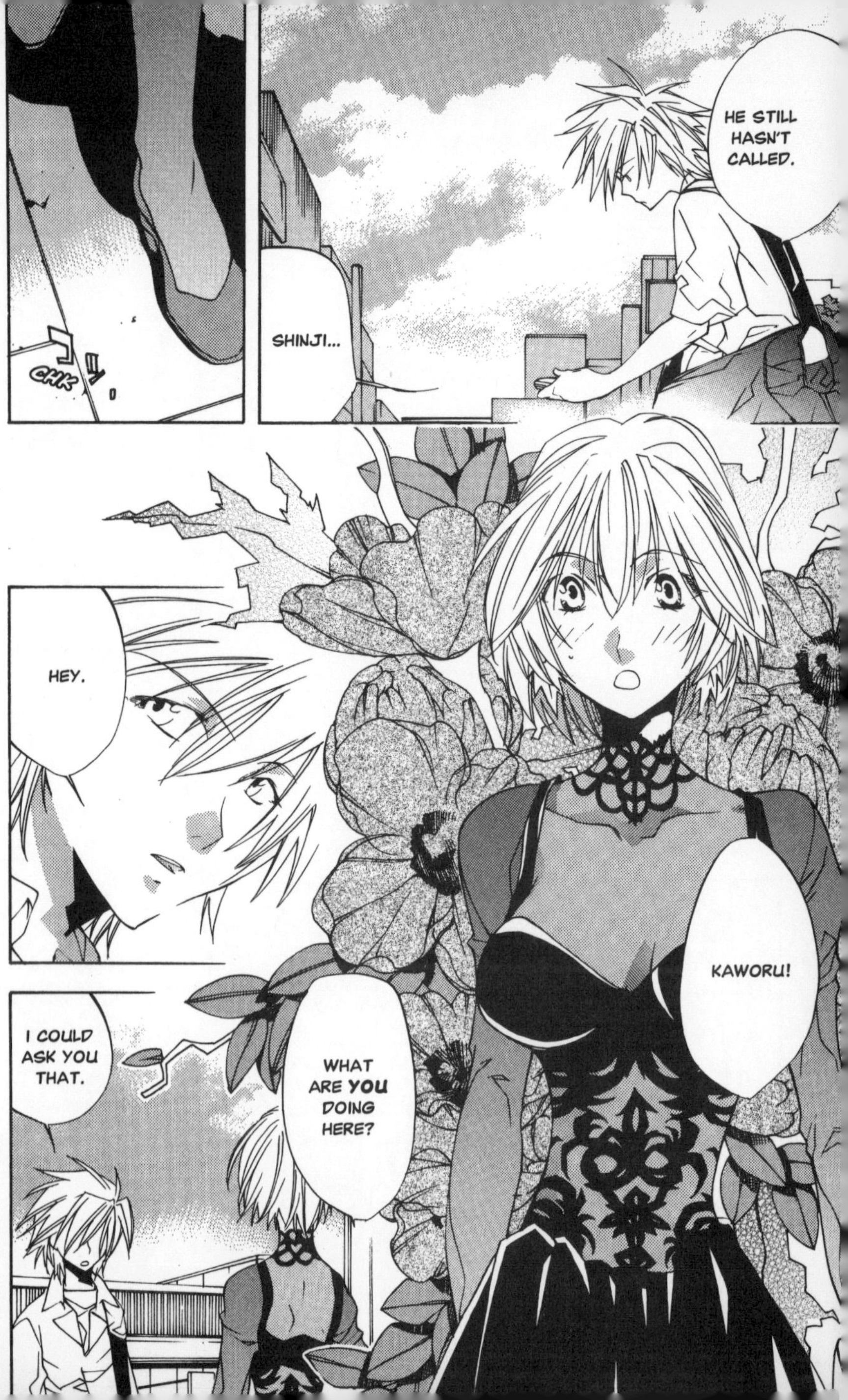

HE STILL HASN'T CALLED.
SHINJI...
CHK
KAWORU!
HEY.
WHAT ARE YOU DOING HERE?
I COULD ASK YOU THAT.

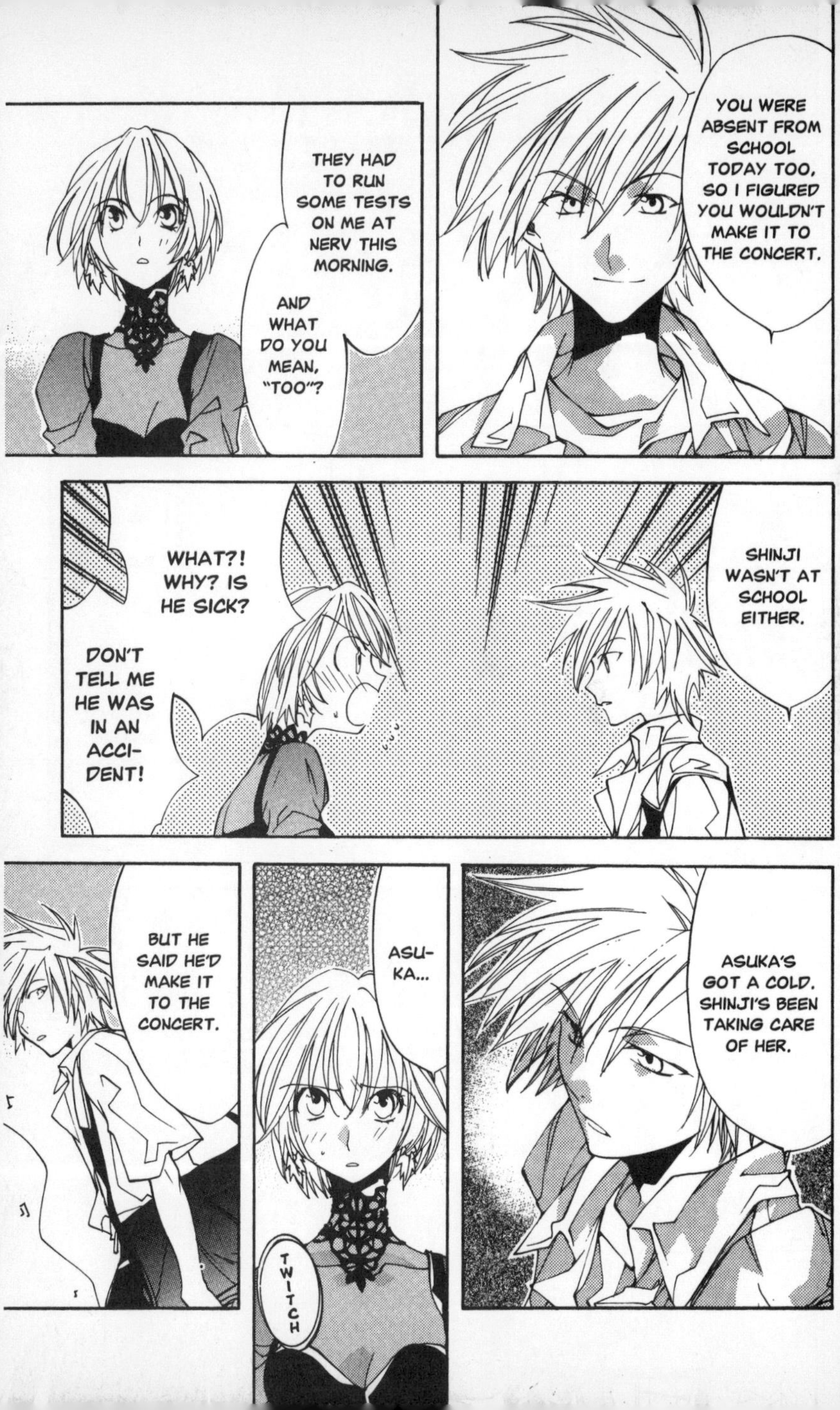
YOU WERE ABSENT FROM SCHOOL TODAY TOO, SO I FIGURED YOU WOULDN'T MAKE IT TO THE CONCERT.
THEY HAD TO RUN SOME TESTS ON ME AT NERV THIS MORNING.
AND WHAT DO YOU MEAN, "TOO"?
SHINJI WASN'T AT SCHOOL EITHER.
WHAT?! WHY? IS HE SICK?
DON'T TELL ME HE WAS IN AN ACCI-DENT!
ASUKA'S GOT A COLD. SHINJI'S BEEN TAKING CARE OF HER.
ASU-KA...
TWITCH
BUT HE SAID HE'D MAKE IT TO THE CONCERT.

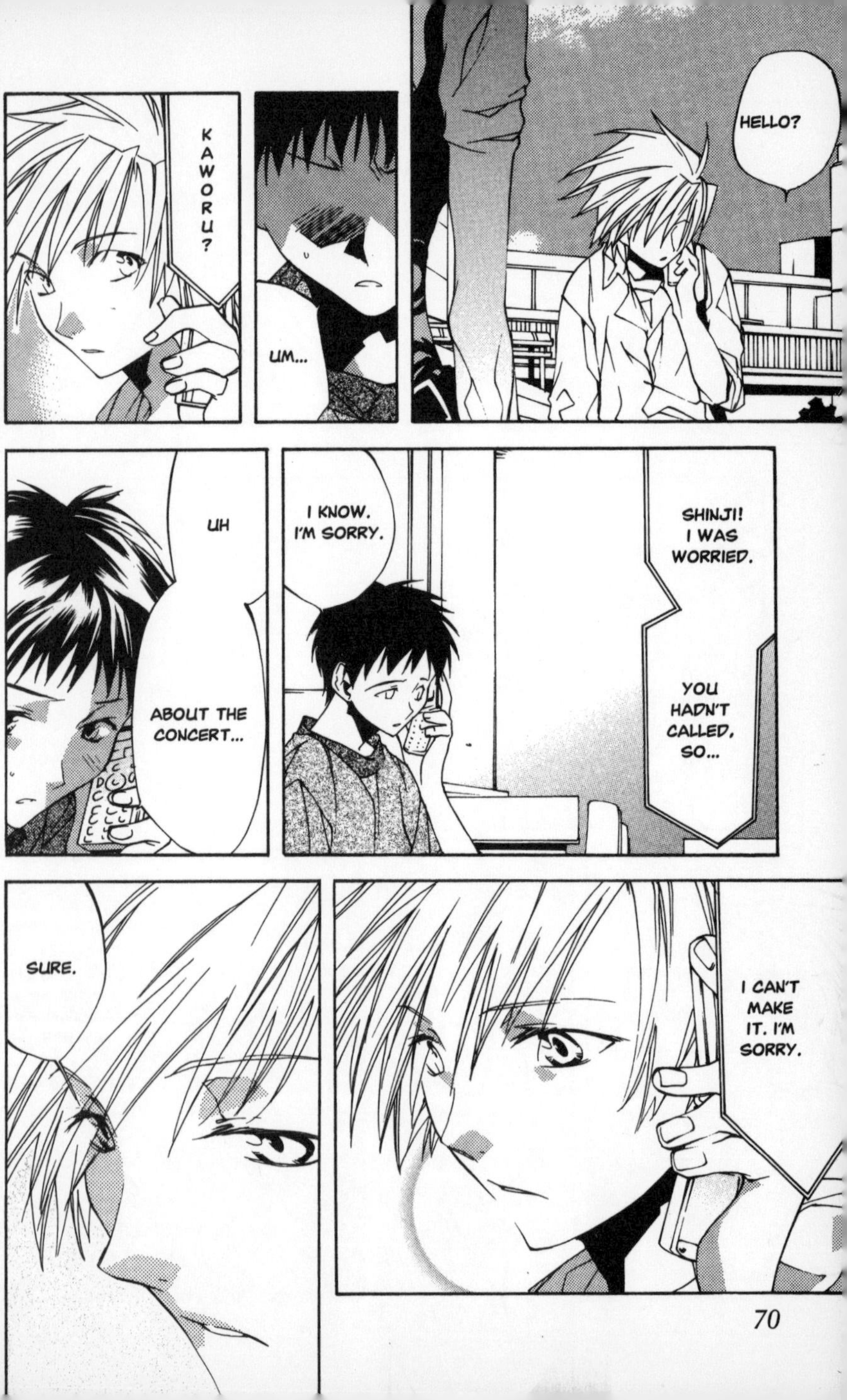
HELLO?
UM...
KAWORU?
SHINJI! I WAS WORRIED.
YOU HADN'T CALLED, SO...
I KNOW. I'M SORRY.
UH
ABOUT THE CONCERT...
I CAN'T MAKE IT. I'M SORRY.
SURE.

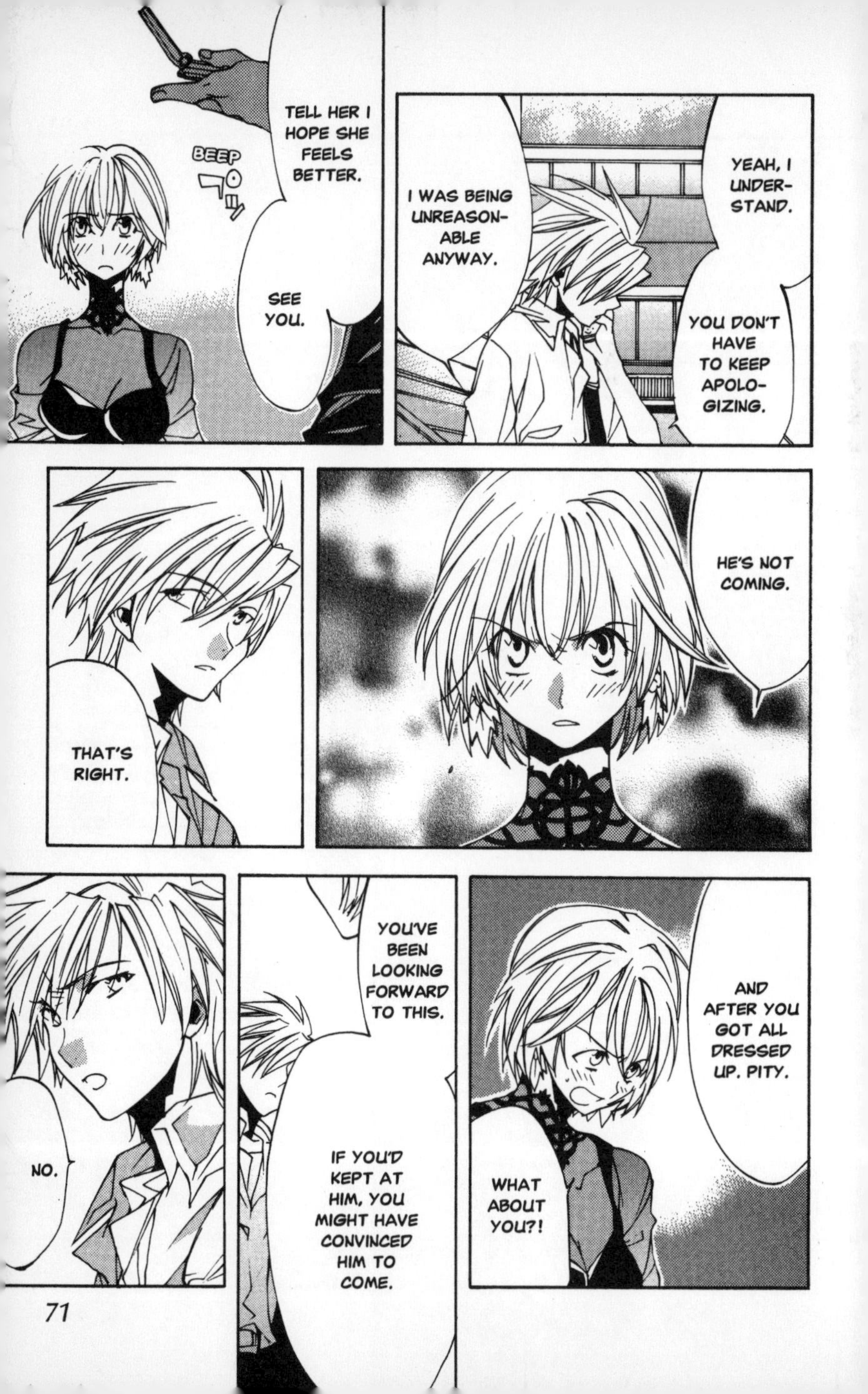
YEAH, I UNDER-STAND.
YOU DON'T HAVE TO KEEP APOLO-GIZING.
I WAS BEING UNREASON-ABLE ANYWAY.
TELL HER I HOPE SHE FEELS BETTER.
SEE YOU.
BEEP
HE'S NOT COMING.
THAT'S RIGHT.
AND AFTER YOU GOT ALL DRESSED UP. PITY.
WHAT ABOUT YOU?!
YOU'VE BEEN LOOKING FORWARD TO THIS.
IF YOU'D KEPT AT HIM, YOU MIGHT HAVE CONVINCED HIM TO COME.
NO.

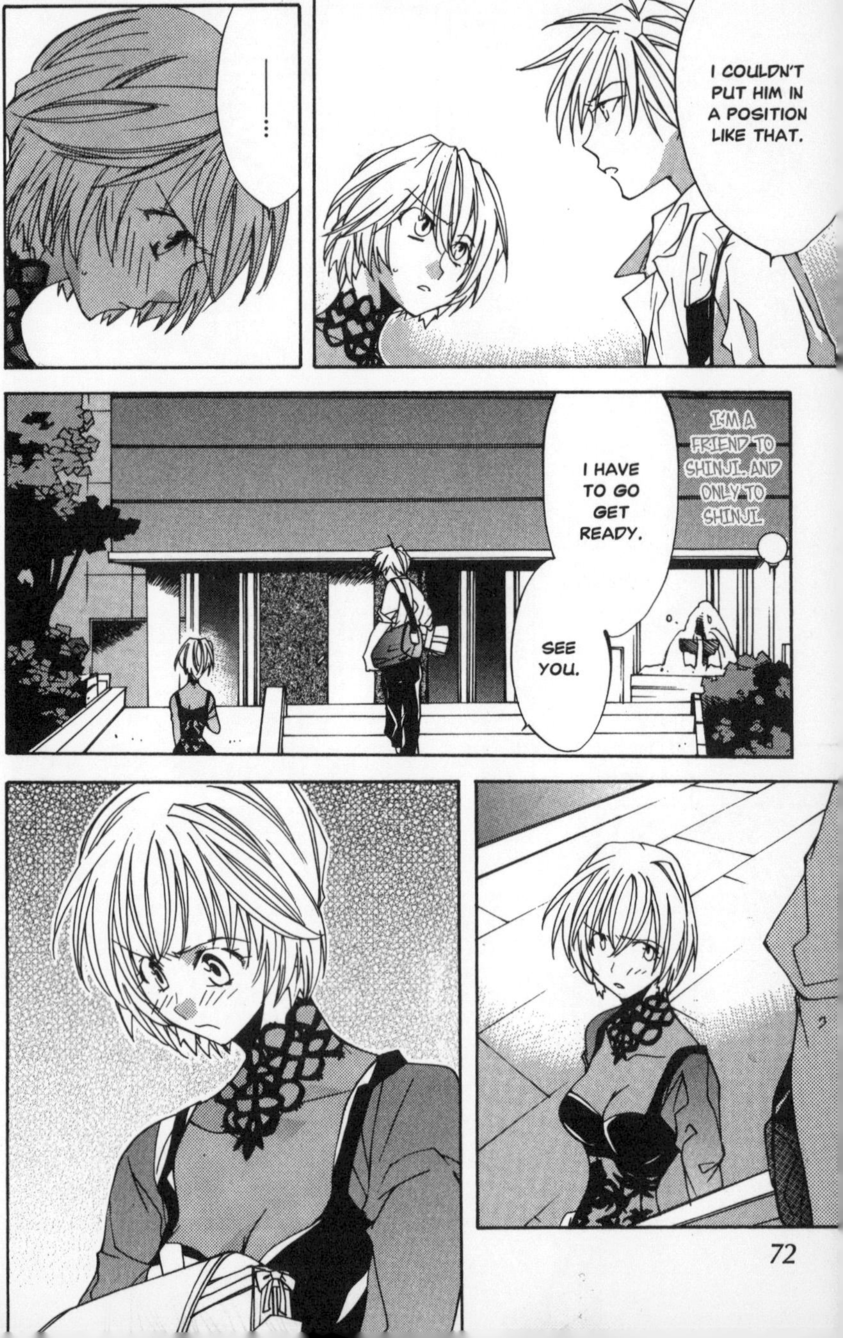
I COULDN'T PUT HIM IN A POSITION LIKE THAT.
……
I'M A FRIEND TO SHINJI. AND ONLY TO SHINJI.
I HAVE TO GO GET READY.
SEE YOU.

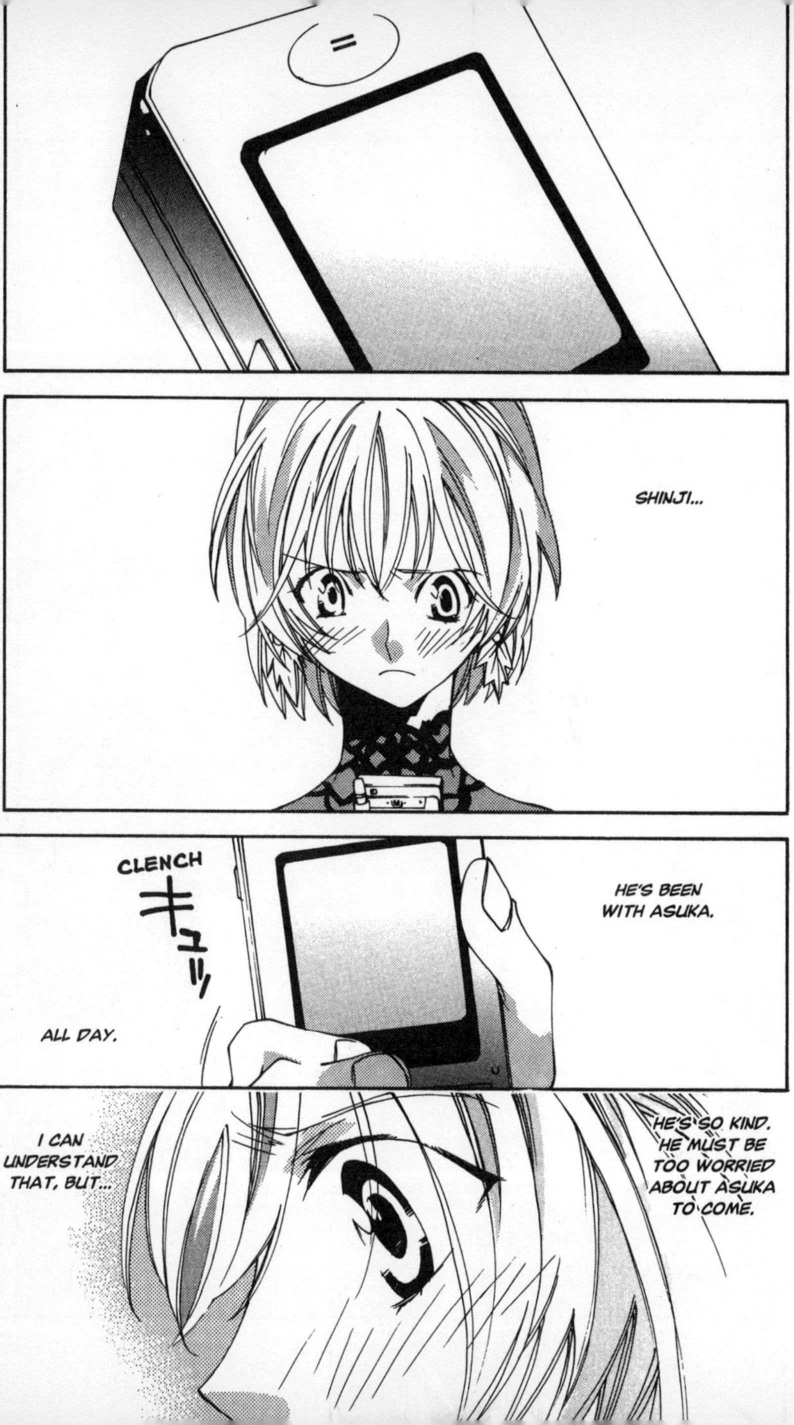
SHINJI...
HE'S BEEN WITH ASUKA.
CLENCH
キュッ
ALL DAY.
HE'S SO KIND. HE MUST BE TOO WORRIED ABOUT ASUKA TO COME.
I CAN UNDERSTAND THAT, BUT...

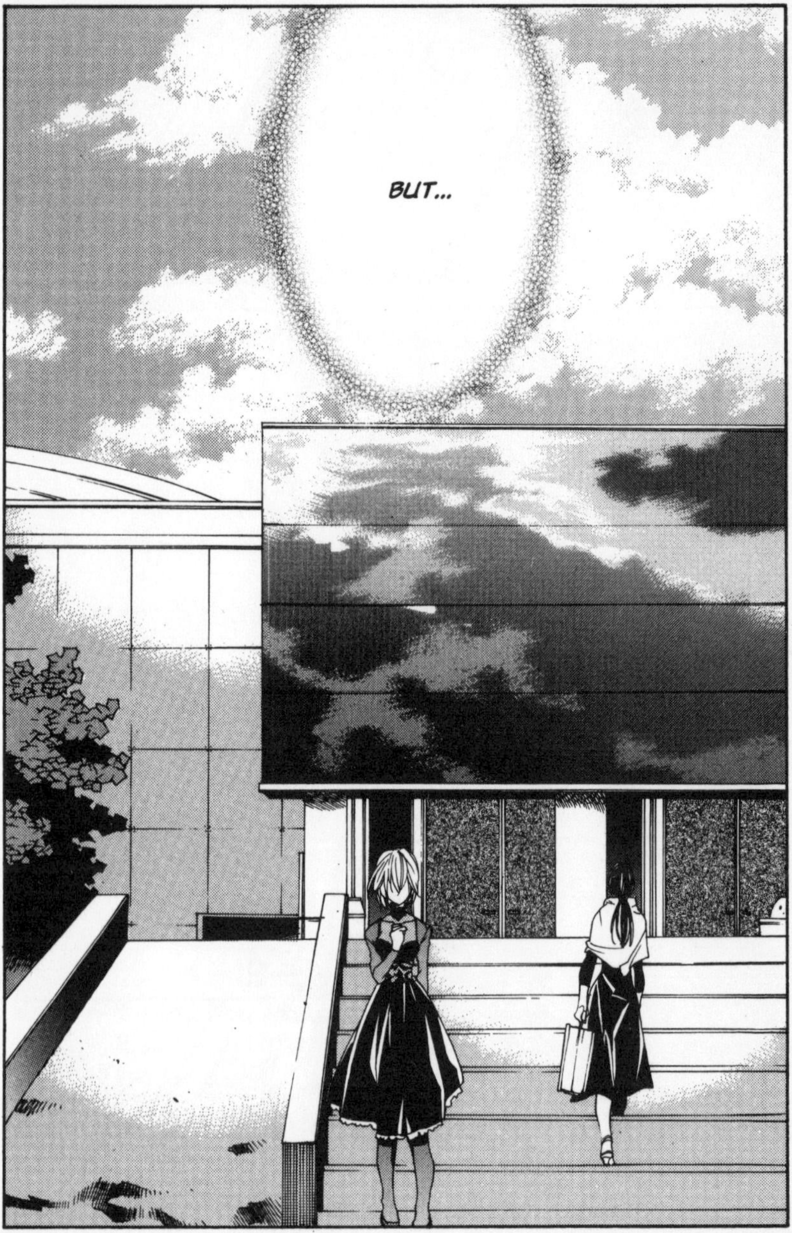
BUT...

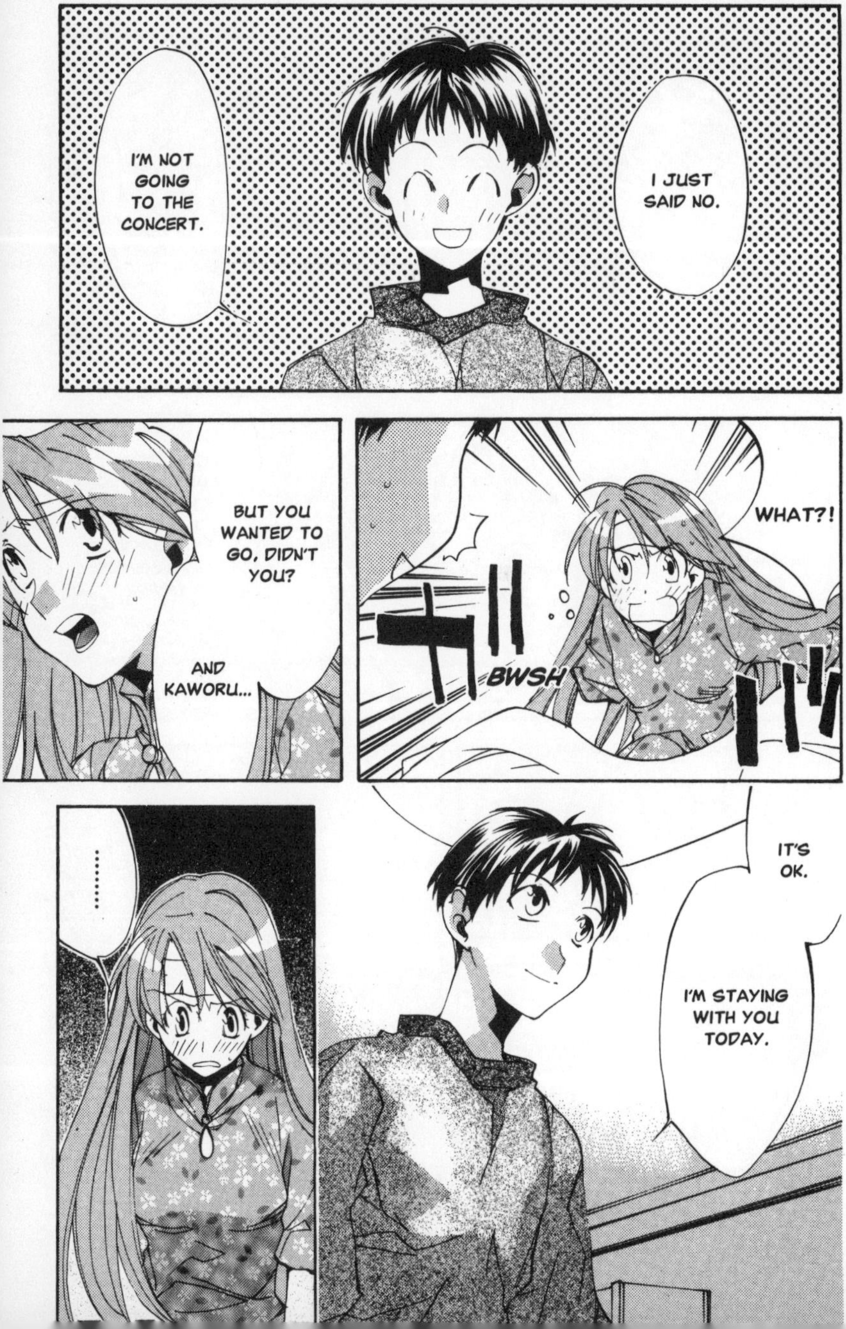
I JUST SAID NO.
I'M NOT GOING TO THE CONCERT.
WHAT?!
BWSH
BUT YOU WANTED TO GO, DIDN'T YOU?
AND KAWORU...
IT'S OK.
I'M STAYING WITH YOU TODAY.
......

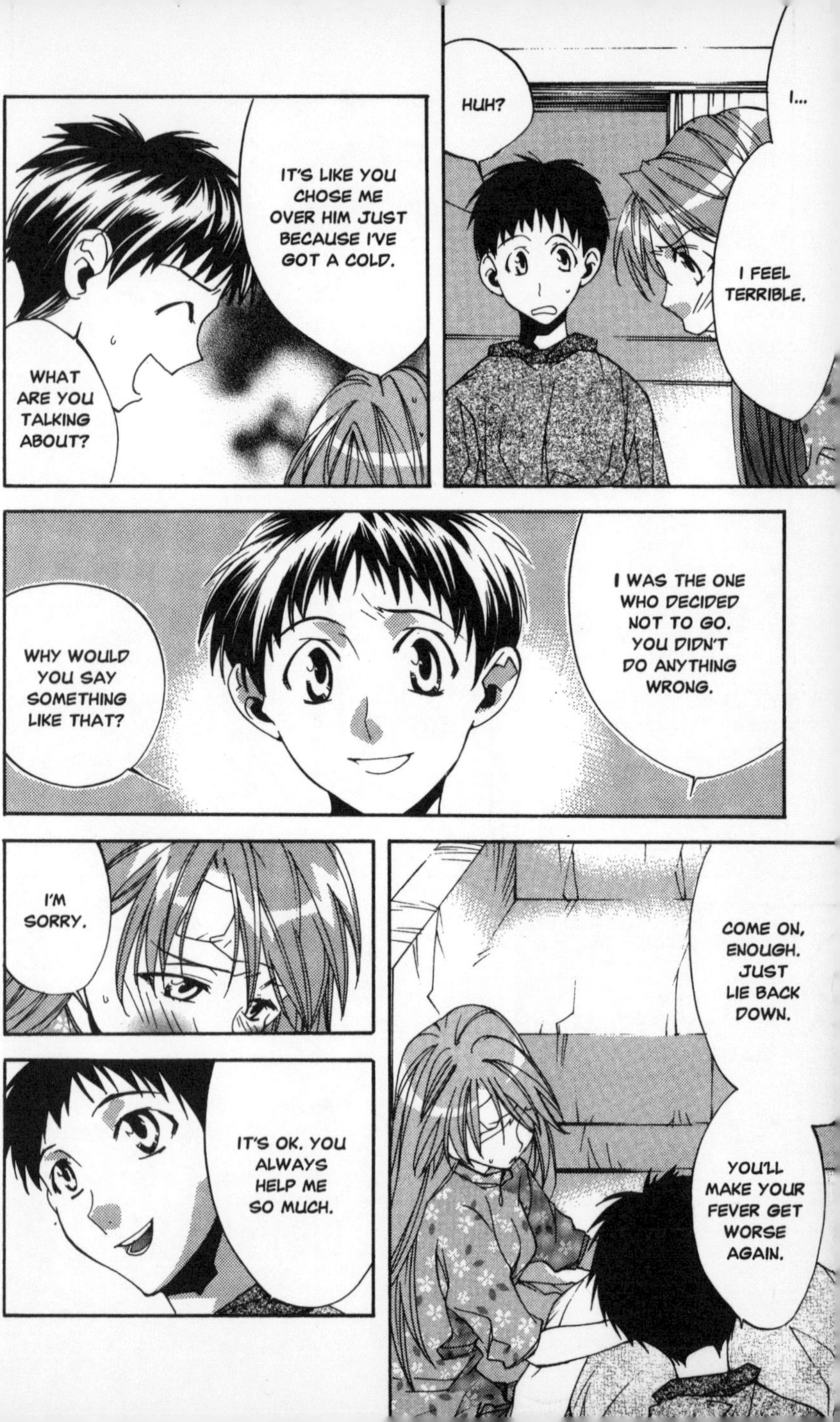
I...
I FEEL TERRIBLE.
HUH?
IT'S LIKE YOU CHOSE ME OVER HIM JUST BECAUSE I'VE GOT A COLD.
WHAT ARE YOU TALKING ABOUT?
I WAS THE ONE WHO DECIDED NOT TO GO. YOU DIDN'T DO ANYTHING WRONG.
WHY WOULD YOU SAY SOMETHING LIKE THAT?
COME ON, ENOUGH. JUST LIE BACK DOWN.
YOU'LL MAKE YOUR FEVER GET WORSE AGAIN.
I'M SORRY.
IT'S OK. YOU ALWAYS HELP ME SO MUCH.

TODAY'S MY TURN TO HELP YOU.

CHK

CHK

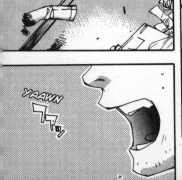

YAAWN

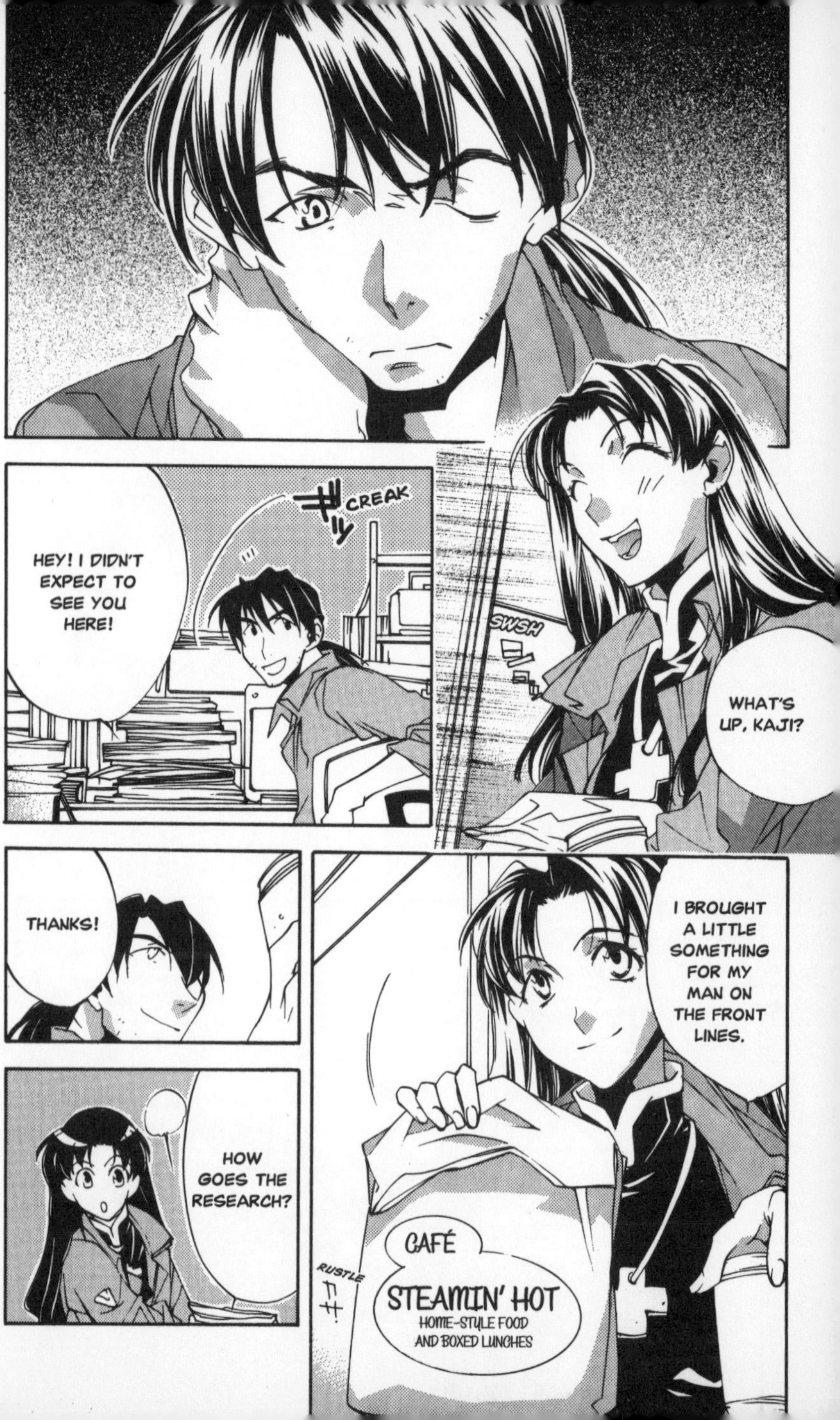
WHAT'S UP, KAJI?
SWSH
CREAK
HEY! I DIDN'T EXPECT TO SEE YOU HERE!
I BROUGHT A LITTLE SOMETHING FOR MY MAN ON THE FRONT LINES.
RUSTLE
CAFÉ
STEAMIN' HOT
HOME-STYLE FOOD AND BOXED LUNCHES
THANKS!
HOW GOES THE RESEARCH?

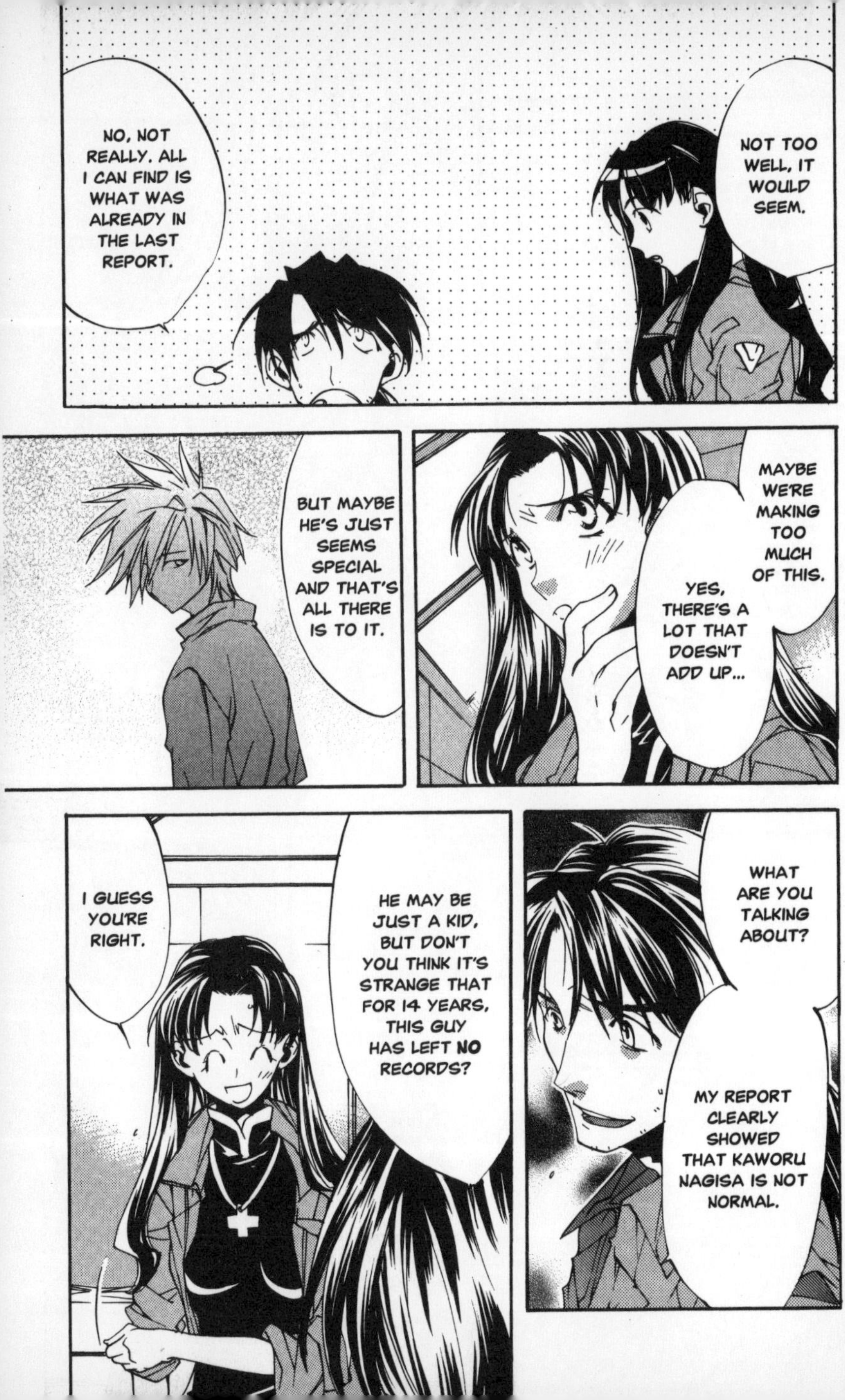
NOT TOO WELL, IT WOULD SEEM.
NO, NOT REALLY. ALL I CAN FIND IS WHAT WAS ALREADY IN THE LAST REPORT.
MAYBE WE'RE MAKING TOO MUCH OF THIS.
YES, THERE'S A LOT THAT DOESN'T ADD UP...
BUT MAYBE HE'S JUST SEEMS SPECIAL AND THAT'S ALL THERE IS TO IT.
WHAT ARE YOU TALKING ABOUT?
MY REPORT CLEARLY SHOWED THAT KAWORU NAGISA IS NOT NORMAL.
HE MAY BE JUST A KID, BUT DON'T YOU THINK IT'S STRANGE THAT FOR 14 YEARS, THIS GUY HAS LEFT NO RECORDS?
I GUESS YOU'RE RIGHT.

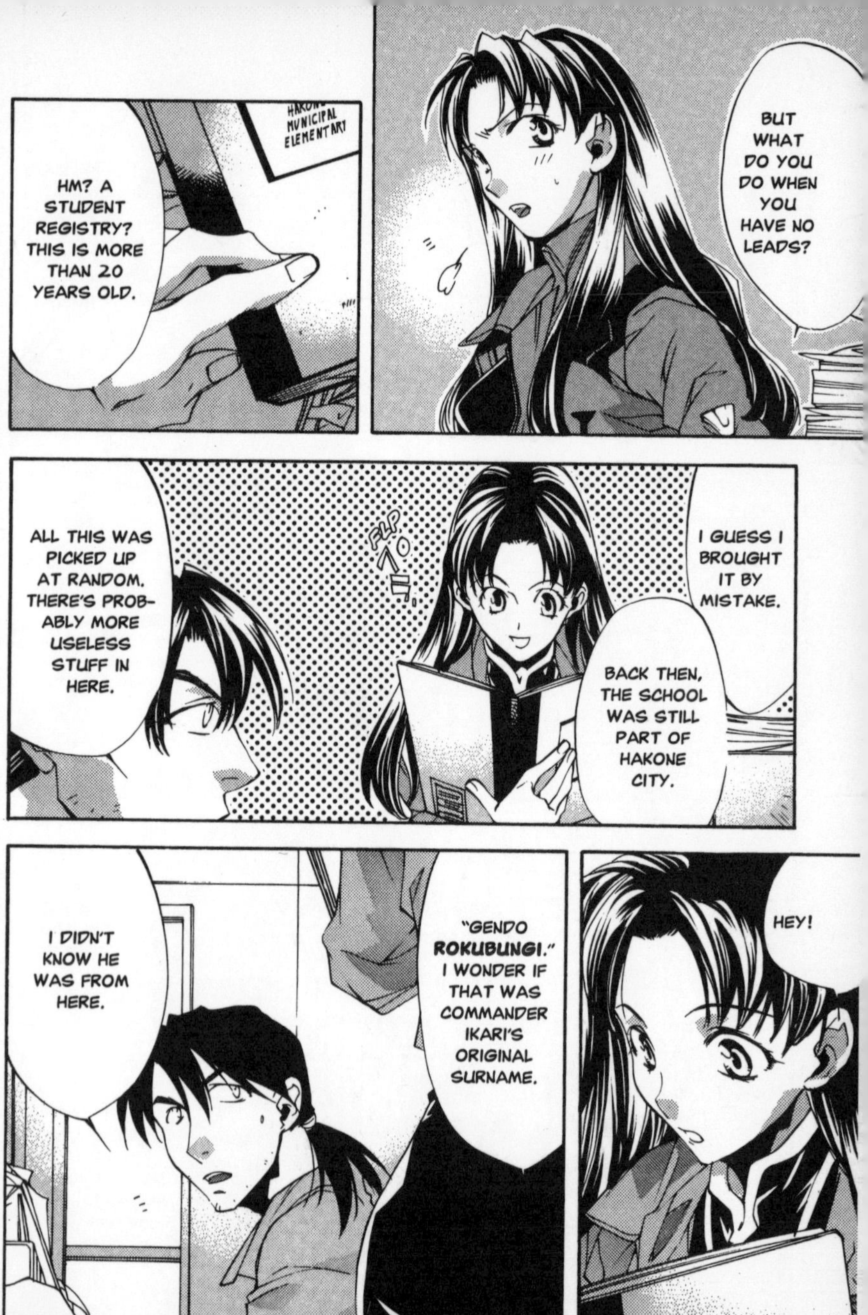
BUT WHAT DO YOU DO WHEN YOU HAVE NO LEADS?
MUNICIPAL ELEMENTARY
HM? A STUDENT REGISTRY? THIS IS MORE THAN 20 YEARS OLD.
I GUESS I BROUGHT IT BY MISTAKE.
BACK THEN, THE SCHOOL WAS STILL PART OF HAKONE CITY.
FLIP
ALL THIS WAS PICKED UP AT RANDOM. THERE'S PROB-ABLY MORE USELESS STUFF IN HERE.
HEY!
"GENDO **ROKUBUNGI**." I WONDER IF THAT WAS COMMANDER IKARI'S ORIGINAL SURNAME.
I DIDN'T KNOW HE WAS FROM HERE.

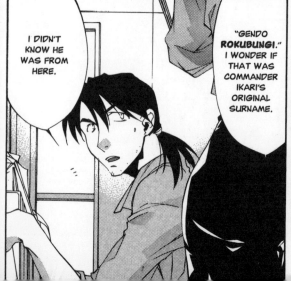

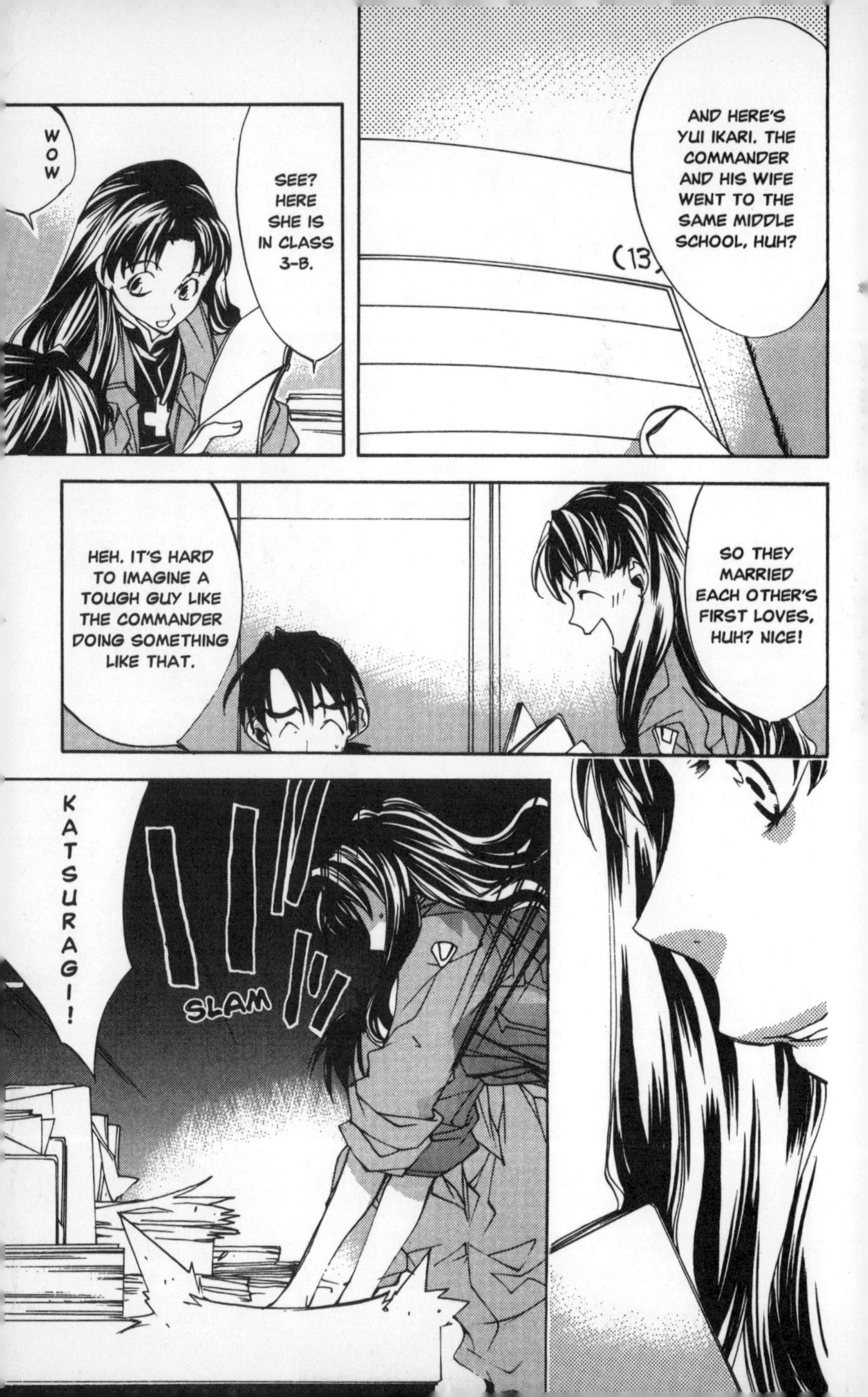
AND HERE'S YUI IKARI. THE COMMANDER AND HIS WIFE WENT TO THE SAME MIDDLE SCHOOL, HUH?
(13)
SEE? HERE SHE IS IN CLASS 3-B.
WOW
SO THEY MARRIED EACH OTHER'S FIRST LOVES, HUH? NICE!
HEH. IT'S HARD TO IMAGINE A TOUGH GUY LIKE THE COMMANDER DOING SOMETHING LIKE THAT.
KATSURAGI!
SLAM

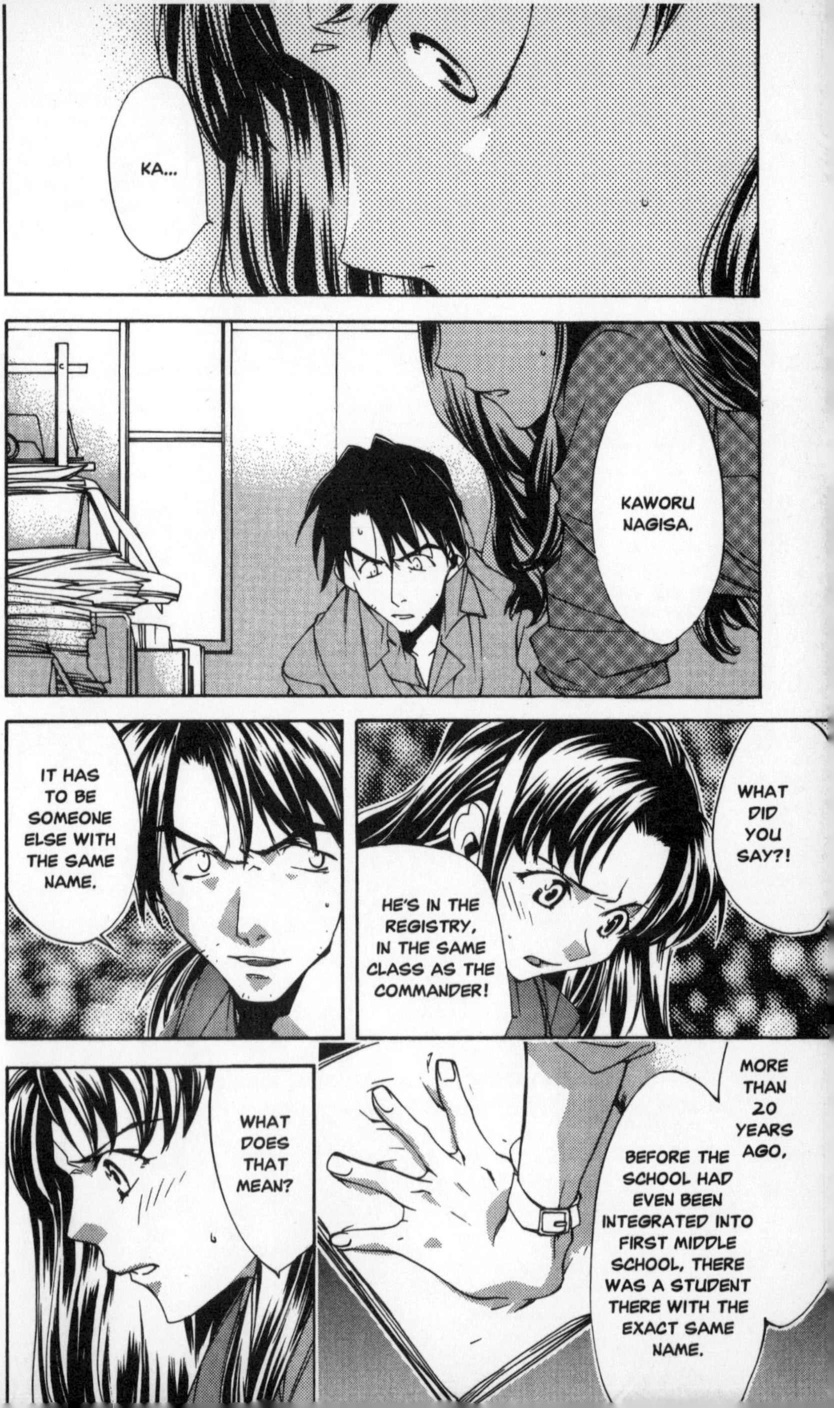
KA...
KAWORU NAGISA.
WHAT DID YOU SAY?!
HE'S IN THE REGISTRY, IN THE SAME CLASS AS THE COMMANDER!
IT HAS TO BE SOMEONE ELSE WITH THE SAME NAME.
WHAT DOES THAT MEAN?
MORE THAN 20 YEARS AGO,
BEFORE THE SCHOOL HAD EVEN BEEN INTEGRATED INTO FIRST MIDDLE SCHOOL, THERE WAS A STUDENT THERE WITH THE EXACT SAME NAME.

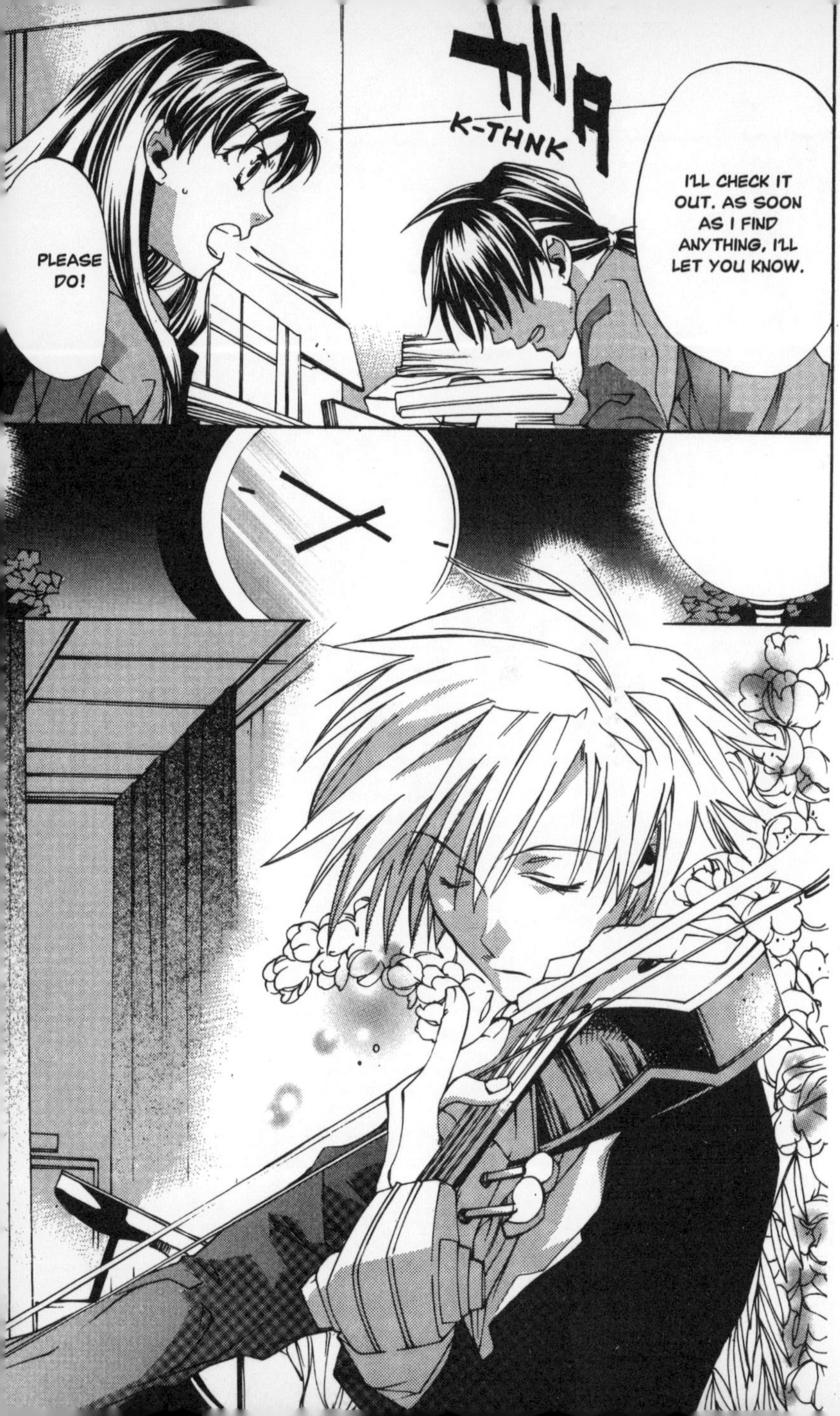
K-THNK
I'LL CHECK IT OUT. AS SOON AS I FIND ANYTHING, I'LL LET YOU KNOW.
PLEASE DO!

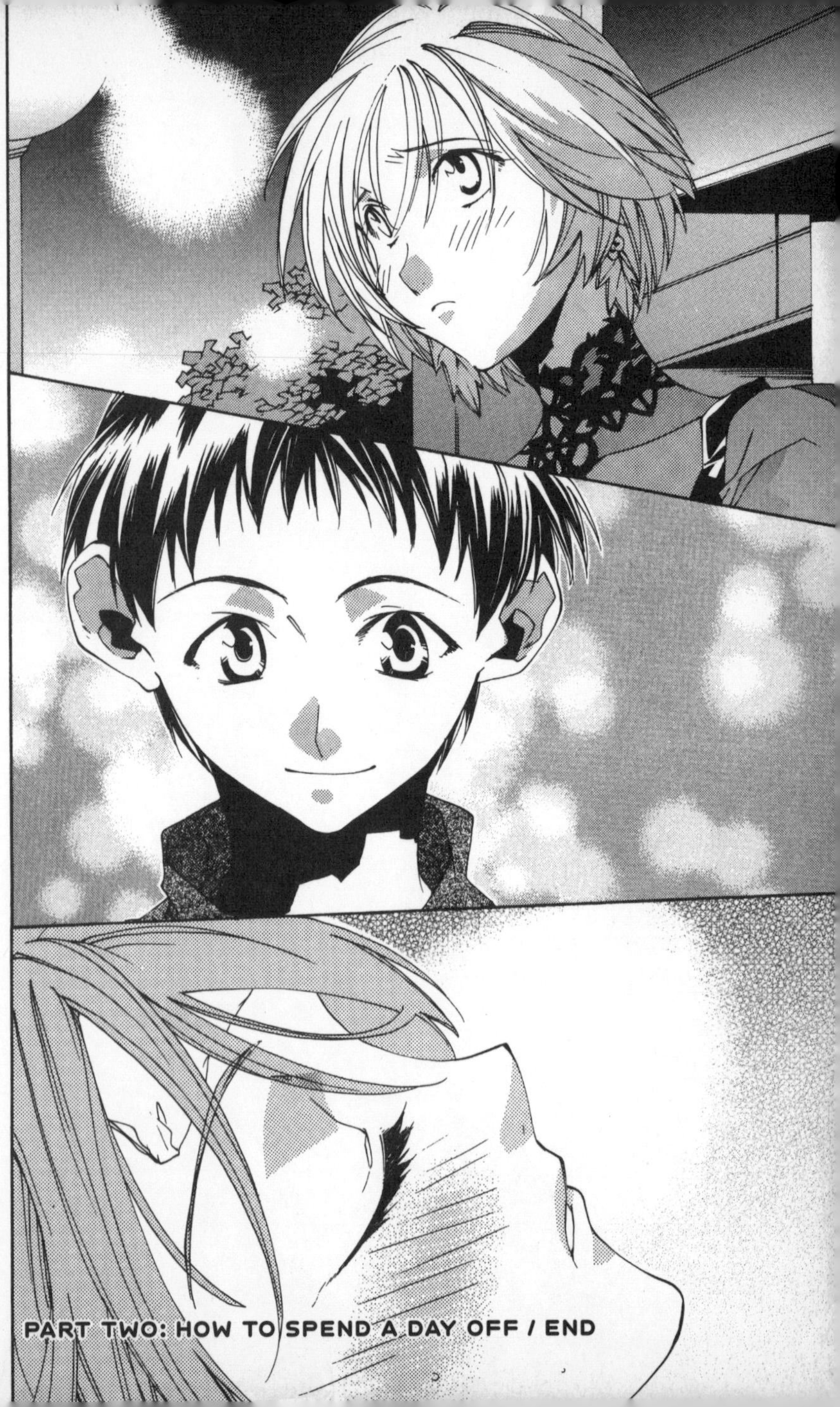
PART TWO: HOW TO SPEND A DAY OFF / END

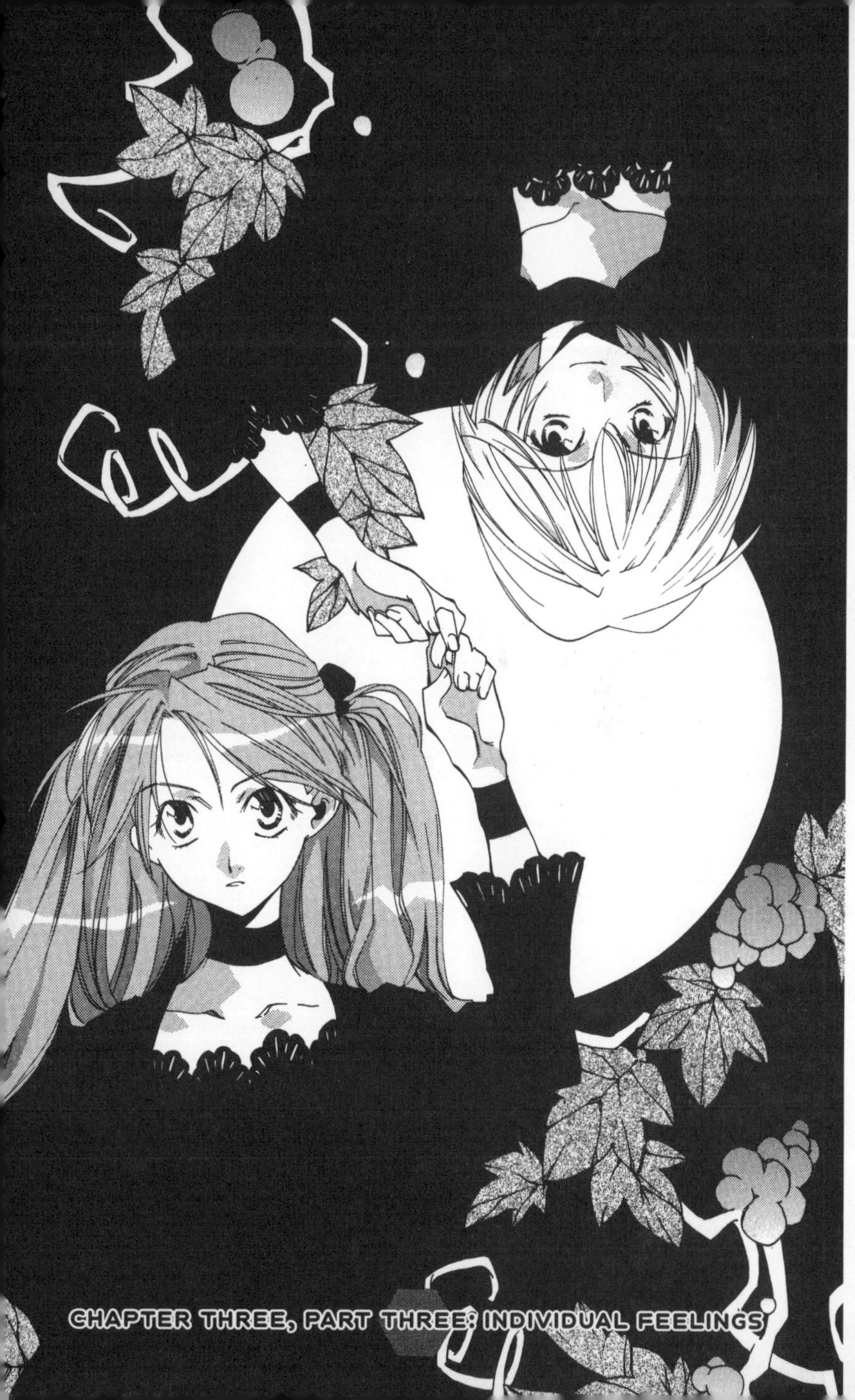

CHAPTER THREE, PART THREE: INDIVIDUAL FEELINGS

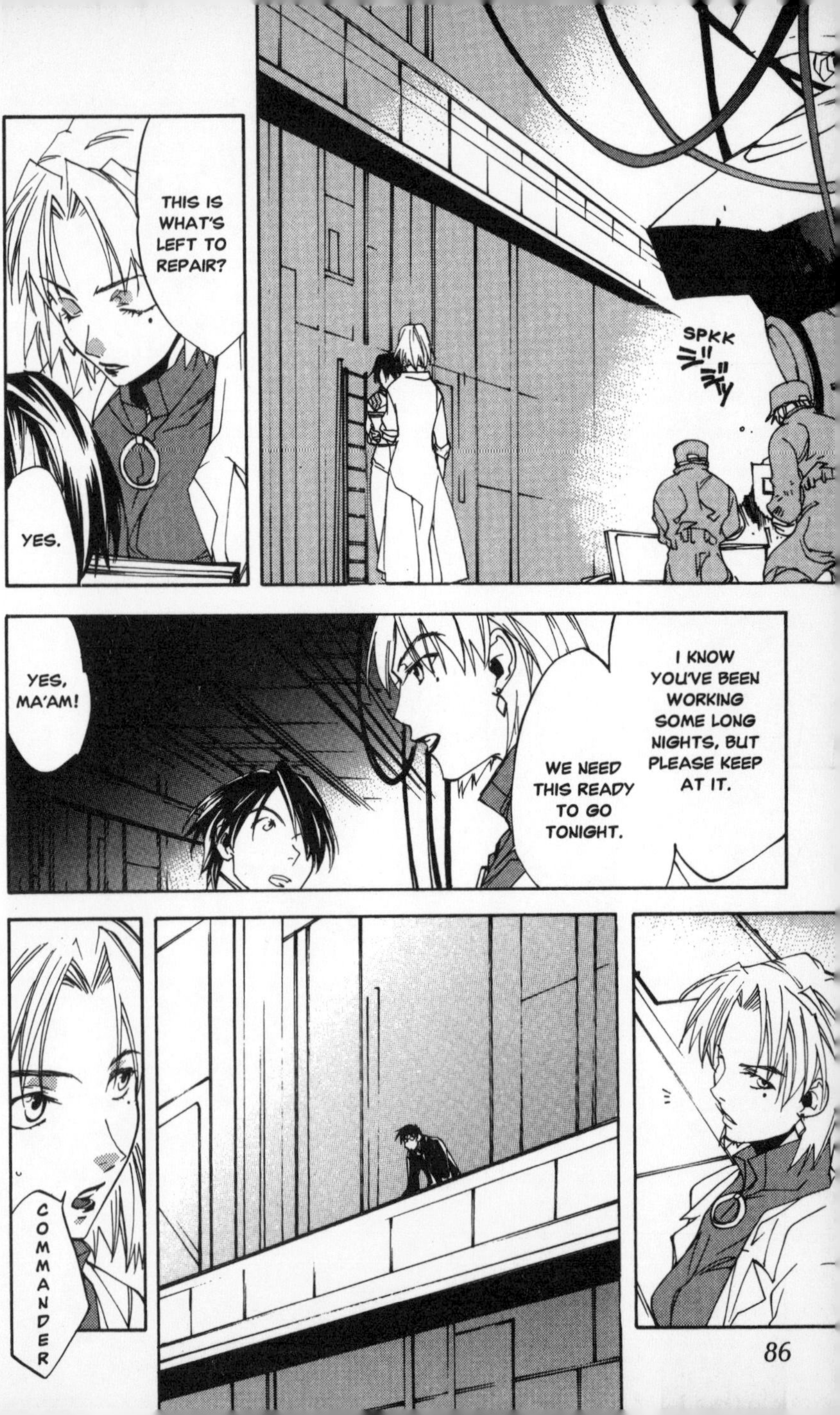
SPKK
THIS IS WHAT'S LEFT TO REPAIR?
YES.
I KNOW YOU'VE BEEN WORKING SOME LONG NIGHTS, BUT PLEASE KEEP AT IT.
WE NEED THIS READY TO GO TONIGHT.
YES, MA'AM!
COMMANDER

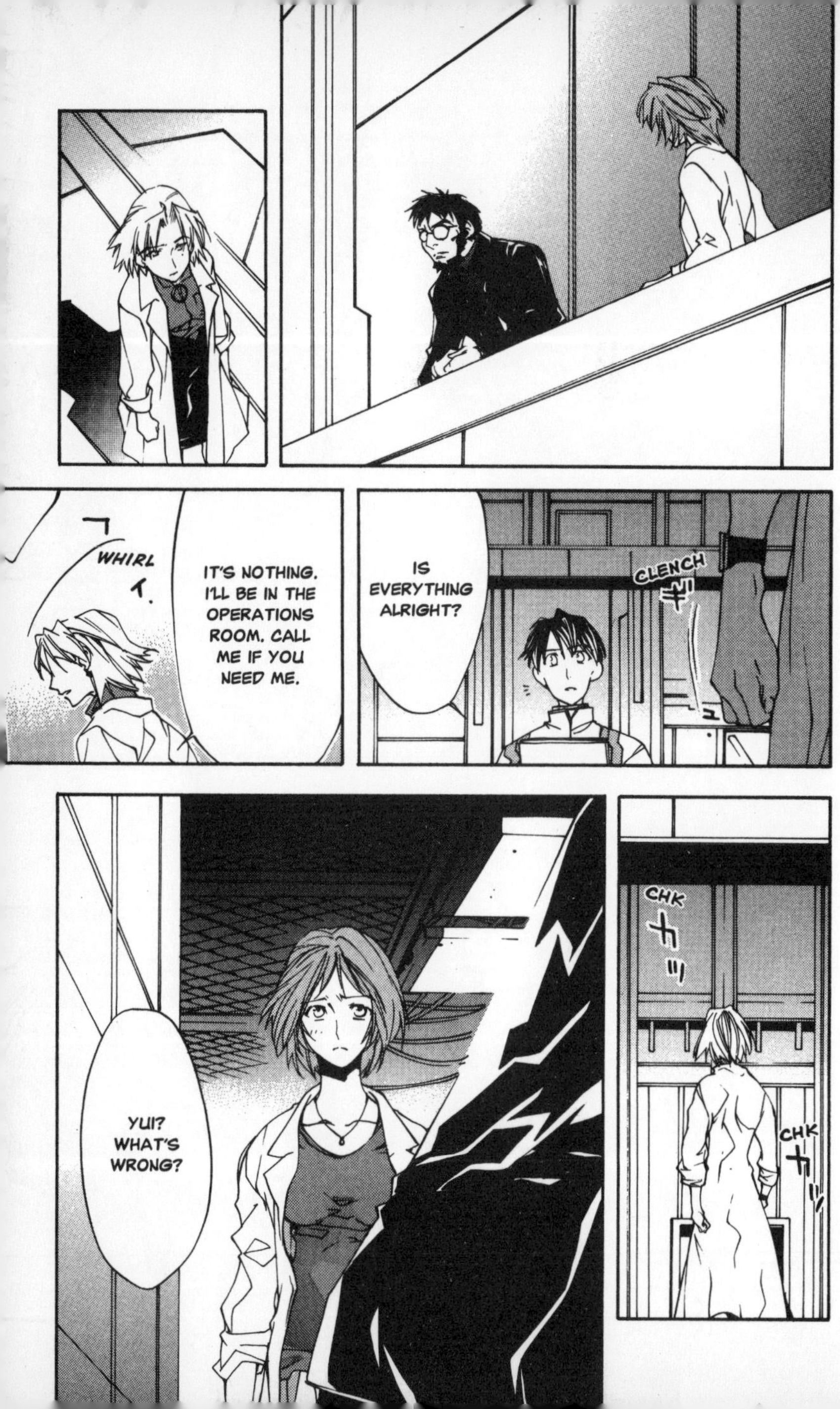
CLENCH
IS EVERYTHING ALRIGHT?
IT'S NOTHING. I'LL BE IN THE OPERATIONS ROOM. CALL ME IF YOU NEED ME.
WHIRL
CHK
CHK
YUI? WHAT'S WRONG?

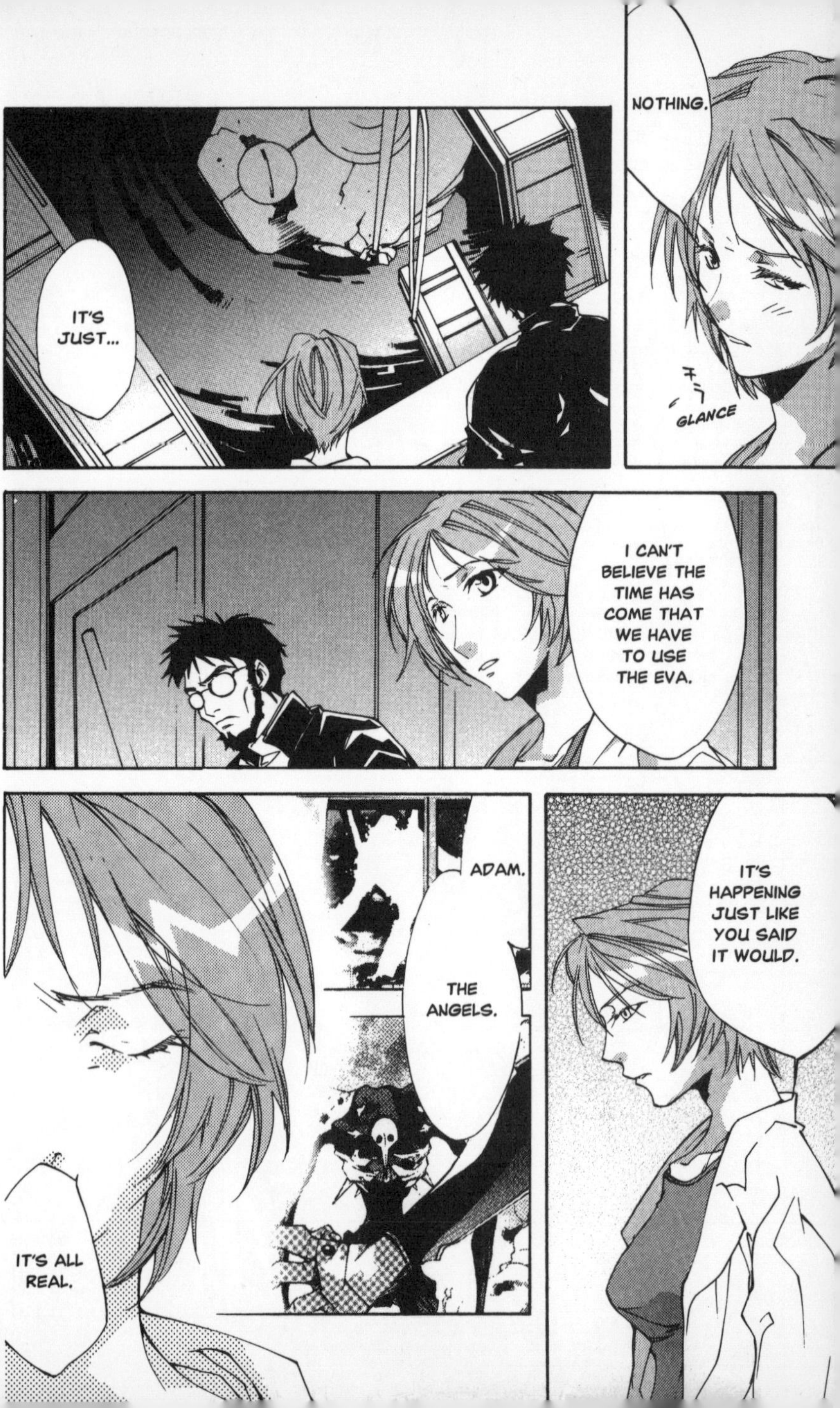
NOTHING.
チラ
GLANCE
IT'S JUST...
I CAN'T BELIEVE THE TIME HAS COME THAT WE HAVE TO USE THE EVA.
IT'S HAPPENING JUST LIKE YOU SAID IT WOULD.
ADAM.
THE ANGELS.
IT'S ALL REAL.

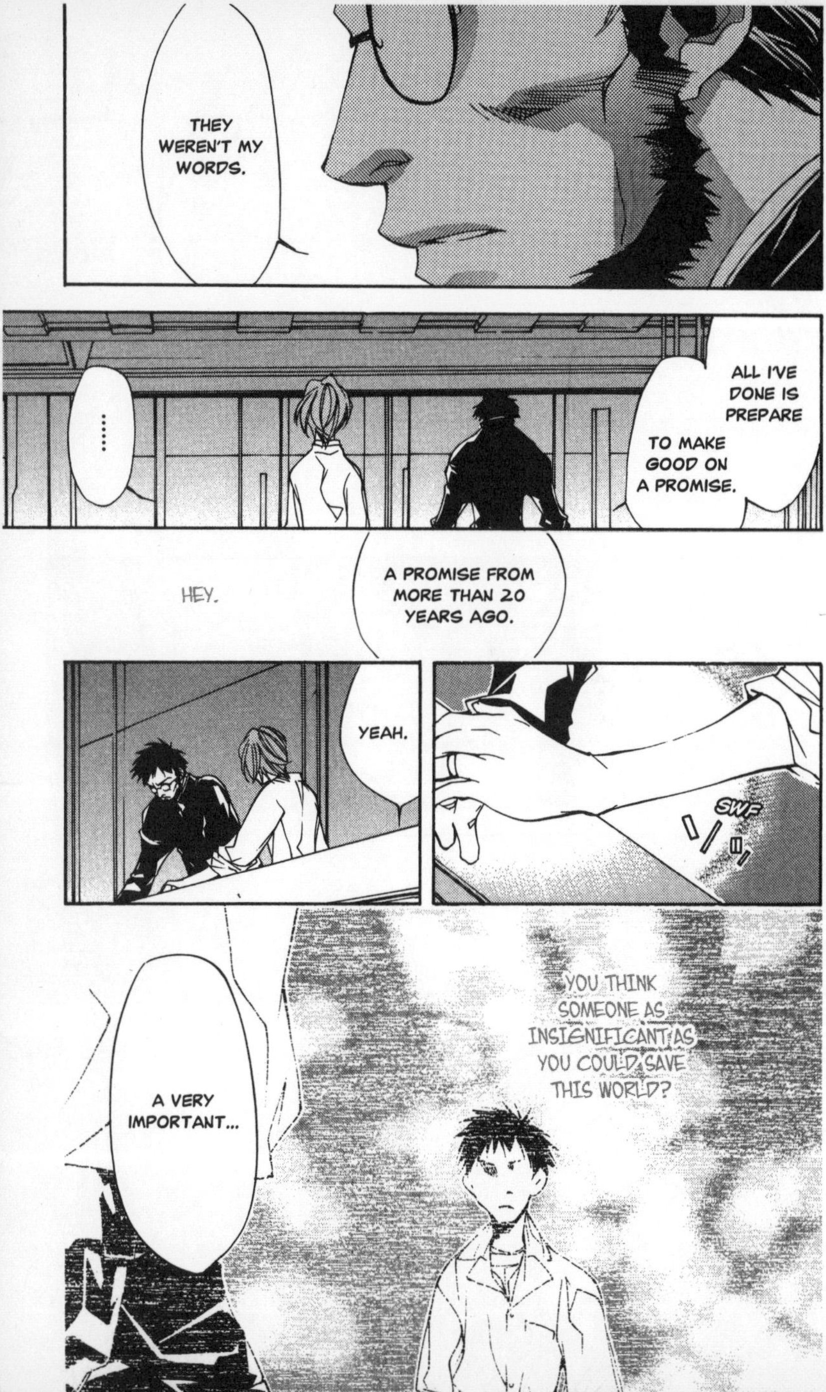
THEY WEREN'T MY WORDS.
ALL I'VE DONE IS PREPARE
TO MAKE GOOD ON A PROMISE.
......
A PROMISE FROM MORE THAN 20 YEARS AGO.
HEY.
SWF
YEAH.
YOU THINK SOMEONE AS INSIGNIFICANT AS YOU COULD SAVE THIS WORLD?
A VERY IMPORTANT...

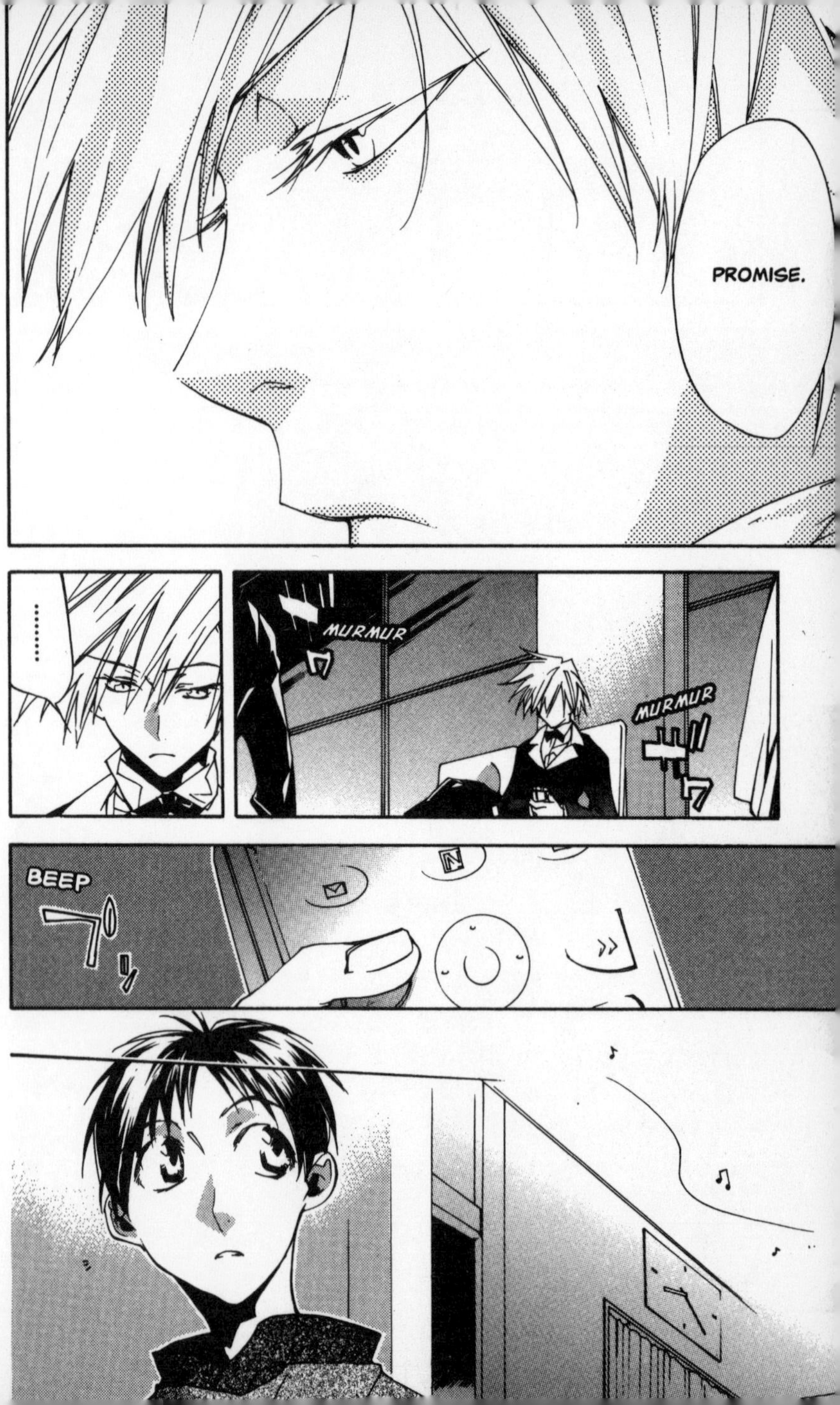
PROMISE.
......
MURMUR
MURMUR
BEEP

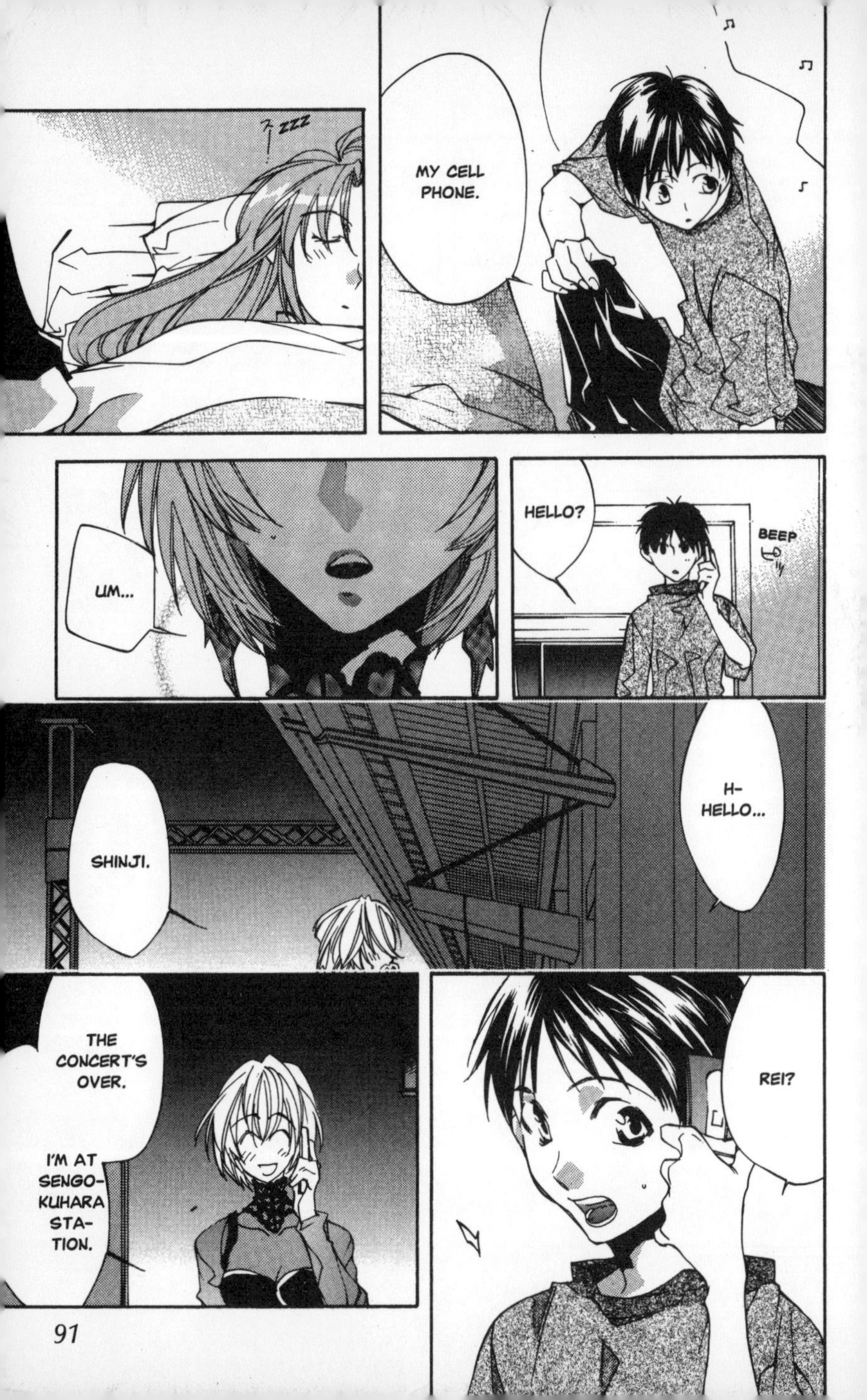
MY CELL PHONE.
ZZZ
HELLO?
BEEP
UM...
H-HELLO...
SHINJI.
REI?
THE CONCERT'S OVER.
I'M AT SENGO-KUHARA STA-TION.

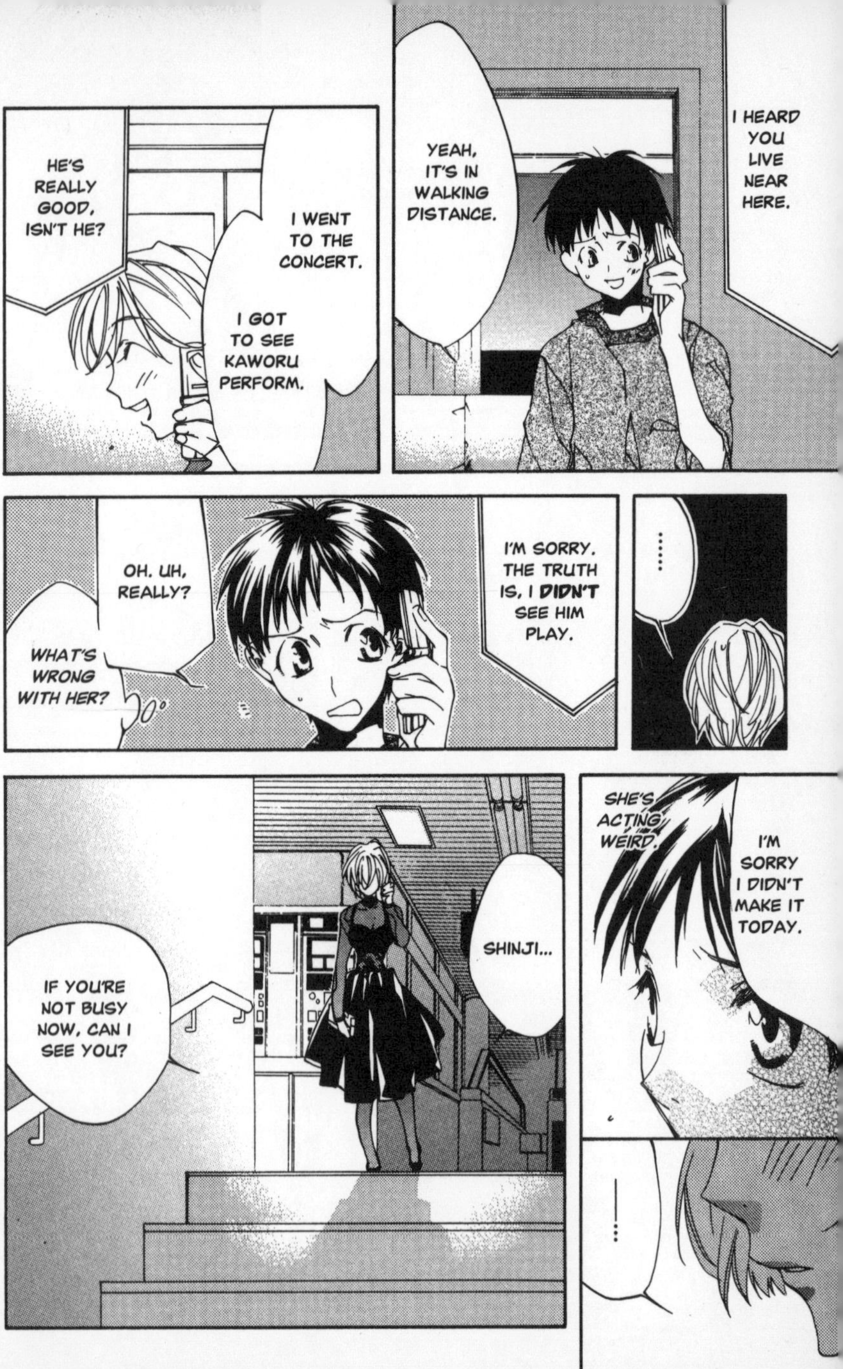
I HEARD YOU LIVE NEAR HERE.
YEAH, IT'S IN WALKING DISTANCE.
I WENT TO THE CONCERT.
I GOT TO SEE KAWORU PERFORM.
HE'S REALLY GOOD, ISN'T HE?
......
I'M SORRY. THE TRUTH IS, I **DIDN'T** SEE HIM PLAY.
OH. UH, REALLY?
WHAT'S WRONG WITH HER?
I'M SORRY I DIDN'T MAKE IT TODAY.
SHE'S ACTING WEIRD.
......
SHINJI...
IF YOU'RE NOT BUSY NOW, CAN I SEE YOU?

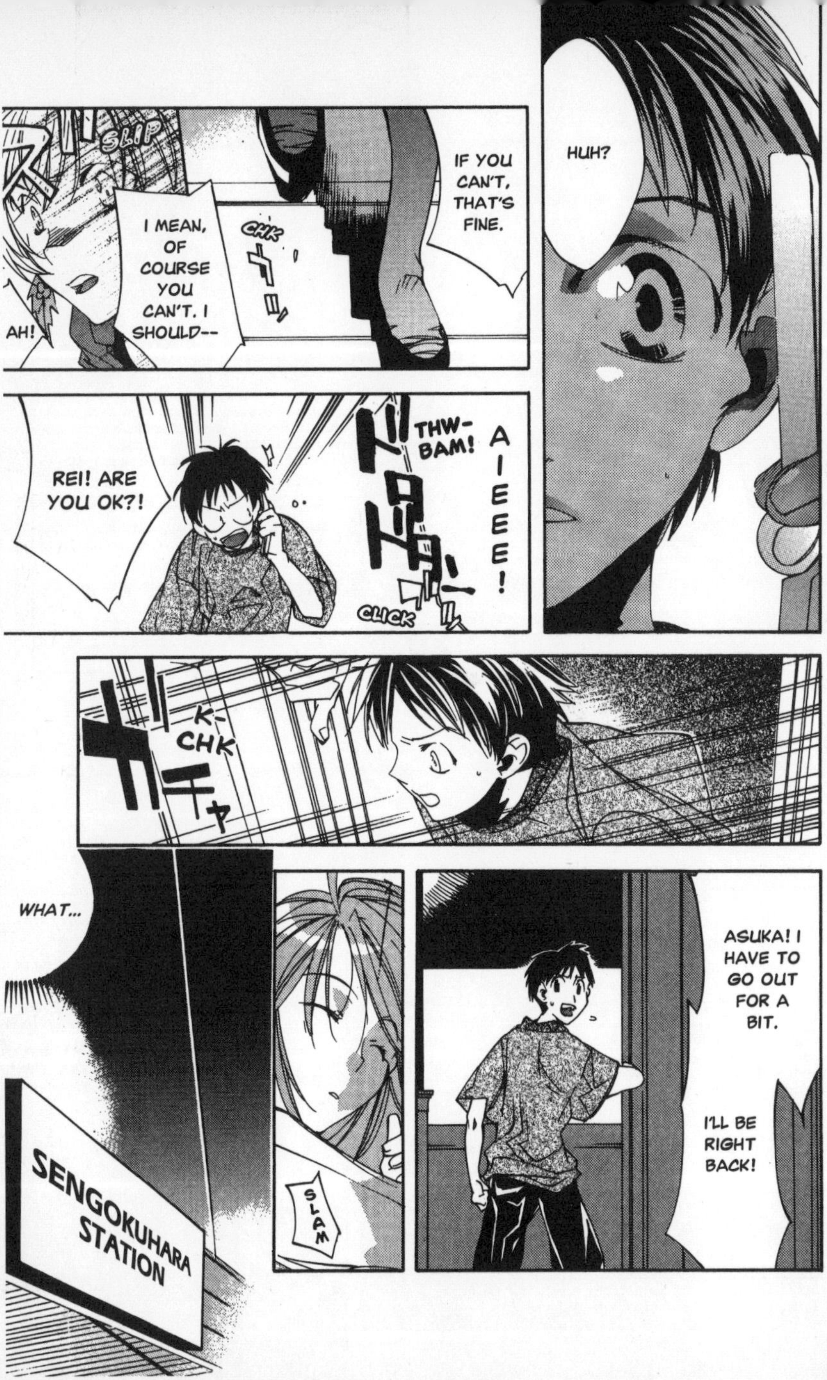
HUH?
IF YOU CAN'T, THAT'S FINE.
CHK
I MEAN, OF COURSE YOU CAN'T. I SHOULD--
SLIP
AH!
AIEEE!
THW-BAM!
CLICK
REI! ARE YOU OK?!
K-CHK
ASUKA! I HAVE TO GO OUT FOR A BIT.
I'LL BE RIGHT BACK!
SLAM
WHAT...
SENGOKUHARA STATION

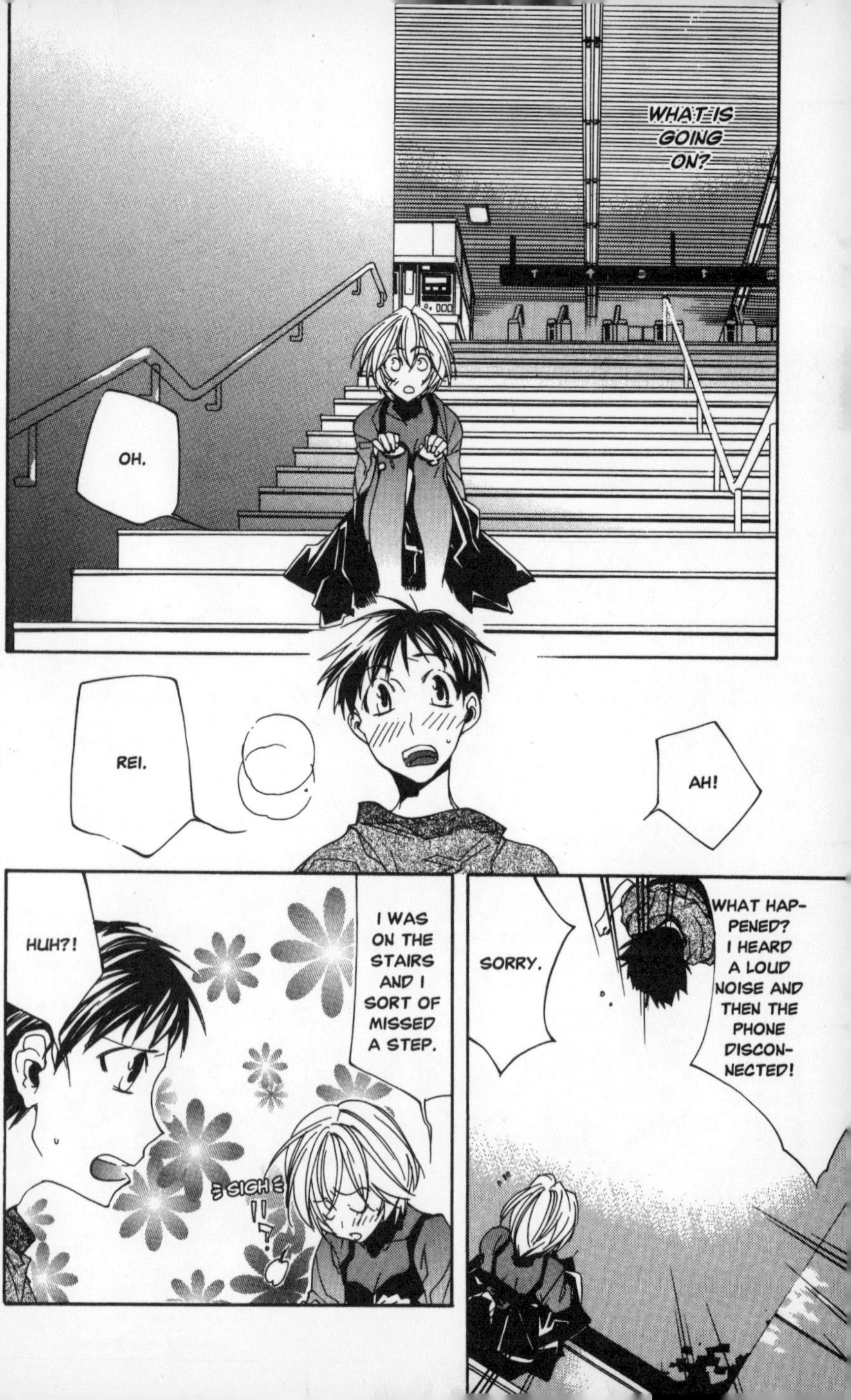
WHAT IS GOING ON?
OH.
AH!
REI.
WHAT HAP-PENED? I HEARD A LOUD NOISE AND THEN THE PHONE DISCON-NECTED!
SORRY.
I WAS ON THE STAIRS AND I SORT OF MISSED A STEP.
HUH?!
SIGH

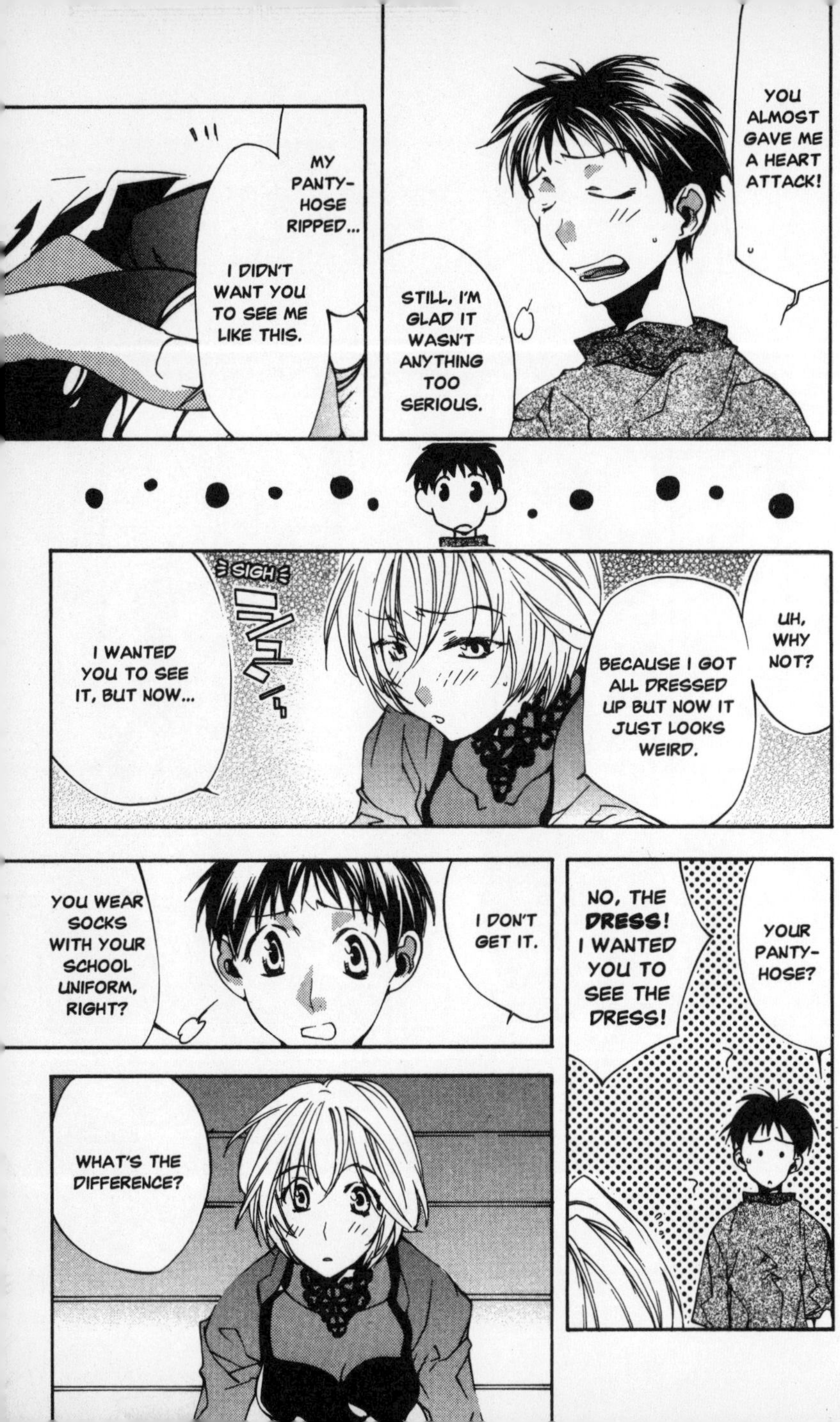
YOU ALMOST GAVE ME A HEART ATTACK!
STILL, I'M GLAD IT WASN'T ANYTHING TOO SERIOUS.
MY PANTY-HOSE RIPPED...
I DIDN'T WANT YOU TO SEE ME LIKE THIS.
UH, WHY NOT?
BECAUSE I GOT ALL DRESSED UP BUT NOW IT JUST LOOKS WEIRD.
SIGH
I WANTED YOU TO SEE IT, BUT NOW...
YOUR PANTY-HOSE?
NO, THE DRESS! I WANTED YOU TO SEE THE DRESS!
I DON'T GET IT.
YOU WEAR SOCKS WITH YOUR SCHOOL UNIFORM, RIGHT?
WHAT'S THE DIFFERENCE?

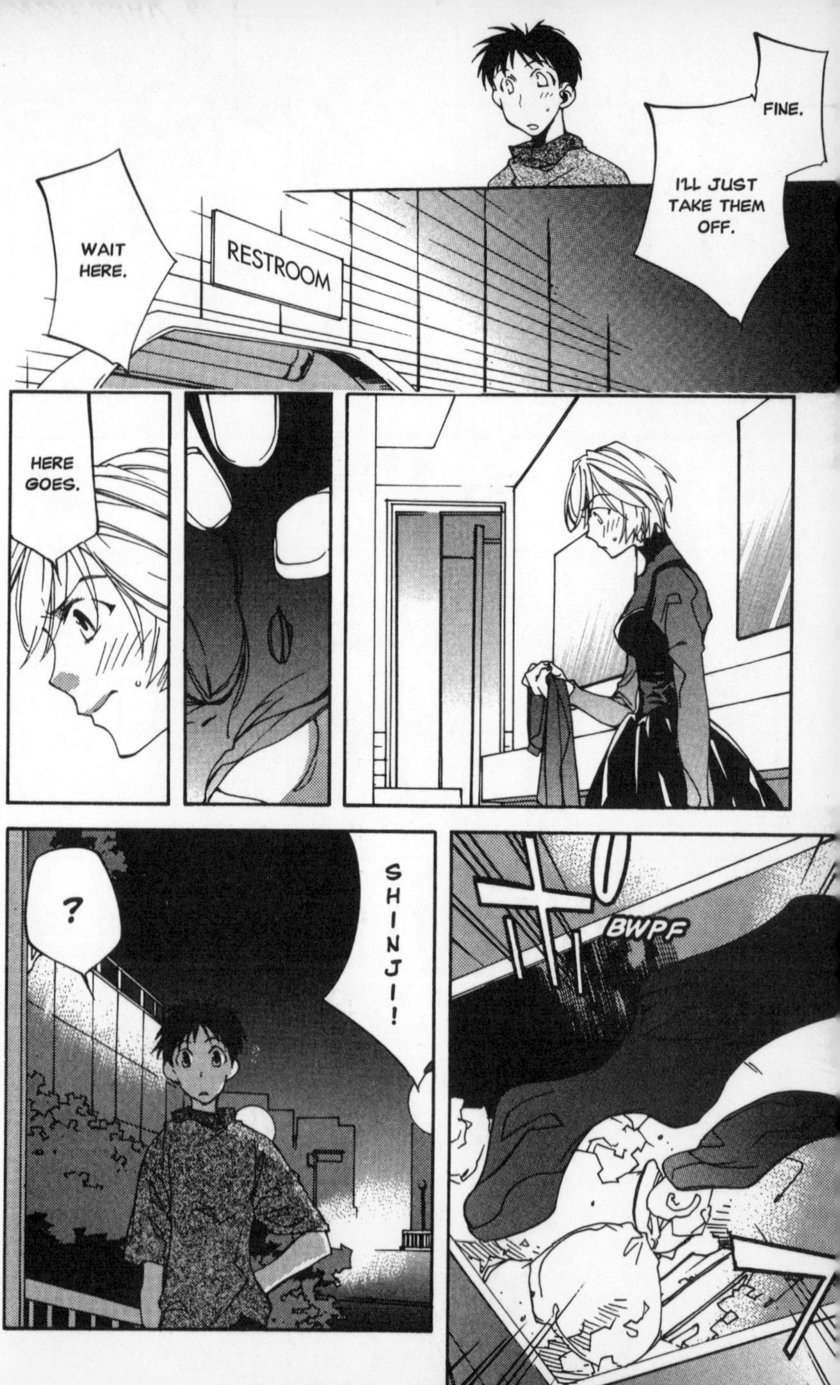
FINE.
I'LL JUST TAKE THEM OFF.
RESTROOM
WAIT HERE.
HERE GOES.
BWPF
SHINJI!
?

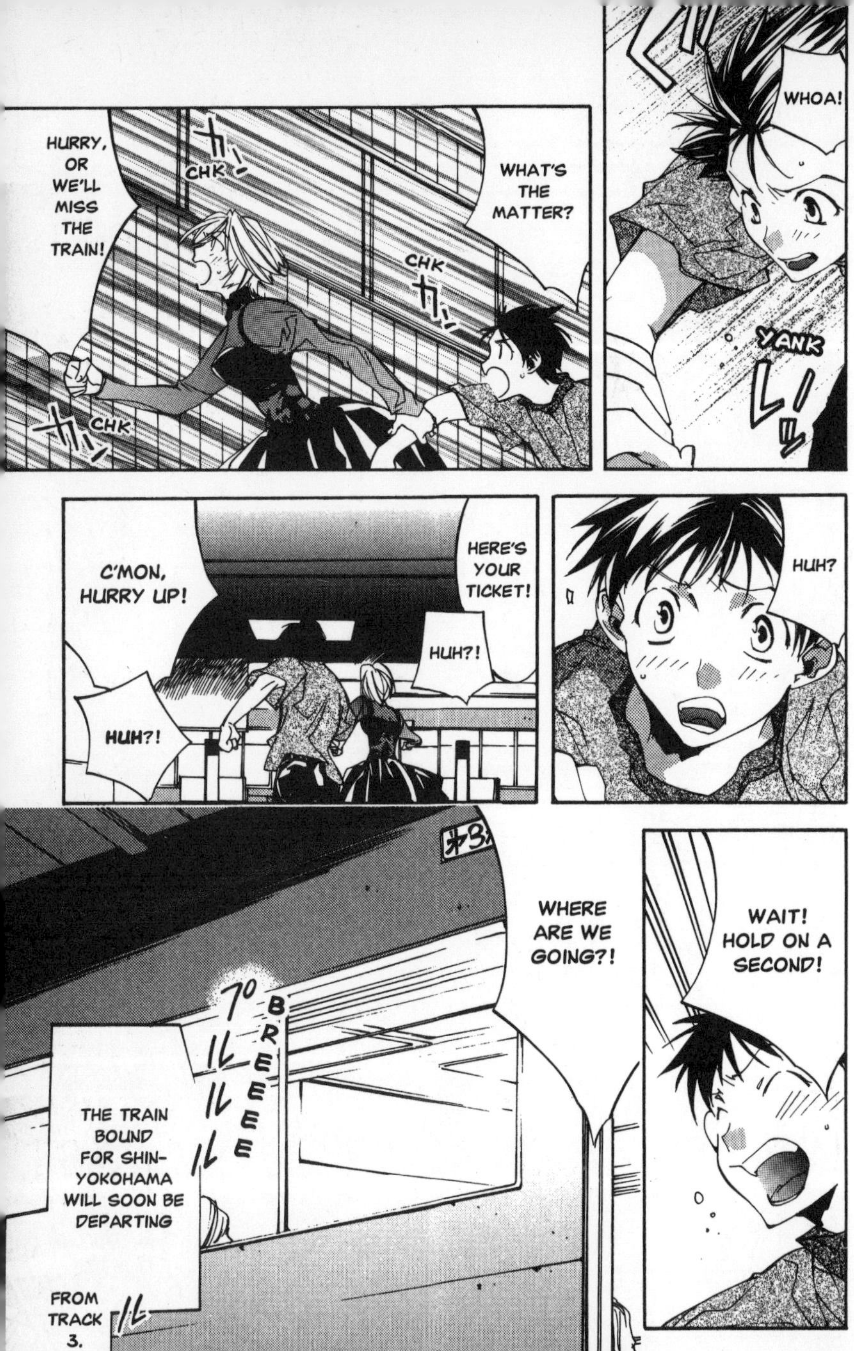
WHOA!
YANK
WHAT'S THE MATTER?
CHK
CHK
HURRY, OR WE'LL MISS THE TRAIN!
CHK
HUH?
HERE'S YOUR TICKET!
HUH?!
C'MON, HURRY UP!
HUH?!
WAIT! HOLD ON A SECOND!
WHERE ARE WE GOING?!
BREEEEE
THE TRAIN BOUND FOR SHIN-YOKOHAMA WILL SOON BE DEPARTING
FROM TRACK 3.

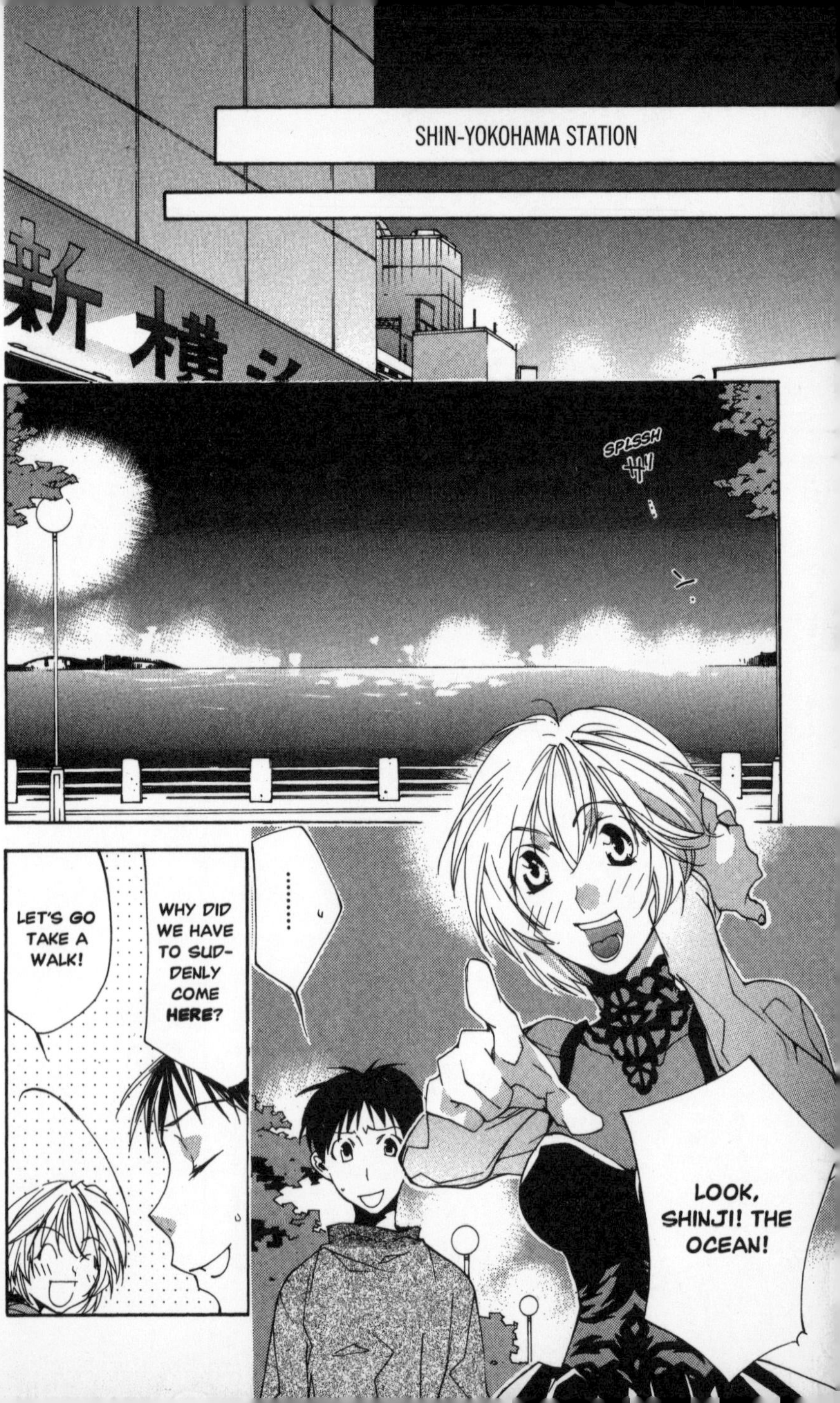

SHIN-YOKOHAMA STATION
新横
SPLSSH
LOOK, SHINJI! THE OCEAN!
....
WHY DID WE HAVE TO SUDDENLY COME HERE?
LET'S GO TAKE A WALK!

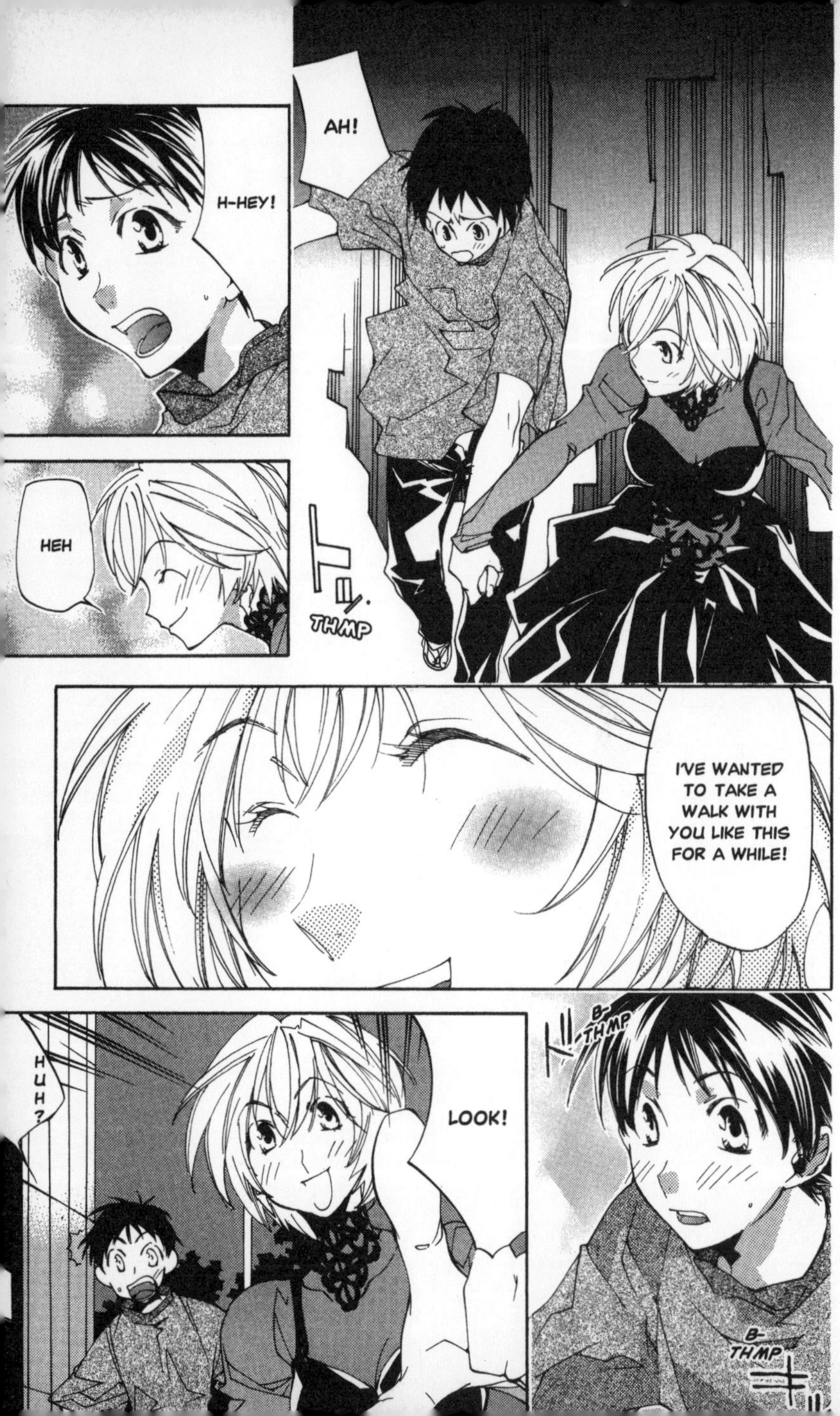

AH!
THMP
H-HEY!
HEH
I'VE WANTED TO TAKE A WALK WITH YOU LIKE THIS FOR A WHILE!
B-THMP
B-THMP
LOOK!
HUH?

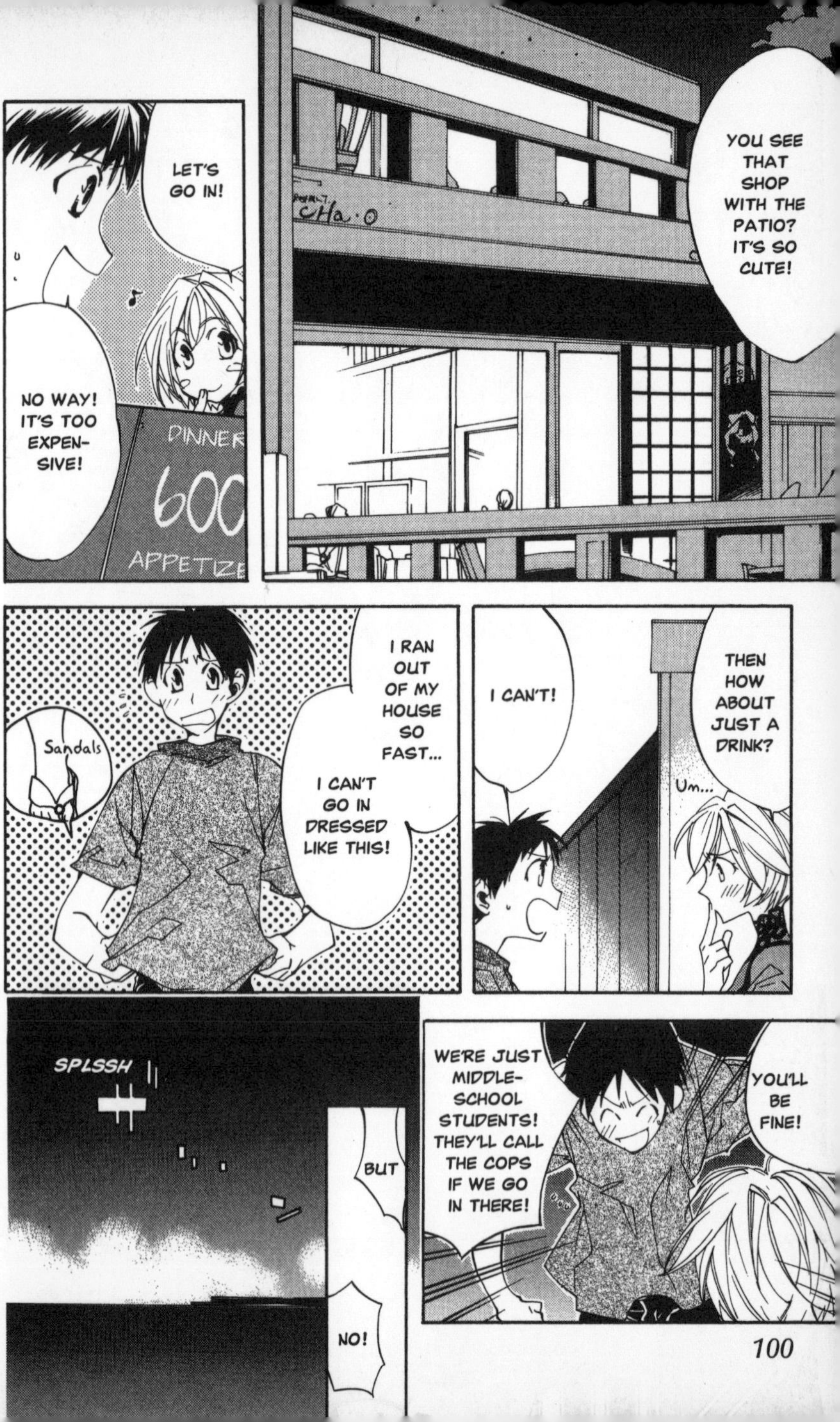

YOU SEE THAT SHOP WITH THE PATIO? IT'S SO CUTE!
LET'S GO IN!
NO WAY! IT'S TOO EXPEN-SIVE!
DINNER
600
APPETIZE
THEN HOW ABOUT JUST A DRINK?
Um...
I CAN'T!
I RAN OUT OF MY HOUSE SO FAST...
I CAN'T GO IN DRESSED LIKE THIS!
Sandals
YOU'LL BE FINE!
WE'RE JUST MIDDLE-SCHOOL STUDENTS! THEY'LL CALL THE COPS IF WE GO IN THERE!
BUT
NO!
SPLSSH

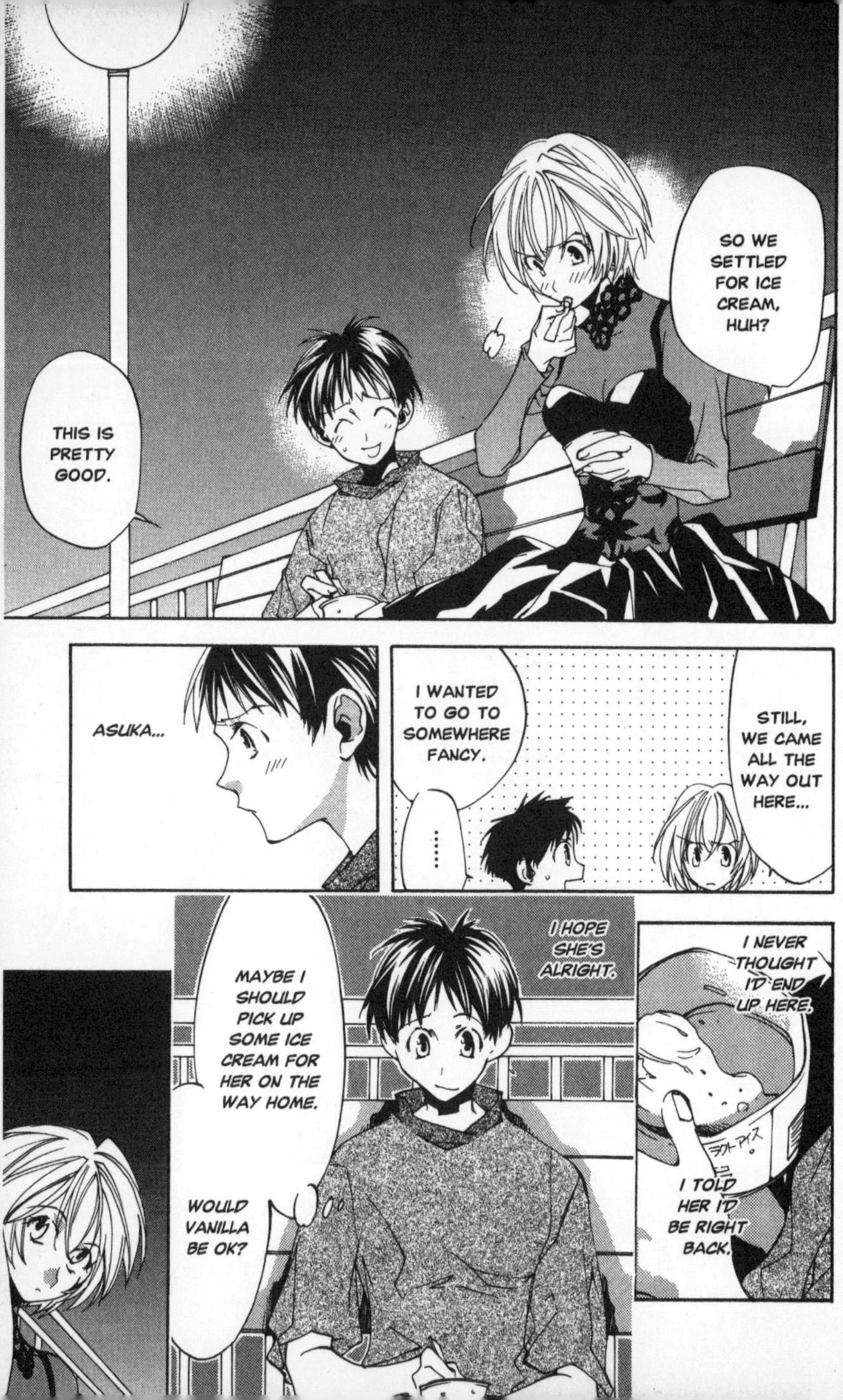
SO WE SETTLED FOR ICE CREAM, HUH?
THIS IS PRETTY GOOD.
STILL, WE CAME ALL THE WAY OUT HERE...
I WANTED TO GO TO SOMEWHERE FANCY.
......
ASUKA...
I NEVER THOUGHT I'D END UP HERE.
I TOLD HER I'D BE RIGHT BACK.
I HOPE SHE'S ALRIGHT.
MAYBE I SHOULD PICK UP SOME ICE CREAM FOR HER ON THE WAY HOME.
WOULD VANILLA BE OK?

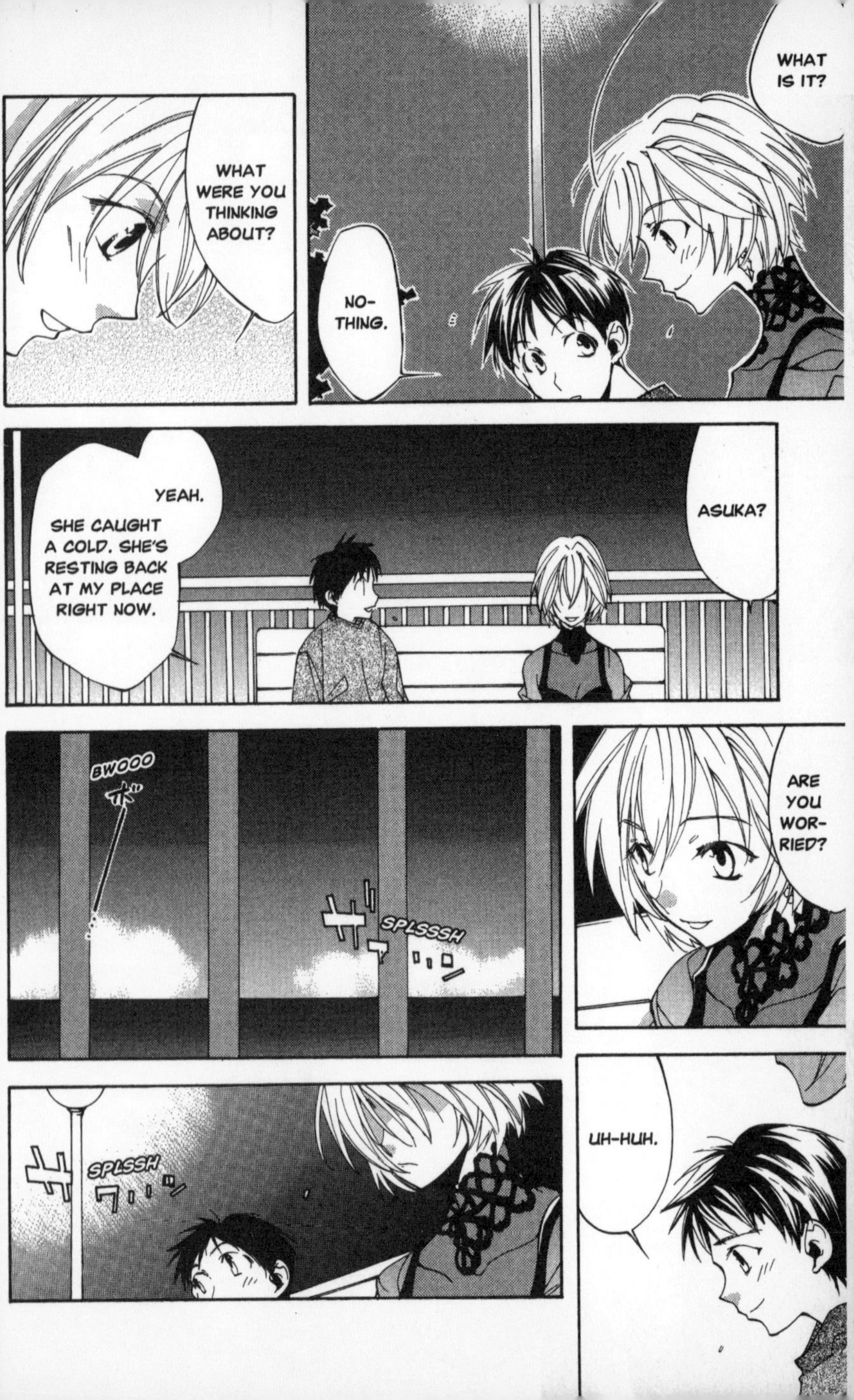

WHAT IS IT?
NO-THING.
WHAT WERE YOU THINKING ABOUT?
ASUKA?
YEAH.
SHE CAUGHT A COLD. SHE'S RESTING BACK AT MY PLACE RIGHT NOW.
ARE YOU WOR-RIED?
BWOOO
SPLSSSH
UH-HUH.
SPLSSH

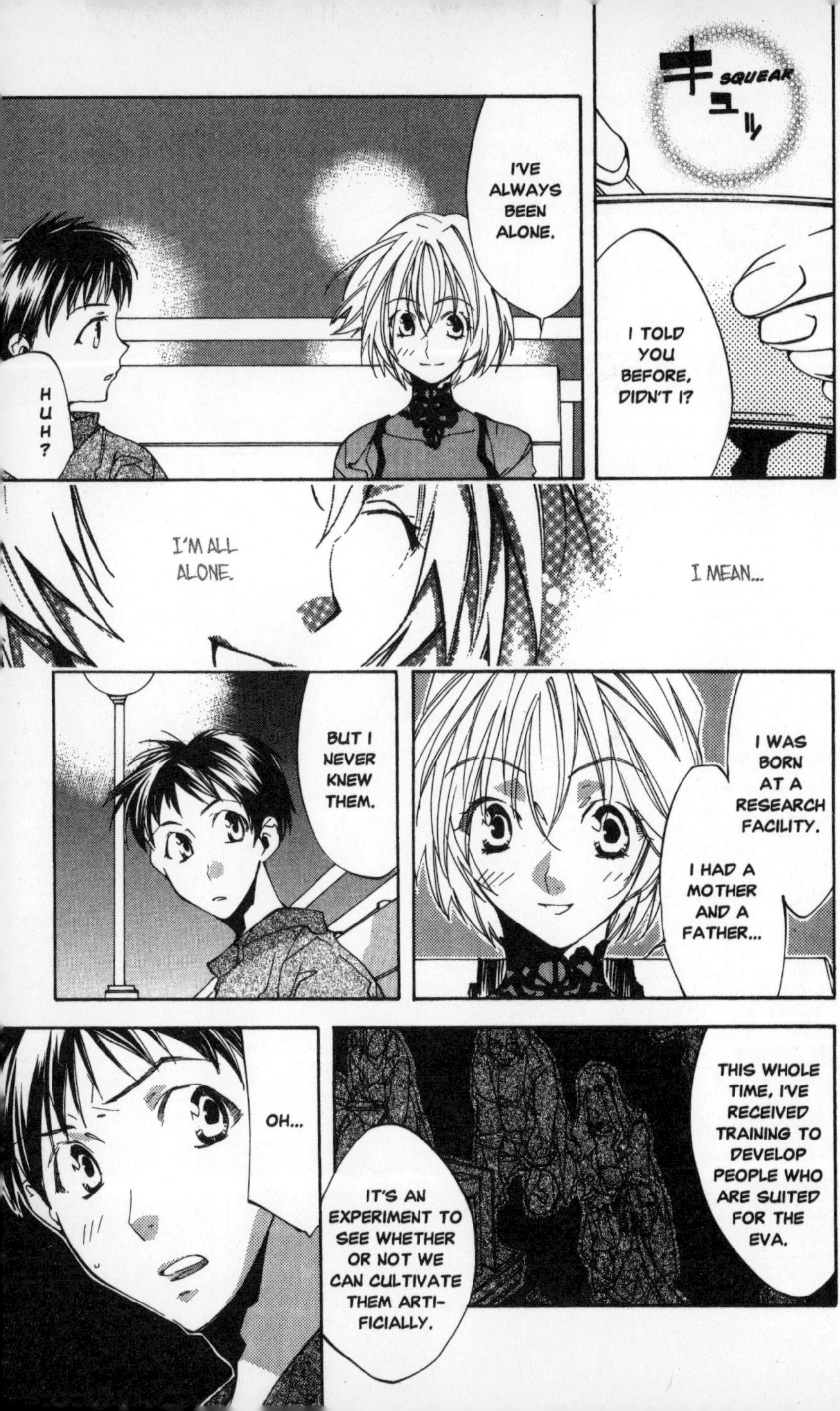
キュル
SQUEAK
I TOLD YOU BEFORE, DIDN'T I?
I'VE ALWAYS BEEN ALONE.
HUH?
I MEAN...
I'M ALL ALONE.
I WAS BORN AT A RESEARCH FACILITY.
I HAD A MOTHER AND A FATHER...
BUT I NEVER KNEW THEM.
THIS WHOLE TIME, I'VE RECEIVED TRAINING TO DEVELOP PEOPLE WHO ARE SUITED FOR THE EVA.
IT'S AN EXPERIMENT TO SEE WHETHER OR NOT WE CAN CULTIVATE THEM ARTI-FICIALLY.
OH...

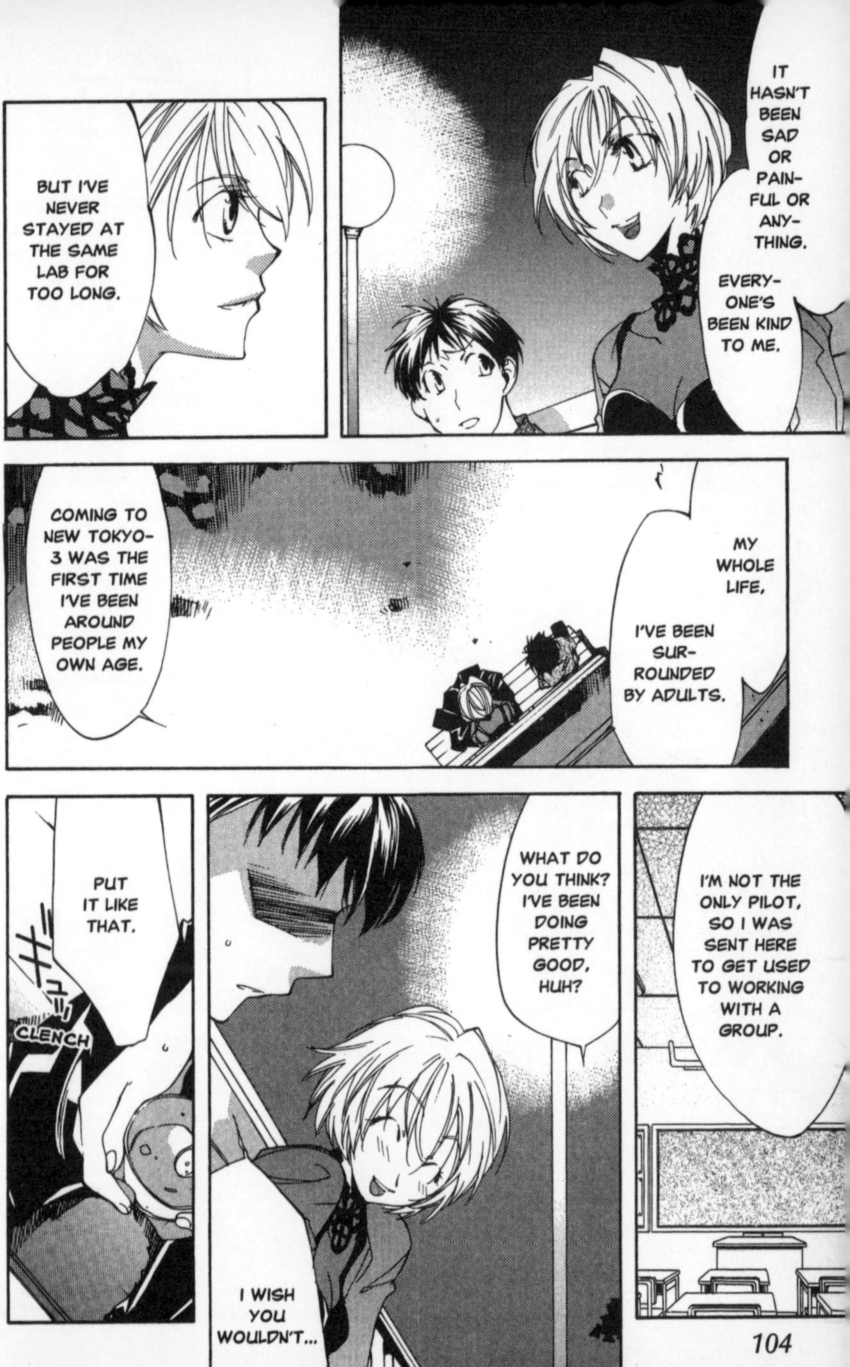
IT HASN'T BEEN SAD OR PAIN-FUL OR ANY-THING.
EVERY-ONE'S BEEN KIND TO ME.
BUT I'VE NEVER STAYED AT THE SAME LAB FOR TOO LONG.
MY WHOLE LIFE,
I'VE BEEN SUR-ROUNDED BY ADULTS.
COMING TO NEW TOKYO-3 WAS THE FIRST TIME I'VE BEEN AROUND PEOPLE MY OWN AGE.
I'M NOT THE ONLY PILOT, SO I WAS SENT HERE TO GET USED TO WORKING WITH A GROUP.
WHAT DO YOU THINK? I'VE BEEN DOING PRETTY GOOD, HUH?
I WISH YOU WOULDN'T...
PUT IT LIKE THAT.
CLENCH

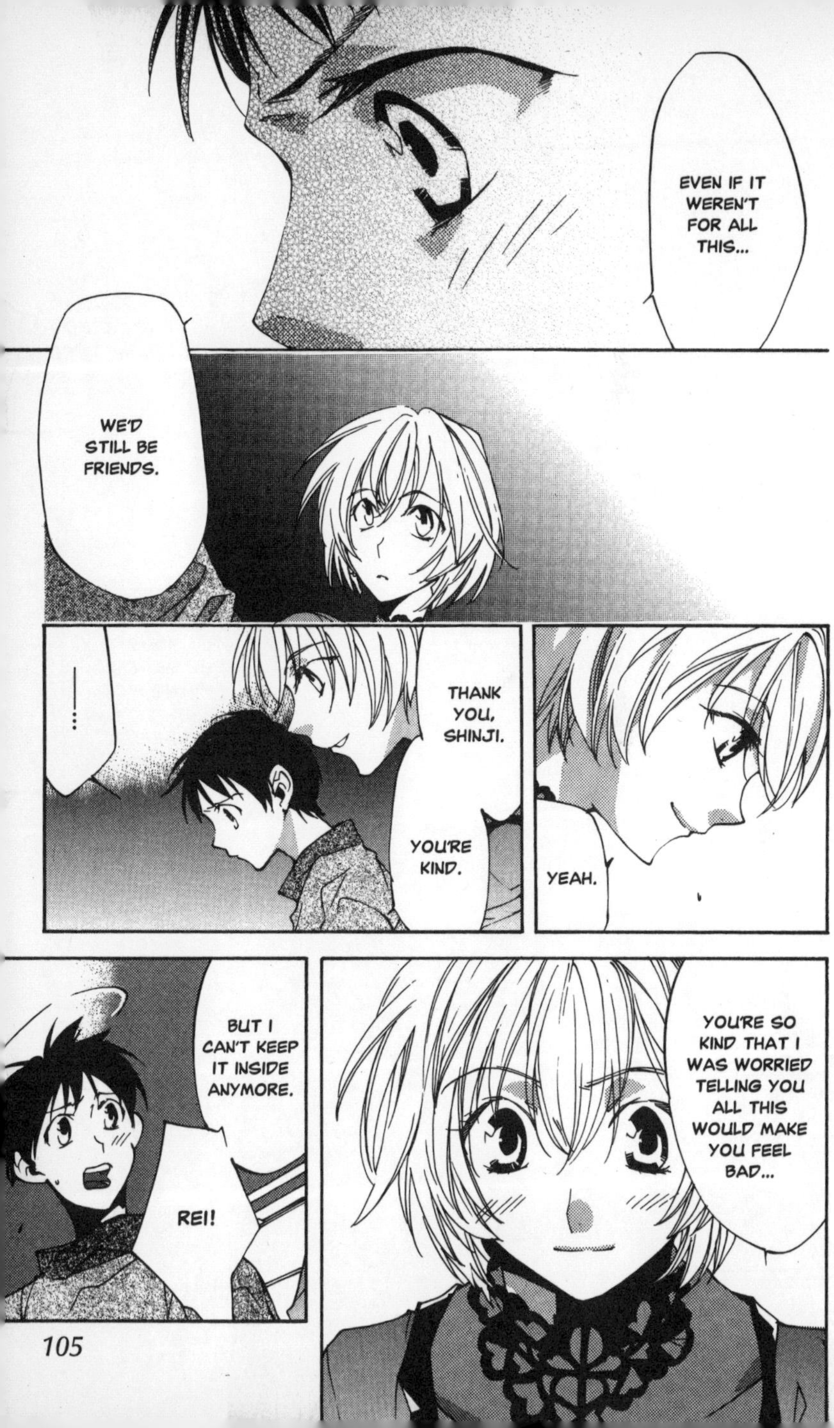
EVEN IF IT WEREN'T FOR ALL THIS...
WE'D STILL BE FRIENDS.
YEAH.
THANK YOU, SHINJI.
YOU'RE KIND.
......
YOU'RE SO KIND THAT I WAS WORRIED TELLING YOU ALL THIS WOULD MAKE YOU FEEL BAD...
BUT I CAN'T KEEP IT INSIDE ANYMORE.
REI!

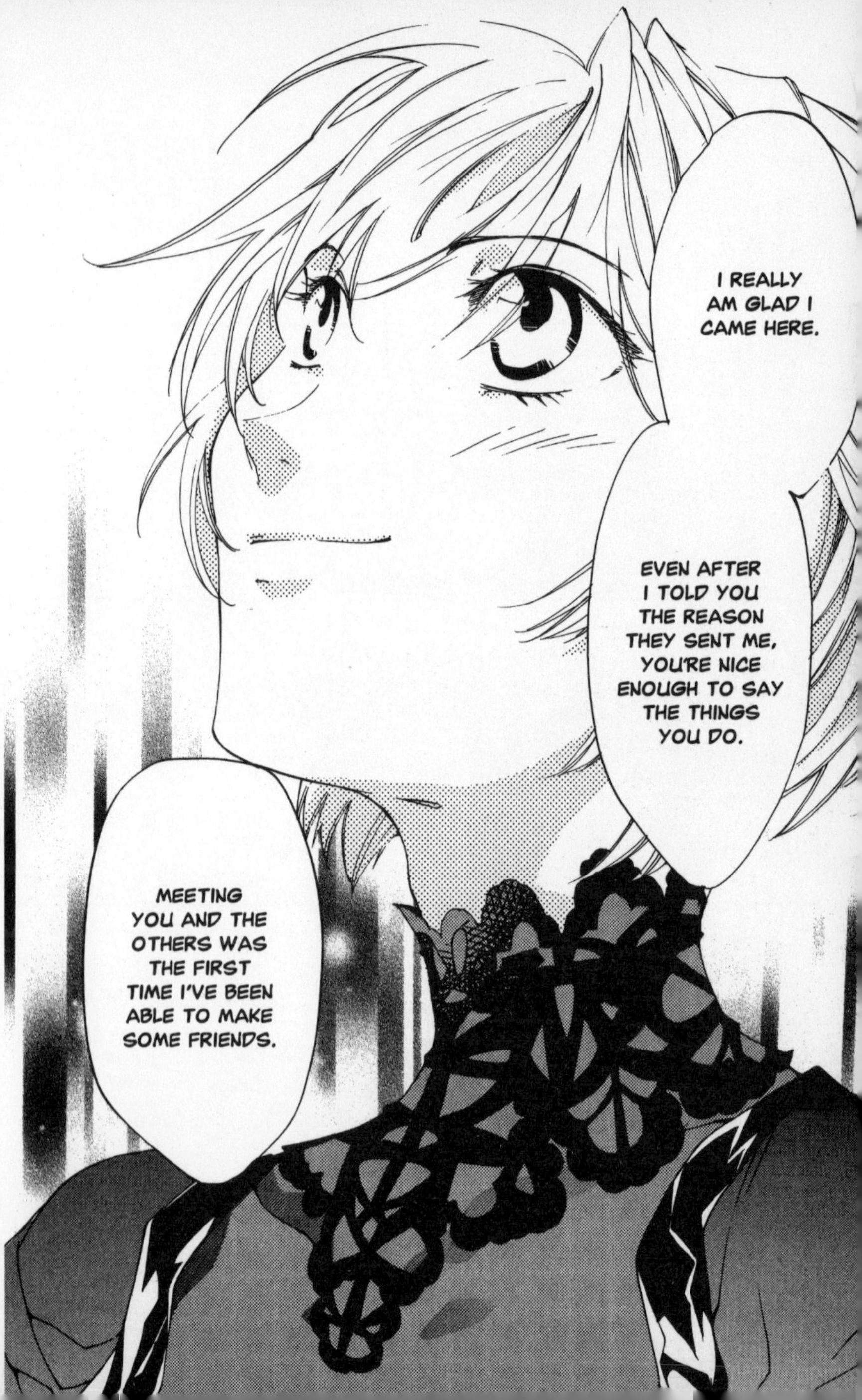
I REALLY AM GLAD I CAME HERE.
EVEN AFTER I TOLD YOU THE REASON THEY SENT ME, YOU'RE NICE ENOUGH TO SAY THE THINGS YOU DO.
MEETING YOU AND THE OTHERS WAS THE FIRST TIME I'VE BEEN ABLE TO MAKE SOME FRIENDS.

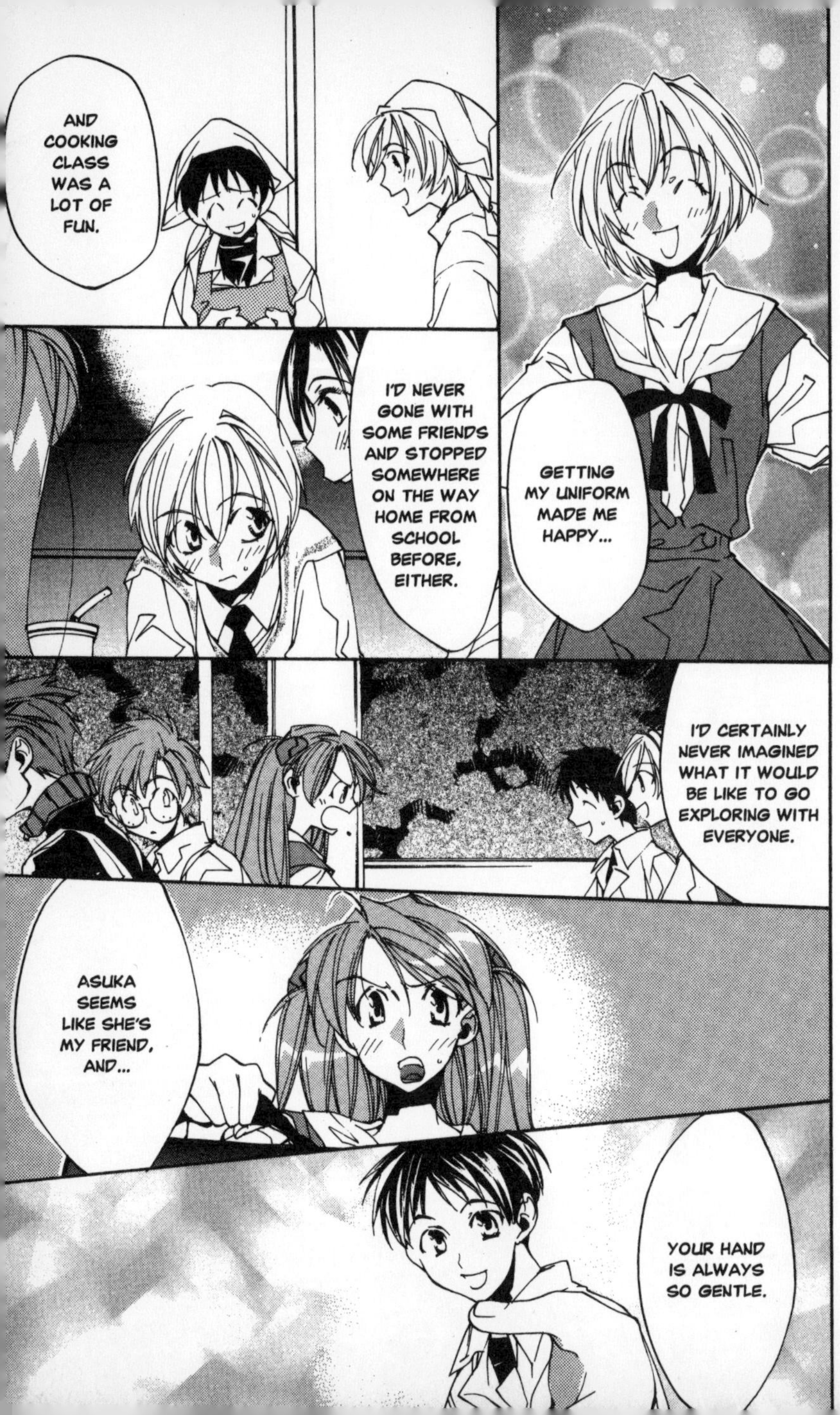
AND COOKING CLASS WAS A LOT OF FUN.
GETTING MY UNIFORM MADE ME HAPPY...
I'D NEVER GONE WITH SOME FRIENDS AND STOPPED SOMEWHERE ON THE WAY HOME FROM SCHOOL BEFORE, EITHER.
I'D CERTAINLY NEVER IMAGINED WHAT IT WOULD BE LIKE TO GO EXPLORING WITH EVERYONE.
ASUKA SEEMS LIKE SHE'S MY FRIEND, AND...
YOUR HAND IS ALWAYS SO GENTLE.

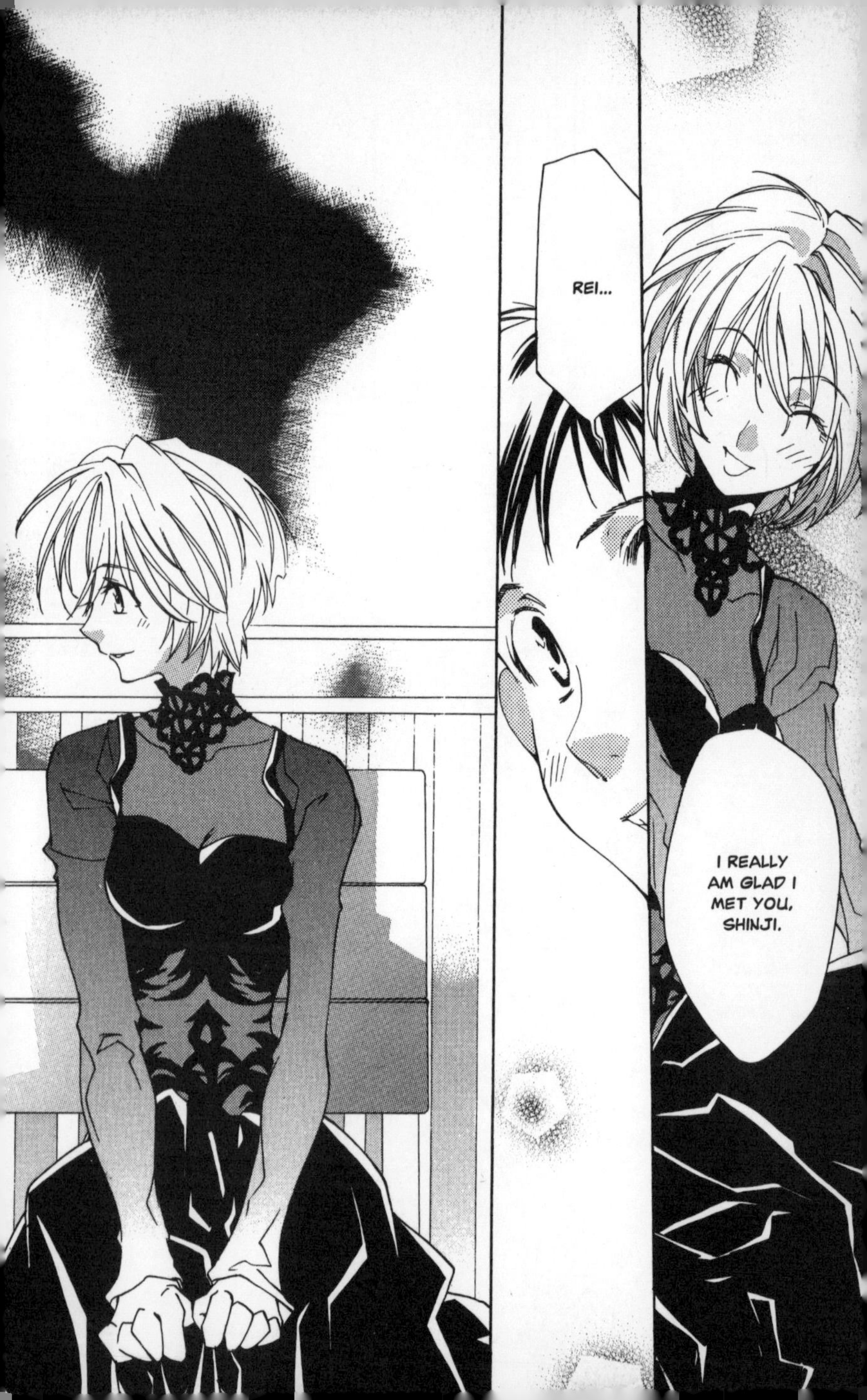
REI...
I REALLY AM GLAD I MET YOU, SHINJI.

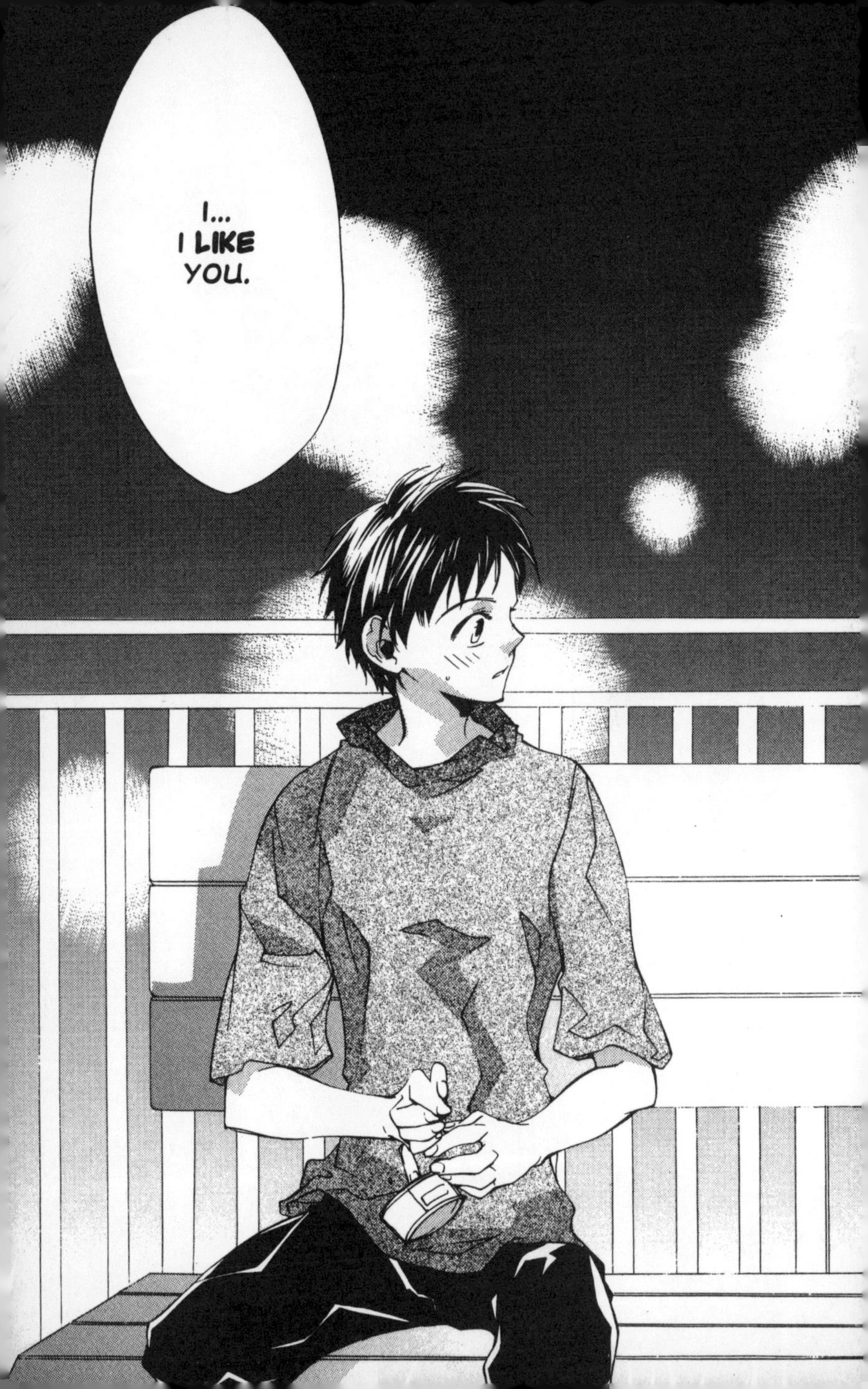
I... I LIKE YOU.

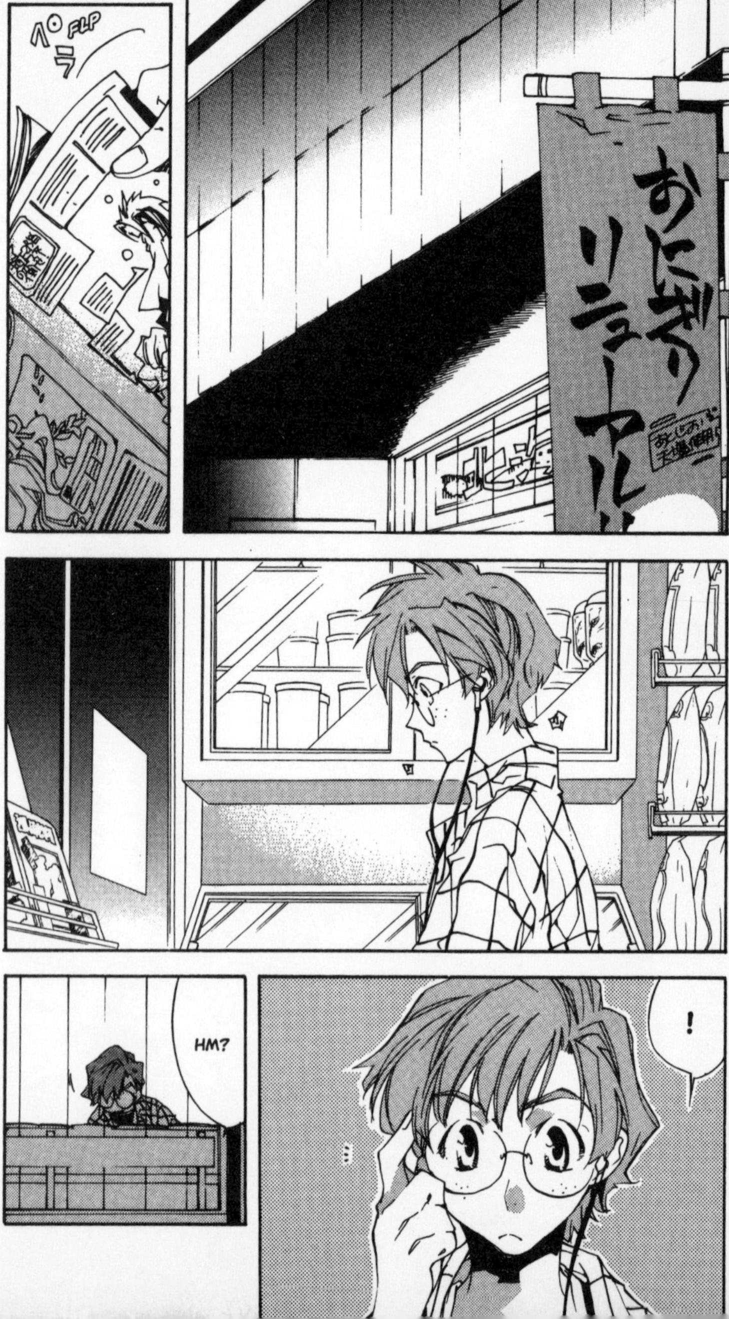
おにぎり
リニューアル
ペラ FLP
!
...
HM?

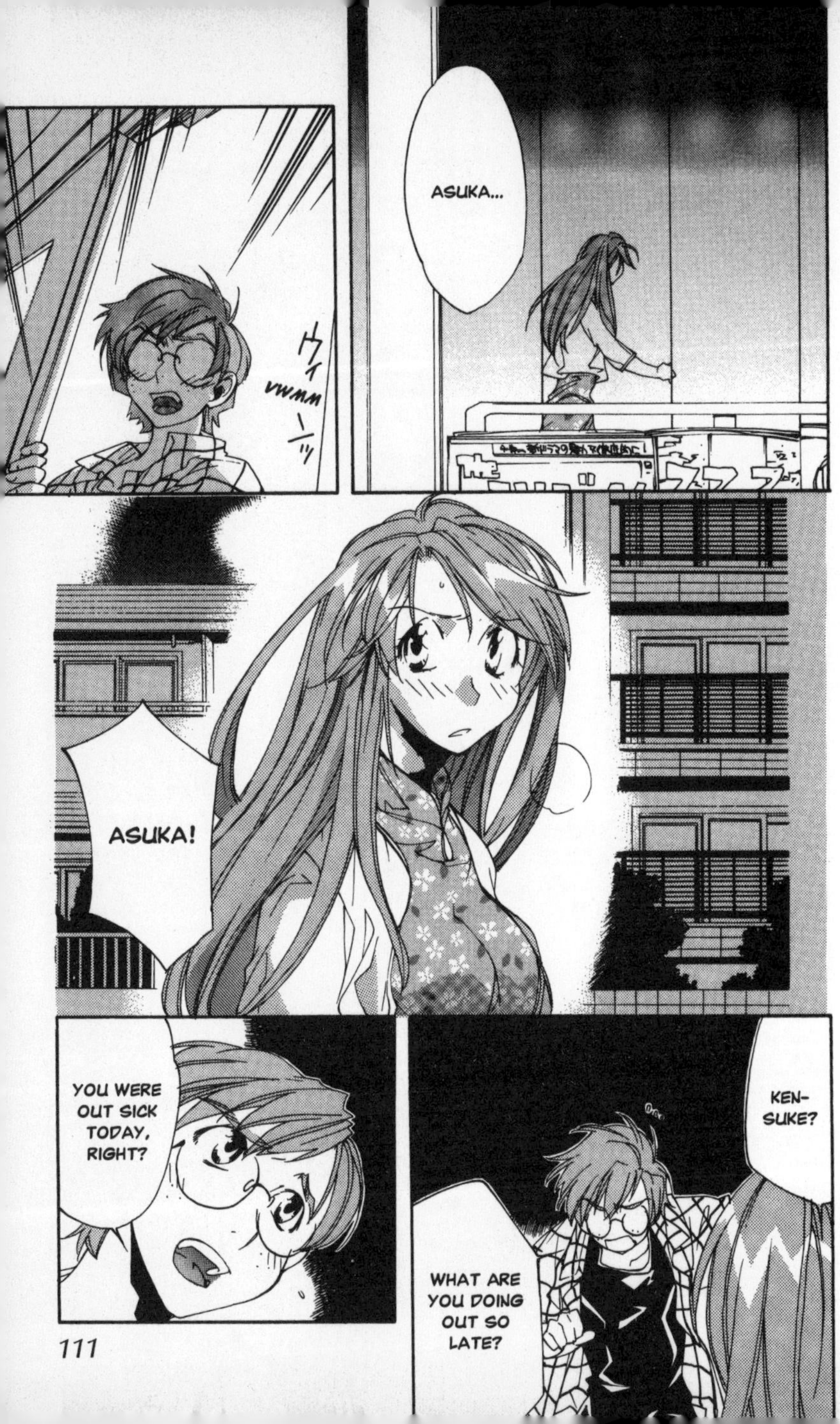
ASUKA...
VWMM
ASUKA!
KEN-SUKE?
WHAT ARE YOU DOING OUT SO LATE?
YOU WERE OUT SICK TODAY, RIGHT?

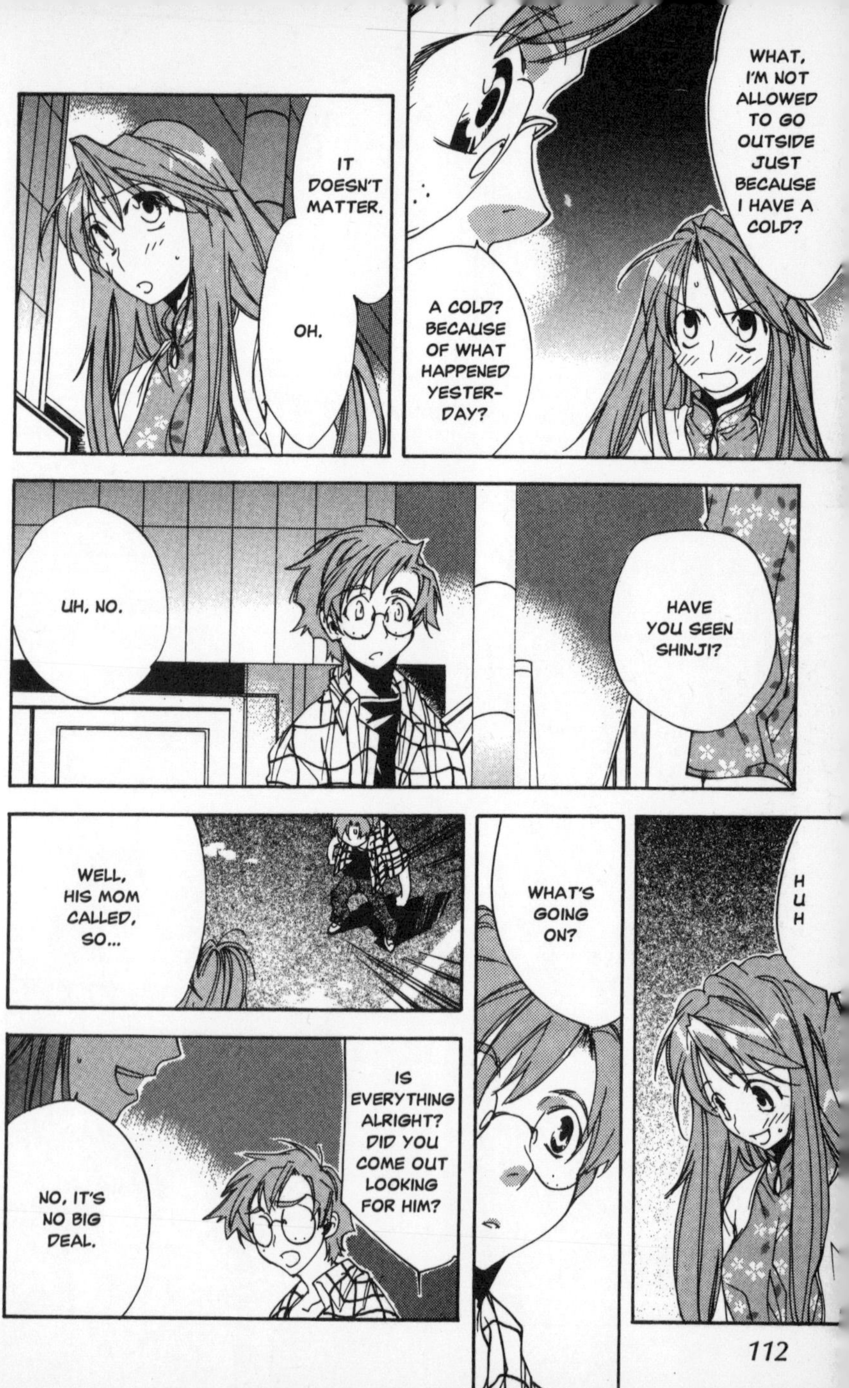
WHAT, I'M NOT ALLOWED TO GO OUTSIDE JUST BECAUSE I HAVE A COLD?
A COLD? BECAUSE OF WHAT HAPPENED YESTER-DAY?
IT DOESN'T MATTER.
OH.
HAVE YOU SEEN SHINJI?
UH, NO.
HUH
WHAT'S GOING ON?
WELL, HIS MOM CALLED, SO...
IS EVERYTHING ALRIGHT? DID YOU COME OUT LOOKING FOR HIM?
NO, IT'S NO BIG DEAL.

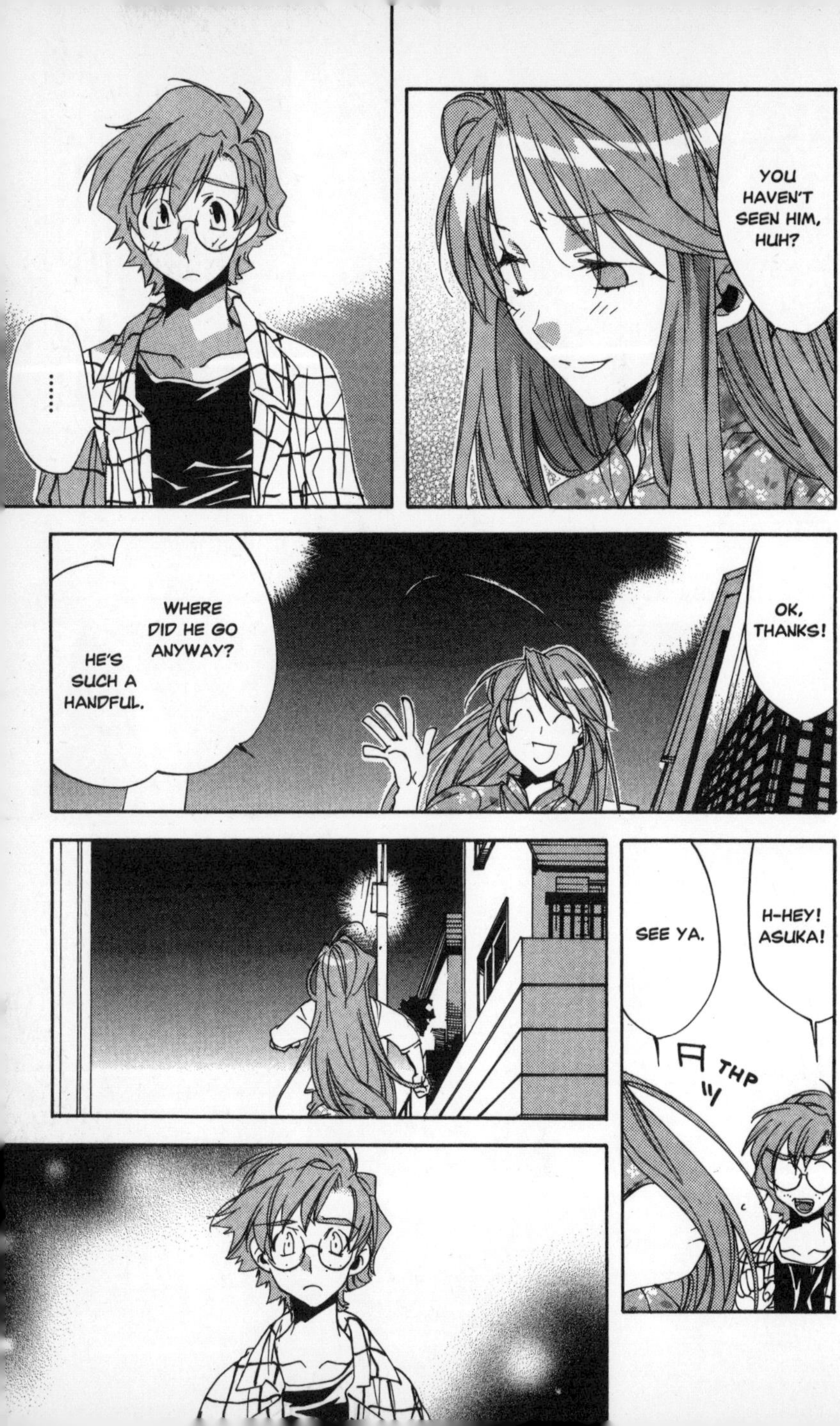
YOU HAVEN'T SEEN HIM, HUH?
......
OK, THANKS!
WHERE DID HE GO ANYWAY?
HE'S SUCH A HANDFUL.
H-HEY! ASUKA!
SEE YA.
THP

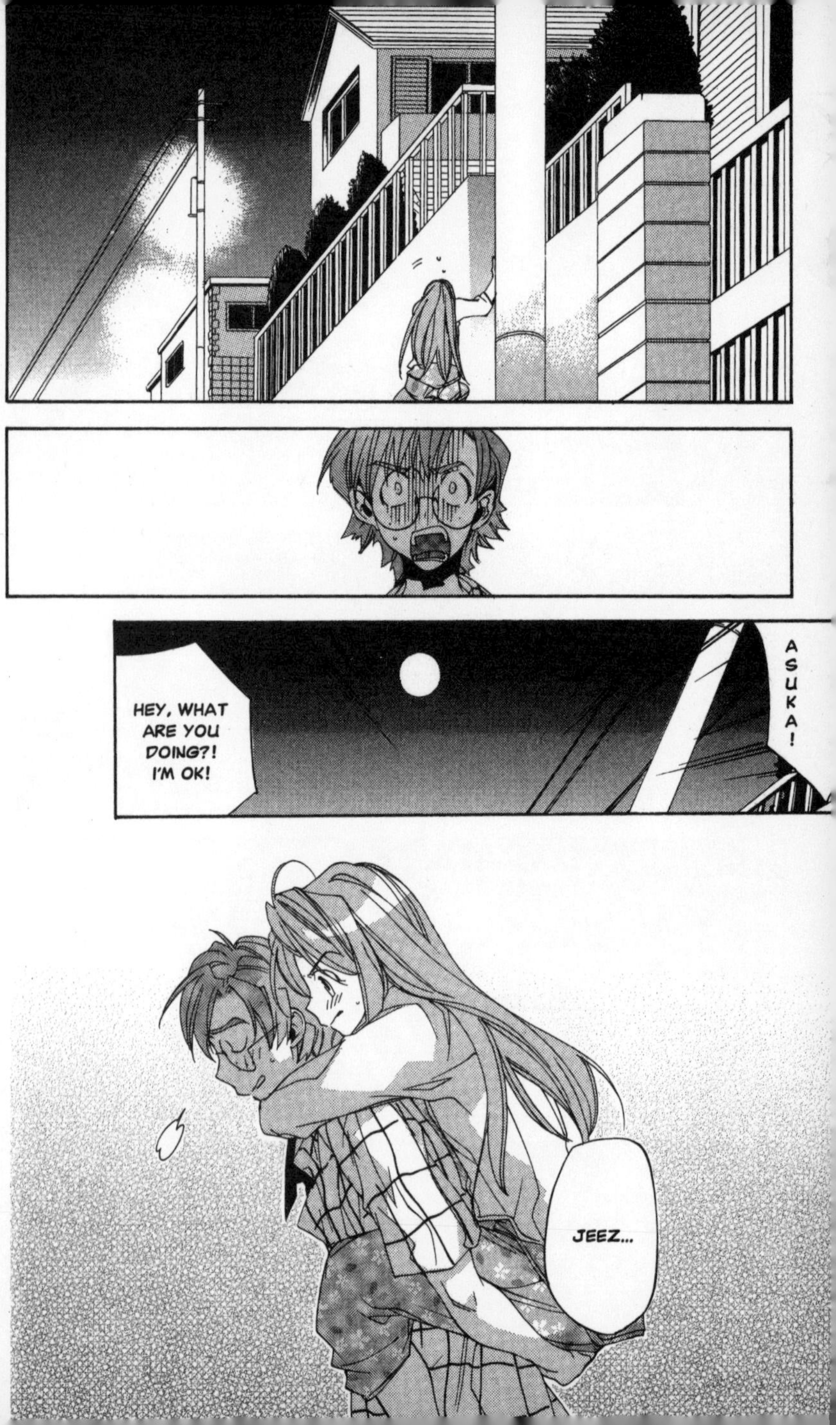
ASUKA!
HEY, WHAT ARE YOU DOING?! I'M OK!
JEEZ...

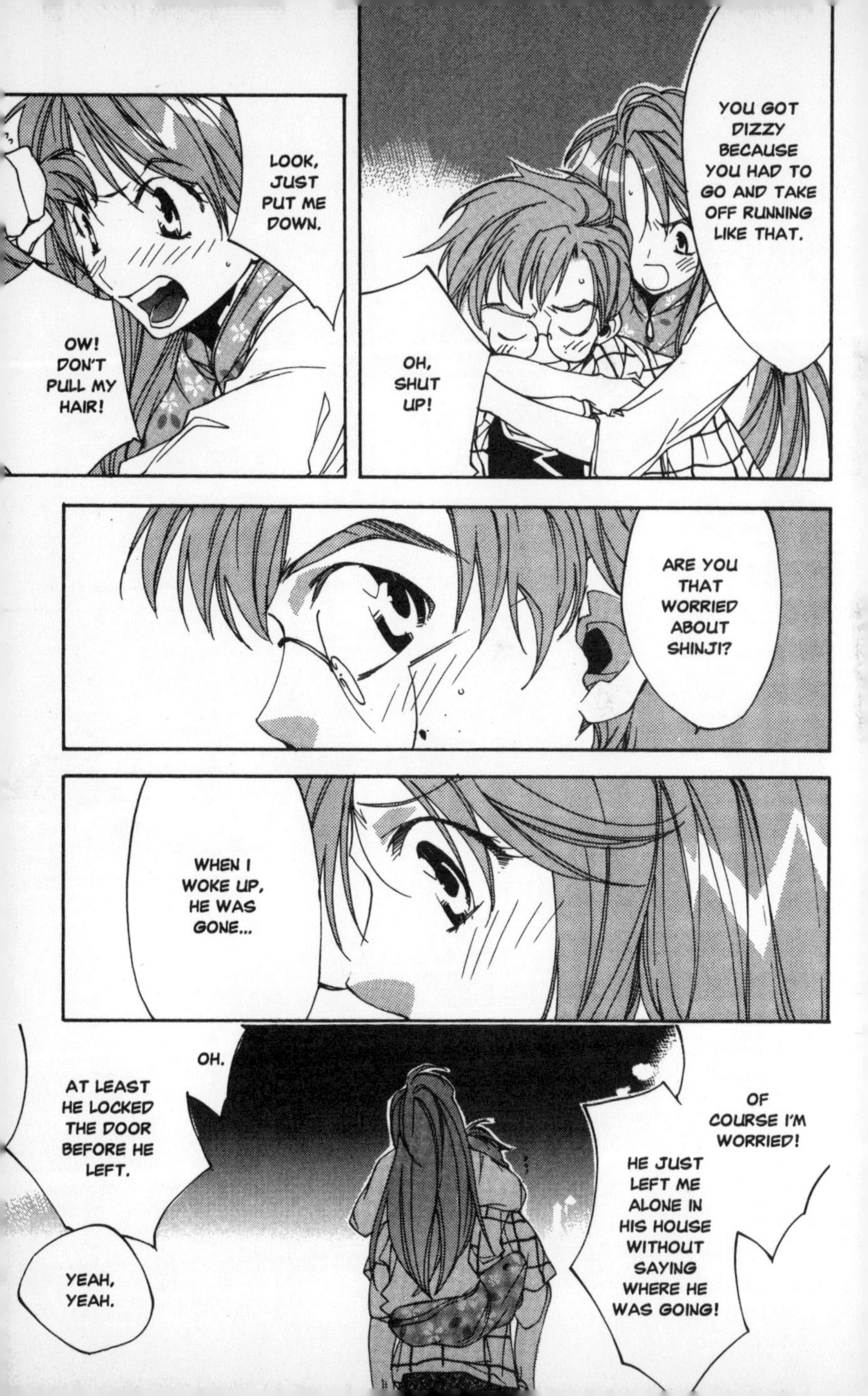
YOU GOT DIZZY BECAUSE YOU HAD TO GO AND TAKE OFF RUNNING LIKE THAT.
OH, SHUT UP!
LOOK, JUST PUT ME DOWN.
OW! DON'T PULL MY HAIR!
ARE YOU THAT WORRIED ABOUT SHINJI?
WHEN I WOKE UP, HE WAS GONE...
OF COURSE I'M WORRIED!
HE JUST LEFT ME ALONE IN HIS HOUSE WITHOUT SAYING WHERE HE WAS GOING!
OH.
AT LEAST HE LOCKED THE DOOR BEFORE HE LEFT.
YEAH, YEAH.

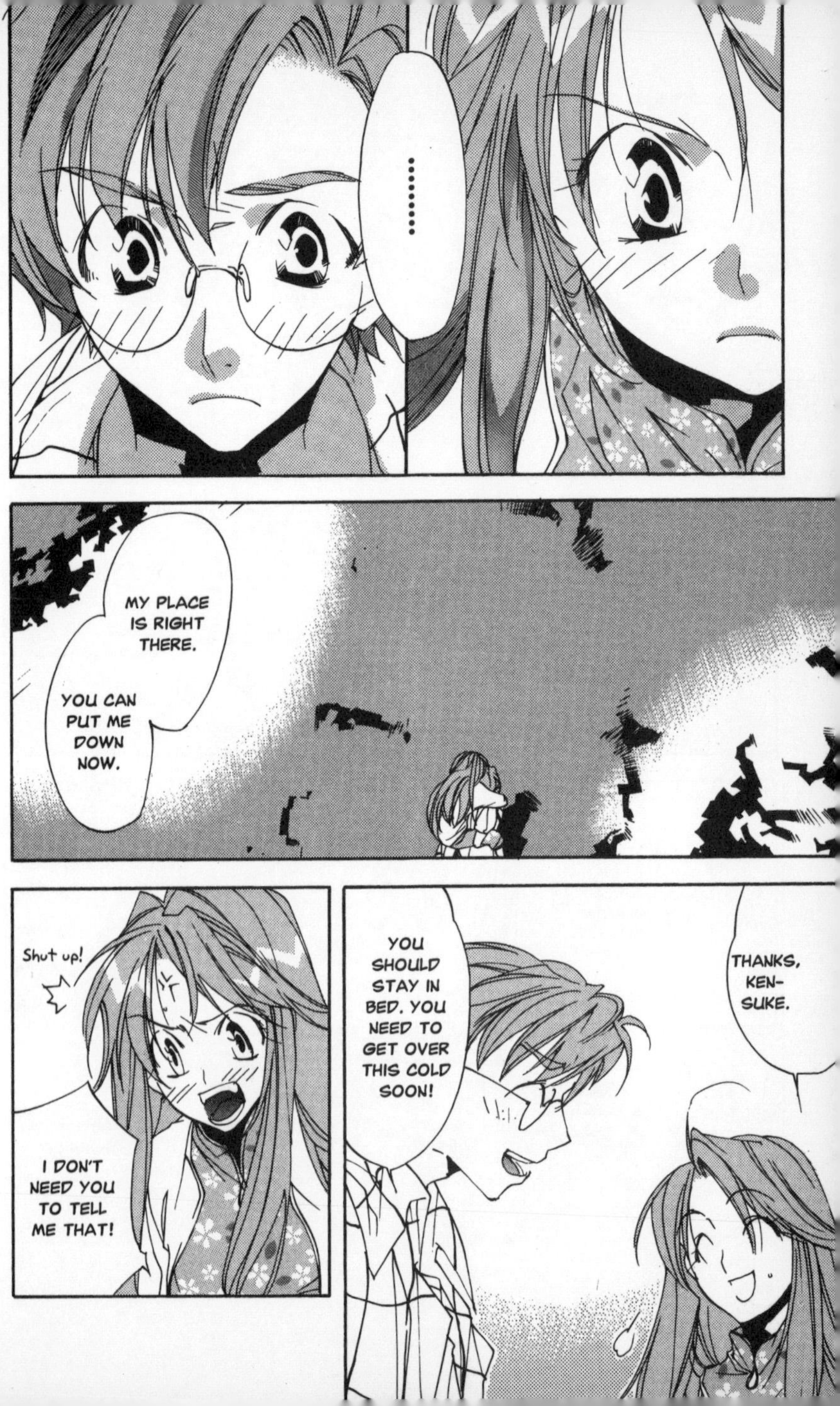
....
MY PLACE IS RIGHT THERE.
YOU CAN PUT ME DOWN NOW.
THANKS, KEN-SUKE.
YOU SHOULD STAY IN BED. YOU NEED TO GET OVER THIS COLD SOON!
Shut up!
I DON'T NEED YOU TO TELL ME THAT!

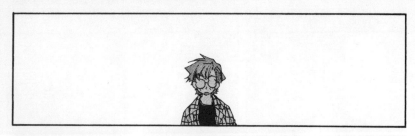

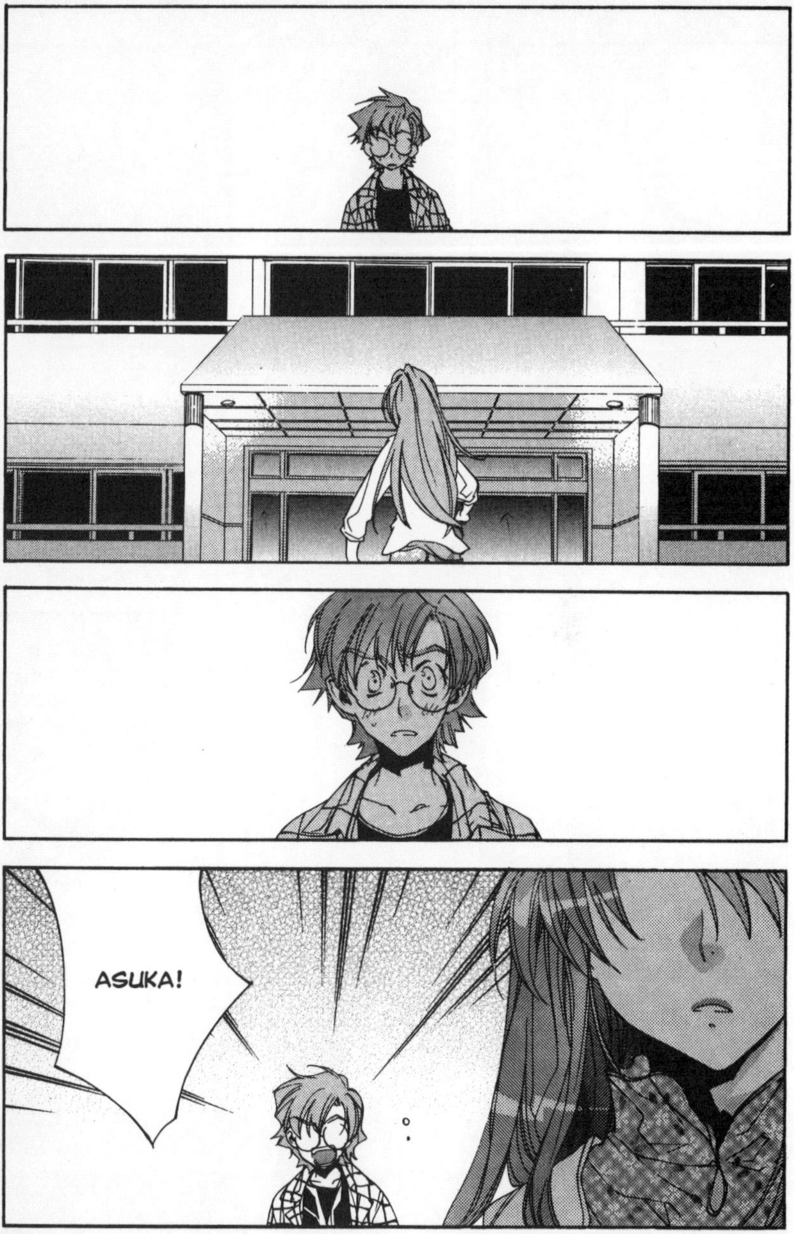
ASUKA!

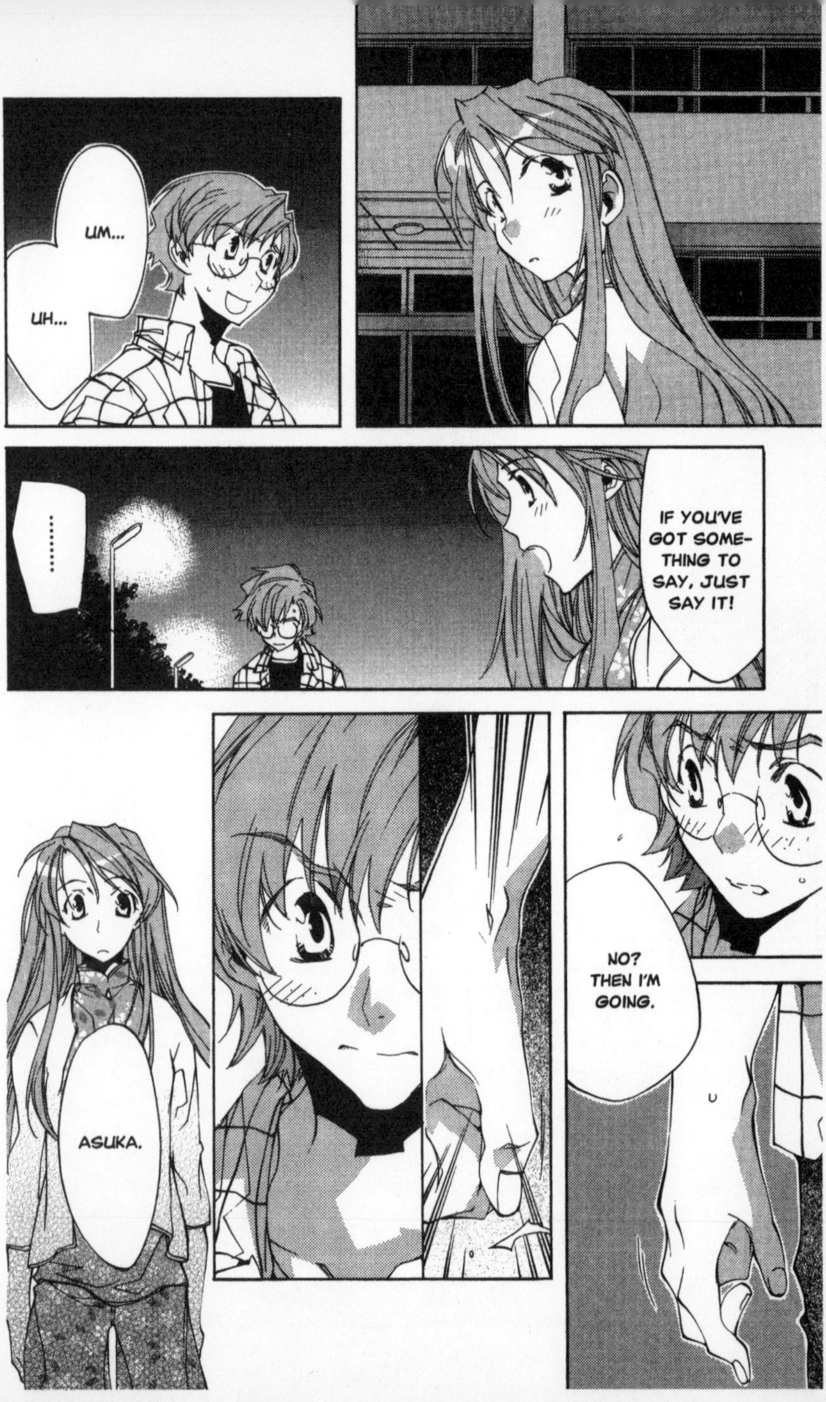
UM...
UH...
IF YOU'VE GOT SOME-THING TO SAY, JUST SAY IT!
....
NO? THEN I'M GOING.
ASUKA.

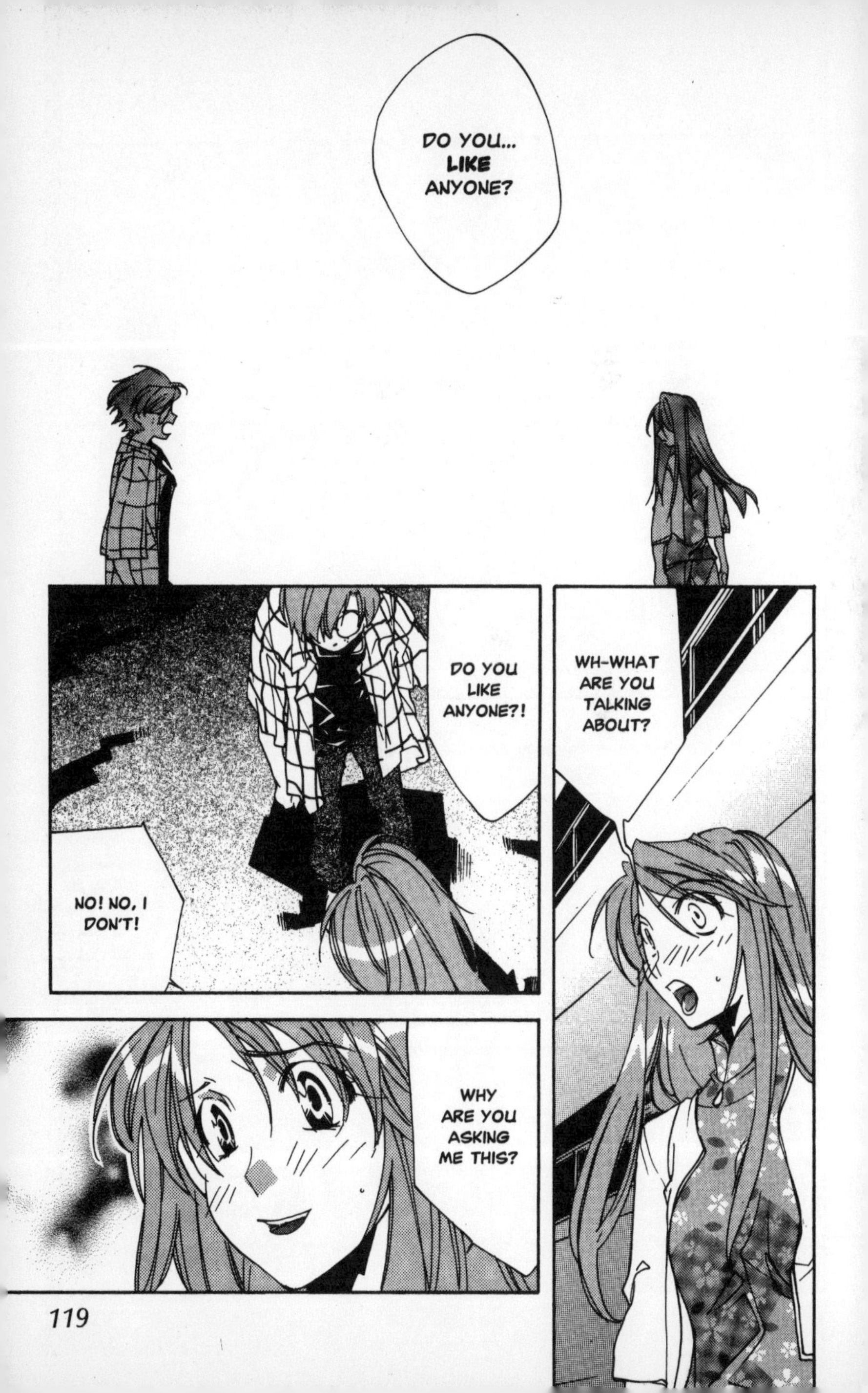
DO YOU... LIKE ANYONE?
WH-WHAT ARE YOU TALKING ABOUT?
DO YOU LIKE ANYONE?!
NO! NO, I DON'T!
WHY ARE YOU ASKING ME THIS?

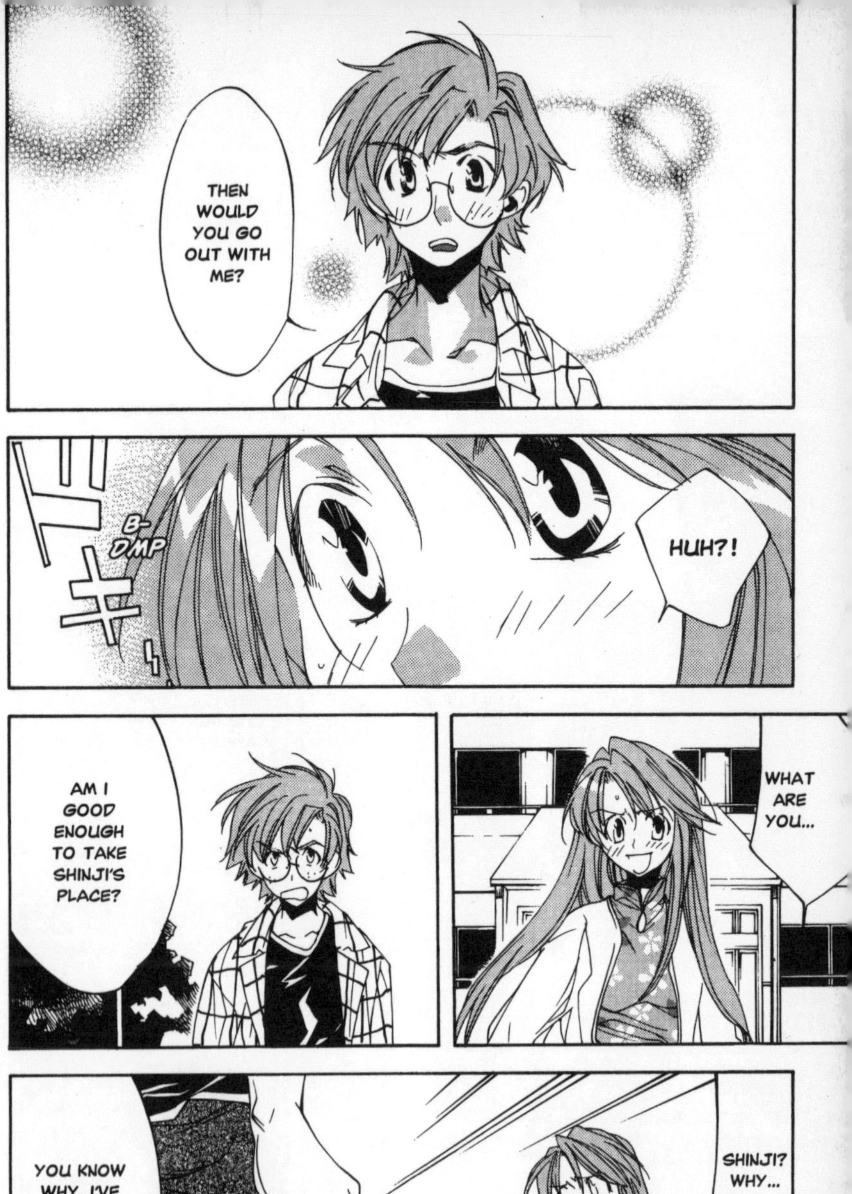
THEN WOULD YOU GO OUT WITH ME?
HUH?!
B-DMP
WHAT ARE YOU...
AM I GOOD ENOUGH TO TAKE SHINJI'S PLACE?
SHINJI? WHY...
YOU KNOW WHY. I'VE SAID ENOUGH.

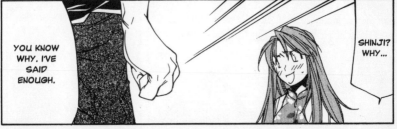

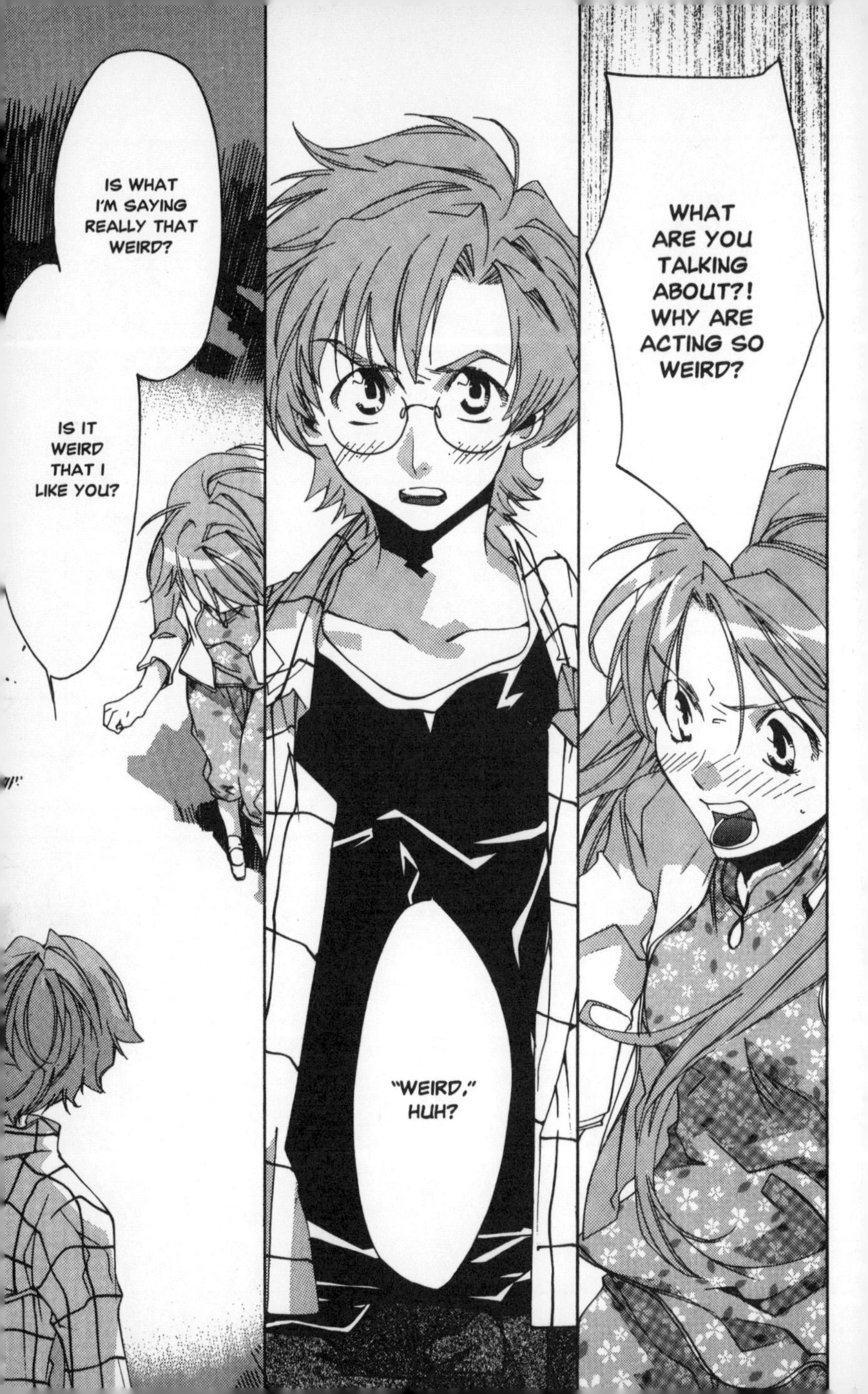
WHAT ARE YOU TALKING ABOUT?! WHY ARE ACTING SO WEIRD?
"WEIRD," HUH?
IS WHAT I'M SAYING REALLY THAT WEIRD?
IS IT WEIRD THAT I LIKE YOU?

DASH

ASUKA!

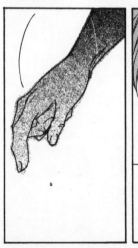

ASU...

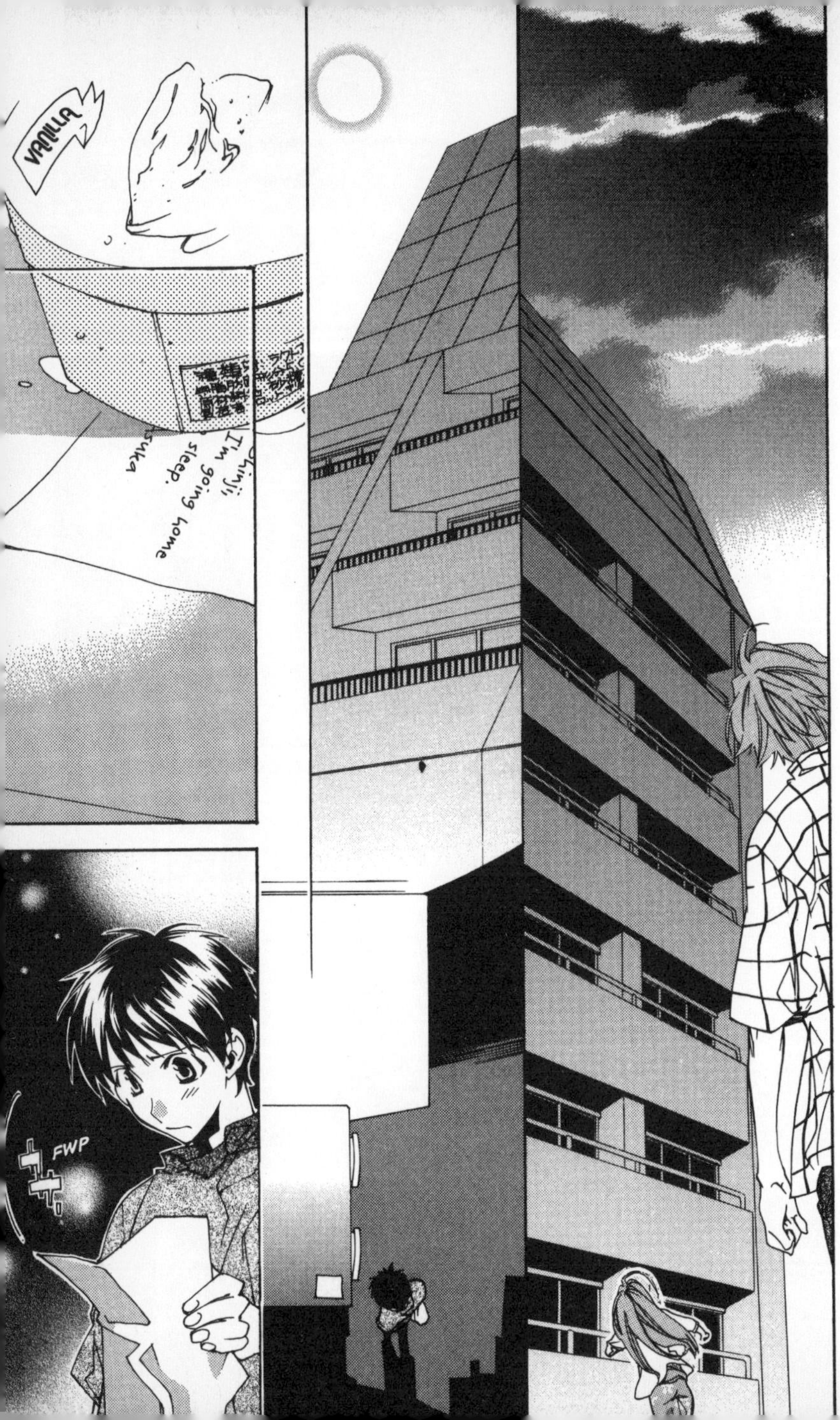
VANILLA
Shinji,
I'm going home
sleep.
suka
FWP

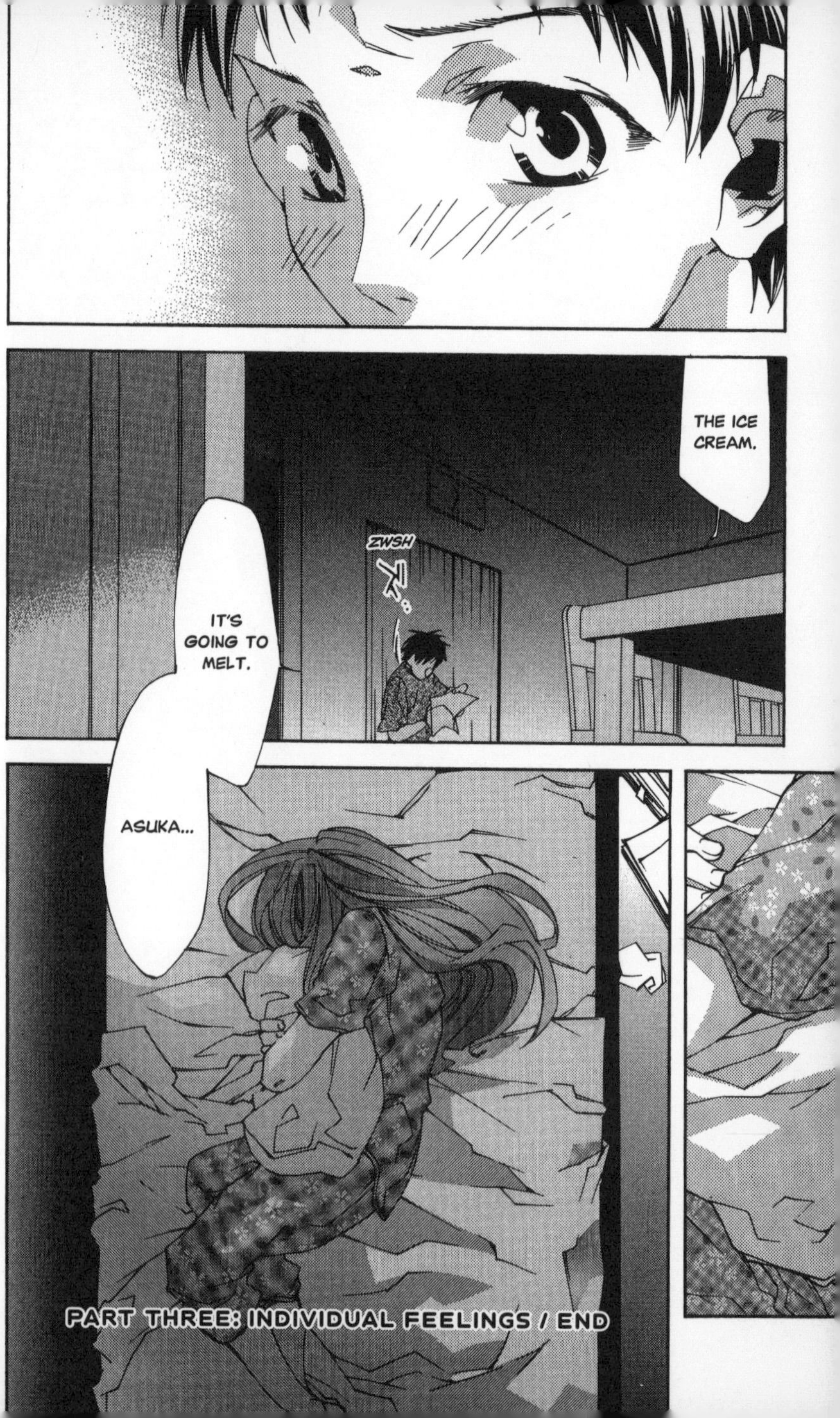
THE ICE CREAM.
ZWSH
IT'S GOING TO MELT.
ASUKA...
PART THREE: INDIVIDUAL FEELINGS / END

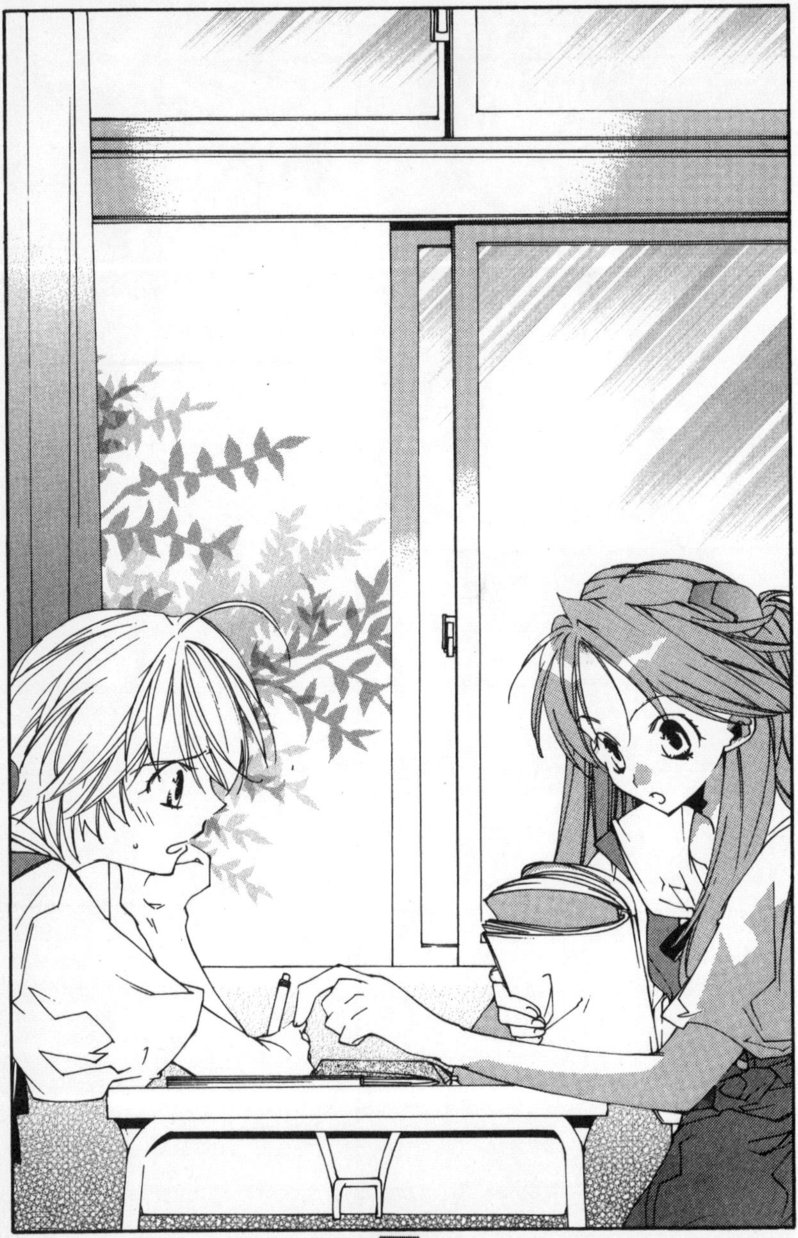

CHAPTER THREE, PART FOUR: THE IDEAL WORLD

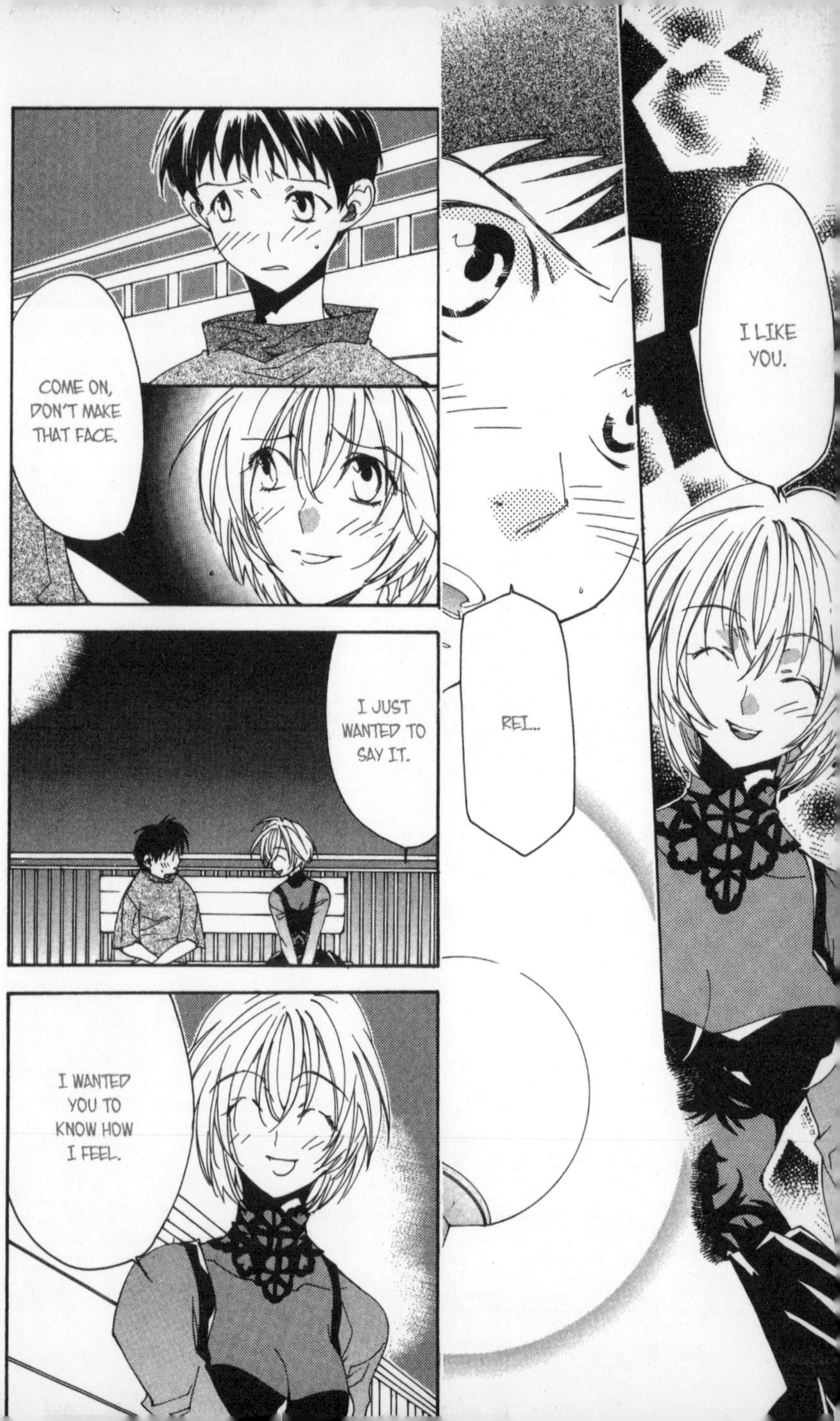
I LIKE YOU.
REI...
COME ON, DON'T MAKE THAT FACE.
I JUST WANTED TO SAY IT.
I WANTED YOU TO KNOW HOW I FEEL.

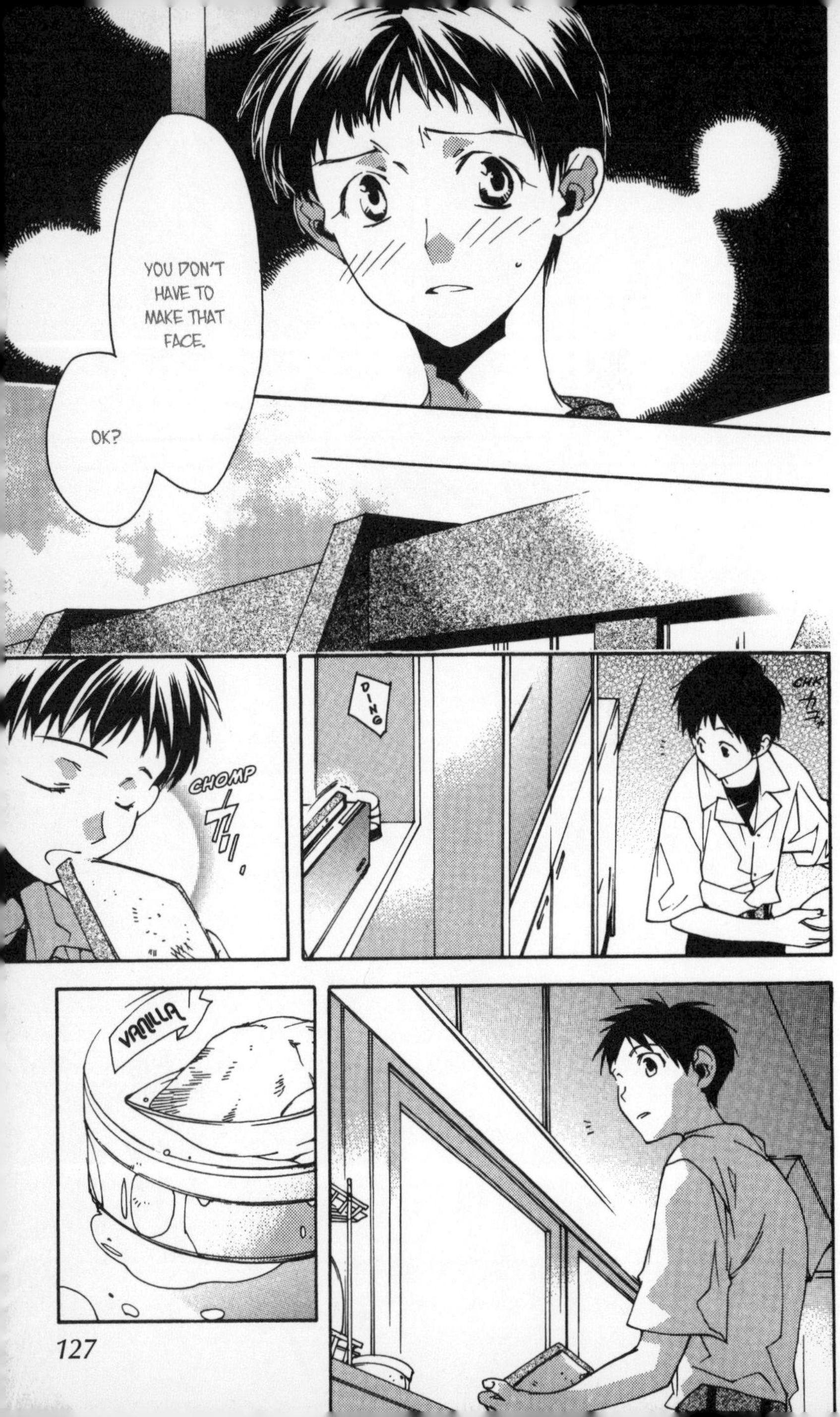
YOU DON'T HAVE TO MAKE THAT FACE.
OK?
CHK
DING
CHOMP
VANILLA

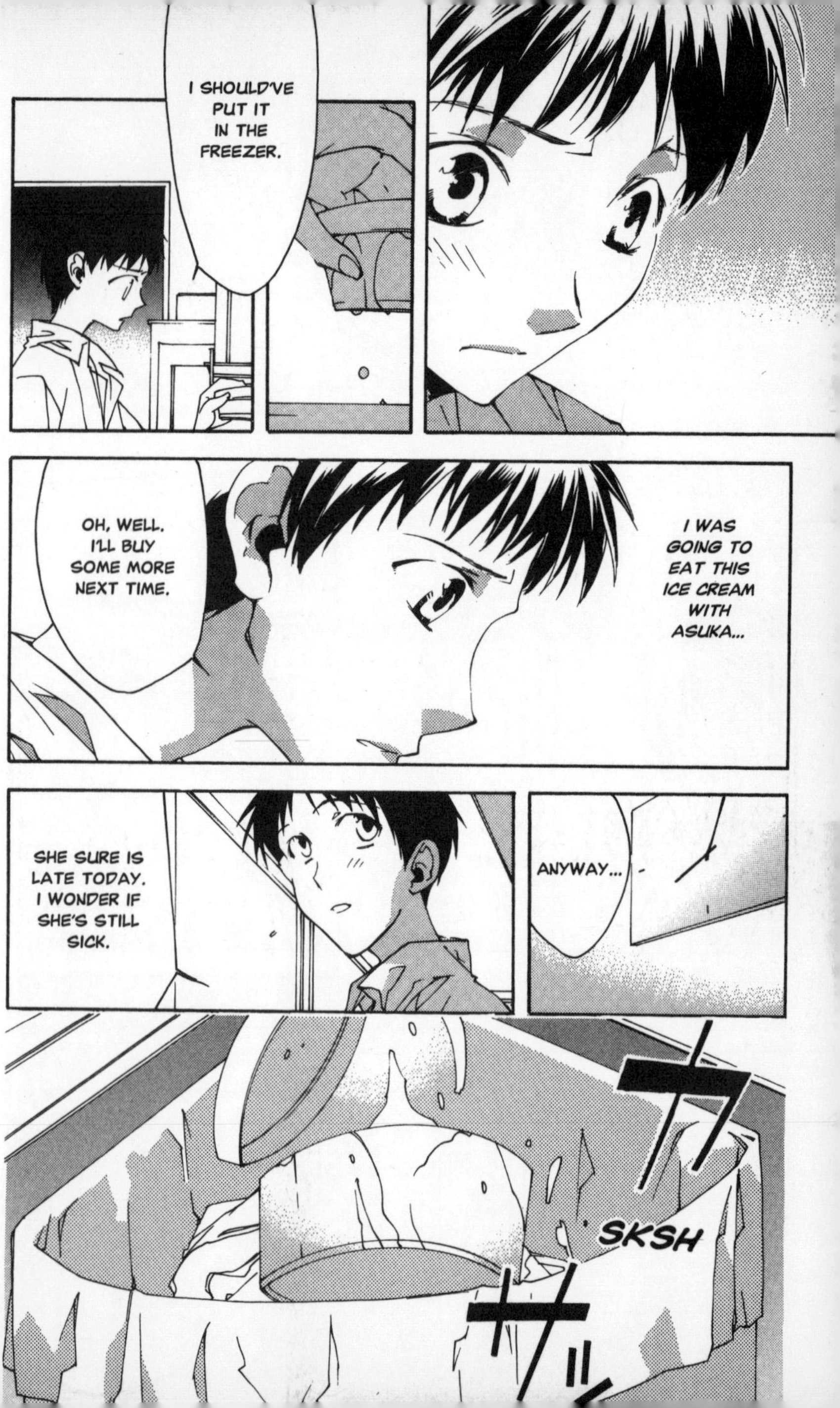
I SHOULD'VE PUT IT IN THE FREEZER.
I WAS GOING TO EAT THIS ICE CREAM WITH ASUKA...
OH, WELL. I'LL BUY SOME MORE NEXT TIME.
ANYWAY...
SHE SURE IS LATE TODAY. I WONDER IF SHE'S STILL SICK.
SKSH

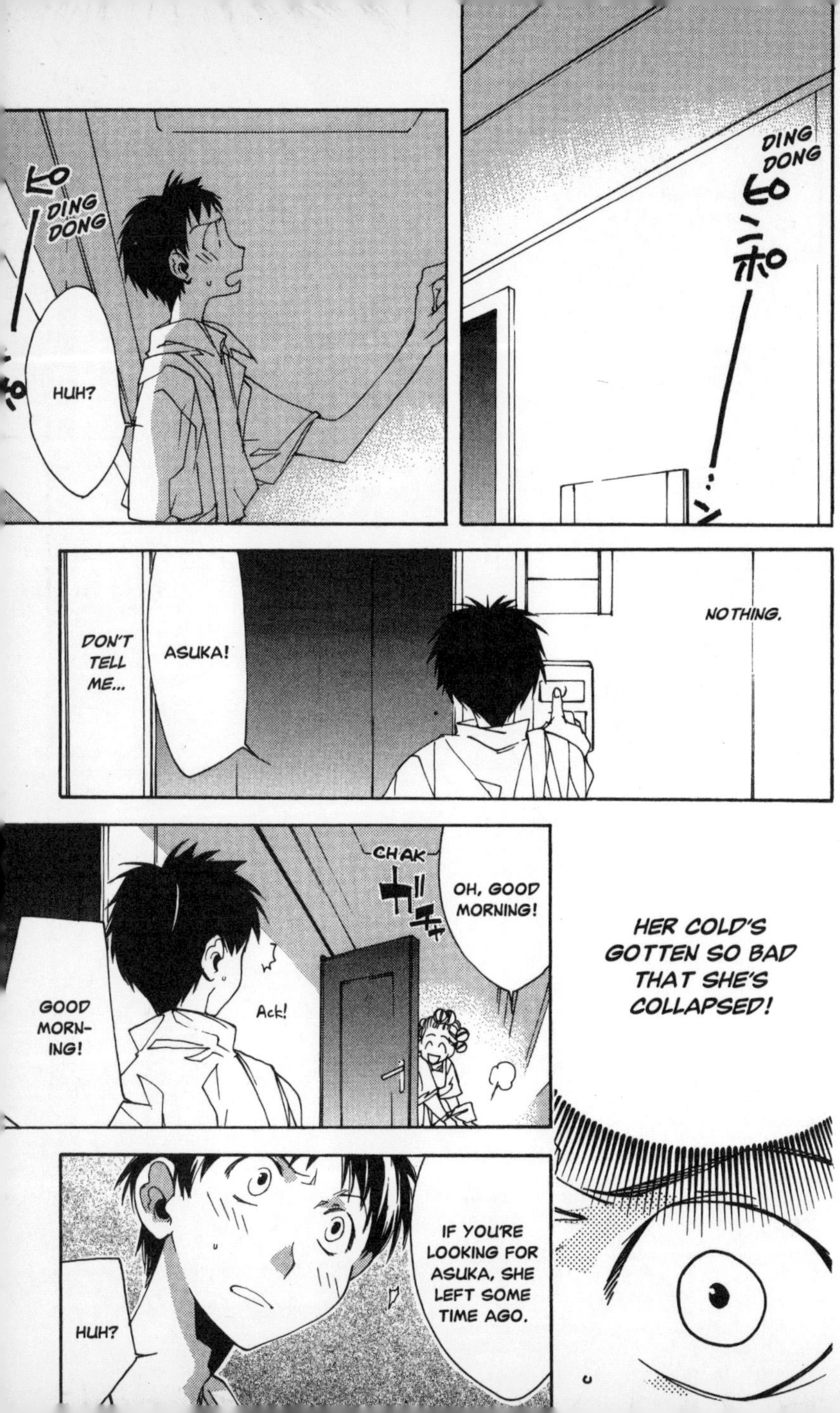
DING DONG
ピンポーン
DING DONG
ピンポーン
HUH?
NOTHING.
ASUKA!
DON'T TELL ME...
HER COLD'S GOTTEN SO BAD THAT SHE'S COLLAPSED!
CHAK
ガチャ
OH, GOOD MORNING!
Ack!
GOOD MORNING!
IF YOU'RE LOOKING FOR ASUKA, SHE LEFT SOME TIME AGO.
HUH?

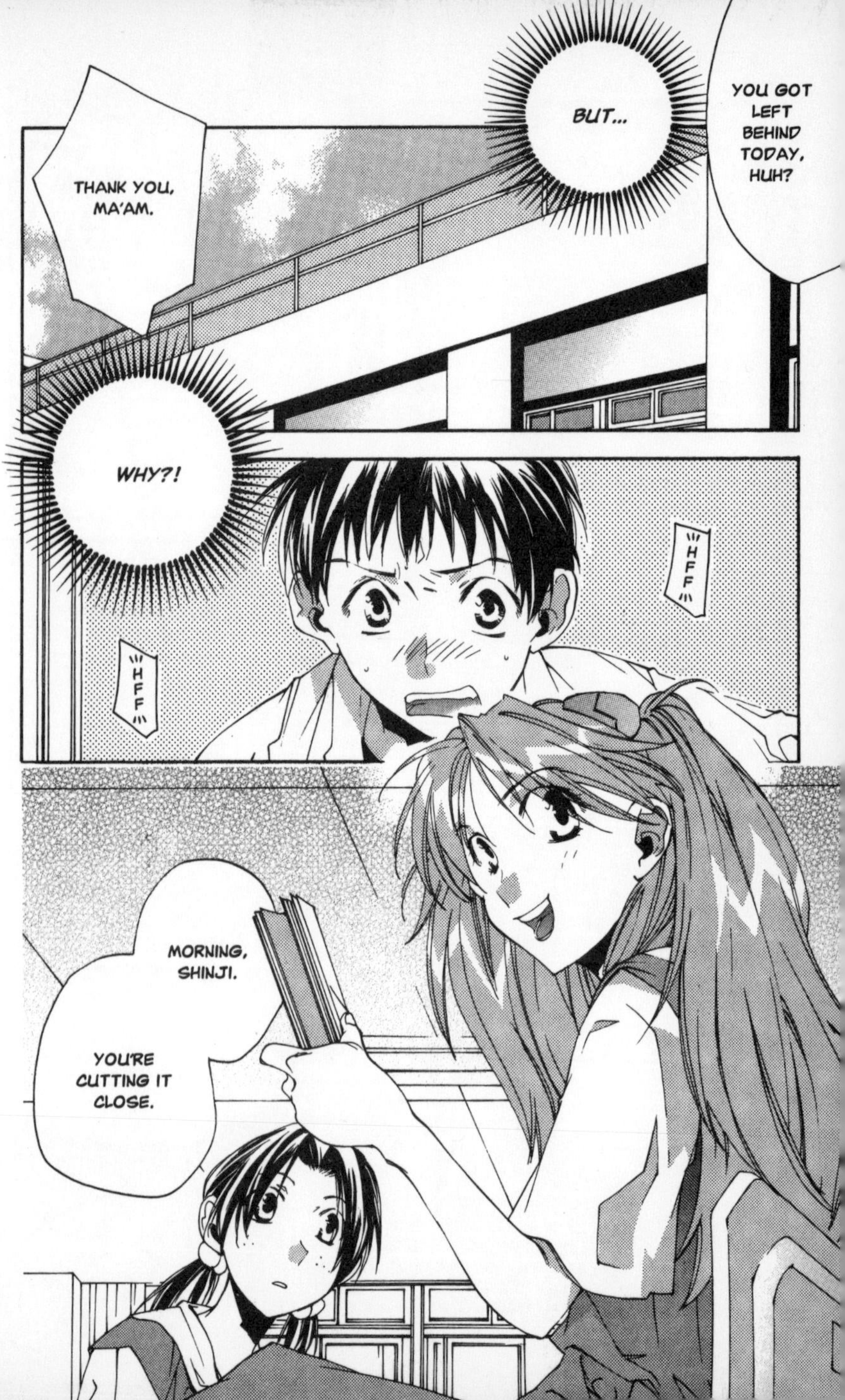
YOU GOT LEFT BEHIND TODAY, HUH?
BUT...
THANK YOU, MA'AM.
WHY?!
HFF
HFF
MORNING, SHINJI.
YOU'RE CUTTING IT CLOSE.

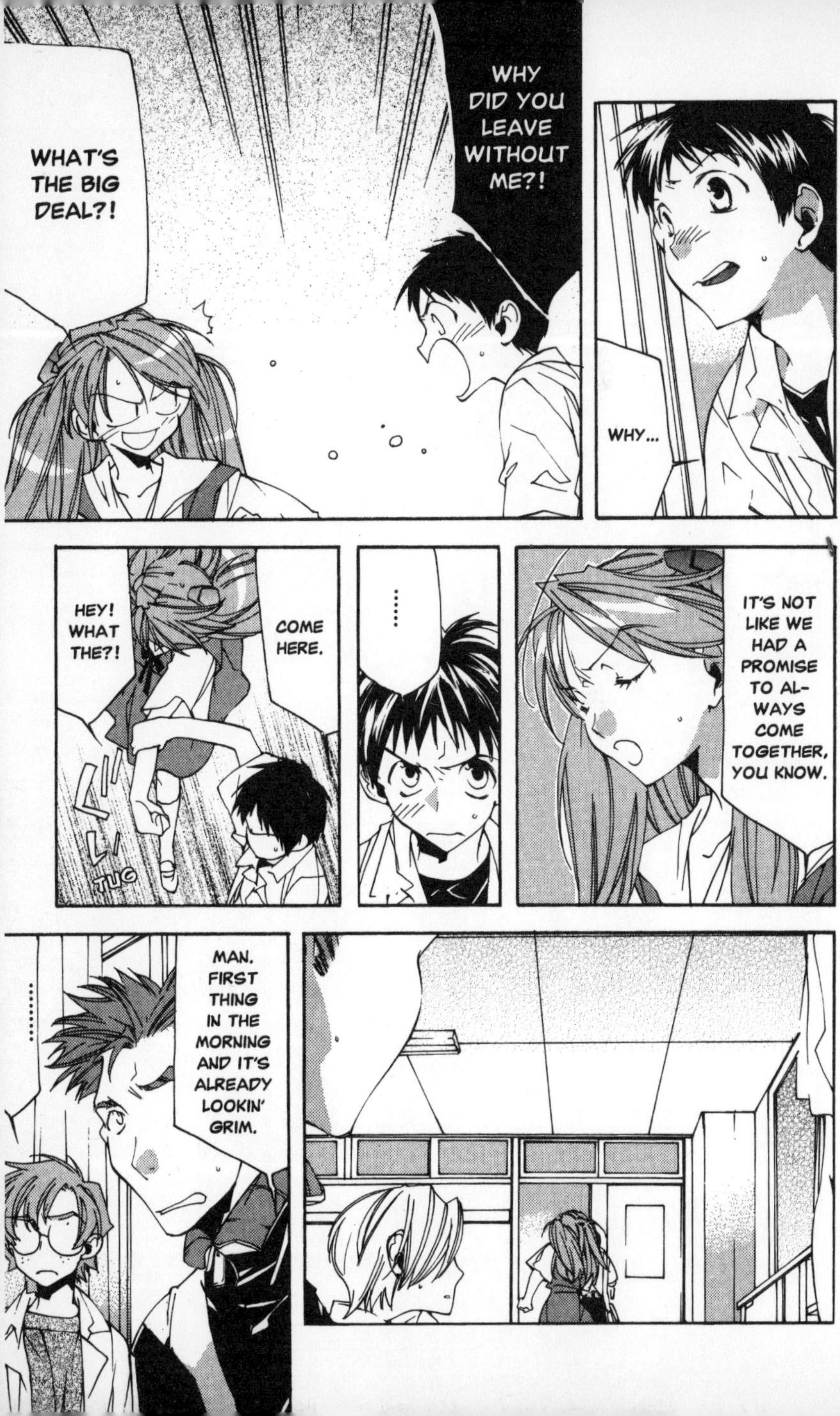
WHY...
WHY DID YOU LEAVE WITHOUT ME?!
WHAT'S THE BIG DEAL?!
IT'S NOT LIKE WE HAD A PROMISE TO AL-WAYS COME TOGETHER, YOU KNOW.
......
COME HERE.
HEY! WHAT THE?!
TUG
MAN. FIRST THING IN THE MORNING AND IT'S ALREADY LOOKIN' GRIM.
......

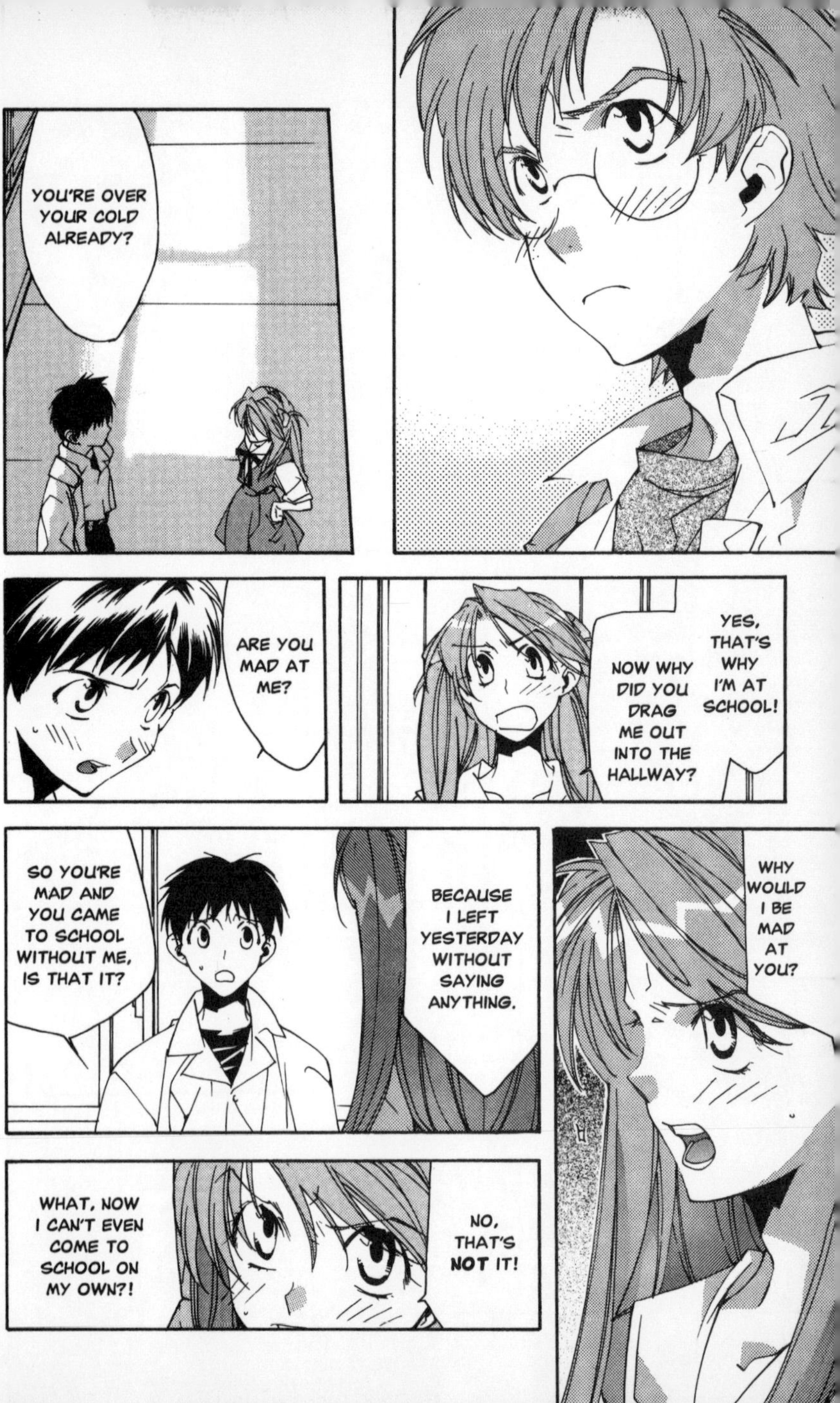
YOU'RE OVER YOUR COLD ALREADY?
YES, THAT'S WHY I'M AT SCHOOL!
NOW WHY DID YOU DRAG ME OUT INTO THE HALLWAY?
ARE YOU MAD AT ME?
WHY WOULD I BE MAD AT YOU?
BECAUSE I LEFT YESTERDAY WITHOUT SAYING ANYTHING.
SO YOU'RE MAD AND YOU CAME TO SCHOOL WITHOUT ME, IS THAT IT?
NO, THAT'S NOT IT!
WHAT, NOW I CAN'T EVEN COME TO SCHOOL ON MY OWN?!

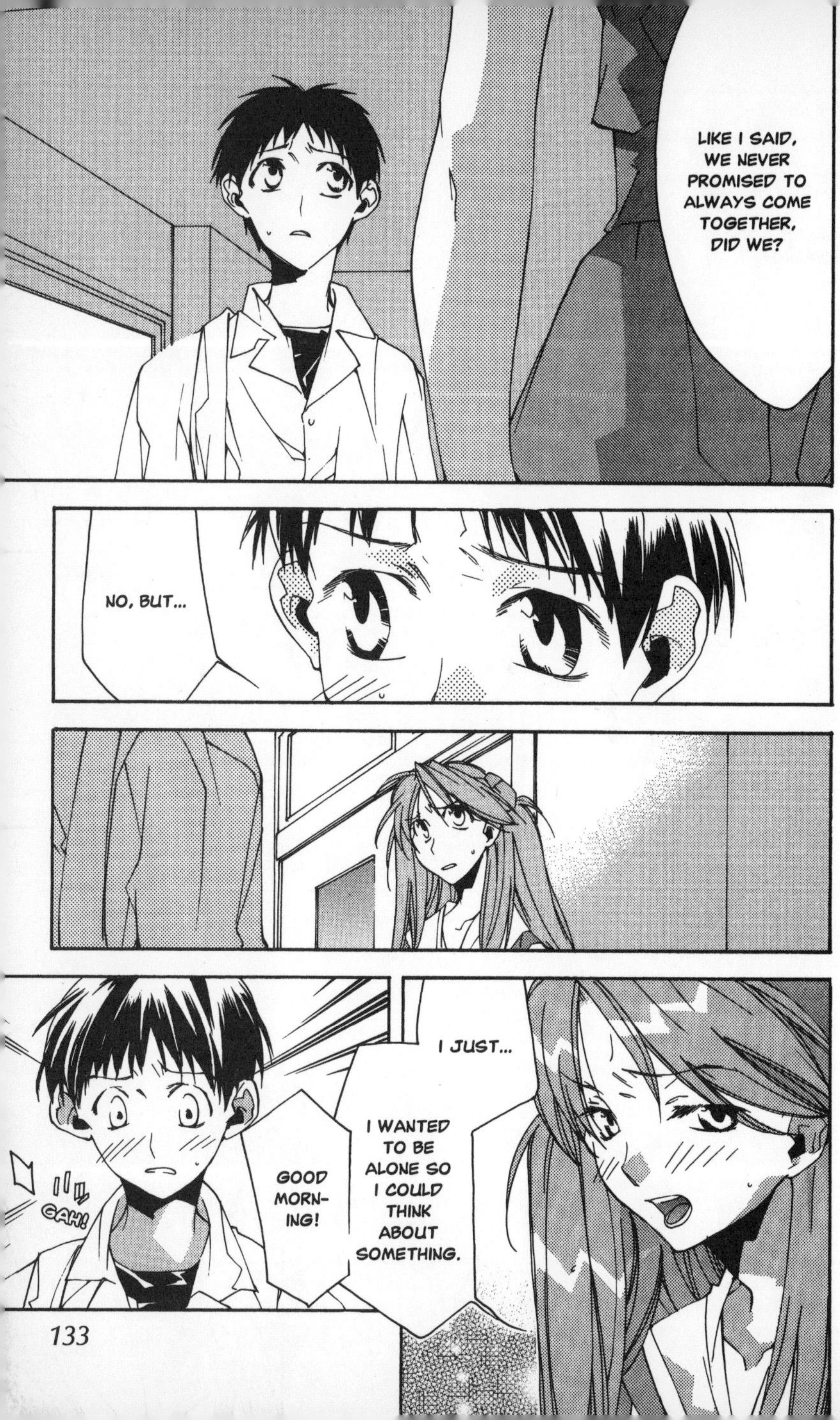
LIKE I SAID, WE NEVER PROMISED TO ALWAYS COME TOGETHER, DID WE?
NO, BUT...
I JUST...
I WANTED TO BE ALONE SO I COULD THINK ABOUT SOMETHING.
GOOD MORNING!
GAH!

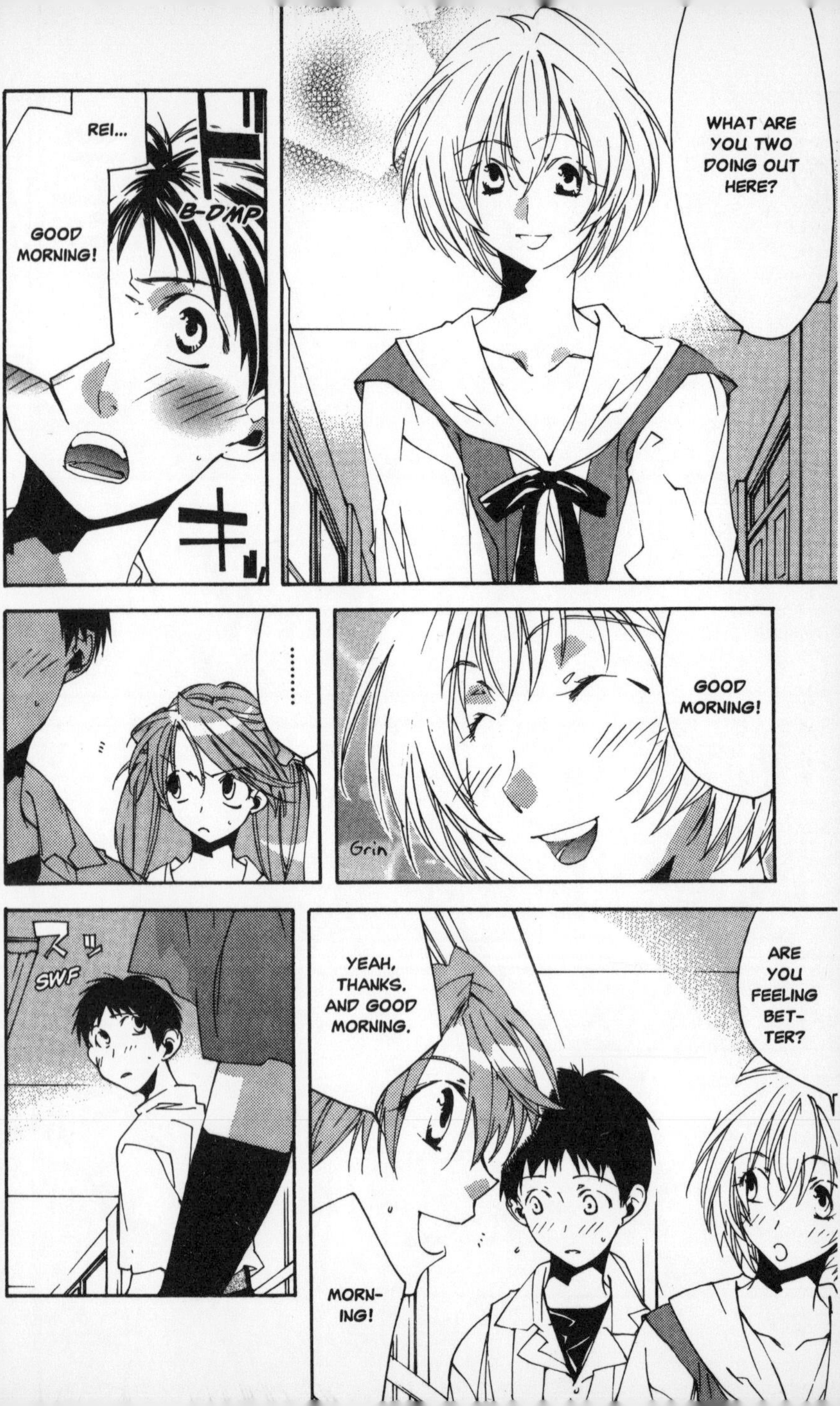
WHAT ARE YOU TWO DOING OUT HERE?
REI...
B-DMP
GOOD MORNING!
GOOD MORNING!
Grin
......
ARE YOU FEELING BETTER?
YEAH, THANKS. AND GOOD MORNING.
MORN-ING!
スッ
SWF

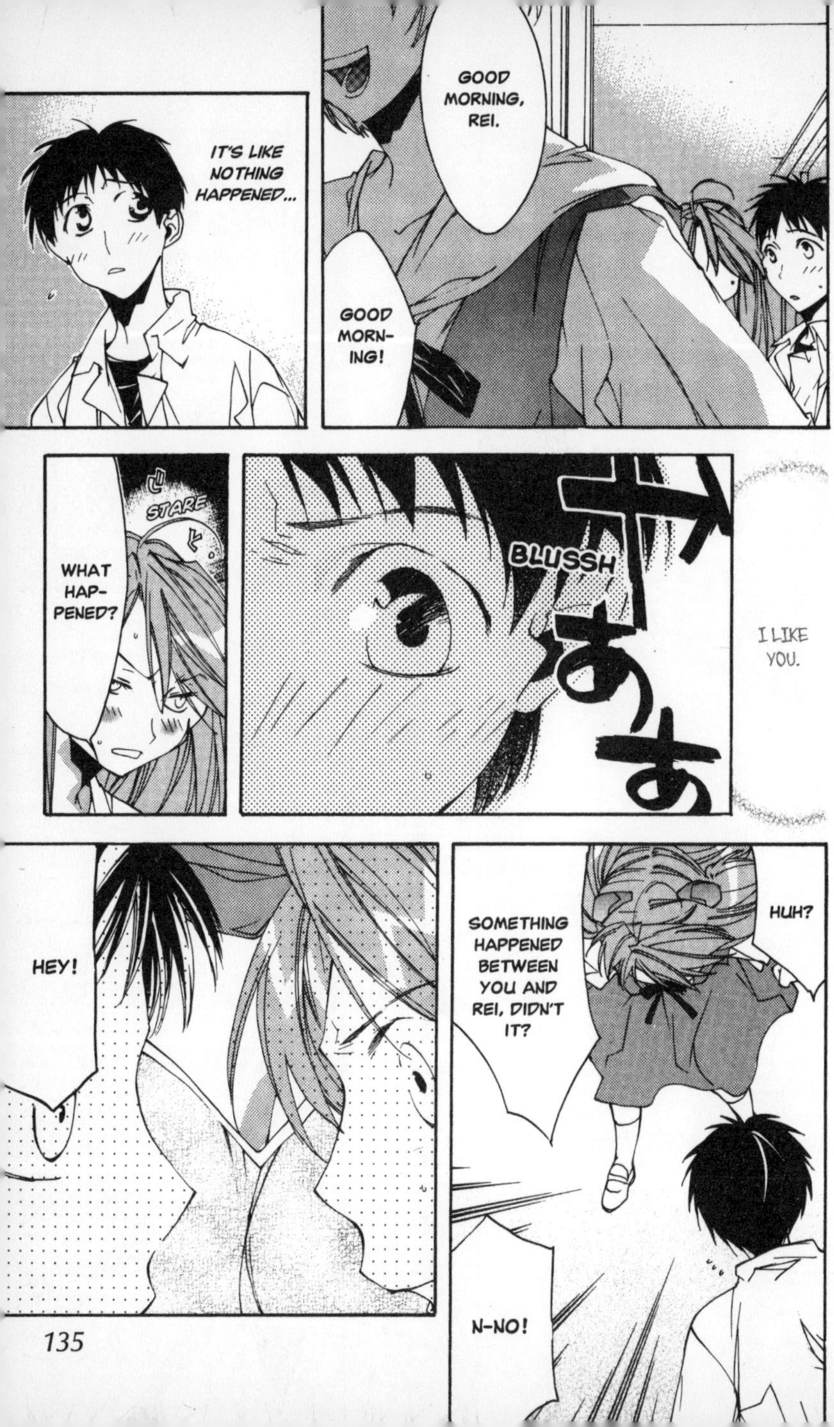
GOOD MORNING, REI.
GOOD MORNING!
IT'S LIKE NOTHING HAPPENED...
I LIKE YOU.
BLUSSH
STARE
WHAT HAPPENED?
HUH?
SOMETHING HAPPENED BETWEEN YOU AND REI, DIDN'T IT?
N-NO!
HEY!

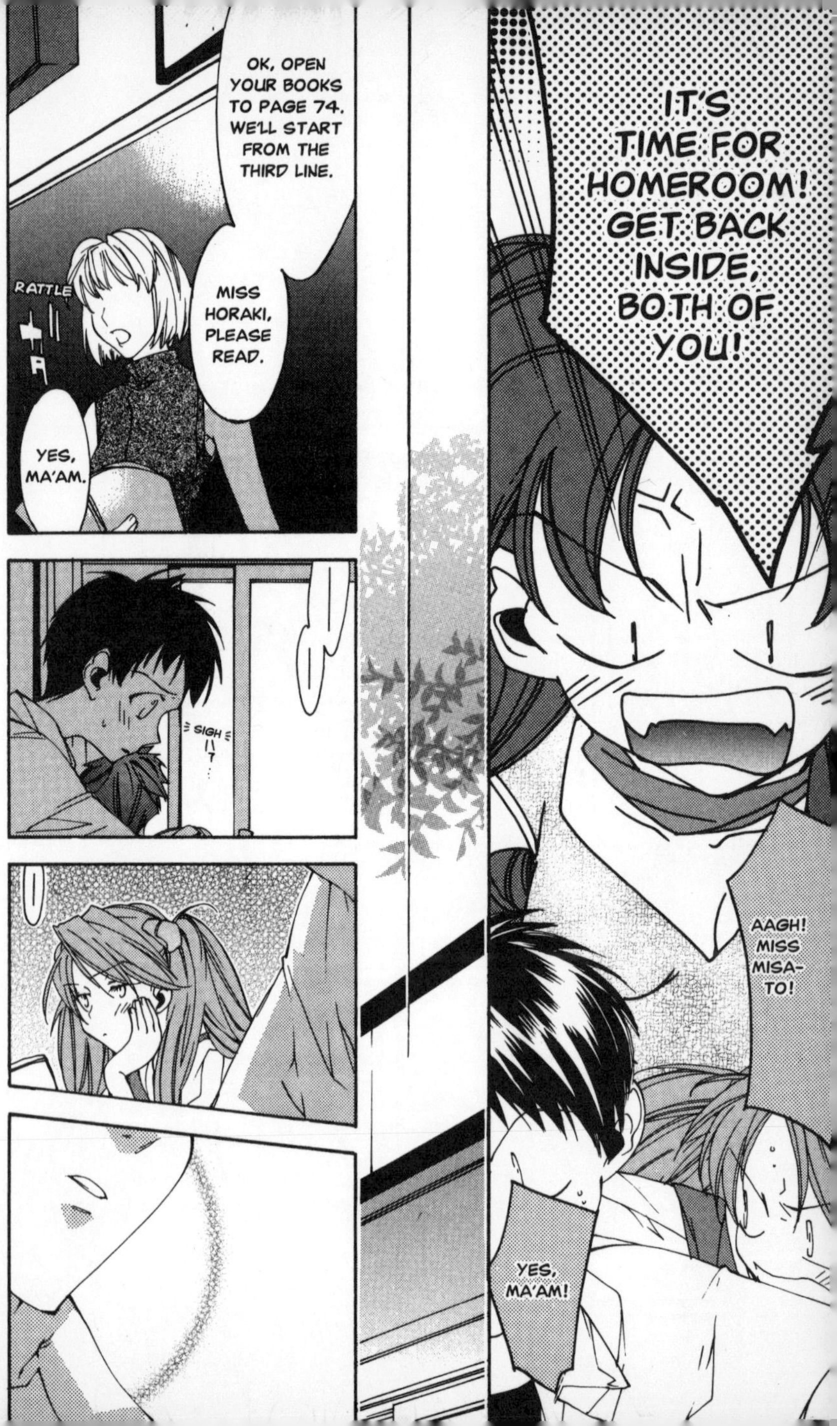
IT'S TIME FOR HOMEROOM! GET BACK INSIDE, BOTH OF YOU!
AAGH! MISS MISA-TO!
YES, MA'AM!
OK, OPEN YOUR BOOKS TO PAGE 74. WE'LL START FROM THE THIRD LINE.
MISS HORAKI, PLEASE READ.
RATTLE
YES, MA'AM.
SIGH

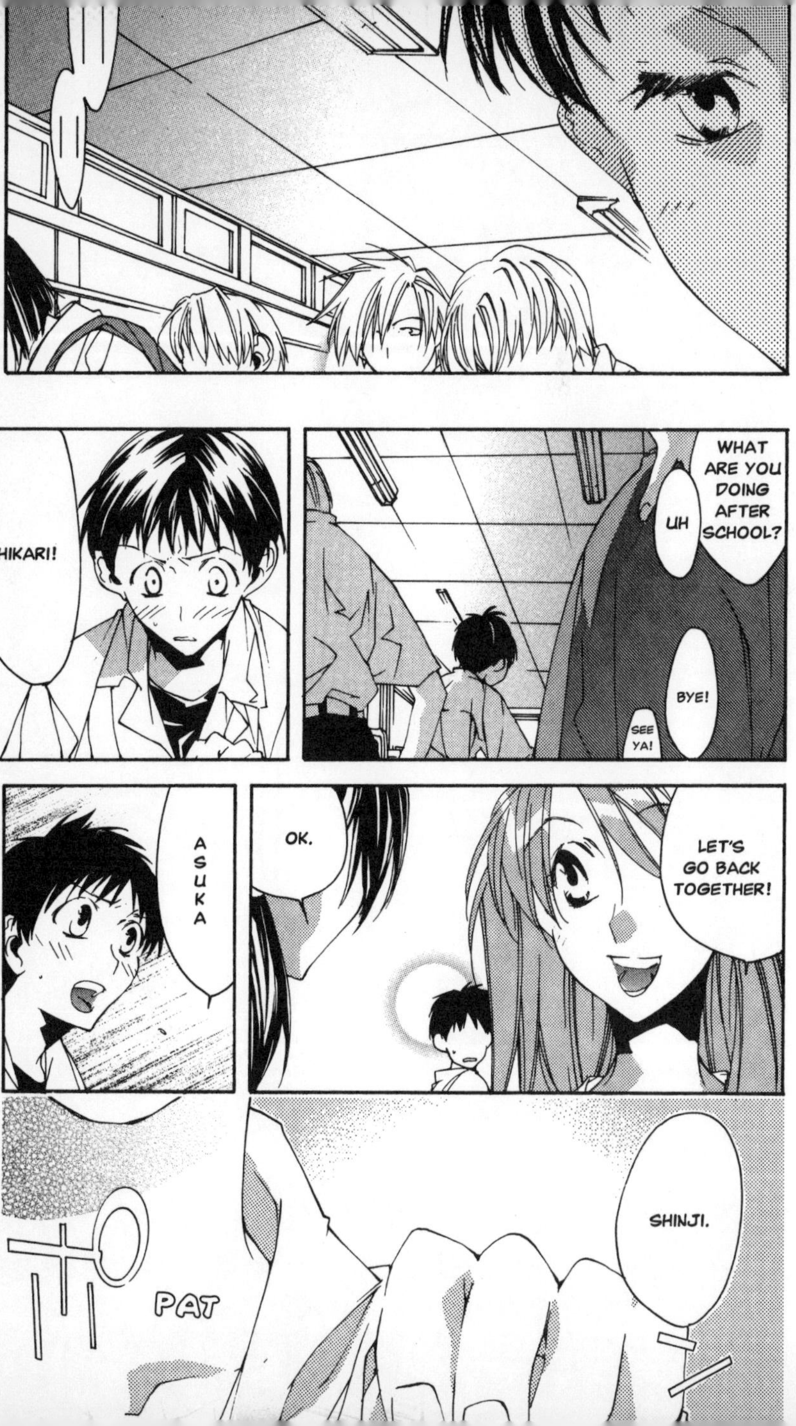
WHAT ARE YOU DOING AFTER SCHOOL?
UH
BYE!
SEE YA!
HIKARI!
LET'S GO BACK TOGETHER!
OK.
ASUKA
SHINJI.
PAT

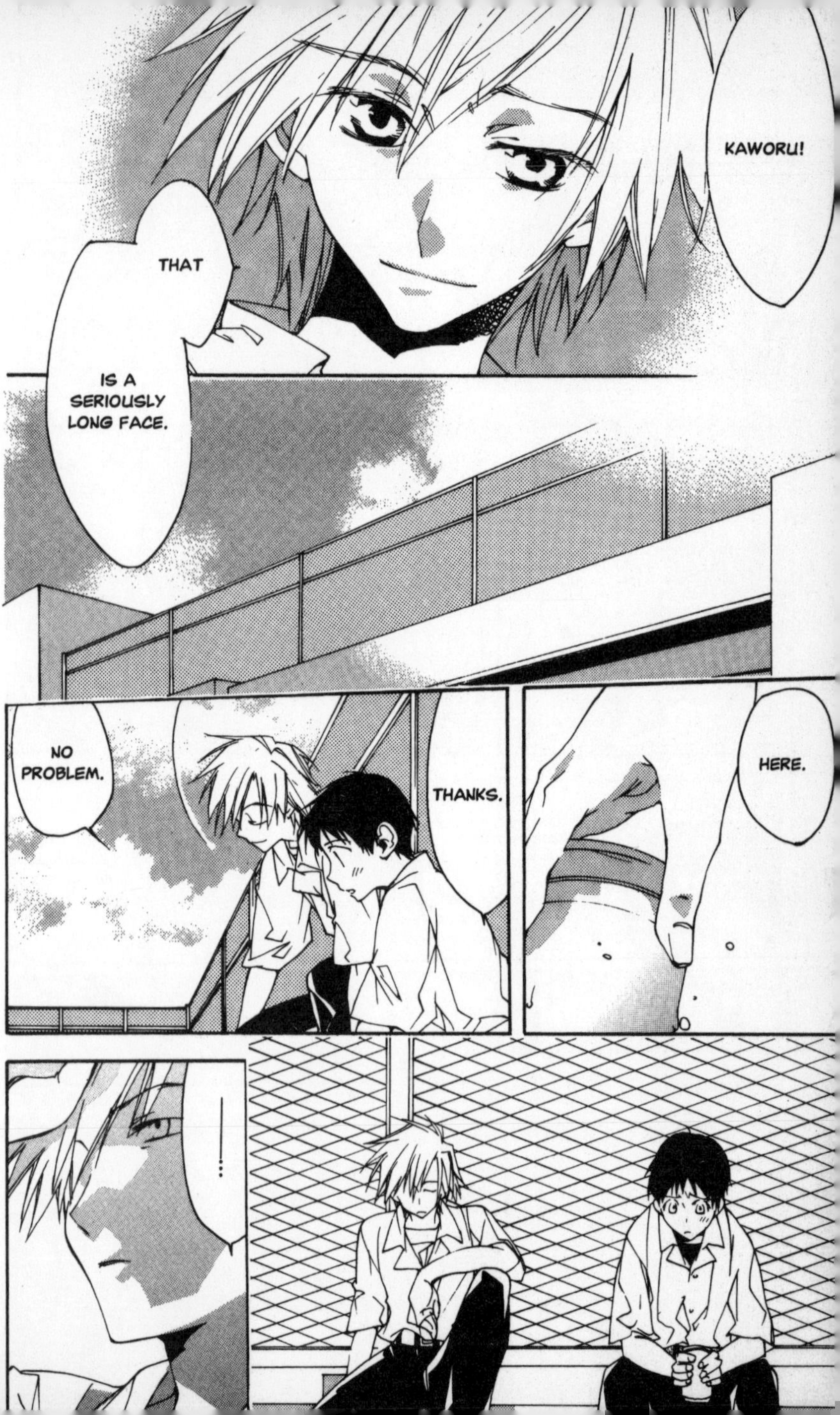
KAWORU!
THAT
IS A SERIOUSLY LONG FACE.
HERE.
THANKS.
NO PROBLEM.
—...

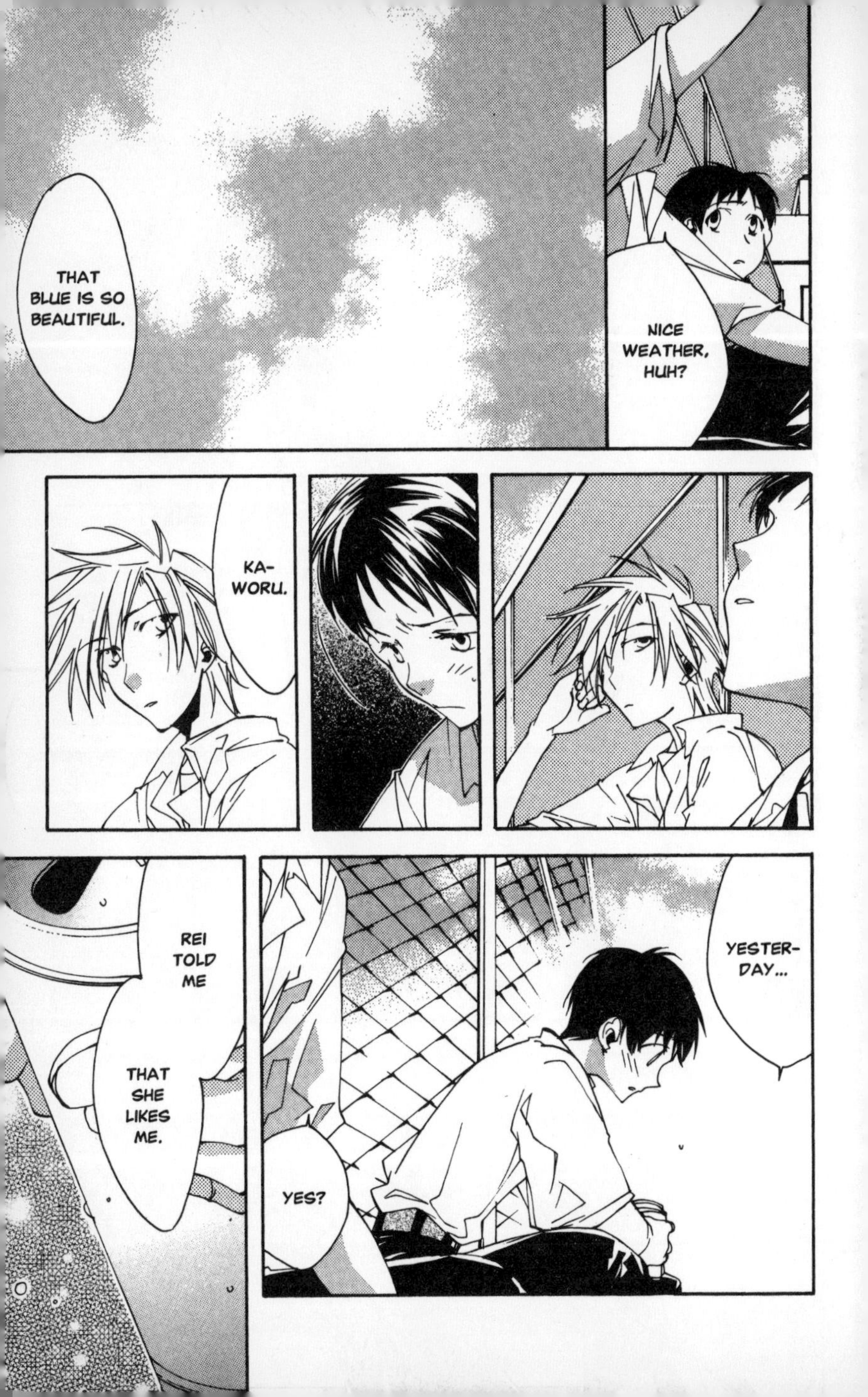
NICE WEATHER, HUH?
THAT BLUE IS SO BEAUTIFUL.
KA-WORU.
YESTER-DAY...
YES?
REI TOLD ME
THAT SHE LIKES ME.

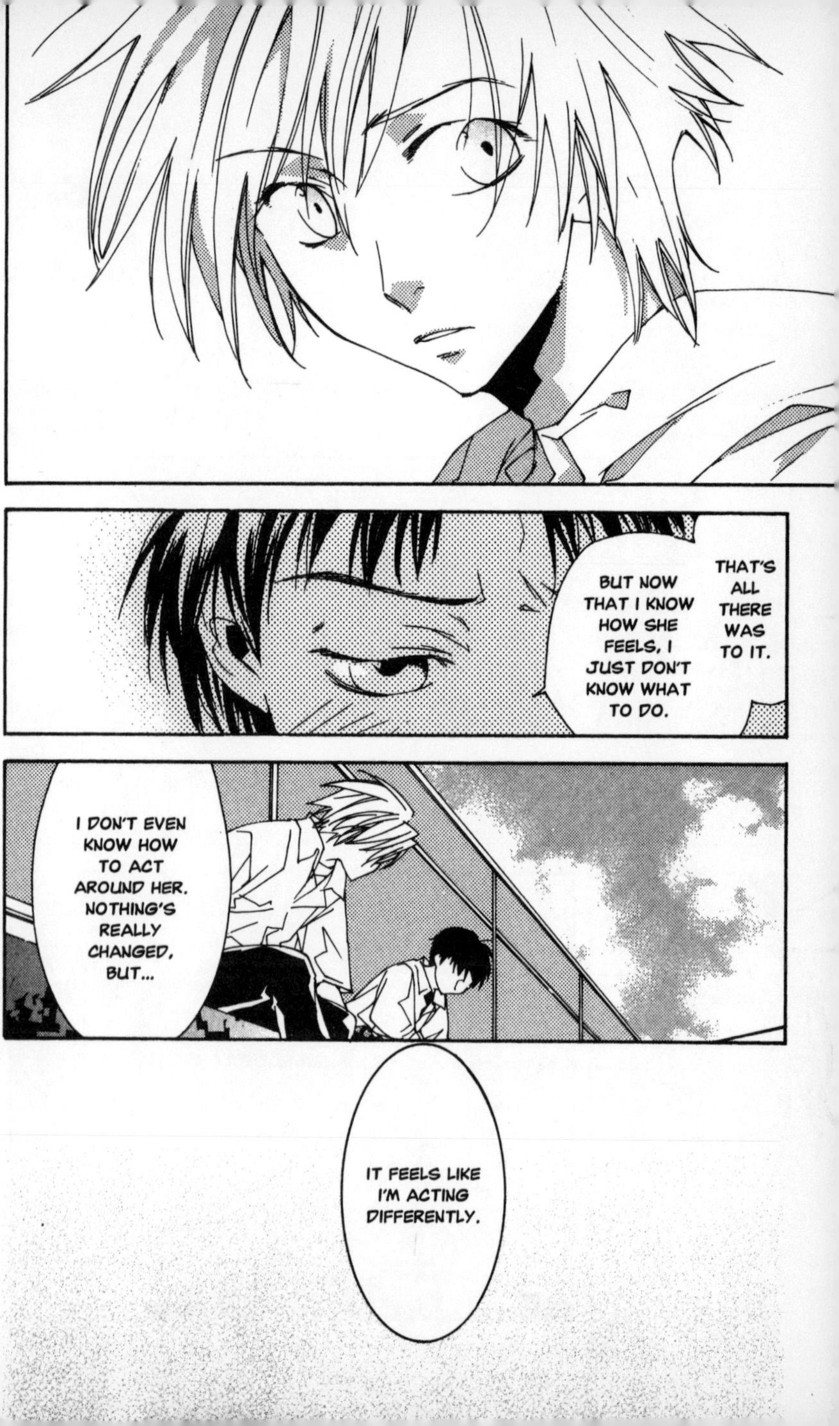
THAT'S ALL THERE WAS TO IT.
BUT NOW THAT I KNOW HOW SHE FEELS, I JUST DON'T KNOW WHAT TO DO.
I DON'T EVEN KNOW HOW TO ACT AROUND HER. NOTHING'S REALLY CHANGED, BUT...
IT FEELS LIKE I'M ACTING DIFFERENTLY.

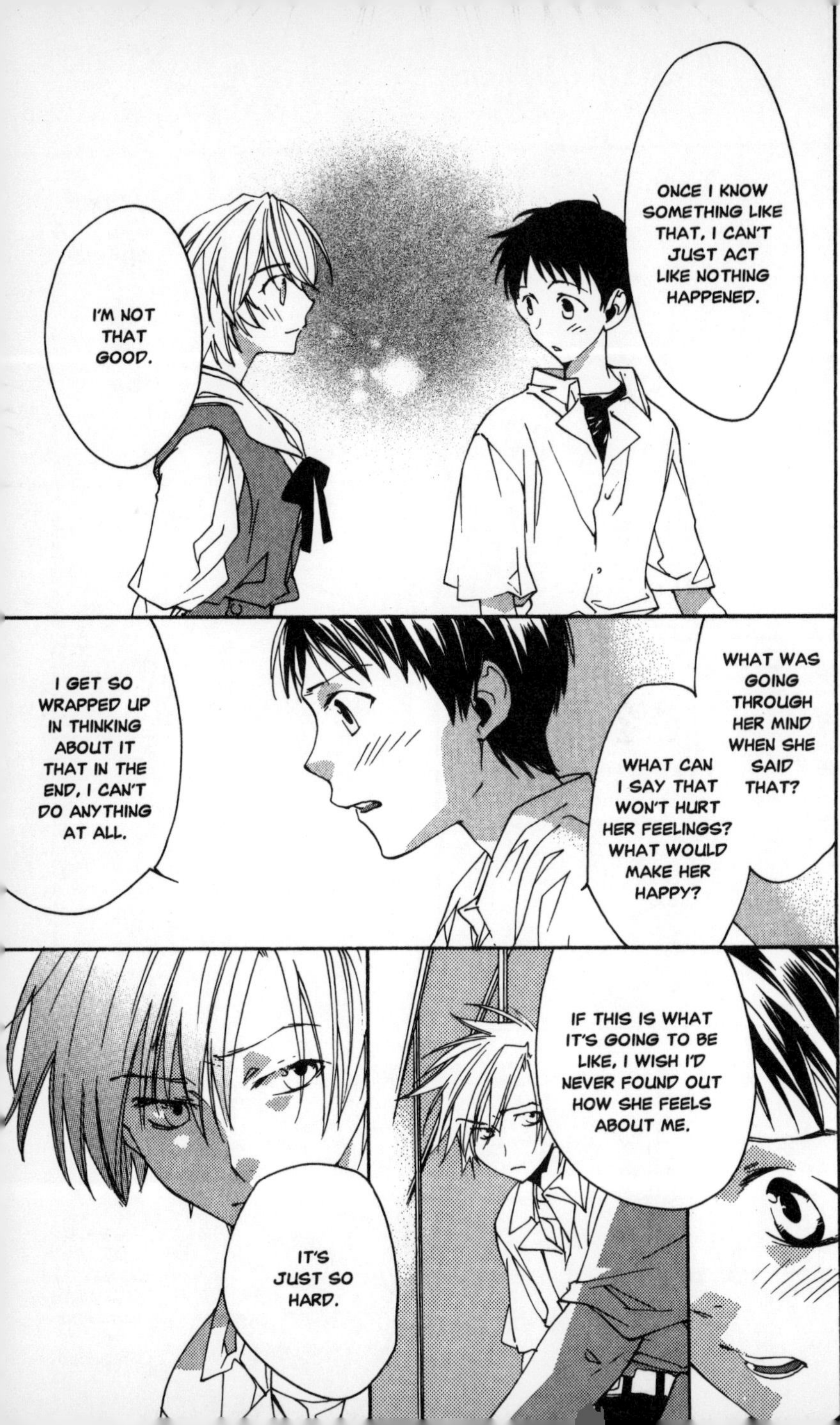
ONCE I KNOW SOMETHING LIKE THAT, I CAN'T JUST ACT LIKE NOTHING HAPPENED.
I'M NOT THAT GOOD.
WHAT WAS GOING THROUGH HER MIND WHEN SHE SAID THAT?
WHAT CAN I SAY THAT WON'T HURT HER FEELINGS? WHAT WOULD MAKE HER HAPPY?
I GET SO WRAPPED UP IN THINKING ABOUT IT THAT IN THE END, I CAN'T DO ANYTHING AT ALL.
IF THIS IS WHAT IT'S GOING TO BE LIKE, I WISH I'D NEVER FOUND OUT HOW SHE FEELS ABOUT ME.
IT'S JUST SO HARD.

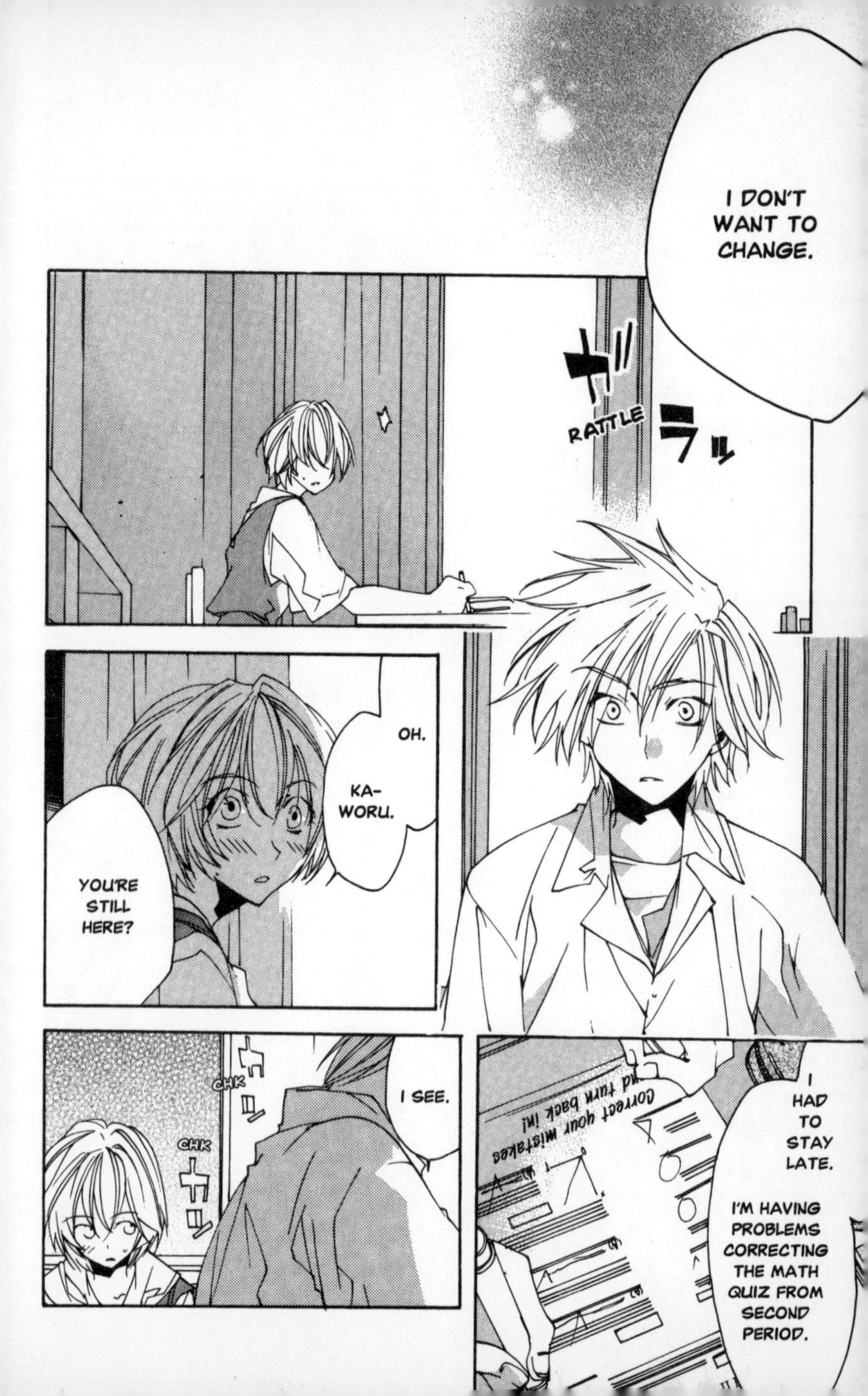
I DON'T WANT TO CHANGE.
RATTLE
OH.
KA-WORU.
YOU'RE STILL HERE?
I HAD TO STAY LATE.
I'M HAVING PROBLEMS CORRECTING THE MATH QUIZ FROM SECOND PERIOD.
Correct your mistakes
nd turn back in!
I SEE.
CHK
CHK

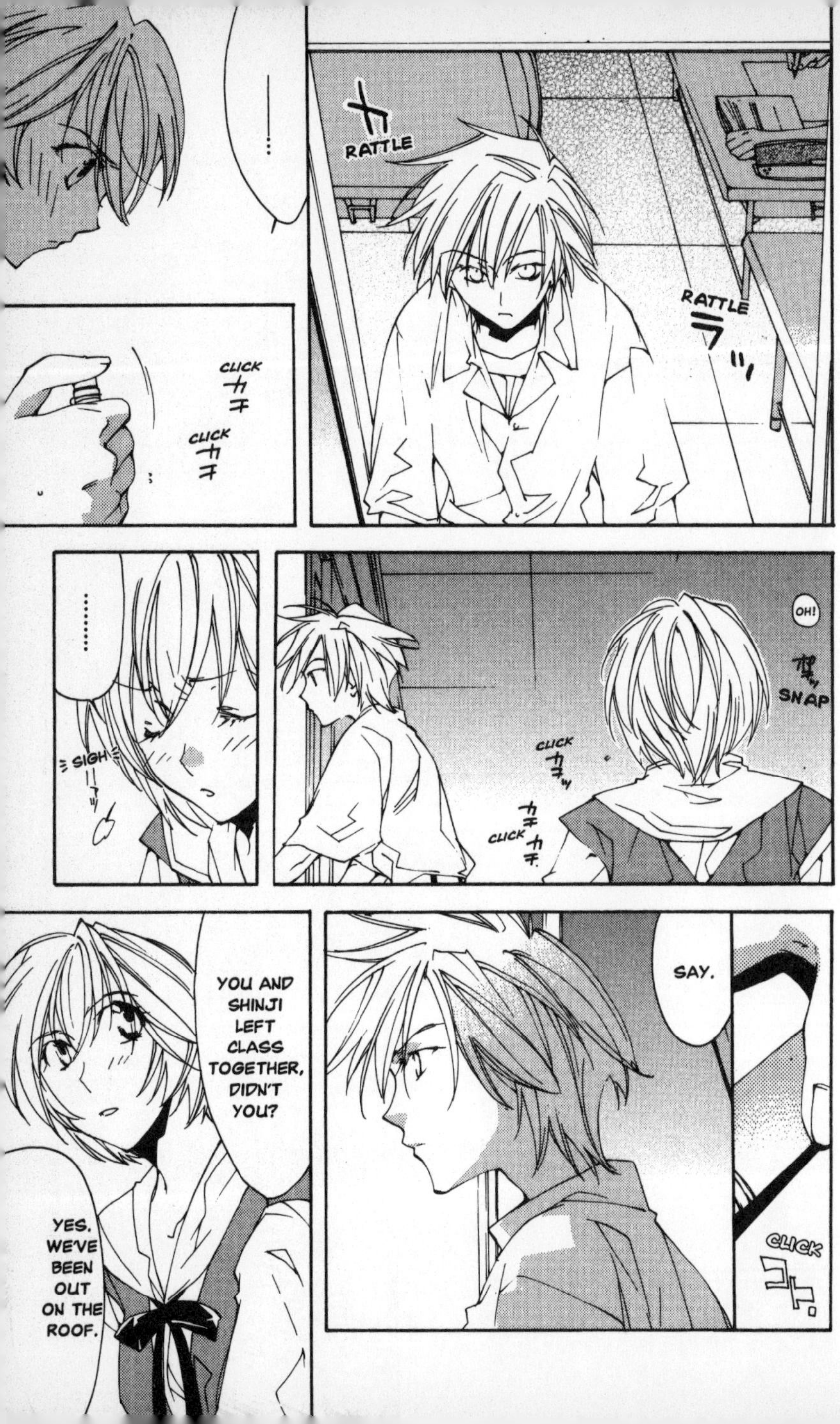
RATTLE
RATTLE
......
CLICK
CLICK
OH!
SNAP
CLICK
CLICK
......
SIGH
SAY.
CLICK
YOU AND SHINJI LEFT CLASS TOGETHER, DIDN'T YOU?
YES. WE'VE BEEN OUT ON THE ROOF.

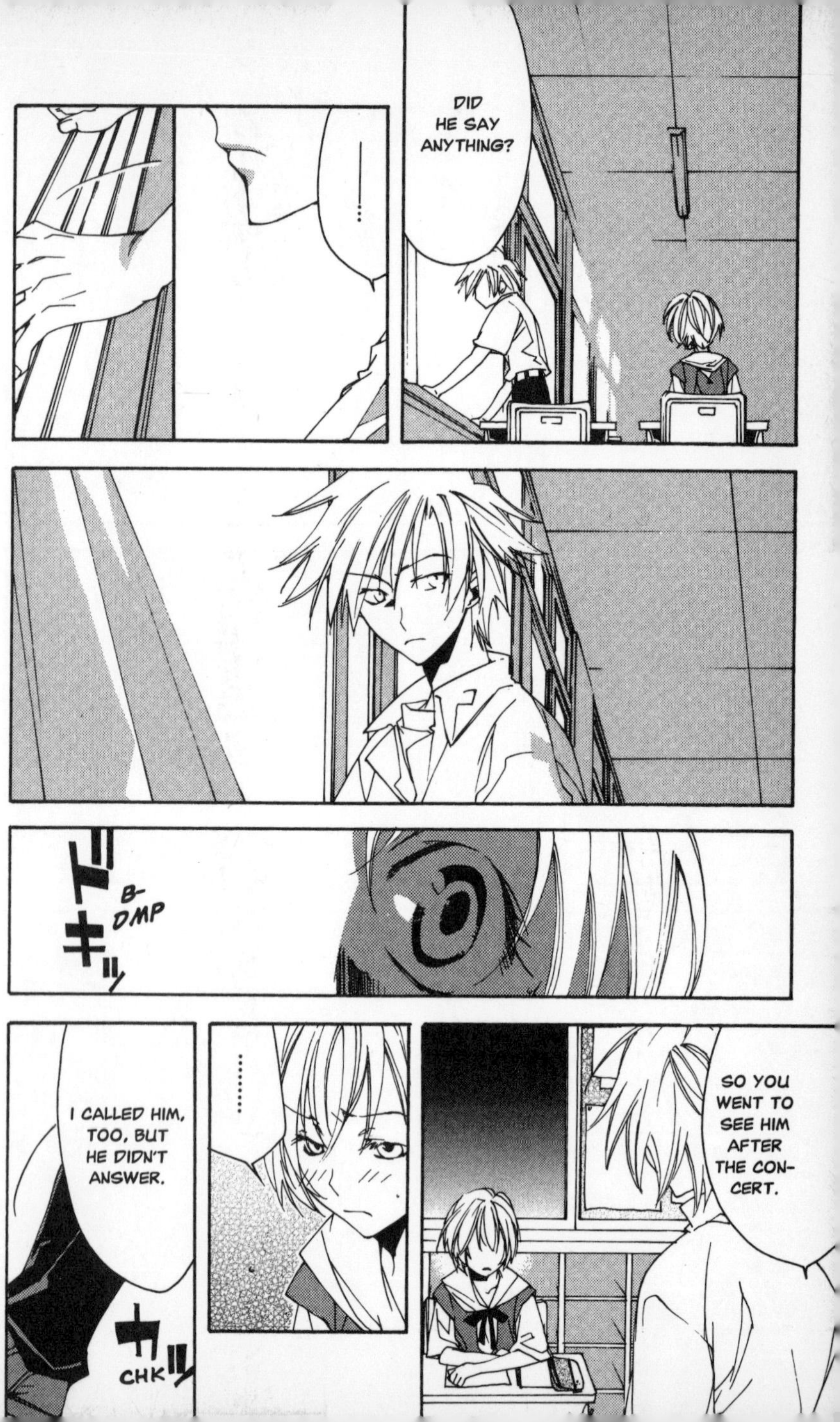
DID HE SAY ANYTHING?
......
ドキッ
B-DMP
SO YOU WENT TO SEE HIM AFTER THE CON-CERT.
......
I CALLED HIM, TOO, BUT HE DIDN'T ANSWER.
カッ
CHK

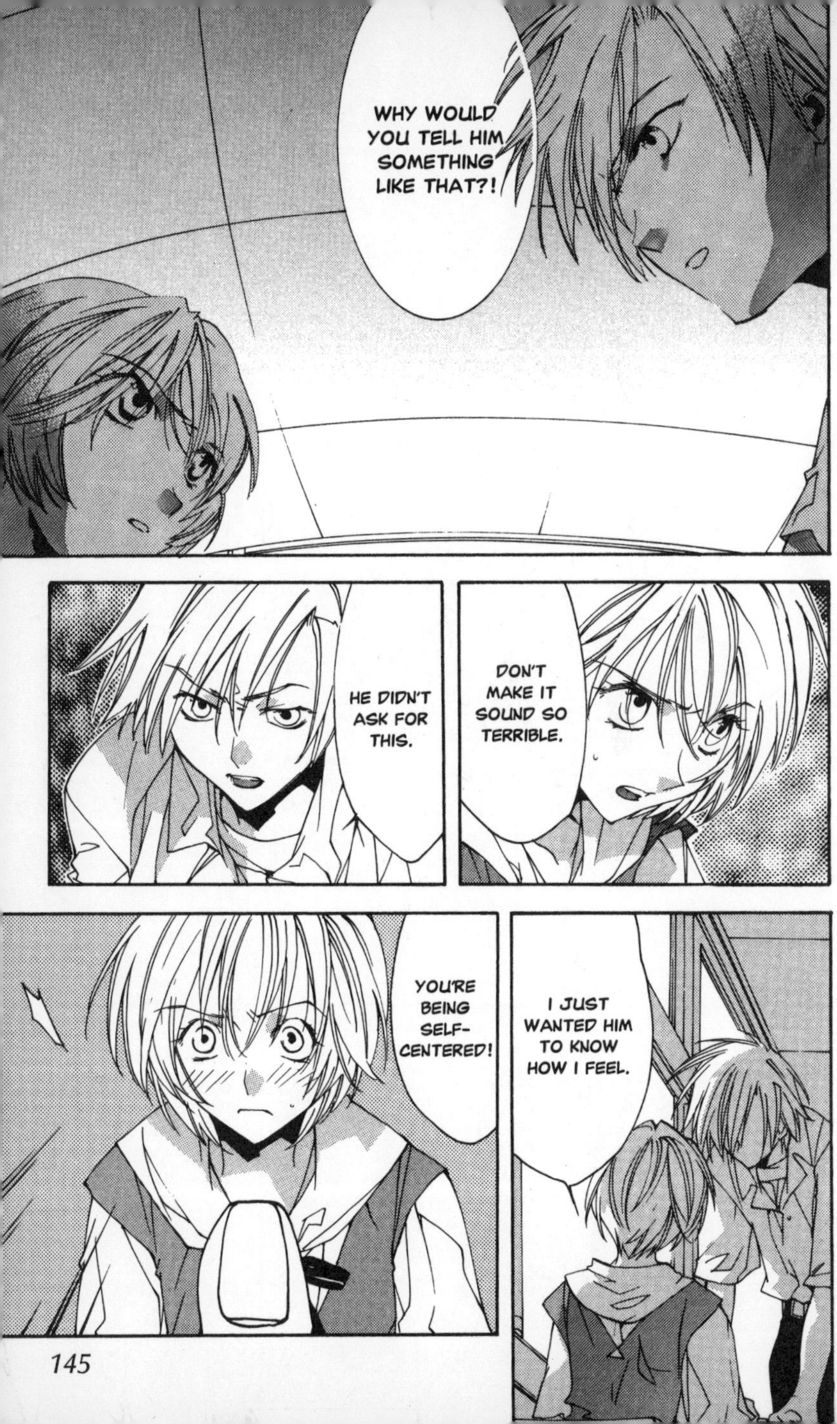
WHY WOULD YOU TELL HIM SOMETHING LIKE THAT?!
DON'T MAKE IT SOUND SO TERRIBLE.
HE DIDN'T ASK FOR THIS.
I JUST WANTED HIM TO KNOW HOW I FEEL.
YOU'RE BEING SELF-CENTERED!

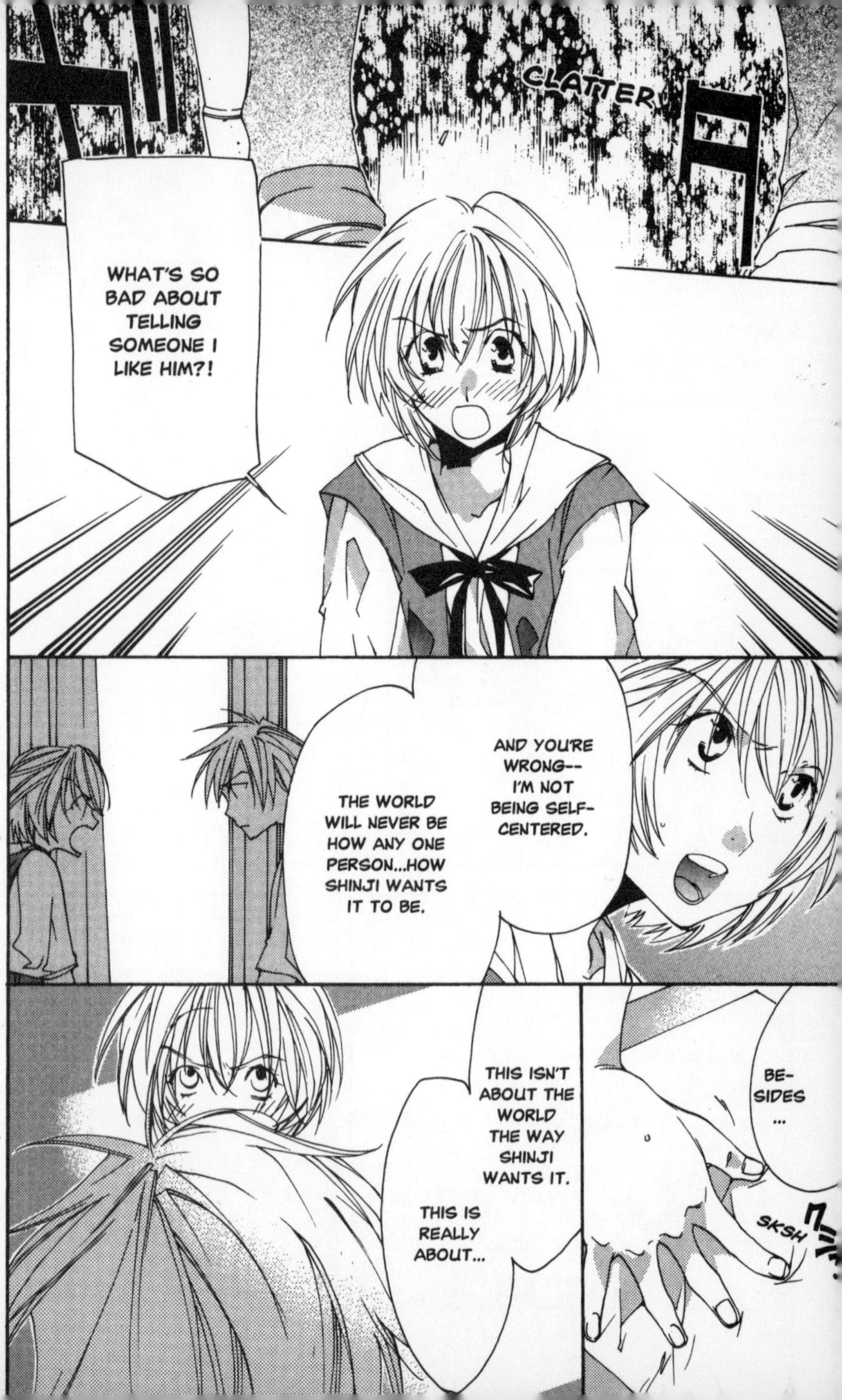
CLATTER
WHAT'S SO BAD ABOUT TELLING SOMEONE I LIKE HIM?!
AND YOU'RE WRONG-- I'M NOT BEING SELF-CENTERED.
THE WORLD WILL NEVER BE HOW ANY ONE PERSON...HOW SHINJI WANTS IT TO BE.
BE-SIDES...
SKSH
THIS ISN'T ABOUT THE WORLD THE WAY SHINJI WANTS IT.
THIS IS REALLY ABOUT...

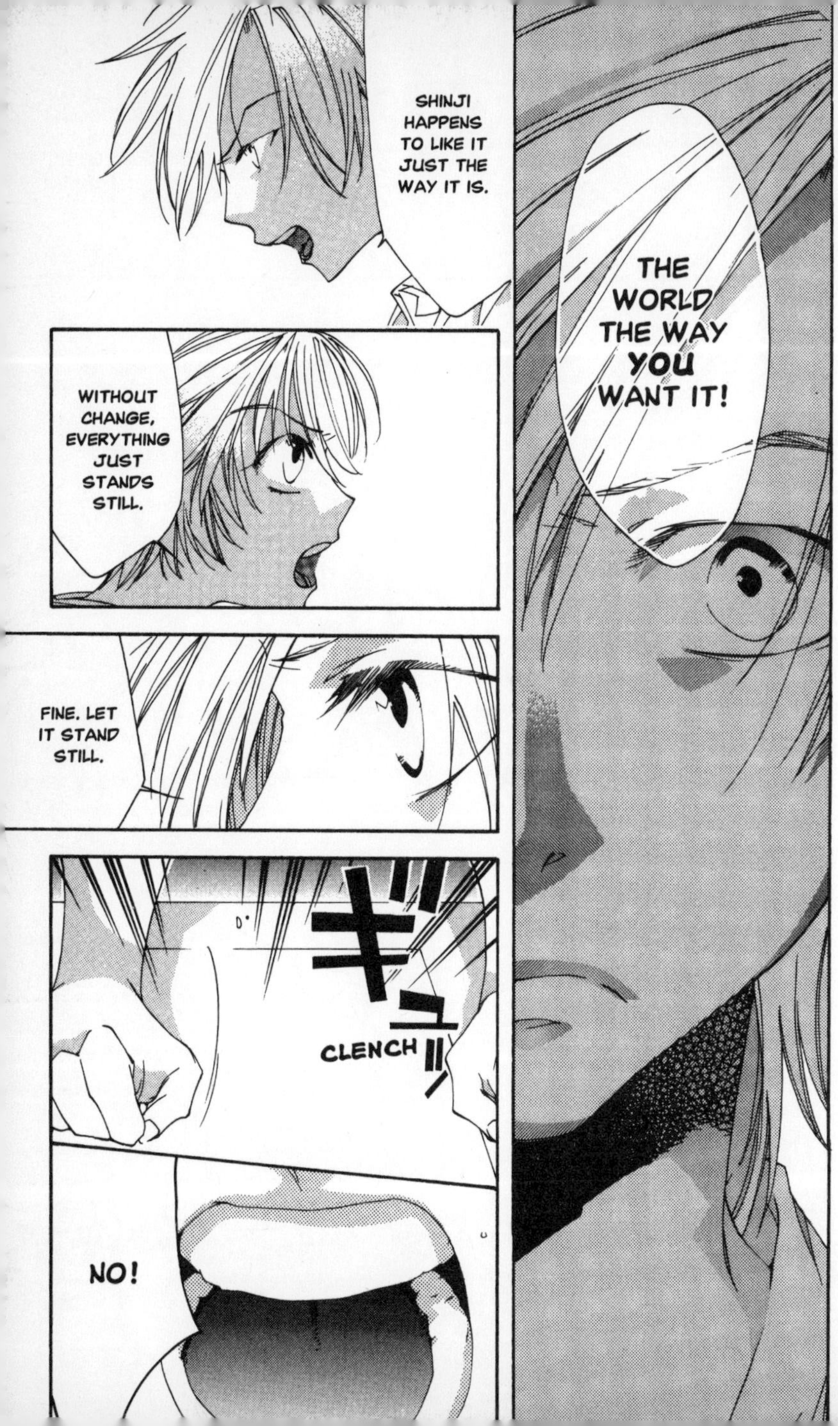
THE WORLD THE WAY YOU WANT IT!
SHINJI HAPPENS TO LIKE IT JUST THE WAY IT IS.
WITHOUT CHANGE, EVERYTHING JUST STANDS STILL.
FINE. LET IT STAND STILL.
ギュ
CLENCH
NO!

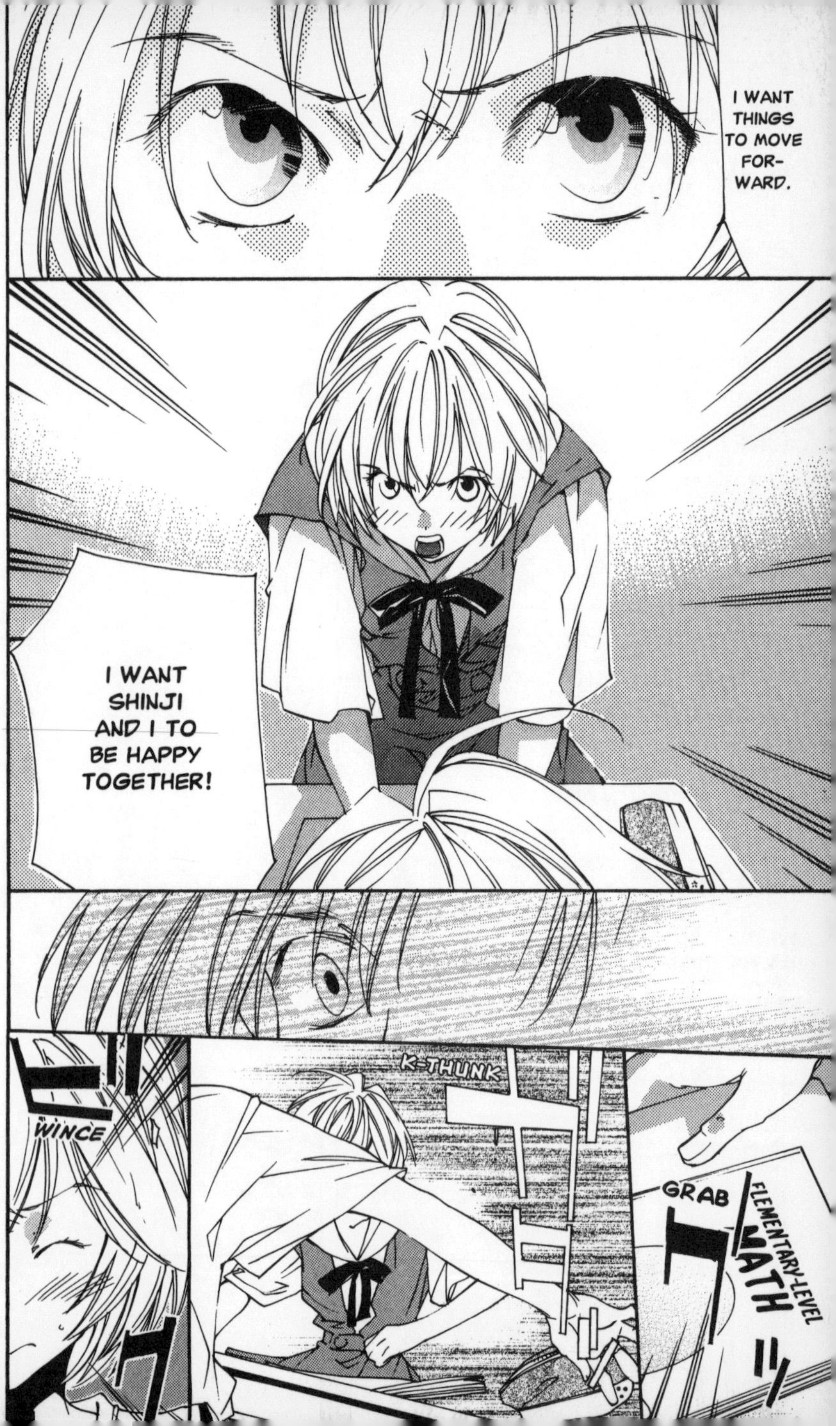
I WANT THINGS TO MOVE FOR-WARD.
I WANT SHINJI AND I TO BE HAPPY TOGETHER!
GRAB
ELEMENTARY-LEVEL MATH
K-THUNK
WINCE

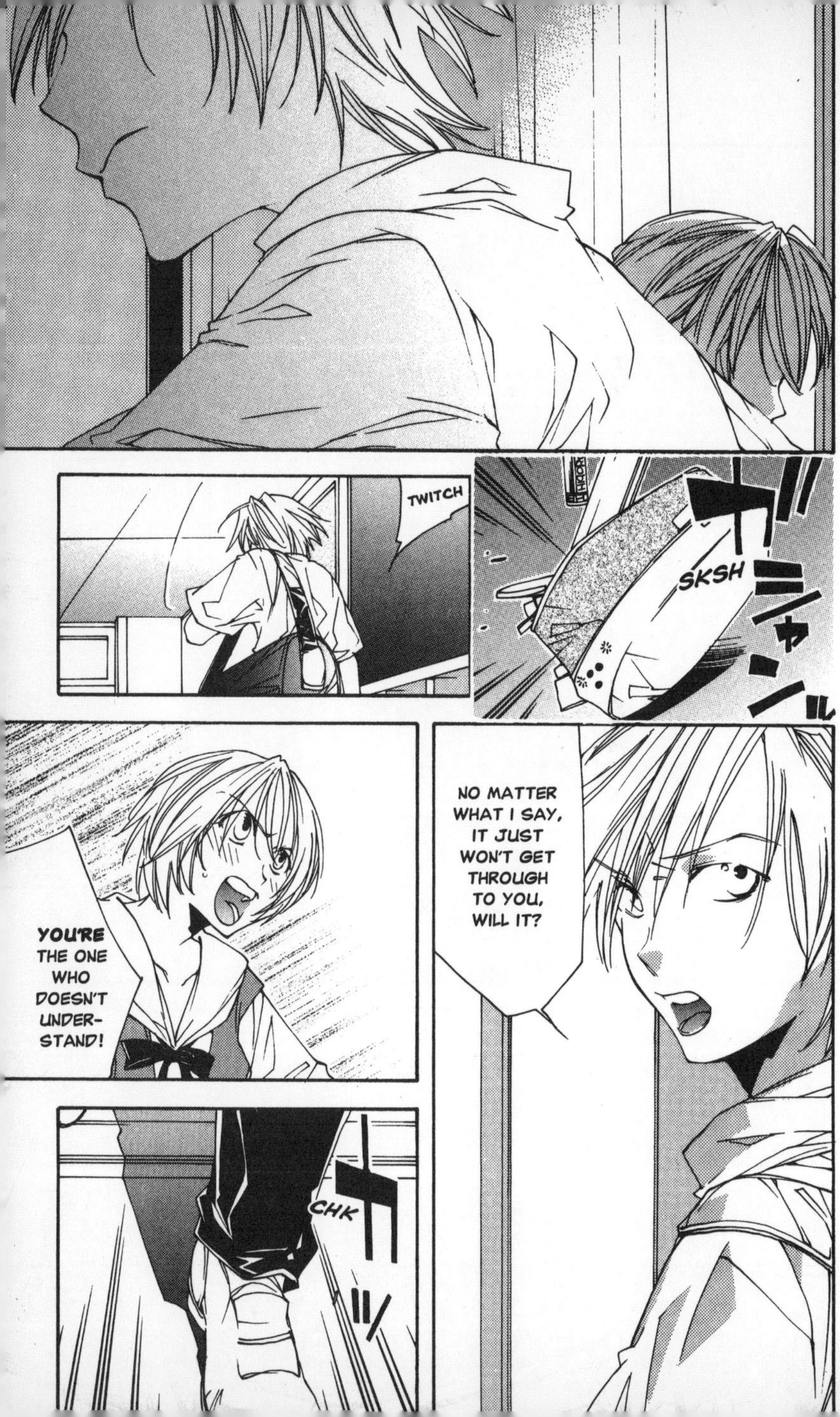
SKSH
TWITCH
NO MATTER WHAT I SAY, IT JUST WON'T GET THROUGH TO YOU, WILL IT?
YOU'RE THE ONE WHO DOESN'T UNDER-STAND!
CHK

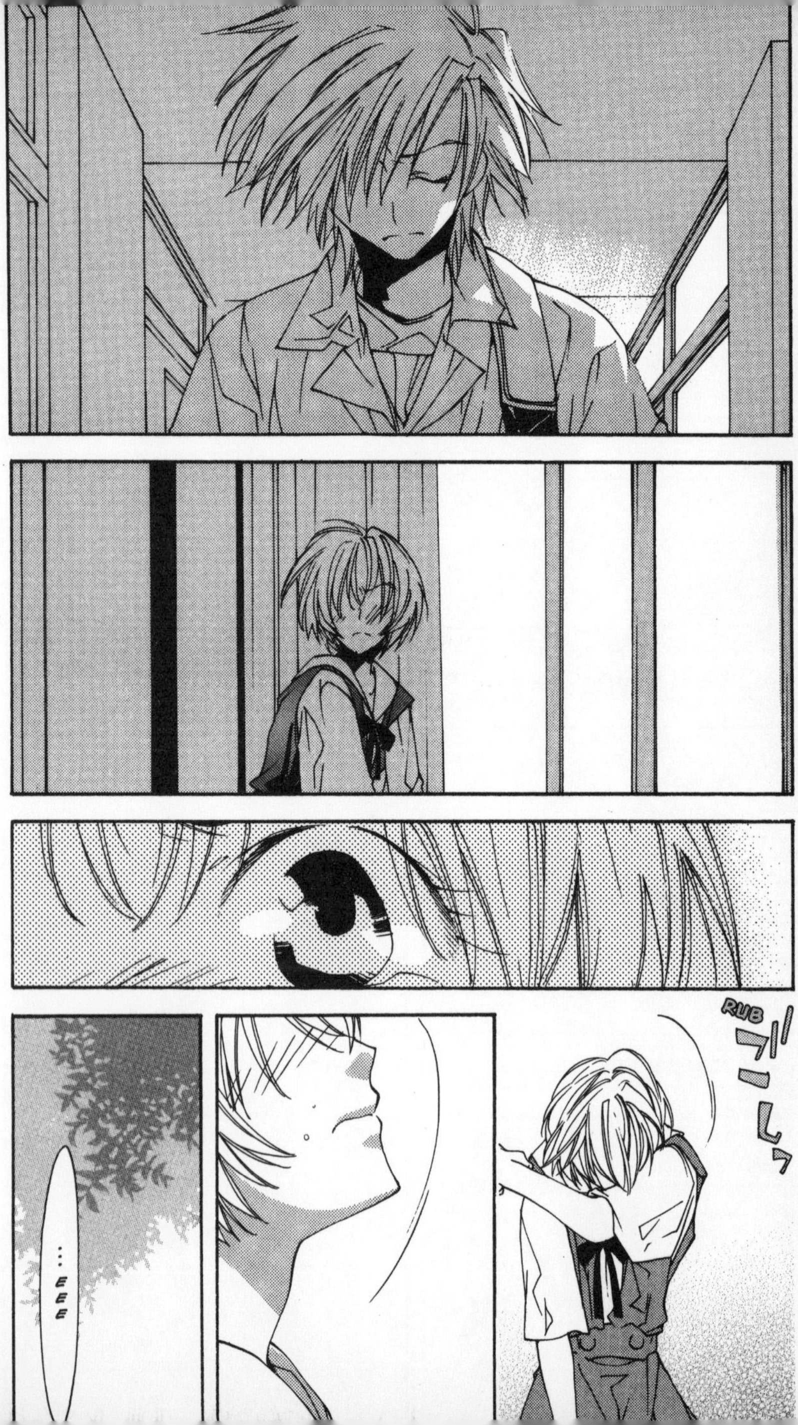
RUB

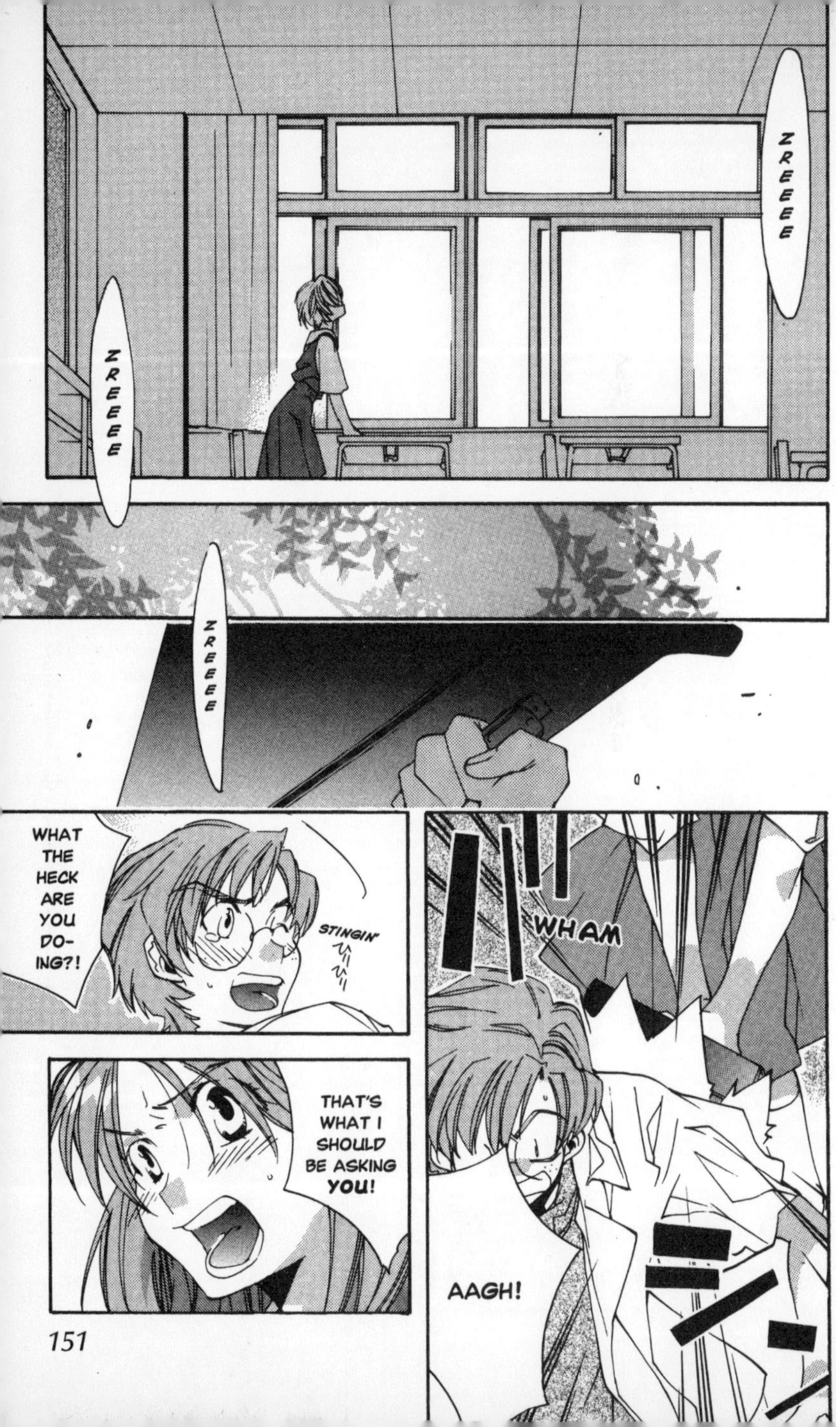

ZREEEE
ZREEEE
ZREEEE
WHAM
AAGH!
WHAT THE HECK ARE YOU DO-ING?!
STINGIN'
THAT'S WHAT I SHOULD BE ASKING **YOU**!

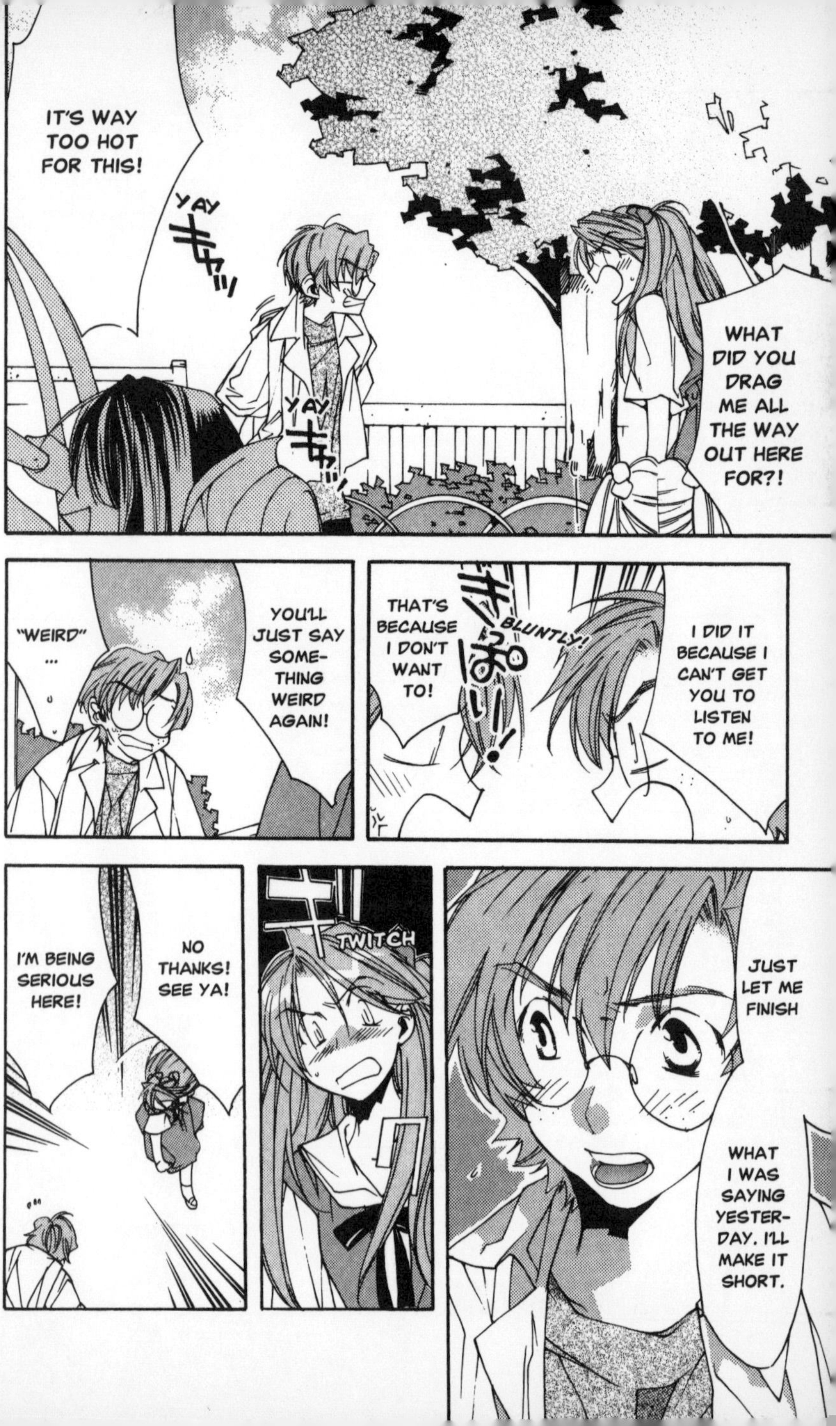
WHAT DID YOU DRAG ME ALL THE WAY OUT HERE FOR?!
YAY
YAY
IT'S WAY TOO HOT FOR THIS!
I DID IT BECAUSE I CAN'T GET YOU TO LISTEN TO ME!
BLUNTLY!
THAT'S BECAUSE I DON'T WANT TO!
YOU'LL JUST SAY SOMETHING WEIRD AGAIN!
"WEIRD" ...
JUST LET ME FINISH
WHAT I WAS SAYING YESTERDAY. I'LL MAKE IT SHORT.
TWITCH
NO THANKS! SEE YA!
I'M BEING SERIOUS HERE!

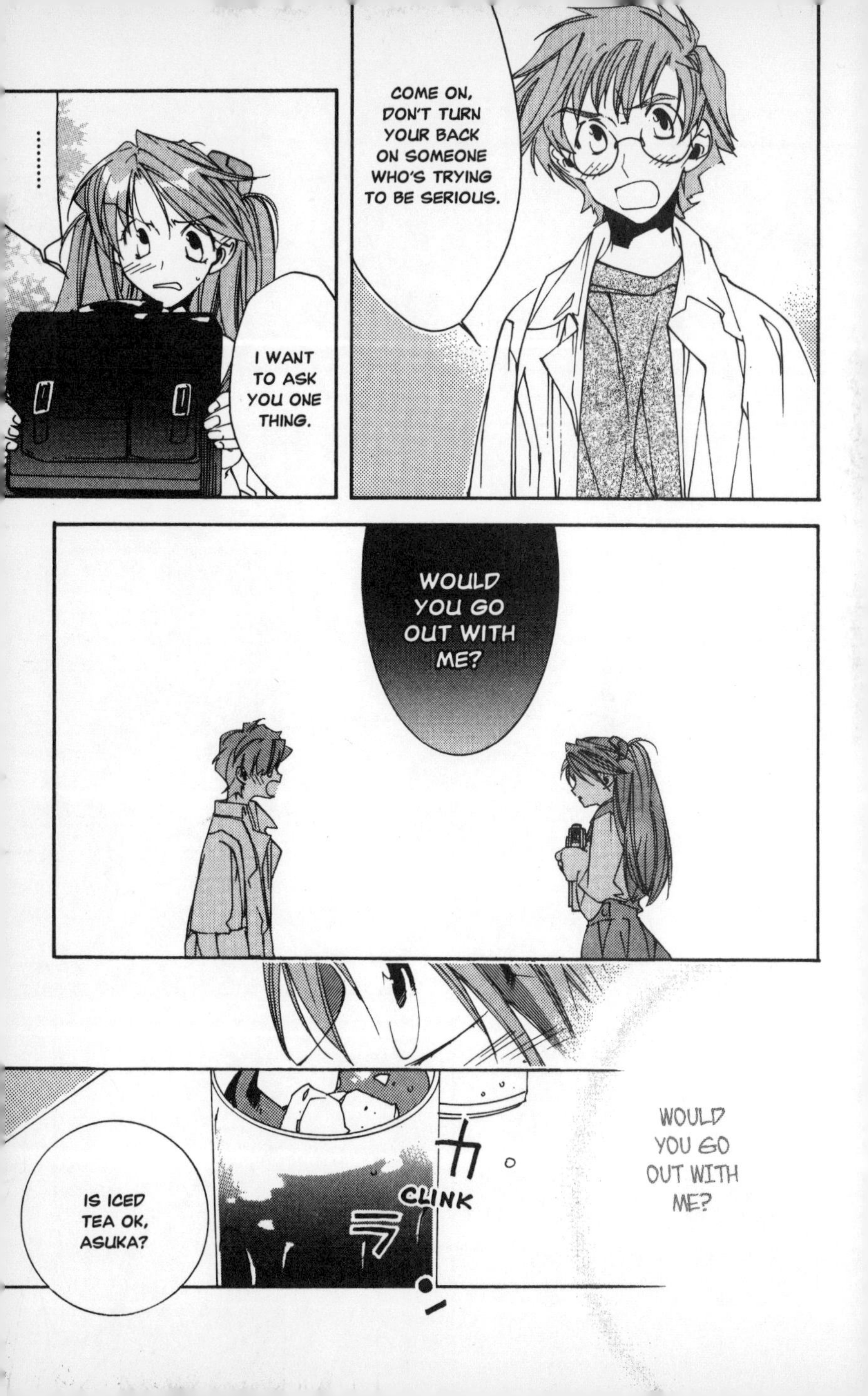
COME ON, DON'T TURN YOUR BACK ON SOMEONE WHO'S TRYING TO BE SERIOUS.
......
I WANT TO ASK YOU ONE THING.
WOULD YOU GO OUT WITH ME?
WOULD YOU GO OUT WITH ME?
CLINK
IS ICED TEA OK, ASUKA?

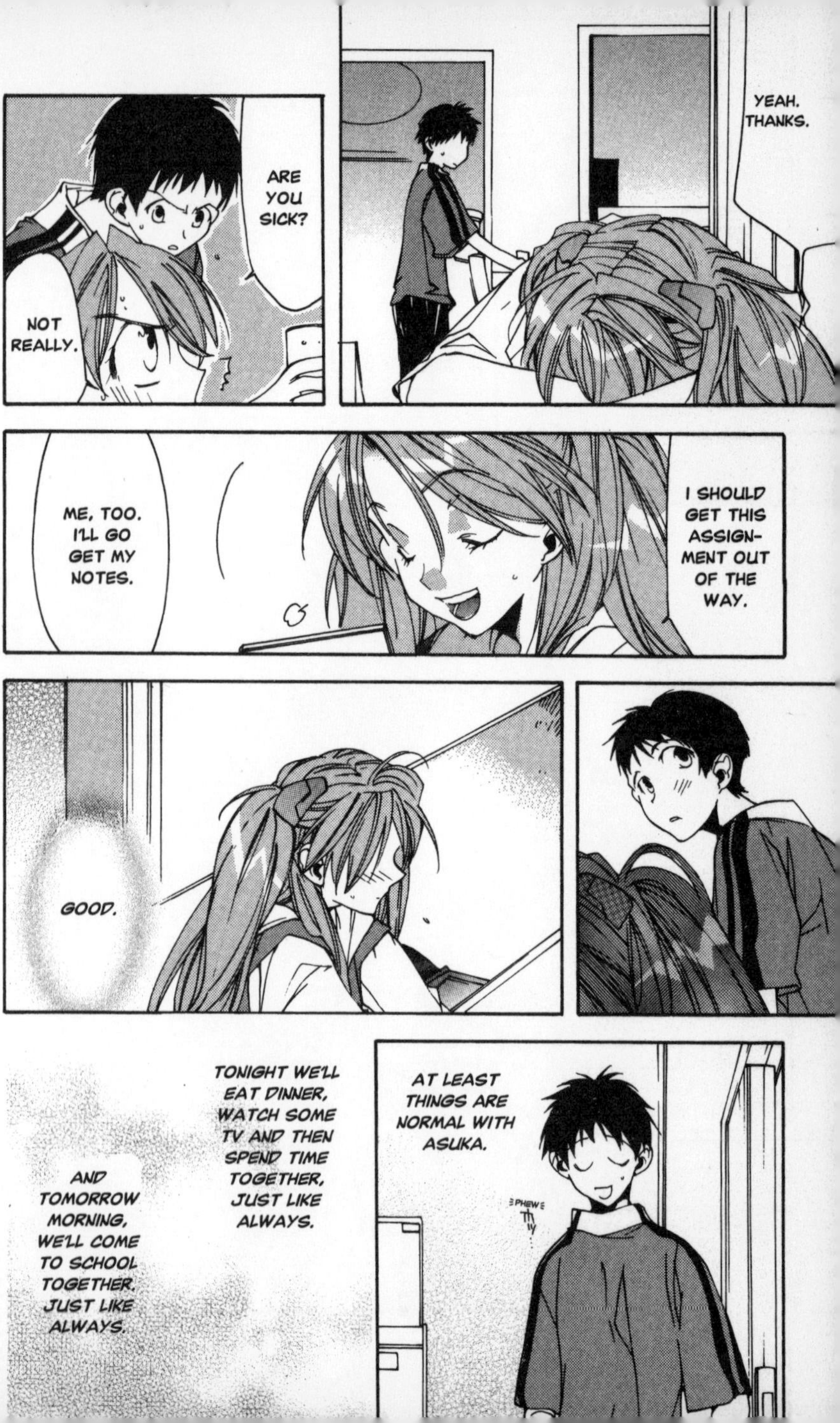
YEAH. THANKS.
ARE YOU SICK?
NOT REALLY.
I SHOULD GET THIS ASSIGN-MENT OUT OF THE WAY.
ME, TOO. I'LL GO GET MY NOTES.
GOOD.
AT LEAST THINGS ARE NORMAL WITH ASUKA.
PHEW
TONIGHT WE'LL EAT DINNER, WATCH SOME TV AND THEN SPEND TIME TOGETHER, JUST LIKE ALWAYS.
AND TOMORROW MORNING, WE'LL COME TO SCHOOL TOGETHER, JUST LIKE ALWAYS.

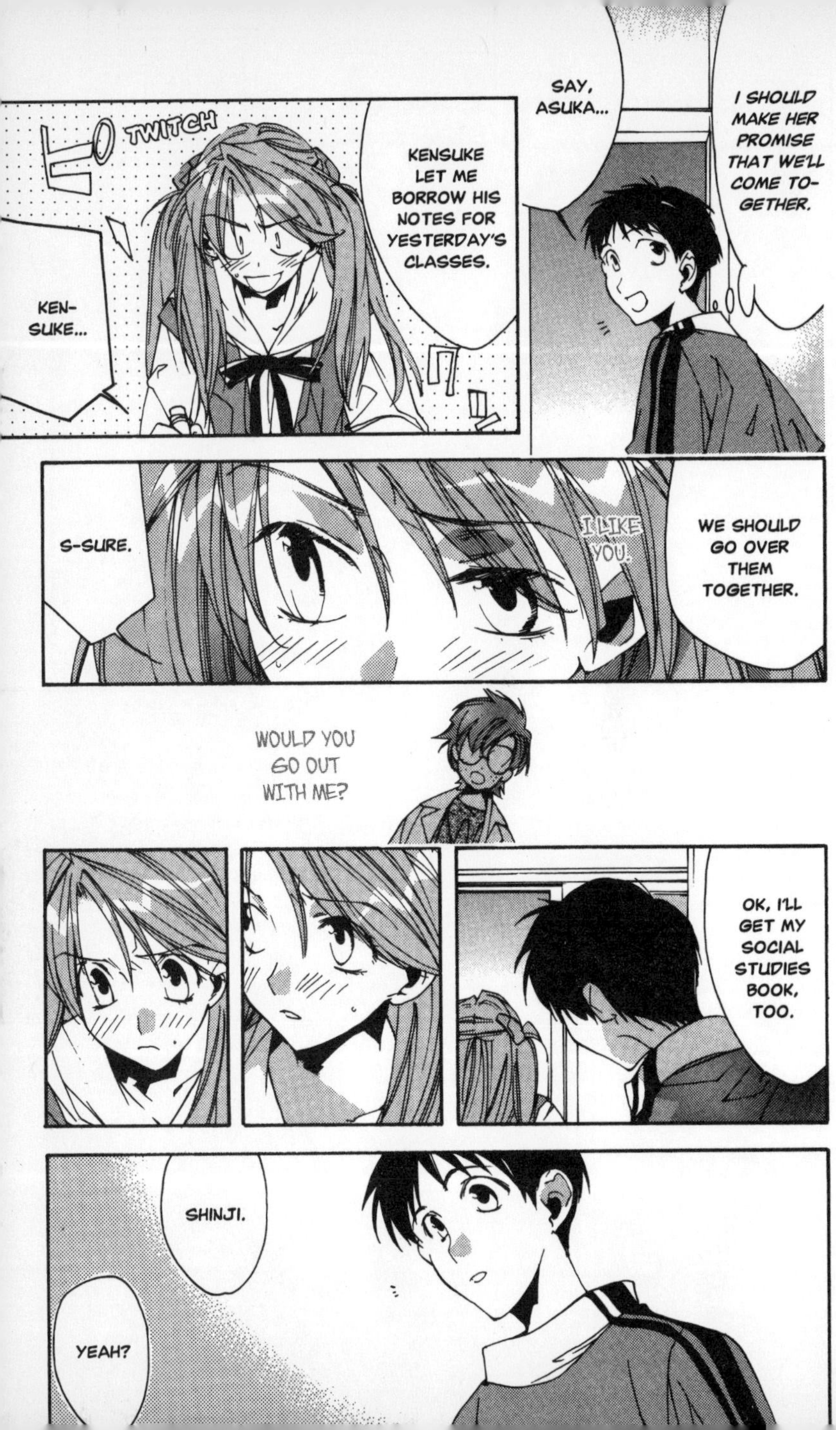
SAY, ASUKA...
I SHOULD MAKE HER PROMISE THAT WE'LL COME TO-GETHER.
KENSUKE LET ME BORROW HIS NOTES FOR YESTERDAY'S CLASSES.
TWITCH
KEN-SUKE...
WE SHOULD GO OVER THEM TOGETHER.
I LIKE YOU.
S-SURE.
WOULD YOU GO OUT WITH ME?
OK, I'LL GET MY SOCIAL STUDIES BOOK, TOO.
SHINJI.
YEAH?

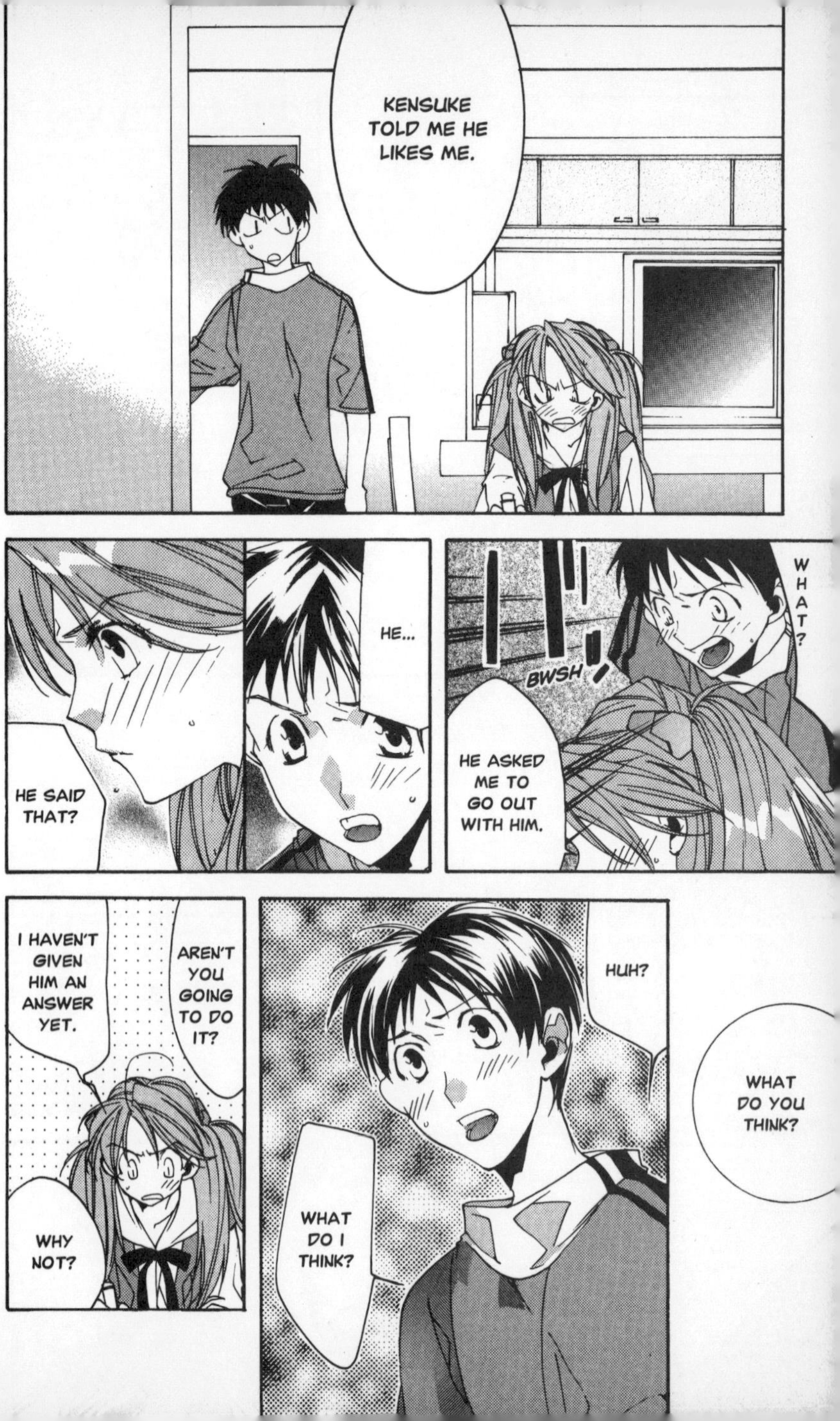
KENSUKE TOLD ME HE LIKES ME.
WHAT?
BWSH
HE ASKED ME TO GO OUT WITH HIM.
HE...
HE SAID THAT?
HUH?
WHAT DO YOU THINK?
WHAT DO I THINK?
AREN'T YOU GOING TO DO IT?
I HAVEN'T GIVEN HIM AN ANSWER YET.
WHY NOT?

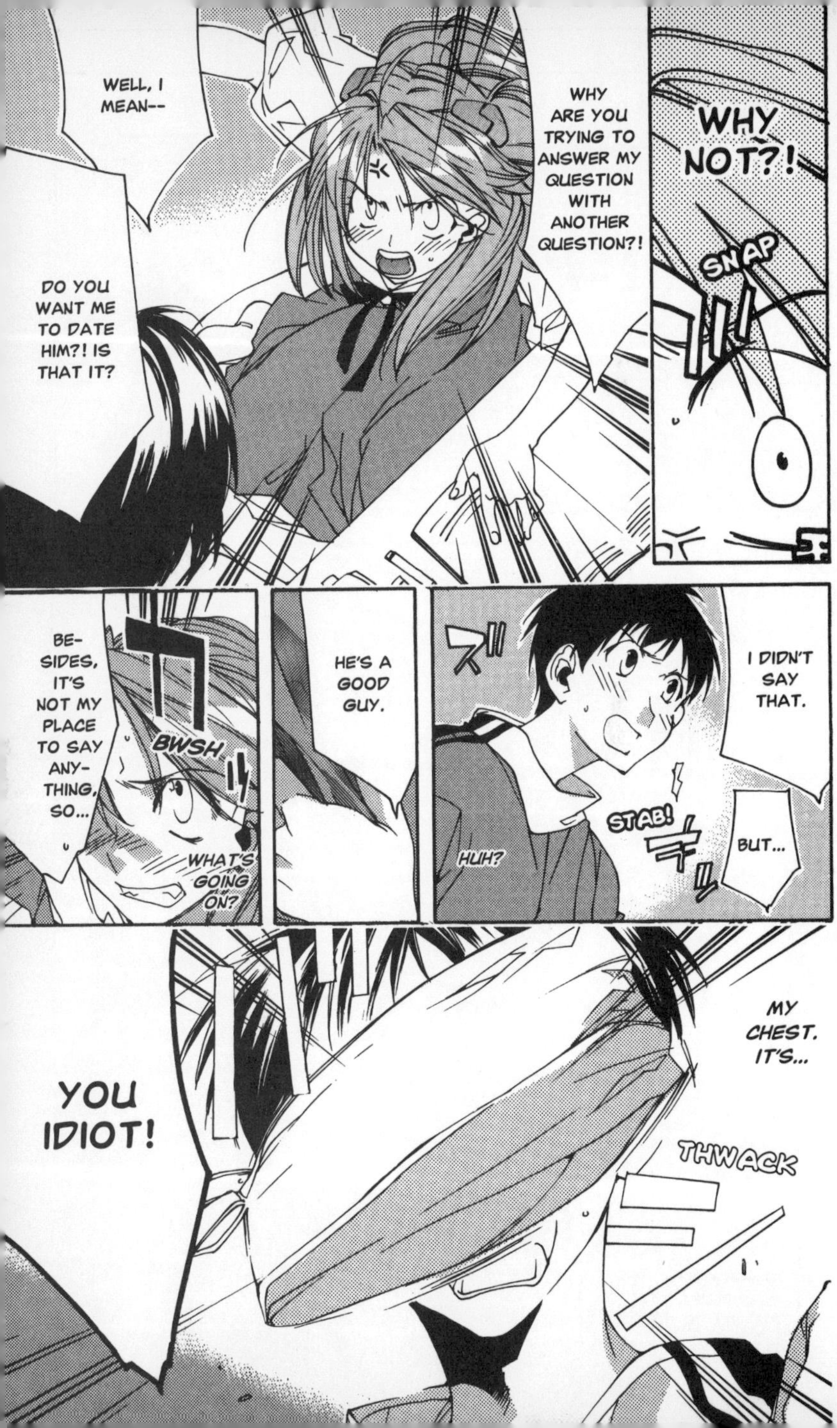

WHY NOT?!
SNAP
WHY ARE YOU TRYING TO ANSWER MY QUESTION WITH ANOTHER QUESTION?!
WELL, I MEAN--
DO YOU WANT ME TO DATE HIM?! IS THAT IT?
I DIDN'T SAY THAT.
STAB!
HUH?
BUT...
HE'S A GOOD GUY.
BE-SIDES, IT'S NOT MY PLACE TO SAY ANY-THING, SO...
BWSH
WHAT'S GOING ON?
MY CHEST. IT'S...
THWACK
YOU IDIOT!

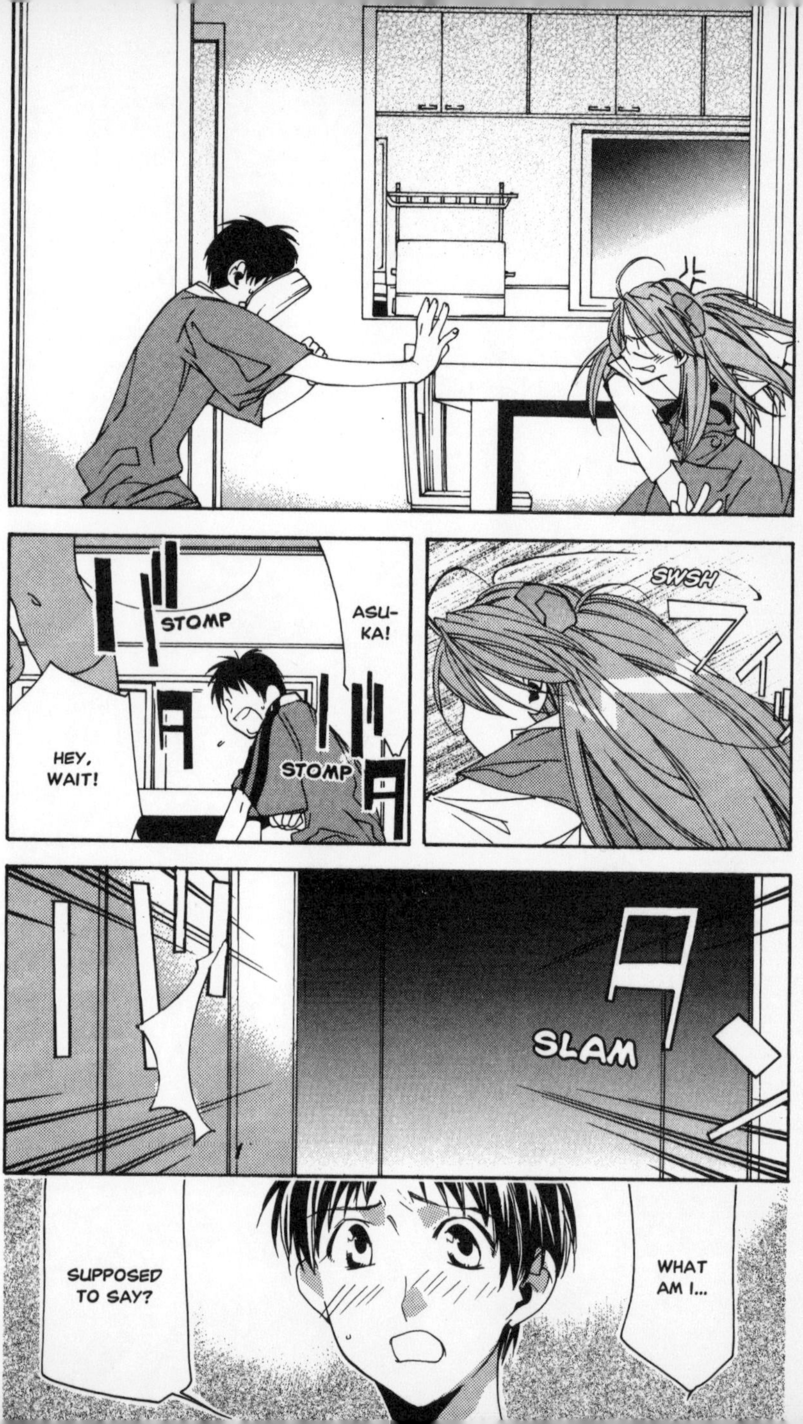
SWSH
ASU-KA!
STOMP
STOMP
HEY, WAIT!
SLAM
WHAT AM I...
SUPPOSED TO SAY?

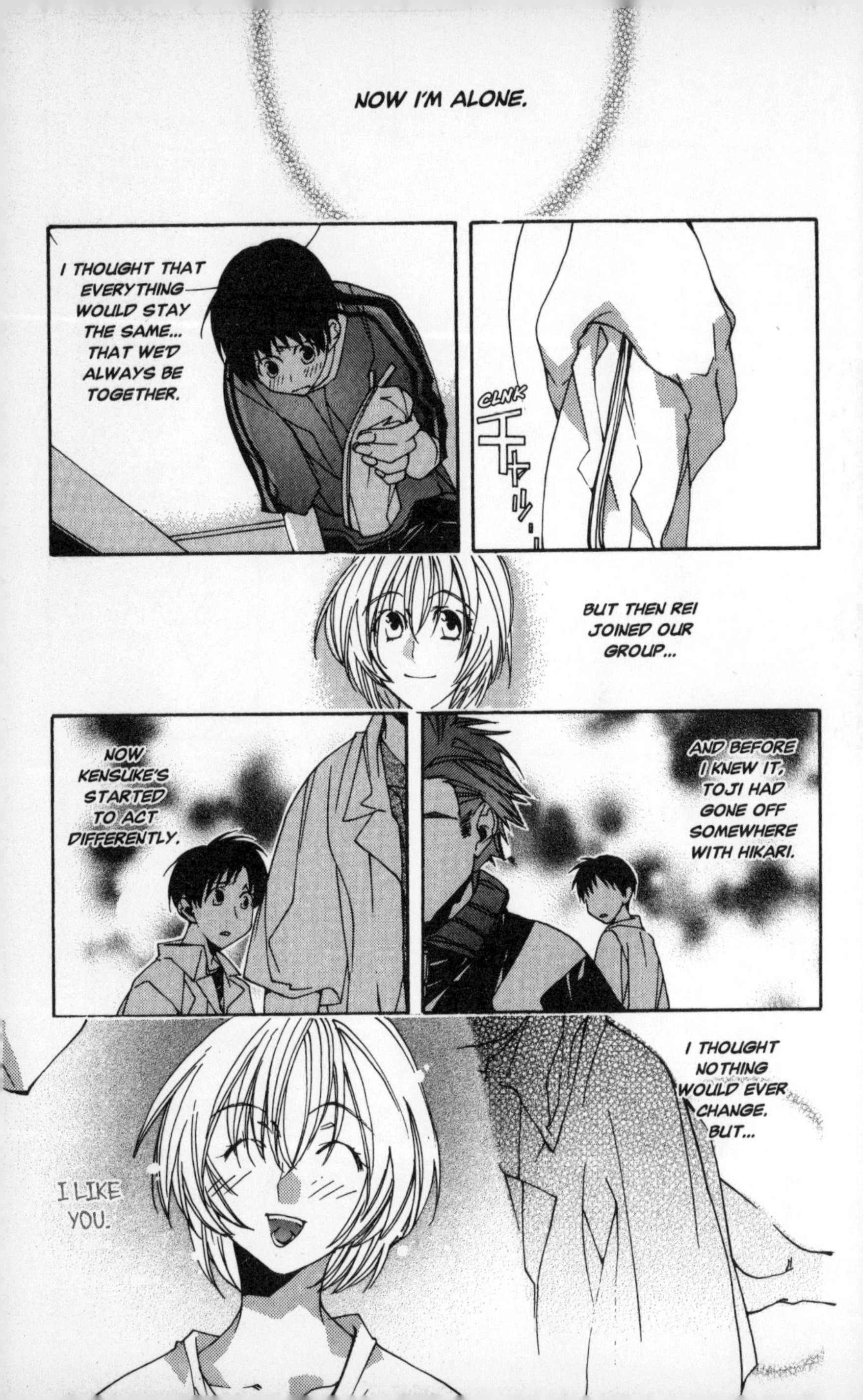
NOW I'M ALONE.
CLNK
チャリ…
I THOUGHT THAT EVERYTHING WOULD STAY THE SAME... THAT WE'D ALWAYS BE TOGETHER.
BUT THEN REI JOINED OUR GROUP...
AND BEFORE I KNEW IT, TOJI HAD GONE OFF SOMEWHERE WITH HIKARI.
NOW KENSUKE'S STARTED TO ACT DIFFERENTLY.
I THOUGHT NOTHING WOULD EVER CHANGE. BUT...
I LIKE YOU.

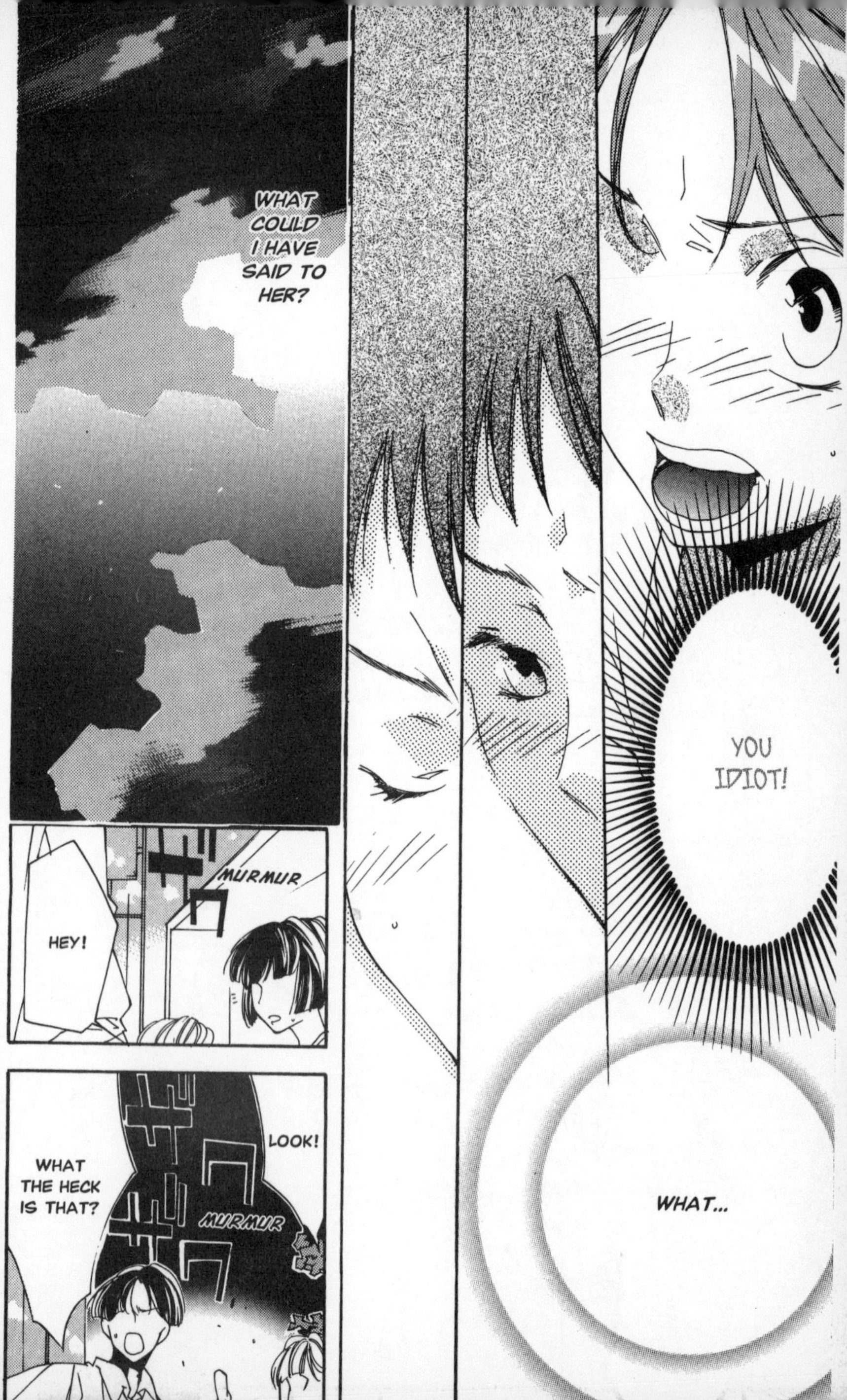
YOU IDIOT!
WHAT...
WHAT COULD I HAVE SAID TO HER?
MURMUR
HEY!
LOOK!
MURMUR
WHAT THE HECK IS THAT?

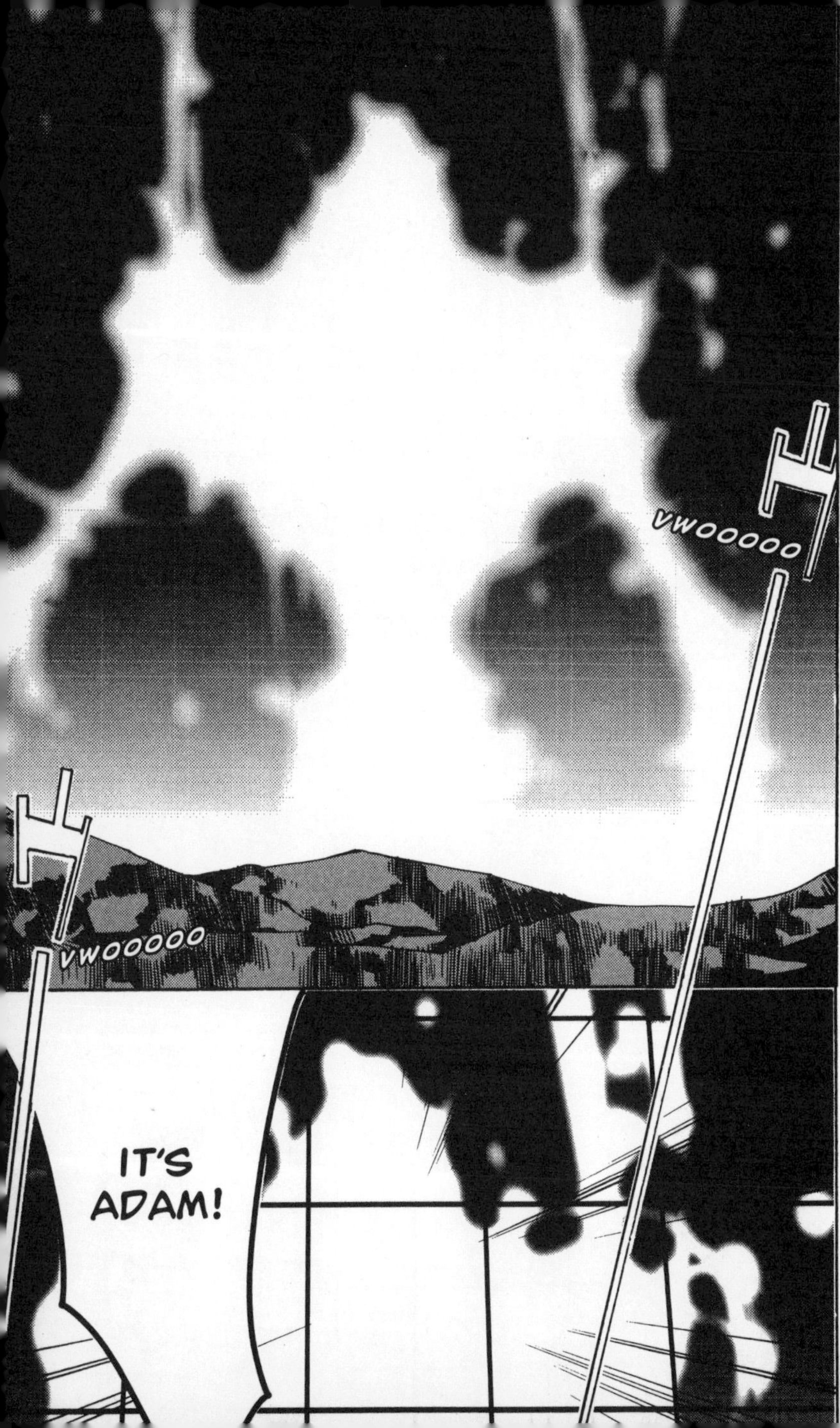
VWOOOOO
VWOOOOO
IT'S ADAM!

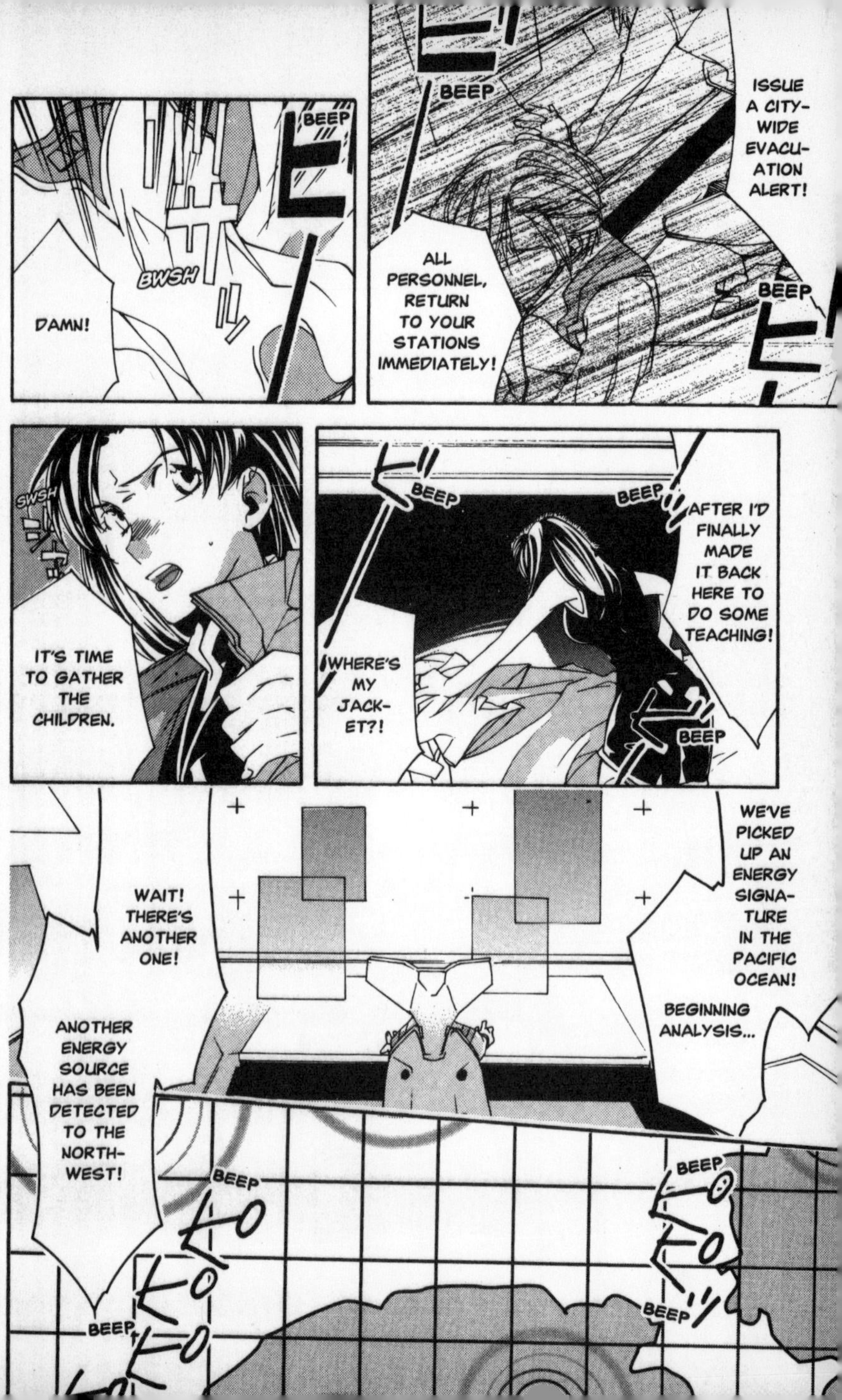
BEEP
ISSUE A CITY-WIDE EVACUATION ALERT!
ALL PERSONNEL, RETURN TO YOUR STATIONS IMMEDIATELY!
BEEP
BEEP
BWSH
DAMN!
BEEP
BEEP
AFTER I'D FINALLY MADE IT BACK HERE TO DO SOME TEACHING!
WHERE'S MY JACKET?!
BEEP
SWSH
IT'S TIME TO GATHER THE CHILDREN.
WE'VE PICKED UP AN ENERGY SIGNATURE IN THE PACIFIC OCEAN!
BEGINNING ANALYSIS...
WAIT! THERE'S ANOTHER ONE!
ANOTHER ENERGY SOURCE HAS BEEN DETECTED TO THE NORTH-WEST!
BEEP
BEEP
BEEP
BEEP

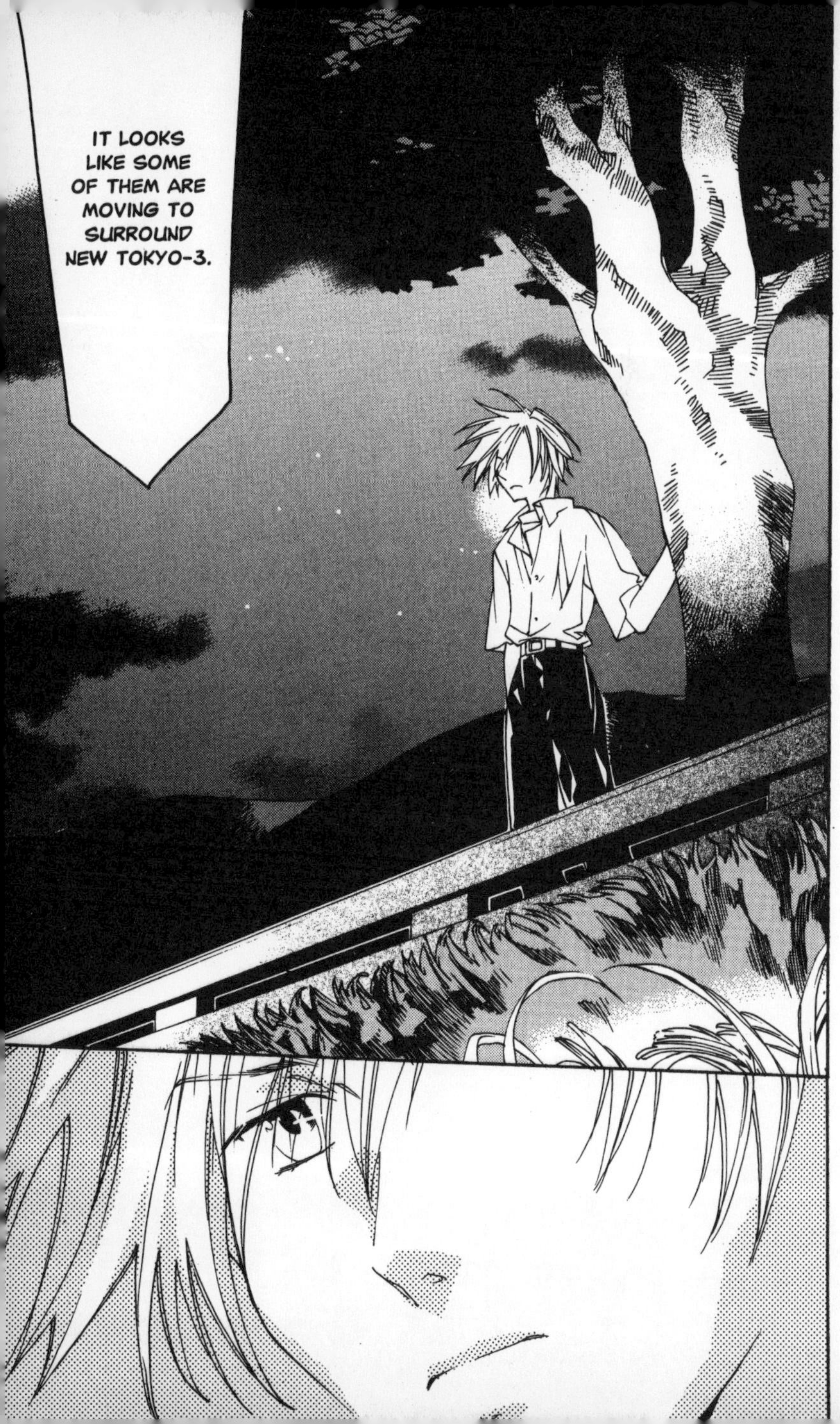
IT LOOKS LIKE SOME OF THEM ARE MOVING TO SURROUND NEW TOKYO-3.

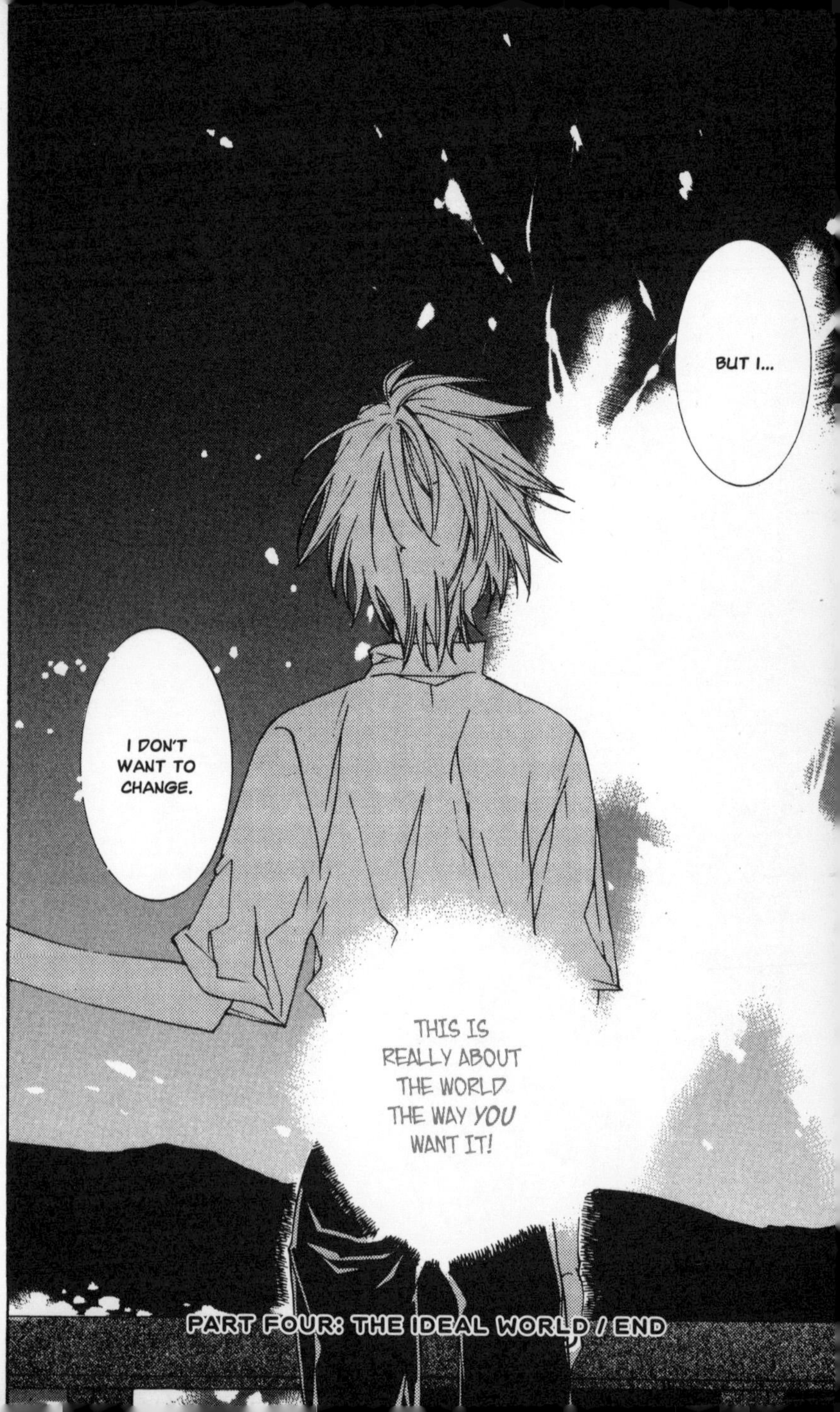
BUT I...
I DON'T WANT TO CHANGE.
THIS IS REALLY ABOUT THE WORLD THE WAY YOU WANT IT!
PART FOUR: THE IDEAL WORLD / END

AFTERWORD

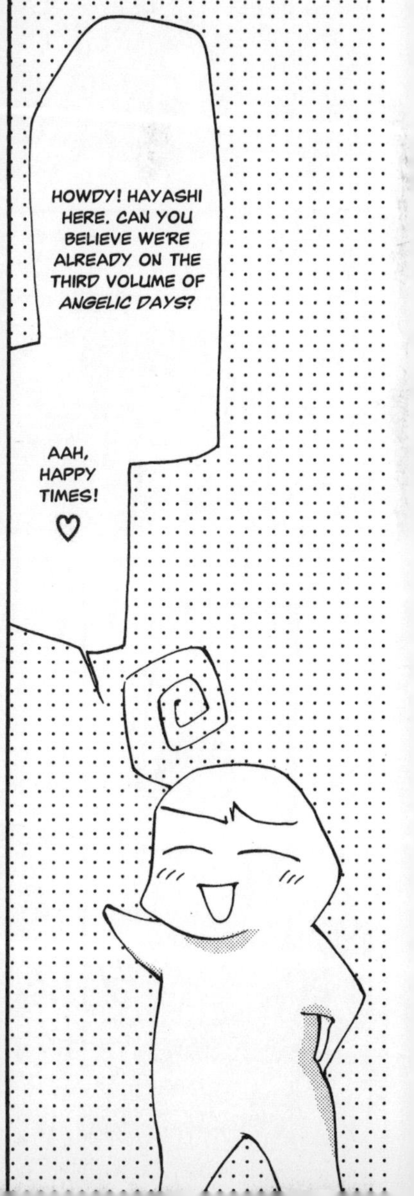

HOWDY! HAYASHI HERE. CAN YOU BELIEVE WE'RE ALREADY ON THE THIRD VOLUME OF *ANGELIC DAYS*?
AAH, HAPPY TIMES! ♡

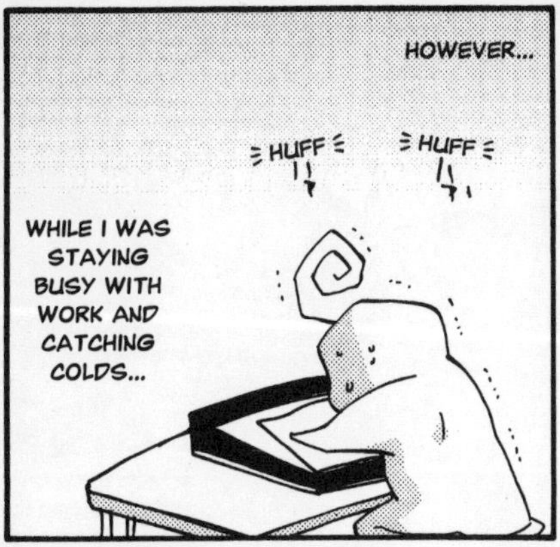

HOWEVER...
WHILE I WAS STAYING BUSY WITH WORK AND CATCHING COLDS...
HUFF
HUFF

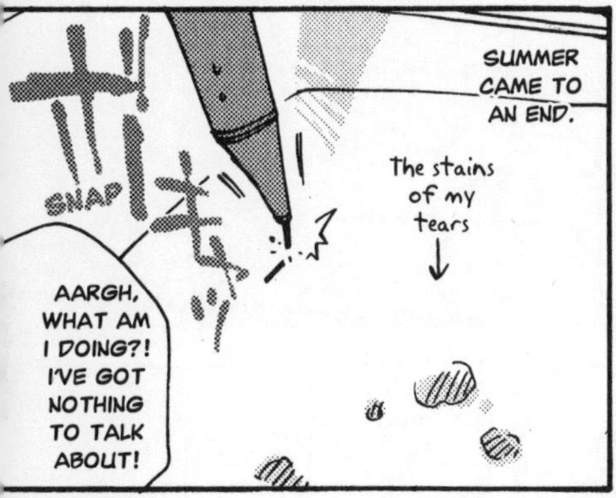

SUMMER CAME TO AN END.
The stains of my tears
SNAP
AARGH, WHAT AM I DOING?! I'VE GOT NOTHING TO TALK ABOUT!

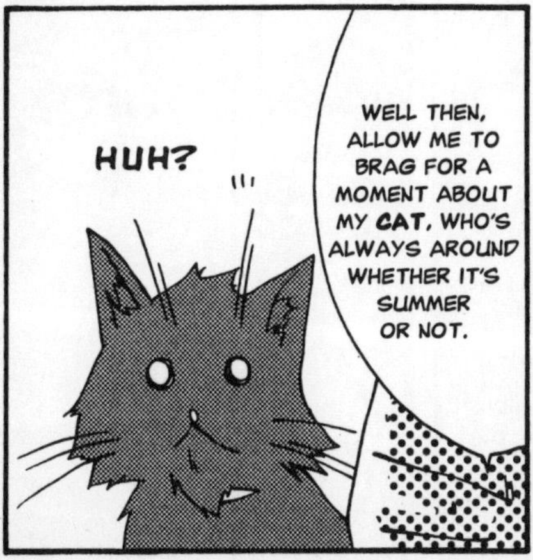

WELL THEN, ALLOW ME TO BRAG FOR A MOMENT ABOUT MY **CAT**, WHO'S ALWAYS AROUND WHETHER IT'S SUMMER OR NOT.
HUH?

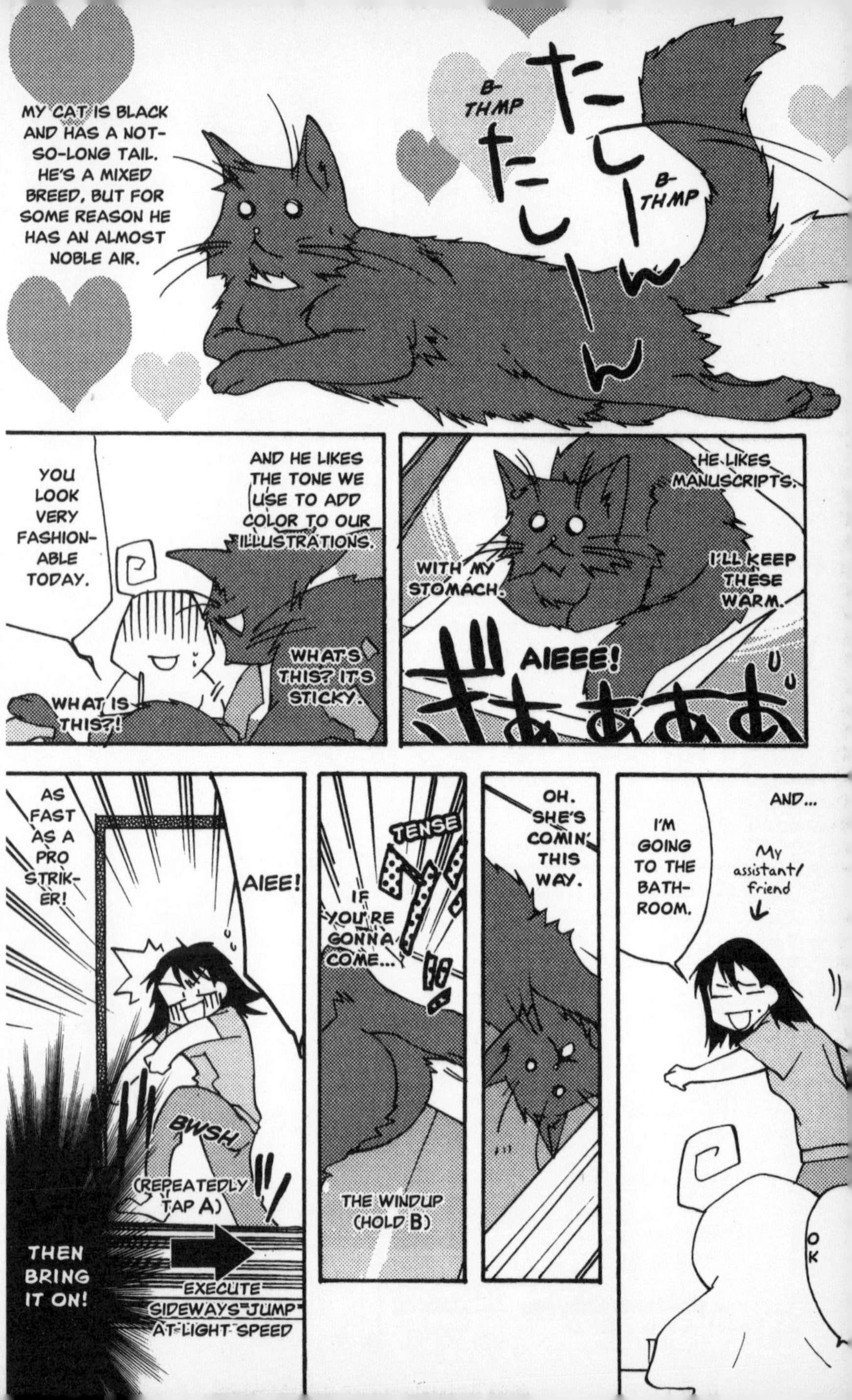
MY CAT IS BLACK AND HAS A NOT-SO-LONG TAIL. HE'S A MIXED BREED, BUT FOR SOME REASON HE HAS AN ALMOST NOBLE AIR.
たーしーん
B-THMP
たーしーん
B-THMP
HE LIKES MANUSCRIPTS.
I'LL KEEP THESE WARM.
WITH MY STOMACH.
AIEEE!
ぎあああああ
AND HE LIKES THE TONE WE USE TO ADD COLOR TO OUR ILLUSTRATIONS.
YOU LOOK VERY FASHION-ABLE TODAY.
WHAT'S THIS? IT'S STICKY.
WHAT IS THIS?!
AND...
I'M GOING TO THE BATH-ROOM.
My assistant/friend
OK
OH. SHE'S COMIN' THIS WAY.
TENSE
IF YOU'RE GONNA COME...
THE WINDUP (HOLD B)
AS FAST AS A PRO STRIK-ER!
AIEE!
BWSH
(REPEATEDLY TAP A)
THEN BRING IT ON!
EXECUTE SIDEWAYS JUMP AT LIGHT SPEED

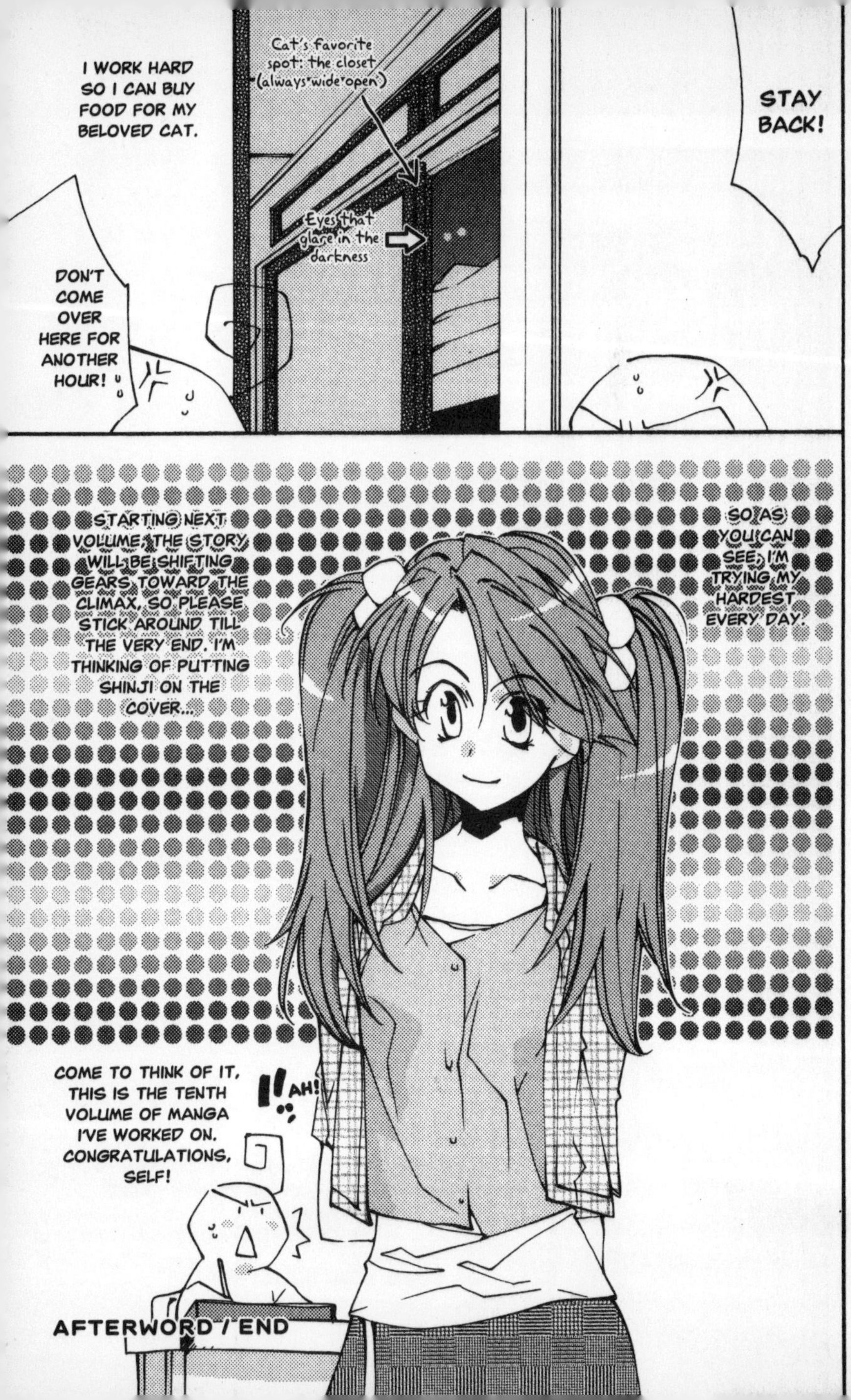

STAY BACK!
Cat's favorite spot: the closet (always wide open)
Eyes that glare in the darkness
I WORK HARD SO I CAN BUY FOOD FOR MY BELOVED CAT.
DON'T COME OVER HERE FOR ANOTHER HOUR!
SO AS YOU CAN SEE, I'M TRYING MY HARDEST EVERY DAY.
STARTING NEXT VOLUME, THE STORY WILL BE SHIFTING GEARS TOWARD THE CLIMAX, SO PLEASE STICK AROUND TILL THE VERY END. I'M THINKING OF PUTTING SHINJI ON THE COVER...
COME TO THINK OF IT, THIS IS THE TENTH VOLUME OF MANGA I'VE WORKED ON. CONGRATULATIONS, SELF!
!! AH!
AFTERWORD / END

NEON GENESIS EVANGELION: ANGELIC DAYS
VOLUME THREE

©GAINAX/Project Eva. • TX   ©2003 GAINAX
Originally published in Japan in 2004 by
KADOKAWA SHOTEN PUBLISHING CO., LTD., Tokyo.
English translation rights arranged with
KADOKAWA SHOTEN PUBLISHING CO., LTD., Tokyo.

Editor **JAVIER LOPEZ**
Graphic Artist **SCOTT HOWARD**
Translator **KAORU BERTRAND**

Editorial Director **GARY STEINMAN**
Print Production Manager **BRIDGETT JANOTA**
Production Coordinator **MARISA KREITZ**

International Coordinators **TORU IWAKAMI & MIYUKI KAMIYA**

President, CEO & Publisher **JOHN LEDFORD**

Email: editor@adv-manga.com
www.adv-manga.com

www.advfilms.com

For sales and distribution inquiries please call 1.800.282.7202

is a division of A.D. Vision, Inc.
5750 Bintliff Drive, Suite 210, Houston, Texas 77036

English text © 2006 published by A.D. Vision, Inc. under exclusive license.
ADV MANGA is a trademark of A.D. Vision, Inc.

ISBN: 1-4139-0350-9
First printing, November 2006
10 9 8 7 6 5 4 3 2 1
Printed in Canada

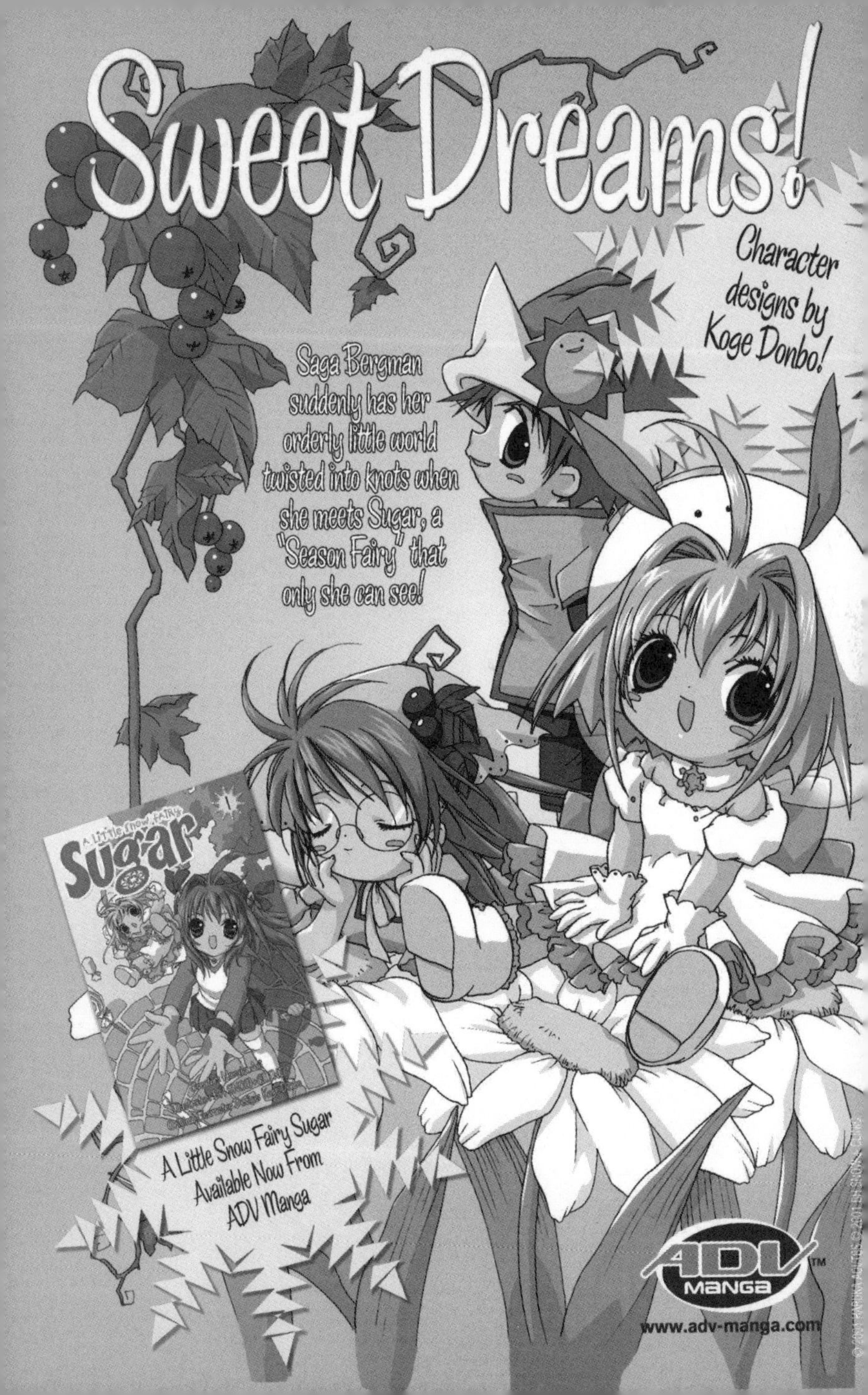
Sweet Dreams!
Character designs by Koge Donbo!
Saga Bergman suddenly has her orderly little world twisted into knots when she meets Sugar, a "Season Fairy" that only she can see!
A Little Snow Fairy Sugar
Sugar
A Little Snow Fairy Sugar Available Now From ADV Manga
ADV Manga ™
www.adv-manga.com

Three people united by
a terrifying secret.

Yuri, a young man who
killed his own mother.

Mitsuba, who will gladly
murder to avenge the
sister that was taken
from him.

Anna, the mysterious
assassin with a
chilling beauty.

Together, they'll
stop at nothing
to bring down
a terrorist
organization...

And along the
way, they'll come
closer to the
truth that binds
them together.

Anne Freaks
The action ends with Vol. 4
In stores December 2006
from ADV Manga

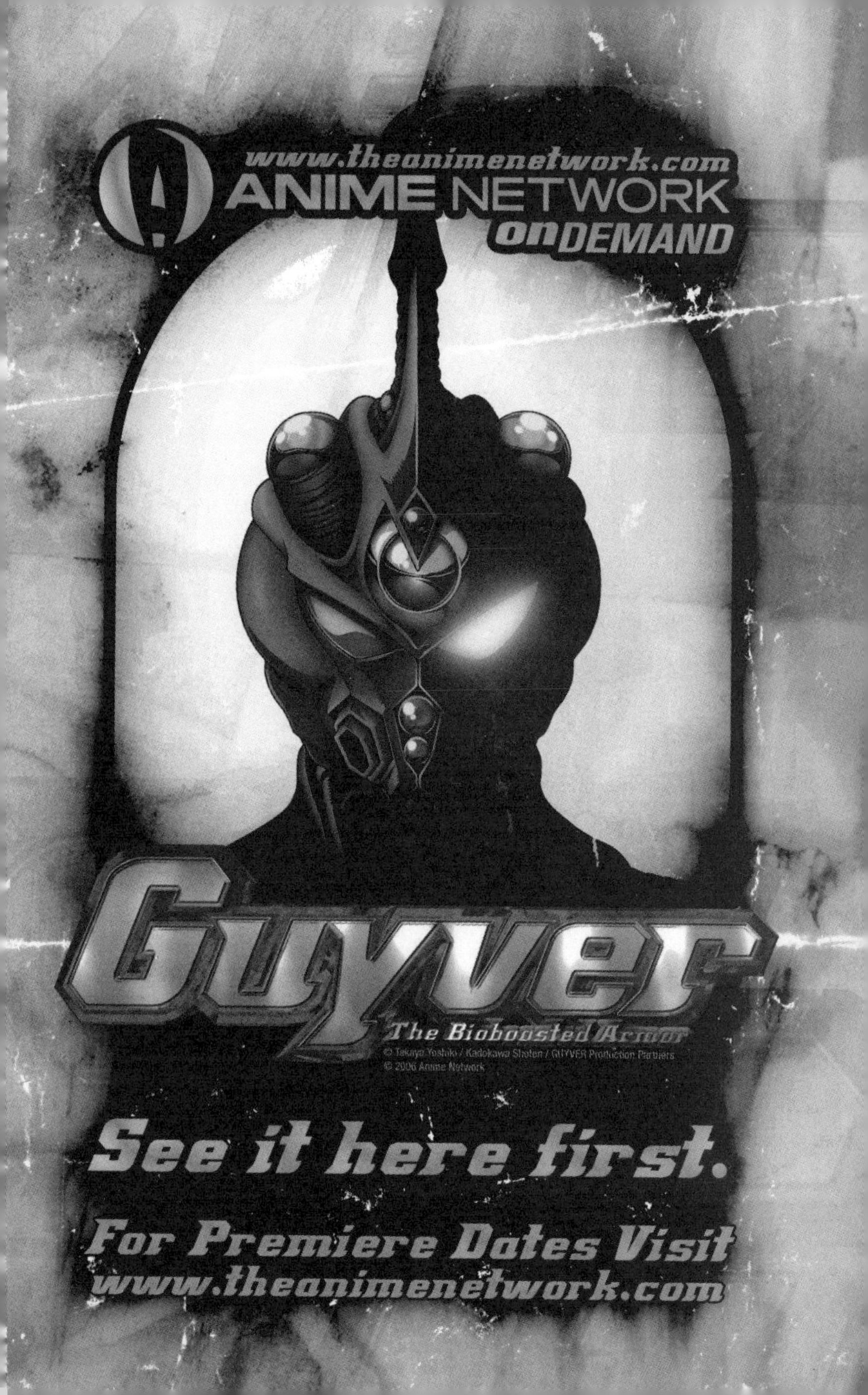
www.theanimenetwork.com
ANIME NETWORK
onDEMAND
Guyver
The Bioboosted Armor
© Takaya Yoshiki / Kadokawa Shoten / GUYVER Production Partners
© 2006 Anime Network
See it here first.
For Premiere Dates Visit
www.theanimenetwork.com